ZEBRA

Books by Clark Howard

Novels

The Arm
A Movement Toward Eden
The Doomsday Squad
The Killings
Mark the Sparrow
The Hunters
The Wardens

Nonfiction

Six Against the Rock
Zebra

ZEBRA

The true account
of the 179 days of
terror in San Francisco

Clark Howard

Richard Marek Publishers
New York

Library of Congrtess Cataloging in Publication Data

Howard, Clark.
  Zebra.

  1. Murder—California—San Francisco.
2. Crime and criminals—California—San Francisco.
3. Black Muslims. I. Title.
HV6534.S3H68   364.1′523′0979461   79-15985
ISBN 0-399-90050-0

Printed in the United States of America

To
Joe Buffer

Fellow Marine,
fellow writer,
and friend,

who was the catalyst
for this one

Contents

PART TWO: Aftermath to Terror

Foreword

In any lengthy work of nonfiction, there are bound to be areas where the facts are not entirely certain—and this book is no exception. Rarely do two people see an event the same way, particularly if that event is sudden, violent, and frightening. A writer is fortunate when he can interview a dozen people regarding a single occurrence and through them develop a consensus of what actually took place. Even then, in the writing of it, he is going to displease some of the people, some of the time.

This book is a reconstruction—as accurate as the author can make it—of a series of particularly terrible crimes perpetrated on randomly selected victims in San Francisco during a 179-day period late in 1973 and early in 1974. All of the victims were white, all of their assailants were black. For reasons which the reader will later learn, the events became known as the "Zebra" crimes.

In order to reconstruct these crimes with all possible accuracy, the author has availed himself of the contents of reams of available written material, and the recollections of dozens of persons connected both directly and indirectly with the case. The written material, which frequently seemed endless but, surprisingly, was rarely contradictory, included the following:

9

Incident Reports made by San Francisco police officers on each crime committed

Police investigation reports made by homicide detectives assigned to each case

Crime laboratory and ballistics reports relevant to each case

Newspaper accounts of the effects of the cases on the San Francisco citizenry and its government

A 609-page transcript of six taped sessions of a confession made by an informer who participated in the crimes

The testimony in the subsequent trial of four men named by that informer as the Zebra crimes perpetrators

Complete criminal and prison records from two states and the federal system on three of the five men involved (the other two had no prior criminal records)

Personal case notes kept by the homicide inspector in charge of the case

And a miscellany of personal notes, letters, and other written material from a variety of sources

The people interviewed include:

The available victims who would agree to discuss the case

Relatives and friends of the victims who did not survive

Police officers assigned to the investigation, including the personal cooperation over a fourteen-month period of the homicide inspector, now retired, who headed the Zebra investigation

Extensive personal interviews at Folsom Prison with two of the men convicted of the crimes

Interviews with relatives and friends of the convicted men and the informer who identified them

Telephone interviews with the informer himself, who has been relocated with a new identity

And lastly, interviews with anonymous and confidential sources who responded to the following classified advertisement in the *San Francisco Chronicle* and *Examiner* newspapers:

ZEBRA. Published author of 12 books wishes to contact anyone having previously unpublished information about the men convicted of the Zebra killings. Particularly interested in anyone who attended a loft meeting. Anonymity, confidentiality, absolutely guaranteed. Communicate anonymously, on cassette, or any way you choose. Contact Boxholder, P.O. Box 5306, Garside Station, Las Vegas, Nevada 89102.

Factual information was obtained from all these sources, information that could be cross-checked and verified with other information from other sources. Analysis and correlation of all this information produced a surprising degree of unanimity. This is not to say that the sources interviewed were never in conflict. The convicted men's stories were naturally at variance with the story told by the informer. With rare exceptions, however, the informer's story proved far more credible—and, more often than not, was supported by circumstantial evidence. That story was accepted by the police, by the prosecutors, and—most important—by the twelve men and women who found the accused men guilty beyond a reasonable doubt. It has, consequently, been given great weight in the story which follows.

But there were still voids. At times the informer and/or other witnesses who were prepared to speak openly were not present. For example, all but one of the men went off alone and committed a solitary crime. In a few cases, the victim survived to give testimony, or a witness was nearby. In other cases, only the solitary killer can be certain of the exact sequence of events. And even when a witness was available, his testimony was limited by what he happened to observe and what he could recall of that observation. And no matter how excellent his memory of observed fact, no witness can tell what was in the killers' mind—or in the victim's.

It would have been possible, of course, just to recount the unquestionable, observable facts and say no more. But that would have been irresponsible writing. The important question is not the who, when, or where of the Zebra murders; the important question is *why* they occurred at all. To answer that question I had to do two things: attempt to fill in the gaps in the observed events, and probe as much as possible the killers' minds.

Of course, only the killers themselves know for sure what was in their minds, or what they did when no witness was present. Everyone else, including myself, must proceed from what we know of their other actions, their background and habits, and what they later said (including, on a couple of lucky occasions, a slip of the tongue when being interviewed). Armed with all of this, we can then try to set down in logical order the most likely version of events. And with all the extrinsic facts available, the margin for error in that endeavor, and the conclusions it produced, have been substantially reduced.

The story which follows is as close to the truth as anyone is ever likely to get. All of the named characters are real people, except two: the person known as Vandyke, who is a composite of several men who conducted unauthorized and illegal secret meetings of Muslim followers; and the character of Willie Fields, from whom the secret laws and other documents of the former Nation of Islam were obtained. Names and identifying characteristics have been changed only where indicated, and for the reasons given. Following the story, an Afterword—"Six Years Later"—has been included to bring the reader up to date on the principal persons involved.

Because the persons who committed the Zebra crimes professed to believe that their deity, Allah, was moving them to do so, and that their acts were for the good of the Black Muslim or Nation of Islam religion, the following, for those unfamiliar with the sect, is a brief history of that religion taken from various Muslim and non-Muslim sources.

The Black Muslims are an independent socioreligious movement made up almost entirely of blacks in the United States. The movement was founded by one Wali Farad, an orthodox Muslim believed to have been born in Mecca around 1877. Farad, or Wallace Fard, as he is also called, migrated to the United States and in 1931 established his first mosque in Detroit. A year later, he founded a second temple in Chicago.

12

Fard's early followers were Negro migrants from the South. Fard preached to them that he was the incarnation of Allah and promised that if they believed in him, their race would someday overcome the white slavemasters and that they would be restored to a position of supremacy among the world's peoples.

Fard was succeeded as leader by one of his lieutenants, Elijah Muhammad, in 1934. Muhammad became known as the Messenger. He had been born Elijah Poole on October 7, 1897, in Sandersville, Georgia. He grew up in nearby Macon, attending public schools, and remained in the state of Georgia until he was twenty-five years old. He was the seventh of thirteen children. During his young manhood he worked for the Southern Railroad Company and the Cherokee Brick Company. In 1923 he married Clara Evans and migrated to Detroit. It was there that he alleged to have met God in the person of Wallace Fard, who, using the name Master Fard Muhammad, was preaching to blacks in the Detroit ghetto.

Elijah Poole was impressed enough with Fard that day to ask to become a follower. Fard gave him the name Elijah Karriem and accepted him as a student minister. Later, because Poole reportedly was the humblest of his disciples, Fard selected Poole as his Supreme Minister.

Black Muslim history states that Master Fard allowed himself to be persecuted. He was sent to jail in Detroit and Chicago; the reasons why are not clear. But for three years he also groomed his Supreme Minister for leadership. Then, in 1934, he disappeared. Elijah Poole Muhammad immediately assumed the title "Messenger of Allah" and began teaching that Fard had, in fact, been Allah Himself. Some of the other Detroit ministers did not believe Elijah, so in 1934 he moved to the mosque in Chicago. Unsuccessful there, he moved a year later to Washington, D.C.

The next few years of Nation of Islam history are vague. It is believed that Elijah went from city to city on the East Coast teaching Islam and recruiting followers, apparently with some degree of success, for he eventually attained sole leadership of the Nation. But the next definite record of him was in May 1942, when he was arrested by the FBI for failure to register for the draft. At that time he said he "would not take part in the war, especially not on the side of the infidels." He served five years in federal prisons, while the Nation of Islam was run by his wife, Clara Evans Muhammad.

In the decade following World War Two, mosques were established in most large cities with sizable Negro populations, and the primary beliefs of the Black Muslims began to be taught with greater zeal. Those beliefs were that the black man was morally and culturally superior, and was destined to rule the earth. The sect condemned Christianity as the chief stratagem of the continued enslavement of nonwhites, and preached that the white race was conceived of devils whose time to reign was coming to an end. It encouraged the reclamation of fallen blacks such as convicts, drug addicts, and so forth, through the study of their true history, through striving for economic independence, and by preparation for the Battle of Armageddon, which they believed would be the final struggle between good and evil, black and white.

The movement established its headquarters at Temple No. 2 in Chicago, when that Midwestern city became the "New Mecca" of the Nation in January 1955. The Nation enjoyed continued growth through the years, and at the time of the Zebra crimes was a thriving religion which was opening numerous black-operated businesses in nearly every large U.S. city in which it had a mosque. Its basic beliefs at that time had not changed: the black man was superior, the white man was a "devil" (Elijah Muhammad) or a "beast" (Malcolm X, a rising young Muslim leader later assassinated).

Then, in 1975, Elijah Muhammad died at the age of seventy-seven.

Poole's son, Wallace Muhammad, succeeded his father as head of the sect. He ultimately relinquished absolute leadership in favor of a governing council, and gradually the old policies of Elijah Muhammad were modified to fit the modern needs of the organization. The old Nation of Islam is now no more; the World Community of Islam has replaced it. Ministers are now "Imams," and the religion no longer espouses black superiority. Today the group welcomes members of all ethnic backgrounds. Recently, the Imam of the San Quentin Prison mosque stated that, "although it will take us quite some time to erase our old image, we will do just that by promoting brotherhood among all men."

That is a laudable goal for the World Community of Islam—or indeed for any of us.

14

Throughout history there have been many stories and examples of man's inhumanity to man. Down through the ages, human beings have destroyed their own kind in an incredible variety of ways, for a multitude of reasons: in the name of gods, philosophies, politics, creeds, *ad infinitum*. Not the most rare of the reasons have been those of race. Hitler slew Jews because they were an "inferior race"—and Pancho Villa executed "Chinamen" in Mexico for the same reasons. The Chinese in turn beheaded "foreign devils" in their own land with little or no provocation; and Idi Amin killed even more promiscuously. The Ku Klux Klan has burned alive black men in the South for reasons of "race" and "white religion"—and the Zebra killers murdered innocent whites in San Francisco because their Black Muslim faith taught them that "blue-eyed devils" were less than human.

Monstrous behavior has never been restricted by race or religion—and never will be. The recounting of that behavior in books, articles, and films must never be restricted either—not by censor, not by conscience. For only in the telling of it might understanding surface.

In this story, as in any story of criminal tragedy, it is left to the reader to decide *why* it happened, where the fault lies. The reader must decide in this case whether the Zebra crimes, by example, are a condemnation of the antiwhite teachings of the former Nation of Islam movement, or whether those teachings were merely an excuse used by a group of psychopaths who would have killed anyway.

It is a hard question to try to answer.

But it would be harder *not* to try to answer it.

We leave it to the reader.

CLARK HOWARD

Author's Note

In this book the reader will encounter two sets of similar characters.

The first set of characters is five previously unidentified men who commit murders during the course of the story. They are given nicknames.

The second set of characters is five men who are eventually accused of being those murderers. These men are identified by their true names.

The two sets of characters are, as indicated, greatly similar. Each set is composed of black men, of varying shades of complexion. They dress in similar fashion, wear their hair in similar styles, have collective characteristics so similar, in fact, that they may become interchangeable, indistinguishable, in the minds of many readers.

Why, then, the two sets of characters?

The author used two sets of characters because he did not choose to judge the men personally. They have already been judged in a court of law. A jury has found them guilty; it is not necessary for the author to do so also.

The use of two sets of characters—one with nicknames, one with actual names—permitted me, in my own mind if nowhere else, the luxury of not having to accuse—or judge—men who still profess their innocence.

PART ONE
The 179 Days

Day 1

The meetings were held in the loft of a San Francisco warehouse. They were conducted by a dignified black man with a Vandyke beard. He wore a business suit and spoke in a quiet, almost ministerial tone.

"The population of the white man in North America has reached one hundred and three million. The population of the black man is only seventeen million. But"—he held a stiff forefinger next to one ear—"the population of the white man throughout the world is only four hundred million, while the population of the black man throughout the world has now reached four and a half *billion.*"

He turned and strolled at a measured pace before one wall of the loft. Facing him, sitting on old but comfortable club chairs and sofas, was an audience of a dozen black men. Their eyes followed him as he strolled.

"There are fifty-seven million square miles of land on the earth. The white man uses only six million square miles; the black man uses nearly four times that amount: twenty-three million square miles."

In two corners of the room, facing the audience, the speaker's bodyguards stood: two large, powerful black men with narrowed, darting eyes that constantly scanned the attentive faces. These men accompanied the speaker everywhere, one of them driving the Continental in which he rode, the other opening doors for him wherever he went.

"So on the earth today," the speaker continued, "there are more black men than white, and the black men occupy and use more land than the white." He stopped strolling and his voice took on a noticeable edge. "Why then has the white man been able to set himself up as our superior? Why has he been able to control our race for four hundred years? To answer that question"—the forefinger went up again—"we must go back in time and learn how the white man came to be."

The speaker returned to the center of the wall and faced his audience. Something seemed to be happening to his eyes; they were becoming wider, and whiter.

"A thousand years ago, near the holy city of Mecca, there lived an evil black leader named Yakub. He desired to create a race of weak people that he and his ancestors could rule forever. To do this, he began to study the black race. He learned that in every black man there exists two germs: a black germ and a brown germ. He found a way to separate the brown germs from the black germs, and he put the brown germs into all the healthy, strong girls among his followers who were at least sixteen years of age. As they produced babies, he had the black ones separated and fed to wild beasts, but he had the brown ones carefully nursed and raised to adults. Then he passed a law that blacks who were alike could not marry; only those who were unlike could marry. Black had to marry brown. Dark had to marry light, and light had to marry lighter.

"Yakub was pleased because he saw his people becoming weaker and weaker, while he and those who ruled with him remained black and strong. For six hundred years there continued this process of grafting brown from black, and lighter brown from darker brown, until finally the original black blood had thinned so much and become so weak that the germ it carried lost all its color and became white. Weak, wicked white."

From the audience came several low grunts of disapproval. The speaker nodded agreement with them.

"By the time the descendants of Yakub realized what had been done, it was too late. The grafted white devils had spread over the earth and were teaching lessons about a new, mysterious god that no one could see until after death. Soon eighty-five percent of the people on earth were being taught about this mystery god. They were being taught by ten percent who were clever and crafty and desired to lead them. Only a scant five percent of the earth's population remained righteously believing in the true god, Allah."

The speaker raised his forefinger like a vengeful sword. "For four hundred years these white infidels have spread their false religion over the land like a great dirty plague, trying to put out the light of Allah. Christians and Jews alike are guilty of setting up rivals to Allah. Both are black-slave-making religions dedicated to the mental destruction of the black man. They are the enemies of Allah and they are the sole people responsible for leading astray nine-tenths of the world's black population!"

"Evil!" one of the men in the audience said loudly.

The speaker's eyes widened even more. His voice grew raspy, hissing. "For four hundred years this grafted white devil has controlled the earth and manipulated the black man. For four hundred years he has castrated black men, raped black women, and *stomped* the heads of little black babies!"

"Devils!" said a voice in the audience. It was the same man who had spoken before. He was a thick-necked black man with a clean-shaven skull and eyes like bullet holes. The only soft feature of his entire presence was his long, almost feminine eyelashes. Under the overhead light, his shiny skull glistened. Call this man Head.

"For four hundred years," the speaker now began to rant, "we, the true followers of Allah, the true Muslims of the earth, have suffered persecution at the hands of this grafted white devil who came from our very own diluted seed! We have been relegated to ghettos, deprived of a decent education, victimized in the labor market, and sent to the white man's prisons!" The forefinger whipped across the audience. "There are some in this very room who can give witness to the injustices wreaked on us in the white man's prisons!"

"Right on!" said Head. He was one who could give such witness.

"All right!" said a young, light-skinned Negro next to him. So

21

light that his skin had faint freckles on it, he was seven years younger than Head, who was twenty-eight, and handsome in a boyish way. Unlike Head, he could *not* give witness to anything about the white man's prison, because he had never even been arrested, much less incarcerated. In the muted overhead light, with the dark contrast of Head next to him, he looked almost yellow-skinned. Call him Yellow.

"But we do not need the white man's prisons to prove to us that the white man is our enemy," the Vandyked speaker continued. "We need only to study our lessons from this—" He removed a small book from his inside pocket. "*Message to the Black Man,*" he said, lowering his voice to a reverent tone to read the book's title. Opening the cover, he recited a prayer on the first page. "In the name of Allah, the Beneficent, the Most Merciful Savior, to whom all praise is due for raising up among us a Divine Leader, Teacher, and Guide, the most honorable Elijah Muhammad. *As-salaam-alaikum.*"

"*As-salaam-alaikum,*" the audience repeated in concert. It was a traditional Muslim saying, "Peace be with you."

"Turn to the subject of Islam in this book and you will find your answer as to who is the enemy of Allah," the speaker said. "Turn to the fourth question and the fourth answer and you will see, you will learn. Listen! The fourth question: 'Does Allah have enemies, and who are they?' The fourth answer: 'The enemies of Allah are known at the present as the white race or European race, who are the sole people responsible for misleading nine-tenths of the total population of the black nation.' That"—he stabbed the air above him with his forefinger—"tells us who our enemy is. Now you tell me!"

"The grafted white devil!" said Head.

"White devils!" said Yellow.

"Whites—whites—whites!" said the others in a low chant.

Only one man in the audience did not respond. He was the third man who sat on the couch with Head and Yellow. He was the same age as Head, and like Head had been in the white man's prison. The two had met in San Quentin; this one had only recently been released. Nothing about his appearance was unusual; he had neither the boyish good looks of Yellow, nor the cold-eyed countenance of Head. He was simply ordinary-looking. What was *ex-traordinary* about him lay under the surface, unseen. It rested in his hands, which were lethal, and his feet, which were deadly. He was an expert at kung fu and jujitsu. Call this one Judo.

"Now that we know the enemy," the speaker said, "what do we do about him?" He smiled, parting the hair around his pink lips. "Simply read the laws of Mohammed. Read the tenth lesson, which asks, 'Why does Mohammed and any Moslem murder the devil?' And answers, 'Because the devil is one hundred percent wicked and will not keep and obey the laws of Islam. His ways and actions are like a snake of the grafted type. Mohammed has learned that he cannot reform the white devils, so they must be murdered. All Moslems will murder the white devil because they know he is a snake. Each Moslem is required to kill four devils, and by bringing and presenting four at one time, his reward is a button to wear on the lapel of his coat, and free transportation to the holy city of Mecca to see Brother Mohammed."

"Praise Brother Mohammed!" the men in the audience said as one voice. Again except for Judo, who remained silent.

"The lessons are clear," the speaker said. His eyes were very wide now, the eyeballs quivering white globes that rolled over the faces before him. "The lessons say who the enemy is!"

"Right on!"

"The lessons say what to do about the enemy!"

"Right on!"

"Kill the grafted snake!"

"Kill it!"

"Kill the evil whites!"

"Kill them!"

"Kill the blue-eyed devils!"

"Kill! Kill! Kill!"

The chant was low, murmured, sloshing across the room like dirty water in a flooded basement. It came from mechanized mouths below mesmerized eyes, robotlike, hypnotic, uncontrollable.

While the chant was going on, the speaker quietly left. His body-

23

guards opened the doors for him and followed him downstairs and out back to where the Continental was parked. They drove away into the night.

Behind, in the loft, the chant went on, created by the voices of all the men who had listened to the speaker. All but one.

Judo.

Anthony Cornelius Harris, number B-35599, sat on a bench on the upper yard at San Quentin and watched the activity around him through narrowed eyes. It was spring of 1973 and Harris was nearing the end of the second year of his second term in prison. This time he was in for burglary; earlier he had served nearly two and a half years for battery on a police officer. The battery had occurred when Harris and his brother Pinky had been fighting on the street in Long Beach. A policeman tried to break them up. Harris, a judo expert, had turned on the officer and disabled him in seconds. Arrested and tried, he was given a six-months-to-ten-years sentence and committed to San Quentin.

Some men hated prison, but Harris did not even dislike it, not really. In a way, being in prison was an easy life. Except for the absence of women, the only thing that disagreed with him was the boredom. He found the life extremely boring at times. Such as now when he had nothing to do but sit on the yard and watch other convicts who also had nothing to do. He had a job in the bookbindery but it only took up part of his day. The rest of the time he was idle. He had tried to enroll in elementary-school classes—he only had a third-grade education—but his request was denied because San Quentin's school enrollment was then out of balance ethnicwise. Too many blacks, not enough whites and Chicanos. Later, perhaps, he was told. So he sat on the yard, bored.

Harris leaned his head back and closed his eyes all the way. His lids shut out the glare of the Northern California sun that burned into the upper yard. He wished he had a nice cold bottle of pop right then. The canteen was open; all he had to do was walk down to the lower yard and buy one, but he only had a couple of dollars in his inmate account, so he decided against it. He rarely had much money for prison luxuries—pop, gum, candy, snack food to keep

24

in his cell—because his wife would not deposit any money in his account unless he allowed her to visit him—and that he would not do. His wife was white; it would have been embarrassing, if not downright dangerous, to let her visit. The way things were in Q at that time—three distinct cliques: white, black, and Chicano—his position as a loner, a judo fighter who wanted to serve his own time, would have been seriously jeopardized if it got around that he had a white wife. For the first few months after he came back for his second rap, he had lived in dread fear that some inmate clerk in the records office would read his package and spread the word about it. Then, judo fighter or not, he would have had to take heavy flak from both the black *and* white convict communities. Better to do without cold pop on a hot day.

As he sat on the bench with his head back and eyes closed, a loudspeaker blared across the yard. "ATTENTION, ALL INMATES! NATION OF ISLAM RELIGIOUS SERVICES FOR ALL BLACK MUSLIMS WILL BE HELD IN THE CHAPEL COMMENCING IN TEN MINUTES! ALL MEMBERS OF THE NATION OF ISLAM RELIGION, AND ALL INMATES DESIRING TO BECOME BLACK MUSLIMS, ARE CORDIALLY INVITED TO ATTEND!"

Anthony Harris opened his eyes. For a moment he stared transfixed at the ground in front of him. Then he sighed quietly, rose, and slowly walked off toward the auditorium. At least it would be something to do.

A little while after the speaker left, the chanting in the loft stopped and the dozen black men dispersed. It was dusk. Head, Yellow, and Judo crossed the rear parking lot to a white Dodge van. Yellow got behind the wheel, Head took the passenger seat, and Judo sat in back on a stack of folded furniture moving pads.

Yellow turned to Head. "Where to, man?"

"Go south on Mission," said Head. He stretched his muscular arms and threw a tight smile over his shoulder at Judo. "I'm glad it's the weekend, man. Gives us lots of time to get even with the motherfuckers for all the nights we spent in Q." He half turned in his seat, waiting for an answer from Judo. When one was not forthcoming, he prompted, "Right, man?"

"Yeah, man, right," Judo replied. He hoped Head did not notice the lack of enthusiasm in his voice. Head could be very vicious when he got mad.

Yellow drove along Mission Street, down the middle of the San Francisco peninsula. Head watched out the front and side windows, his bullet-hole eyes looking, scanning, searching.

"Hey, man, tell me some more about Q," said Yellow with boyish enthusiasm. It was a regular question with him. He was the kid asking the big guys about the service. Never having been arrested, he had a morbid curiosity about prison. It fascinated him.

"Ain't nothin' to tell, man," said Head. "It's a fucking white man's joint. I'm just glad I be out, man. I been waiting a long time to pay my respects to my white enemies."

"Hey, man, you tell me about it," Yellow said to Judo.

Judo sighed. The question was getting old. "What you want to know now, man?"

"Did you hate it in there?"

"I didn't hate it. It wasn't too bad."

Head threw him a contemptuous look. "Man, what the fuck's the matter with you? You been in that fucking place two times and all you can say is, 'It wasn't too bad.' Shit." He looked back at Judo. "You better get your head on right and start thinking vicious, man. You a black man and you've gone through four hundred fucking years of slavery." Head twisted around in the seat. "Sometimes I wonder about you, man. Sometimes I wonder what kind of heart you got."

"Don't worry none about it," Judo replied with an edge. "Ain't nothing the matter with my heart."

"We'll see," said Head. He faced forward again and his expression became set. "We each gonna try to get one white kid tonight. It be the first of four that we all need."

"Say, man, I want to ask you about that," said Judo. "The man tonight, he say four white *devils*. He don't say nothing about no kids. How come you looking for kids?"

"Because the man, he only be talking about what it take to be a regular Muslim. What *we* talking about is what it take to be a Death Angel."

26

Judo rolled his eyes upward. The Death Angels. They were back to that shit again.

Leaving that first Muslim meeting in San Quentin, Anthony Harris was approached by a thick-necked black man with a clean-shaven skull and eyes like bullet holes. His name was Jesse Lee Cooks. He was serving the last year of a seven-and-a-half-year sentence for armed robbery.

"Say, brother, what's happening?" Cooks asked.

Harris shrugged. "Ain't much."

"You the one knows judo and that stuff, ain't that right?"

"I know some, yeah."

"How 'bout teaching it to me?" Cooks asked.

"I don't know, man," Harris said hesitantly. "It takes a long time to learn."

"Hey, baby, I got the time, you know what I mean?" Cooks said. He smiled, but it was not a pleasant smile; it was cold, mechanical.

"What about the guards?" Harris asked, looking for a respectable way out.

"Fuck the guards," said Cooks. "Prisoners got rights too, man. Long as we don't do no disrupting, they can't stop us."

"What do you want to learn?" Harris asked. Maybe he could teach Cooks a few simple holds and throws, and let it go at that.

"I want to learn how to bust a heart with a punch to the chest," the thick-necked black said. "And how to come up behind somebody and snap their neck. I want to learn how to kill, man." He took Harris by the arm and led him to a private corner. "See, man, in San Francisco they got what's called the Death Angels. It's a special part of the Muslims. The job of the Death Angels is to off white chumps, see? But you got to prove that you can kill before they'll let you in. So I want to learn how to kill. How 'bout it, brother?"

Harris shrugged resignedly. "I guess," he said. Why not? he asked himself. It was better than being bored. And it did not look like he was going to get into the prison school.

So he began teaching judo and kung fu to Jesse Lee Cooks.

* * *

"Turn up Tingley Street," Head told Yellow. "There's usually white kids out playing in this neighborhood."

Yellow turned off Mission into Tingley.

"I still don't see why we need kids," Judo said from the rear of the van.

"Oh, man," Head said irritably. He slapped Yellow on the arm. "Explain it to the dude, will you?"

Yellow glanced at Judo in the rearview mirror. "Offing white kids is the quickest way to get into the Death Angels," he said. "See, they figure it's harder for a grown man to kill a kid or a woman than it is for him to kill a man. Killing mens is easy. To get into the Death Angels, you gots to kill nine white men. Killing women is harder, so you only gots to kill five. Killing kids is the hardest; alls you need is four of them."

"Turn here and go over to the next street," Head instructed.

Yellow drove over to Theresa Street. They cruised the block, searching. There were no children out.

"Try the next street," Head directed. "Just keep going."

Yellow drove down Cotter Street. No children.

"Next street." Head's voice was surly; his patience was thinning.

Yellow drove along Francis Street. Near the corner they saw two white children in front of the steps of a house, and a third white youngster coming down the steps to meet them.

"Perfect," said Head. "One for each of us." He patted Yellow's arm. "Pull over and park, brother."

The girl coming down the steps of her home at 41 Francis Street was eleven-year-old Michele Denise Carrasco. She was a slender child with huge, dark eyes and a quick, tentative smile. Her dark hair was parted in the middle and fell to each shoulder.

Inside the house, Michele's brother Greg was having a birthday party. Michele was out on the steps to see her friend, twelve-year-old Marie Stewart. The two girls attended nearby Corpus Christi School together. On this evening, Marie's fifteen-year-old brother Frank, a Unity Junior High School student, had walked over to Michele's house with his sister. The two of them were waiting on the

28

steps when Michele came out. As they began talking, all of them noticed two black men walking toward them. The youngsters continued talking until the men came up to them and stopped.

"Say," Head said to Michele Carrasco, "where's Mission Street?"

Michele pointed toward the corner. "Up there, one block," she said.

Head looked around nervously. His hands played with the front of his black leather jacket. The other man, Judo, slipped one hand inside the black Nehru coat he wore.

"Where's Mission Street?" Head asked again.

Michele frowned. "I told you: down there one block."

Her words were barely out when Head drew a gun from his waistband. He grabbed the girl roughly by her arm. "Just be quiet," Head warned, pointing the gun at her. "Just be quiet and follow us."

Judo was on the curb, blocking any possible escape by Frank and Marie Stewart. He still had one hand inside his Nehru coat.

The youngsters were marched three abreast along the sidewalk. Head walked on the inside, continuing to hold Michele's arm, the gun at her back. Judo kept to the outside, his free hand holding Frank Stewart's elbow.

"Hey, have you guys been drinking?" Frank asked. Maybe it was some kind of joke.

"Shut up!" Head snapped.

They walked toward the van, which was parked facing them on Francis just off the next cross street, Alemany Boulevard. Yellow was standing beside the van waiting for them. He was shifting his weight from foot to foot as if he had to go to the bathroom.

"Get the door open," Head told Yellow as they approached. Yellow hurried to the side of the van.

"Listen, is this a joke?" Michele asked. The black man was hurting her arm and had a wild look in his eyes. He forced her toward the back of the van.

Suddenly Frank Stewart jerked away from Judo and yelled, "Cops!" His sister, who was in the middle being held by no one, darted to his side. They both started running.

"Oh, man!" Head said angrily to Judo.

29

With the black man's attention momentarily distracted, Michele jerked her own arm away and also started running. Because the black men and the van were between her and her house, Michele had to run in the opposite direction. She ran to the nearby corner and hurried down Alemany Boulevard.

Back at the van, Head glared at Judo. "Man, you fucked up!"

"No worse than you, motherfucker!" Judo snapped.

Yellow was already getting behind the wheel. "Come on, let's get the fuck out of here!" he said in a breaking voice. Now he *did* have to go to the bathroom; several drops of urine had already spotted his trousers.

Michele was still running. Down Alemany one block to Santa Rosa; around another corner and down another street; unable to run home, she was heading for the next safest place she knew: the rectory of Corpus Christi Catholic Church.

Frank and Marie Stewart were safe by now. They had reached the Carrasco home and the police were being called. On the next street over, at the church, a priest named Father Gerald took the terrified Michele by the hand and started walking her home.

And in the van, Yellow was making a U-turn and swinging north on Alemany Boulevard to get out of the area. Next to him, Head was muttering, "Motherfucker! Motherfucker!"

Judo, in the back, was trying to keep his trembling hands out of sight.

Anthony Harris had first learned to fear Jesse Lee Cooks after he began teaching him judo in San Quentin. Cooks was different from anyone Harris had ever known—although in what *way* he was different, Harris was not certain. At times, Harris thought it was simply because Cooks was more dangerous than other men, but there were times too when he was certain that it was because Cooks was less *sane* than other men. The man's capacity for evil thinking seemed to Harris to be without bounds.

"What I plan to do someday," Cooks told him, "is raid a white orphanage and take all the little white kids by their feet and swing them like a baseball bat and smash their brains out against the wall."

Another time he said, "I'd like to raid one of those hospitals

30

where old white people live. You know, man, one of those places where they just sit around all day slobbering all over theyselves. Man, I'd like to just go through a place like that and off them all, every one of the old motherfuckers. Use a blade and really hack them up."

It never occurred to Harris that perhaps Jesse Cooks's dreams of carnage were all founded in cowardice. Cooks always planned to attack children or old people or women. Never anyone who might fight back. Always the weak, the helpless.

Harris continued to train Cooks nevertheless. He also began training other members of what was called the San Quentin Mosque of the Nation of Islam. As Harris had skeptically predicted, the prison guards did not like what he was teaching, but—as the institutionwise Cooks had told him—there was nothing they could do about it. The judo sessions were quiet and orderly; they broke no rules, caused no trouble. Still, the guards must have had uneasy feelings as they patrolled the exercise yard and watched someone like Jesse Lee Cooks learning to gouge out eyes, crush a larynx, snap a neck, and burst a heart with a single powerful blow to the chest.

While Harris was teaching, he was also learning. After formally becoming a member of the mosque, he was invited to attend lectures which came into the prison on cassettes. The lectures preached black superiority, reminded those who listened of the preceding four hundred years of abuse, and openly encouraged active revenge against white devils. Prison officials often found the contents of the tapes repugnant, but they were unable to suppress them. Muslimism was a religion, and freedom of religious choice was a guaranteed right—even for convicts.

Gradually the taped lectures and other indoctrinations began to have a collective effect on Anthony Harris. He began to think less and less of his white wife, and daydreamed about marrying a black girl. He also shunned going to school when an opening finally became available. "I changed my mind," he told the counselor. "I don't want any part of the white educational system."

When he was being evaluated for possible future parole, Harris was asked to give his version of the crime that sent him to prison for the second time. "I was living with my wife in an apartment down in Santa Ana," he said. "A couple of guys my brother knew needed a place to stay, so I let them stay with us. Then me and my wife, we went down to San Diego for the weekend, see. An' when we come back, our TV and stereo and some of our furniture had been pawned to this here pawnshop, and the two friends of my brother was gone. My old lady was pretty upset about it, but I didn't have no money to get the stuff back. Well, she kept bitchin' and yelling about it, so finally I said okay, goddamn it, I'll go out and *steal* the money to take the stuff out of pawn."

He had gone out that night and burglarized the Charles Haynes Realty Company in Long Beach. His loot amounted to one hundred dollars petty cash and a few postage stamps. A month later, while riding in a car with two other men, the three of them were arrested on suspicion of armed robbery because they fit the description of a holdup trio. The charge was subsequently dropped, but during the proceedings the Haynes Realty burglary came up and was eventually blamed on Harris. He confessed and pled guilty to one count of second-degree burglary. He was sentenced to serve from six months to fifteen years, and returned to prison as a second-termer.

In San Quentin, Harris first worked in Food Service, dishing out food in the dining room. Then he was assigned to Waterfront and worked on the docks. Eventually he was moved to Vocational Bookbinding. That was when he had asked to go to school but was refused because too many blacks were already enrolled. He also asked to learn to be a baker, thinking it would be a good occupation when he was released. But the counselors told him he was not smart enough for that trade. Finally he drifted into the Black Muslims.

In mid-August of 1973, Anthony Harris said good-bye to Jesse Lee Cooks when the latter was paroled. Harris himself was scheduled for parole within the next two months.

The two Black Muslims instinctively knew they would see each other on the outside.

After the fiasco with the three white children, the men in the van were nervous and shaken. Head was furious with Judo.

"Man, you fucked up!" he accused again, his naturally petulant mouth puffed into a sullen pout.

"No more than you did," Judo replied, detesting the weakness he could hear in his own voice.

Head picked up at once on that weakness. "You got piss for blood, man! You not fit to be a Death Angel!"

"Fuck you, motherfucker," said Judo. It was all he could think of to say.

"Quit bitchin' at one another," Yellow said. He glanced at Head. "Tell me where to go, man."

Head looked out the window to get his bearings. They were on the Bayshore Freeway now, heading north, passing San Francisco General Hospital. "Keep on going," Head told him. "All the way to the end of the freeway." He ignored both of them then and sat muttering to himself.

Yellow followed the curving, turning freeway toward its terminus near the Embarcadero. The men did not speak to each other for the fifteen minutes or so that the drive took. Yellow concentrated on his driving, keeping the van in a middle lane and well within the speed limit. Judo laced his fingers together and gripped tightly to control his trembling. He silently cursed Head for being so accurate in his evaluation. Judo *had* been frightened back there; in prison vernacular, he *did* have piss for blood. He glanced up and saw that Head's lips were still moving as the bald man continued to mutter under his breath.

Yellow drove off the freeway and cruised along Battery Street. "Where to now?" he asked Head.

"Man, I don't give a shit where," Head replied crossly. He spotted a lone white man waiting to cross the street at Battery and Vallejo. "Pull over right there," he said. "I'll kill that motherfucker right on the corner."

Judo's mouth dropped open. "Man, you crazy! You just *asking* to go back to Q." He slapped Yellow on the shoulder. "Keep driving, man."

"I said stop here!" Head repeated. He snatched the pistol from his belt but did not point it at anyone.

"No, keep driving, man!" Judo ordered. "I ain't going back to the shithouse on account of this crazy motherfucker." Judo looked into Head's eyes and saw the glare of murder! He slipped one hand under his Nehru coat in case Head lost control and decided to start shooting. The feel of his own gun was reassuring.

"Hey, man, he's right," Yellow said to a now extremely agitated Head. "This ain't no place to do one. Besides, I want a woman or a kid; it takes too many men to get Death Angel wings."

Death Angel wings were awarded to each man who killed four white children, five white women, or nine white men. Upon completion of the required quota, a new member's photograph was taken and a pair of black wings were drawn extending from the neck. The photo was mounted on a board along with pictures of other successful candidates, and the board was displayed on an easel at the loft meetings. At that time, there were fifteen accredited Death Angels in California. To achieve their collective membership, they had already quietly killed throughout the state 135 white men, 75 white women, 60 white children—or enough of a combination thereof to give each of them his required four, five, or nine credits. This was October of 1973. The California attorney general's office had already secretly compiled a list of forty-five of those killings which had taken place in the cities of San Francisco, Oakland, Berkeley, Long Beach, Signal Hill, Santa Barbara, Palo Alto, Pacifica, San Diego, and Los Angeles; and in the counties of San Mateo, Santa Clara, Los Angeles, Contra Costa, Ventura, and Alameda. All of the victims were white. All the known suspects in the killings had been associated with the Black Muslim movement. The killings were even then continuing throughout the state.

"Come on, man, I want me a white woman or a kid, hear?" said Yellow. "I don't want to fuck with no men." He drove past the man on the corner. Head muttered something but did not object further.

Yellow turned left off Battery and began cruising the Telegraph Hill area.

In their apartment at 399 Chestnut Street, Richard Hague and his wife Quita decided to go for a walk after dinner. It was a pleasant evening. Richard put on a light cardigan; Quita pulled a yellow-and-orange South American woolen shawl around her shoulders, over the sweatshirt and cardigan she already had on. They left the apartment and walked west on Chestnut, toward Columbus Avenue.

Richard Hague, age thirty, was a mining engineer employed in the San Francisco office of Utah International Company. Quita, two years younger, was a reporter for the Industrial City press in South San Francisco. The previous month they had celebrated their seventh wedding anniversary.

As they walked downhill on Chestnut, they held hands.

Richard and Quita Hague were white.

"There you are, man," Head said to Yellow when he saw the young white couple. "There's a woman for you and a man for me."

"What about him?" asked Yellow, bobbing his chin toward Judo and speaking as if he were not even present.

"His heart ain't ready," Head replied with a sneer.

"Fuck you, man!" Judo snapped.

"Pull over there by the corner," Head instructed, ignoring Judo.

Yellow parked on the north side of Chestnut, near the corner of Powell. The young white couple was walking along the south side of the street, toward the same corner.

"You stay with the van like before," Head told Yellow. He turned to Judo. "You gonna help or not, man?" he asked coldly. Head and Judo locked eyes. Head's question was a direct challenge and Judo knew it.

"I'm right behind you, man," said Judo. At that moment he hated Head.

Head and Judo got out of the van and strolled across the street. They stepped onto the sidewalk a hundred feet in front of the white couple. They separated: Head stood at the curb, Judo leaned against a fence across the sidewalk. The white couple would have to walk between them.

Quita Hague frequently had trouble with people mispronouncing her name. Most people pronounced it as it was spelled, coming up with something like "Quee-ta." The correct pronunciation was "Kee-ta." She had developed a clever way to point out the correct pronunciation: She would say, "Just think of me as 'Quita Banana.' " It worked like a charm.

Quita was a vivacious, outgoing young woman with a keen, often infectious sense of humor. She was quick to laugh at her own misfortunes, such as running out of gas on the Bayshore Freeway at midnight. Her pixie grin and freckles often caused people to mistake her for Irish. But her maiden name was Pirelli-Minetti, and one of the things she was most proud of in life was that her grandfather, a vineyard specialist, had been one of the earliest graduates of Stanford University, in the class of 1906.

As she walked with her husband this evening, Quita was looking forward to Christmas. She liked Christmas better than any other holiday. It was still two months away, but she habitually started thinking about it early. Whenever the season approached, she was always reminded of the first Christmas she and Richard had spent together. They had been married four months and were living in South West Africa where Richard was employed as a geologist. There was no such thing as an evergreen Christmas tree to be found, so Quita decided that they should decorate a camelthorn bush, which had an abundance of small green leaves as well as countless tiny thorns. It, along with an uncommonly tough turkey and sweltering temperatures, did little to bring them any of the traditional holiday spirit. They ended up celebrating Christmas at a local swimming pool to escape the heat.

It had not been much of a first Christmas, but for the sentimental Quita it was a memory she cherished.

She held Richard's hand a little tighter as they walked down Chestnut—toward two black men lounging on opposite sides of the sidewalk.

As the Hagues started to walk between them, Head reached out and grabbed Richard by the arm. "Hold it, man. Don't move. You coming with us."

Judo stepped away from the fence and leveled a gun at them. He was standing downhill, looking up at them. Richard froze. But not Quita.

"No, no, no," she said, frightened, her voice breaking. She bolted past Judo and ran several yards downhill.

Now Head drew a gun. He pointed it at Richard's chest. "Get on back up here, woman," he said to Quita, "or I'll kill him."

The eyes of Quita Hague and her husband met for a split instant in the dull gray of the streetlight.

"They already have us," said Richard. "Let's cooperate. They won't hurt us."

Reluctantly, hesitantly, Quita walked back up to where her husband was being held. Judo took her arm.

"Over to that van," Head said. Still holding Richard's arm, he guided him across the narrow street. Judo followed a step behind with Quita.

Yellow saw them coming. He hopped out and ran around to open the cargo door on the passenger side.

"Get in there," Head ordered, shoving Richard toward the van. Hague climbed into the van. "Move over there and lay down," said Head. "On your stomach." Hague crawled over and stretched out facedown next to the furniture pads stacked in the bed of the van.

"Now you." Head nodded to Quita.

"No!" she said, terrified again. She started to run a second time. Yellow, younger and faster than either Head or Judo, reached out and grabbed her by the hair. He jerked her back and slammed her against the side of the van. She groaned and started to go limp.

"Get in there!" Yellow snapped, grabbing her under the arm, up close to the shoulder, and manhandling her into the van. He made her stretch out behind the passenger seat, facedown like her husband was lying. "You lay there, bitch!" he said in his ugly, boyish voice. The urine had dried on his trousers now and he felt better. More like a man.

Then suddenly he heard something that made even his bowels queasy.

"Shit, man!" Judo hissed. "A fucking cop car is coming!"

Police officers Bruce Marovich and Ben McAllister were proceeding slowly down Chestnut toward Powell. McAllister was driving the black-and-white radio car; Marovich was in the passenger seat, routinely checking the street. As they passed the middle of the block, Marovich observed some activity on the sidewalk next to where a light-colored Dodge van was parked. He frowned, studying the situation, as the radio car slowly passed the van. Marovich had been a policeman for more than five years. He could see nothing really suspicious occurring at the van, and yet—

"Hold it a minute," he said to McAllister. "Back up next to that white van."

McAllister backed up. As they halted parallel to the van, Head walked around to them.

"What's going on?" Marovich asked out the passenger window.

"Everything's okay, Officer," Head said with a smile. "We had a flat and we're fixing it."

Behind Head, Marovich could see another black man. He was vaguely aware of still a third person around by the open cargo door. But nothing seemed out of order. The two blacks he could see up close were neatly dressed, well-groomed men; certainly not hubcap thieves.

Marovich thought about it for a moment. Then he said, "Okay."

He nodded to his partner and they drove on, continuing their patrol.

Minutes later, the van was on the freeway again, heading south toward the railroad yards below the Central Basin. Yellow was driving. Head was in the rear, astraddle Richard Hague, tying his hands behind him with heavy twine. Judo was next to him, astraddle Quita. Her hands were already tied. Judo had her rolled onto her side; one hand was up under her sweat shirt, feeling her breasts.

Yellow glanced in the rearview mirror and saw Head looking through Richard Hague's wallet. "We not allowed to steal, man," he said.

"You just drive," Head snapped. "I ain't doing nothing but just looking." He closed the wallet and shoved it back into Richard's pocket. Then he rolled Hague over and started going through his front pockets.

Hague raised his head and saw that Judo was doing something to Quita. "What are you doing to her?" he asked.

Judo, angered at being watched by the white woman's husband, reached over and hit him in the mouth. "Shut up, motherfucker!" He glanced at Head. "Man, make him keep his fucking face down."

"Keep your face down, motherfucker!" Head ordered.

Hague raised his head again, blood running over his bottom lip from Judo's backhand. "What is he doing to her?"

Head reached behind him and picked up a straight lug wrench. "I done told you to keep your white motherfucking face down!"

He swung the lug wrench and smashed Richard Hague's jaw. Hague's head flopped back as if his neck were broken; blood gushed from his nostrils. Head hit him again, breaking his jaw in two more places. "I told the motherfucker once," he mumbled. "I don't tell no motherfucker twice." He hit him with the lug wrench a third time.

"Rick—" Quita said. It was little more than a plaintive whisper.

"Shut up, bitch," said Judo. He had Quita on her back now, sweat shirt and cardigan pushed up around her neck, fondling her exposed breasts with both hands.

Head got off the unconscious Richard and moved over to them. He put his hand between Quita's legs and started rubbing her through her jeans. Quita's hands were tied behind her back and she was lying on them. She had made fists and was arching her body up to relieve the pain in her wrists. Head thought she was pushing her lower body up because he was rubbing her. "You like that, baby?" he asked with a lewd grin. He looked around Judo at her face. "You suck dick, baby?"

"Hey, man," said Yellow at the wheel, "we supposed to kill the white devils, not fuck with them."

Head ignored him. He was trying to unbuckle a wide leather belt that Quita wore on her jeans, but he could not manage it because Judo was sitting too far back on her. He tried to get his hand to the zipper to unzip the fly, but he could not reach that either. "Shit, man," he said in frustration. He unzipped his own trousers and released his erection.

Yellow looked over his shoulder. "We don't supposed to be fucking with these white devils," he warned again. "We only supposed to kill them."

Head had one hand curled around his hard penis. "Ain't no rule says I can't fuck a white devil before we kill her," he argued. "Ain't that right, man?" he asked Judo, slapping him on the shoulder.

"Don't ask me, man," Judo replied. "I don't know no rules." Judo maneuvered around until he was not on top of Quita anymore but was kneeling beside her, near her neck. He bent and sucked one of her nipples.

At the wheel, Yellow was becoming increasingly agitated. This was not the way it was supposed to be. Not sucking on the white devil's tits or trying to get inside her clothes. He glanced at the next off-ramp sign: PENNSYLVANIA AVENUE. There were lonely, isolated railroad spurs just east of Pennsylvania Avenue. Yellow stepped down on the accelerator and changed to the off-ramp lane.

Quita Hague's face was turned to the wall of the van. Tears streamed down her cheeks, trailing into her mouth and onto her neck. Her hands felt numb. She could feel Judo's lips sucking her nipple raw; she could see Head walking toward her face on his knees, trousers open, black penis erect. And from the front of the van was the constant, whining voice talking about killing white devils.

"Please—please—" she begged. "Rape me—take my money—but please don't kill me—please—"

"We won't, baby," said Head, "leastwise, not until we through with you—"

Yellow got off the freeway, doubled back up Pennsylvania to Twenty-third Street, and drove under the freeway toward the industrial area. As he had surmised, the neighborhood was quiet, devoid of activity. Past Indiana Avenue he drove, to Minnesota. He swung into Minnesota, feeling gravel replace pavement under the tires. In seconds he was past Twenty-fourth Street. He drove alongside a single-track railroad spur until it turned down a narrow alley of warehouses and loading docks. There he jammed on the brakes and skidded to a halt.

"That white devil belongs to me!" he yelled.

Yellow leaped from behind the wheel and ran to the cargo door. He threw it open with a vengeance and reached under the back of the passenger seat. When he drew his hand out again, it held a sixteen-inch machete. He made several chops at the air with it, as if testing it.

"Say, man, be careful with that motherfucker," Head said, covering his erection protectively.

"This white devil is mine!" Yellow declared again. His voice was a loud hiss; the boyish features of his face were distorted: lips twisted, eyes narrowed to slits, Adam's apple throbbing. "I want her! She's mine!"

"Yeah, right, man, take her," Judo agreed quickly. "Just watch out with that fucking sword."

Yellow took Quita Hague by her thick, dark hair and dragged her

40

from the van. She came out on her side and fell heavily to the ground. Yellow dragged her up to her knees, dragged her *on* her knees for several yards, then angrily, impatiently, pulled her to her feet.

"Oh, please—oh, no—" she pled, choking and crying.

Yellow jerked viciously at her hair to make her keep up. She stumbled, staggered, almost fell. Her tied wrists were raw from the twine, her knees throbbing from falling on them and being dragged on them, her scalp a mass of pain as her hair was literally being pulled out by the roots. But she probably felt none of that agony because her entire being had to be laced with the terrible fear of impending death. She could see the machete in Yellow's hand. She must have known what he was going to do with it.

"Oh, please—oh, no—"

When Yellow got her where he wanted her, next to the railroad spur, he let go of her hair and used a hip throw to drop her to the ground. Judo, watching from next to the van, realized that it was a throw he himself had taught Yellow when he, Judo, first came out of prison. It was one of the basic jujitsu throws. Easy to execute. Particularly easy when applied to a terrified woman, forty pounds lighter, with her hands tied behind her back.

"Oh, please—oh, no—"

Yellow grabbed her by the hair again and dragged her across one of the rails. When he let go, a handful of her hair came out, entwined in his fingers. Yellow stared at it in revulsion; he frantically shook his hand until the hair came loose and drifted to the ground.

"Now your head is mine, white devil," Yellow said.

"Oh, please—oh, no—please—"

It was the last time Quita would beg for her life.

Yellow raised the machete high in the air and brought it down with all his strength on the throat of Quita Hague.

Head and Judo were standing by the parked van when Yellow came running back over to them.

"I did it! I did it!" Yellow shouted triumphantly. He threw his hands into the air, still holding the bloody machete, and did a brief victory dance. It was, Judo thought, not unlike the quick little dances that football players do in the end zone following a touchdown. Judo stared at Yellow's wild-eyed, frenzied grin. "You

41

ought to see the blood gushing out of that devil's neck!'' Yellow said. "It's wonderful, wonderful! I got to get a picture of it!'' He shoved the machete into Head's hand and ran around the van. From under the driver's seat, he removed a Polaroid camera with flash attached. He hurried back to the railroad spur with it.

Head stared at the bloodstained blade he held. "Blue-eyed devils,'' he muttered. "I wanted that bitch to suck my dick.'' He peered in at Richard Hague in the van. "I bet she sucked *his* dick,'' he said indignantly. "Blue-eyed motherfucker!''

With sudden ferocity, Head reached in with the machete and hacked at the unconscious Richard Hague's face. He hacked twice. Three times. Then, drooling slightly over his puffy lips, he dragged the limp form out of the van and across the ground.

Judo, wide-eyed, watched Head walk away, pulling Richard Hague by one arm behind him. Crazy, Judo thought, the motherfucker is crazy.

When Head approached the railroad spur, he saw a flashbulb explode. Then another. Yellow taking pictures of his kill, he thought sullenly. He gots a woman and I only gots a man. Shit.

Head dragged Richard Hague to the opposite side of the tracks from where Quita lay. A man's better than nothing, he thought. Leastwise, better than what Judo was getting tonight. As indifferently as if he were chopping wood, Head began hacking away at Richard Hague's face.

Across the tracks, Yellow finished taking pictures. He too thought briefly about Judo, waiting back at the van; Judo, who would get credit for no kill tonight. Then Yellow remembered a ring he had seen on Quita Hague's finger: a white gold ring with a green stone. He knew that Death Angels were not supposed to steal from their victims, but he decided to take the ring anyway— for Judo. His friend was getting married in a few days; maybe he could use the ring. Bending, Yellow rolled Quita sideways enough to expose her limp, tied wrists, and worked the ring off her finger.

As Yellow stepped back across the tracks, he saw Head still hacking away. "Hey, brother, you want a picture of that devil?'' he asked.

"Don't need no picture, man,'' Head muttered. "If I say I killed the motherfucker, then I killed him. Don't need no picture.''

"Okay, brother.'' Yellow hurried back to the van.

When he was alone again, Head took Richard Hague's wallet and slipped it into his own pocket. No one would ever know, he told himself.

Several minutes later, Head returned to the van, tossed the bloody machete into the back, and got in.

Without headlights, the van drove slowly away from the railroad spur and the carnage that had been spread over it.

Shortly after eleven o'clock that night, John Battenberg and his wife Beverly were in their car driving west on Twenty-fifth Street. Battenberg was a forty-one-year-old professor of art at San Jose State University. As the Hagues had done earlier, the Battenbergs decided to get some air before going to bed. Unlike the Hagues, they drove instead of walking.

As their car passed the intersection of Minnesota Avenue, the Battenbergs saw a figure lurch from the shadows and stagger toward the street.

"Looks like he's drunk," said Beverly Battenberg.

"Looks like," her husband agreed. Then John Battenberg took a closer look. "Wait a minute. That man's hands are tied behind his back—"

Battenberg pulled over and got out of the car. He hurried toward the lurching figure.

It was Richard Hague.

In shock, badly hacked about the face and head, Hague had done the incredible: he had clung to life, struggled to his feet with hands still tied, and set out on foot looking for help for his wife.

Battenberg was appalled at what he saw. Richard Hague's head was horribly mutilated. The flesh had been hacked open down to the bone. His skull was open and exposed. Ghastly strips of skin hung from his face, dripping steady rivulets of blood. He was muttering incoherently.

Battenberg untied Hague's hands, dropping the rough twine to the ground. He guided Hague to his car. Not sure where the nearest hospital was located, he drove to the nearby Potrero District police station.

The van, meanwhile, had sped south on the freeway. It parked behind an apartment in the Hunters Point section. Judo went to the door of the apartment and knocked. The door was answered by a plump, round-faced young black woman dressed in Muslim robes.

"*As-salaam-alaikum,*" Judo said, speaking the Muslim greeting.

"*As-salaam-alaikum,*" she replied.

"I need a favor," Judo said. "My friends and I need a place to wash up."

The woman noticed dark spots on his Nehru coat and the pink shirt he wore under it. "What have you been doing?" she asked.

Judo smiled. "We been out killing white folks," he said. His voice was half serious, half joking. He took the young woman's hand. "Listen, I don't want you mixed up in this. You go on in the bedroom and stay until they're gone. Don't ask no questions, hear?"

She studied his eyes for a long moment, then she nodded and went into her bedroom.

Head and Yellow washed up in the bathroom, scrubbing the Hagues's blood off their hands and arms. Then the three men filled a small garbage can with water and took it out to the van. They removed the furniture pads and sluiced down the cargo floor, cleaning out Richard Hague's blood. Yellow used the excess water to wash off the machete, and put it back under the passenger seat.

When Yellow and Judo were away from Head momentarily, Yellow gave Judo the ring he had taken from Quita Hague. "Just so's the night won't be a complete loss for you," he said. "Maybe you can use it at your wedding."

"Thanks, man," Judo said. "I appreciate it."

In the light of the kitchen, Judo examined the ring. Inside the band it was engraved: REH to QPM 9–17–66 ALL MY LOVE.

Judo rubbed several tiny specks of red off the white gold and slipped the ring into his pocket.

At the police station, John Battenberg ran up to the first occupied patrol car he saw and banged on the window. "I've got a man over here who may be dying!"

Officers Donald Hensic and John Chestnut hurried to the Battenberg car. They took one look at Richard Hague and immediately radioed a request for a Code Three ambulance—emergency lights and siren. Within ten minutes, Hague was on his way to San Francisco General Hospital.

The two policemen, along with another team and a sergeant, returned with the Battenbergs to the intersection of Twenty-fifth and Minnesota. They began to search the area. The first thing they found was the length of twine that John Battenberg had taken off Richard Hague's hands. Next they found a small pool of still-wet blood where Richard had lain. Then they found several patches of brown hair lying between the rails.

Finally they found Quita.

Back at the Hunters Point apartment, Head and Yellow had left and Judo and the Muslim girl were alone.

"You shouldn't be over here without a chaperone," she told him. "We're not married yet."

"We will be in three days," Judo said. "Anyway, I got a present for you and I wanted us to be alone when I gave it to you."

He put Quita Hague's white-gold-and-emerald ring on her finger.

"Oh, honey, it's so pretty!" she praised, holding the back of her hand up to see how it looked on her. "My, it must have cost something!"

"It wasn't cheap," Judo said.

At the railroad spur, Quita Hague was being photographed in death for the second time. Standing around her body were men from the Crime Lab, Photo Lab, Operations Center, and Homicide details, and a representative from the coroner's office. Quita was still lying across one rail of the tracks. Her hair, face, and upper torso were matted with her own drying blood. Her head lay back at a grotesque angle, its neck open, almost severed from the body. Her windpipe and most of her major neck arteries had been cut open, and her backbone and spinal cord had been lacerated.

Her hands were still tied behind her back.

Quita Hague was pronounced dead at 11:45 P.M.

At the end of Day One, there were two victims.

Quita Hague was dead, hacked to death.

Richard Hague was still alive, in shock, his face and head horribly mutilated.

Day 4

Jesse Lee Cooks alighted from a Market Street bus with a white bakery bag in one hand. The bag contained two dozen freshly baked cookies, so fresh that several grease stains had spotted the bag. Jesse had brought the cookies from the place where he worked, the Muslim-owned Shabazz Bakery. He had been employed there as a baker's helper since his parole from San Quentin the previous summer.

On this day, Jesse felt good. The cookies he carried were for his friends, Anthony Harris and Larry Green. They were a peace offering to make up for some differences that had arisen between them. Jesse had no family nearby, no girlfriend, no one who really liked him and wanted to be his friend. He knew he was difficult to get along with; he was moody, surly, hot-tempered. He had never kept a friend for very long, not in his entire life. But with Anthony Harris and Larry Green he was going to try.

Despite outward appearances, Jesse liked Anthony Harris. Anthony had been straight with him in San Quentin, had taught him all the judo and kung fu that he knew. He was a good man, Anthony was, even if he didn't have the right kind of heart yet. That would

46

come in time, Jesse was sure of it. All Anthony needed was a little experience. A little exposure.

Larry Green now, he was something else. Just a kid, barely twenty-one, but that little motherfucker had a *heart.* No experience at all; never even been busted. So curious about prison; always asking those dumb fucking questions about life inside. (Jesse knew he was the right one to ask, however. Jesse's rap sheet read like a tour itinerary of jails and penitentiaries. Federal prisons at Lompoc, Terre Haute, Marion, McNeil Island, San Pedro. County jails in Denver, Omaha, Chicago, Los Angeles. Then San Quentin.)

Jesse's expression always hardened whenever he thought about his years in prison. He had hated those years. He was determined never to go back. No more prison for him; they'd have to kill him next time.

For the first time in his life, Jesse Lee Cooks felt as if he had *direction.* The Muslims in San Quentin had been the beginning of it. Then his job at Shabazz. And the good friends he had made since he got out. At last Jesse felt he was *somebody.* He felt a part of *something.*

He walked with a slight strut as he crossed Market Street and headed toward the Black Self Help Moving and Storage Company. That was another Muslim-owned business, where both Anthony and Larry worked. Jesse had thought several times that it might be nice if he could work there also, then he and his friends could be together more. He knew he could probably get on if he cared to apply; he was bigger and stronger than most of the men who worked there now. But he liked his job at the bakery: it was clean work, everything smelled so good when it was baking, and he liked to watch the women come in to make purchases. Not like the moving company: dusty, musty, all that heavy lifting.

Jesse walked around to the rear of Black Self Help. It looked oddly inactive. Anthony and Larry were nowhere to be seen. Or anyone else for that matter. He walked in the back door, into the storage area. Only one person was on the premises, a man named Dwight.

"Say, brother, where everybody at?" Jesse asked.

"Took off early for the wedding, man."

"Wedding? What wedding?"

"Brother Anthony and Sister Carolyn," said Dwight.

Jesse frowned. He knew that Anthony Harris and Carolyn Patton were engaged, but he had not known when their wedding would take place. "That's tonight, huh?"

"Yeah, man."

Jesse nodded. No one had told him. "Larry gone to it too?"

"Sure thing. Larry, he the best man."

Jesse stared into space for several moments. Not even Larry had mentioned it to him.

"Say, man, you going to the wedding?" Dwight asked.

Jesse shook his head once. "I got something else to do," he said self-consciously. He started to leave, then turned back. "You want a bag of cookies?" he asked.

"Sure thing," said Dwight.

"They good," Jesse emphasized. "I helped bake 'em myself."

"Say, man, thanks," said Dwight, accepting the bag and opening it.

Jesse shrugged. He did not know how to respond to a thank you. Still self-conscious, he simply bobbed his chin at Dwight and left.

Outside, walking along Market Street, minus the carefree strut now, Jesse's expression slowly turned mean. I should have known, he thought. I should have known they wouldn't be my friends.

Not after last night.

It was the first loft meeting following the Hague kidnap-killing. Head had the floor and was complaining bitterly about Judo's participation.

"The man don't have the *heart* for Death Angel business," he proclaimed.

"Can you elaborate on that for us?" asked the man with the Vandyke, who was moderating the meeting. He was flanked, as usual, by his bodyguards.

"You want to hear more, I'll tell you more," said Head. He ignored Judo, who was glaring at him from the audience. "First, he fucked up when we had three white kids almos' in the van. He let one of them break away, then they *all* broke away. Next, when we had the two white devils down on the railroad track, he didn't even help. He didn't do nothing. The man just don't have the fucking heart."

The moderator looked at Judo, raising his eyebrows inquiringly. "Your reply, brother?"

Judo stood. "I got as much heart as he has. It's just that this is all new to me. I'm not used to it. I haven't been out of prison very long; it's taking me a while to adjust."

Yellow looked up at Judo and winked. That was exactly the right thing to say. Exactly as they had rehearsed it the night before.

"Anyhow," Judo added, and this was not rehearsed, "he's just pissed off because *his* white devil didn't die." Judo turned his eyes to Head, who was now glaring back at him. He decided to rub salt in Head's wound. "He had the sucker knocked out and his hands tied behind his back. He had a machete big enough to chop down a fucking tree. He had all that going for him and he couldn't even kill the devil."

There were several smiles and a few chuckles from the audience as the men saw Head's discomfiture. Head's lips were pursed as far out as they would go, and his forehead was drawn into a tight scowl. "At least I tried, motherfucker," he said to Judo. "More than you did."

In the audience, Yellow raised his hand for permission to speak. The moderator nodded. All eyes turned to Yellow with interest: he had a new, higher status because of what he had done to Quita Hague. Rising, he stood next to Judo.

"I think maybe we might be pushing this brother too fast," he said. "After all, like he told us, he just got out of the white man's prison a while back. We can't expect to push him out front right away and have him score a kill." He glanced at Judo and grinned. "Anyhow, he getting married soon, you know, and he nervous about it. He don't know can he handle her or not."

There were some raucous laughs from the audience. The moderator smiled through his Vandyke. Even Head could not contain the flicker of a grin.

"All in all," Yellow continued, "I don't think this brother did too bad for his first time out. I vote we overlook what happened with those three white kids. This brother will do all right if we give him time."

"I'm inclined to agree," said the moderator. He motioned for Head, Judo, and Yellow to sit down. From his coat pocket he took a neatly cut, one-column newspaper clipping headlined:

Clark Howard

He read aloud from the clipping. " 'A young woman was hacked to death and her husband severely slashed after they were abducted by three men . . . Police say Mrs. Hague . . . had been nearly decapitated by a single stroke to her throat by a heavy-bladed weapon, probably a machete . . . Richard Hague found staggering around . . . taken to San Francisco General Hospital . . . underwent several hours of surgery . . . deep, savage slash wounds . . . in serious condition . . .'" He stopped reading and said, "In light of our younger brother's splendid kill, I think we will not cloud the event with any internal discipline or reprimand. Suffice it to say that he"—the moderator raised both hands and pointed proudly to Yellow—"is well on his way to becoming a respected Death Angel, while his two participating brothers"—he gestured toward Head and Judo—"have some catching up to do."

There were a few more laughs from the group, good-natured now instead of derisive.

"One final point, however," the moderator said, looking at the clipping again. "The police say the motive for the killing might have been robbery, since Hague's wallet was missing. Do any of you know anything about that?"

Yellow and Judo looked suspiciously at Head.

"Don't be looking at me, motherfuckers," Head muttered. "I don't know nothing 'bout no fucking wallet."

The moderator allowed a moment of silence to pass. Then he said, "Of course, it could have been lost somewhere during the night, or a policeman may have stolen it. I bring it up simply to emphasize that we"—he spoke the word loftily—"are not thieves. Nor are we rapists. What we do, we do to avenge four hundred years of abuse. Always remember that."

Before he left, the moderator took Judo aside and spoke to him in private. "I don't want you to be discouraged by this temporary setback," he told him in confidential tones. "I know a lot about you, and I feel that you have great potential. I think that if you work hard and apply yourself, you can become an important man

50

in the Nation of Islam. Men of your caliber are needed in New Mecca.''

The moderator departed then. On the way out to his car, he put the Quita Hague newspaper clipping back into his pocket and removed another one. This one was headlined: VICIOUS SLAYING A MYSTERY. The moderator's eyes skimmed the story: Oakland police trying to identify a young woman viciously hacked to death . . . found near the Oakland Coliseum . . . throat deeply cut by a hatchet or ax . . . numerous deep hack wounds in her body . . . two fingers missing from her left hand . . .

The moderator sighed wearily. Two fingers. Why couldn't they just take Polaroid shots like everyone else?

"Let's run across the bridge to Oakland boys," he told his bodyguards.

As the big, shiny Continental pulled away, Head watched sullenly from an upstairs window. He was pouting. He felt cheated.

After finding the Black Self Help premises nearly deserted, Jesse Lee Cooks wandered down Market Street with no particular destination in mind. He was angry, blue, moody—and the overall feeling was coated with self-pity. No friends, he kept telling himself. Nobody he could depend on. Nobody.

Not that he cared, he tried to convince himself. He didn't *need* anybody. He could make it alone just fine. Fuck them all.

After he walked around for a while, he became hungry. He entered the first fast-food restaurant he came to and ordered a cheeseburger and Pepsi at the counter. The white girl who waited on him had large breasts that pushed out the front of her uniform blouse. Jesse stared at them while he waited for his food.

He took a table near the rear, as far away as he could get from the few other customers in the place. As he ate, he brooded—about many things: not being invited to Anthony's wedding, not having any real friends, not being able to see his kids, all the years he had spent in prison, not ever seeming to be able to do anything right—

That was an old story with Jesse. Not being able to do anything right. God knows he *tried* to do right. But sometimes other forces seemed to take over. Like the time back in 1958 in East St. Louis, when he was twelve years old. "Go out to play, Jesse Lee," his mother told him. "I want to lay down and rest."

"Yes, Momma."

"And you mind, take care of those other children and see they don't go off and be hurt."

"Yes, Momma."

The other children were his brothers Johnny and Tommy, who were ten and eight, and his sister Glory, who was seven.

When he got outside, Jesse had an overwhelming urge to go back into the house. But it was not like *he* was going back in; it was like *somebody else* was doing it and he was only watching. *Somebody else* sneaked back inside; *somebody else* crept up to the bedroom door and peeked in at his mother napping on the bed; *somebody else* slipped quietly into the room—and with a pillow, *somebody else* tried to smother the dozing woman.

Somebody else.

They committed Jesse to the Illinois State Training School for delinquent boys. Located at St. Charles, Illinois, it was commonly called "Charleytown." The boys lived in barracks called "cottages," which were named after U.S. presidents. They kept Jesse there until he was fourteen. It was one of the most terrible, frightening experiences of his life—as well as one of the most educational. For Charleytown is one of the best training schools for young criminals in the nation. It might have been "somebody else" who got sent up, but it was Jesse Lee Cooks who came out—reform-school tough and reform-school smart.

He stayed out eight months, then was returned for shoplifting. This time they kept him until he was sixteen. When he got out again, the family moved to Omaha. Jesse was enrolled in Technical Junior High School. He attended through the ninth grade, then dropped out.

Young Jesse was a natural nomad; he liked to move around, to go places—even if he had no purpose for going, no goal in mind. His favorite place to wander to was Denver, 540 miles away. It was a nice hitchhiking trip. But trouble was usually waiting for him there. The Denver police arrested him for "investigation" whenever they saw him in town. Then, when he returned home, the Omaha police did the same, on "suspicion."

In 1963, Jesse met Rosetta. He was eighteen, she sixteen. They married and began having children. Four children were born in a five-year period. They took them and moved to Los Angeles, looking for—well, something better.

Trouble still waited. Jesse was arrested for fighting, for ignoring traffic citations, for "investigation." Times got hard for him. The only job he could find was as a parking-lot attendant, and that did not pay enough to feed four kids. Jesse finally decided that he could not make it. Not that way, at least. He decided to try another way.

On September 11, 1965, Jesse and a friend entered the Boy's Market in the early afternoon and handed a note to the woman in the cashier's booth. The note read: "Give me all the money. A gun is pointed at you." The cashier handed over approximately one thousand dollars. Jesse and his partner fled. They got away clean. It had been easy.

A week later they tried it again, at a Ralph's Market. The woman in the cashier's booth read a note with the same instructions on it, then she snatched up an intercom mike and started screaming for the store manager. This time there was no chance to flee; a number of store employees came down on them and held them until police came.

Charged with second-degree robbery, Jesse managed to get out on bail. Now trouble began to mushroom on him. He needed money to fight the robbery charge, redeem the bail bond, take care of Rosetta and the kids. He was desperate.

The first bank he held up was the Bank of America at Western and Washington. He got less than $700. The next one was the Bank of America at Pico and Vermont, only two miles away. There he got $1400—and also got caught. He was later identified in the first bank robbery.

The federal courts work faster than state courts. Before California could schedule him for trial on the two supermarket holdups, the government had tried and convicted him for the bank robberies. He was sentenced to seven and a half years in prison.

The Federal Bureau of Prisons apparently did not know what to do with Jesse. They first sent him to the Federal Correctional Institute at Lompoc, California. He remained there nine months. Then he was transferred to the U.S. prison at Terre Haute, Indiana. He stayed there two and a half months. Next came the big federal pen at Marion, Illinois: nine months. Then to McNeil Island, where they kept him for nearly two years. Finally, he was sent to the Federal Correctional Institute at San Pedro, California. From there he was paroled and given back to the State of California to serve a one-year-to-life sentence for the market holdups.

California sent him to San Quentin. He served fourteen months and was paroled.

When Jesse got home, he found that his wife had born two illegitimate children while he was in prison. He refused to live with her. Instead he went back to Omaha to live in the home of his parents. He got a job with a construction company.

Jesse had four years to do on parole. He only managed one. Then he yielded to his nomadic nature, took his girlfriend, and left town. He went to New Orleans, stayed there four months, then moved on to Chicago. In March of 1973 he was taken into custody by the U.S. marshal in Chicago on a charge of unlawful flight to avoid confinement. Returned to California, he was turned over to the state and sent back to San Quentin as a parole violator.

Back in the California prison, Jesse was assigned to the Short Term Program for parole violators. He was scheduled for counseling, vocational aptitude testing, and institutional work assignments which would, in theory, prepare him for rerelease. The officials in the program were certain that they could have him ready to reenter society within six months.

During those six months, however, Jesse joined the prison mosque of the Nation of Islam.

And met a jujitsu and kung fu expert named Anthony Harris.

Head had nothing to do. He was loitering around Black Self Help, hoping someone would show up. But no one had. Even Dwight, who had been there earlier, was gone.

There was nothing to do. Nothing. Head was edgy, restless.

Then the white woman came along.

It was about eight thirty. She got off a bus at Van Ness and Market, and started walking down Market toward the street on which she lived. She was a slim, pretty woman, twenty-seven years old. She wore a tailored blue dress under an off-white raincoat. In one hand she carried her purse and a briefcase.

54

She walked past Black Self Help. Head fell in a short distance behind her.

Before she got to her street, the young woman noticed the husky black behind her. She thought perhaps he was following her, but she could not be sure. She quickened her pace slightly. Head noticed it; he quickened his pace also.

The young woman glanced around. There was practically no one on the street, certainly no one close enough to help her. But she was almost home. She hurried faster. Head hurried after her.

At last she reached her building. She ran up the outside steps, door keys in hand. She unlocked the outer door and was about to enter when she felt a strong hand on her wrist and the cold metal of a gun barrel on the side of her neck.

"You best be quiet," Head told her, "or I'll kill you."

The young woman felt her mouth go dry. "I'll be quiet," she said.

Ellen Linder* had already made up her mind to live. She decided it the instant she felt Head's grip on her wrist. She *would* be quiet—and do anything else he told her to. Ellen had a degree in psychology from an Eastern university, and was then studying advanced psychology at a nearby California school. With the black man's viselike fingers holding her right hand immobile, she was mentally gearing up to use everything she had ever learned to deal with whatever kind of mind she was now facing.

"I'll be quiet," she said again.

Head took the gun away from her neck and put it in his coat pocket. "Come on," he said.

He guided her down the steps to the sidewalk. They walked to the corner and into a very dimly lit parking lot.

"In here," he said, walking her onto the lot. He took her purse and briefcase and tossed them into some bushes.

"My money is in that purse," Ellen said.

*Due to the nature of this incident, the victim's name and identity have been altered.

"I'm not after your money," he told her. "Now keep quiet or I'll kill you. Take off your coat."

He tossed her coat into the bushes also.

"Take off your underpants."

Ellen slipped out of her panties and handed them to him. Head tossed them after the other things.

They moved into the shadows of the lot.

"Get down on your knees," he said. Ellen complied. Head was very close to her. She heard the zipper as he opened his trousers. She felt his thick penis brush her lips. "Suck it," he ordered.

Ellen closed her eyes, blanked her mind as much as possible, and ministered to him with her mouth.

Presently they were interrupted by several people coming onto the lot. "Shit," said Head. He zipped up his trousers and pulled Ellen to her feet. "Come on."

They walked around the corner and up two blocks. Head walked with his arm around her as if they were intimates.

"Where you been tonight?" Head asked.

"I'm on the board of directors of a youth group," she told him. "I was at a meeting."

"Youth group? What kind of youth group?"

"A church group. Nondenominational."

Head frowned. He did not know the meaning of that last word. He decided to change the subject. "Where at you work?"

She told him, and what she did.

"Sounds interesting," Head allowed. "I'm a boxer myself. Out here from St. Louis."

They came to one of the city's miniparks and Head guided her to a bench. Ellen studied him in the artificial illumination of the streetlight. He seemed to want to talk. She led him on, encouraged him. The conversation eventually evolved to racism.

"Oppression of black people has got to stop," he told her. She noted that his tone lacked conviction; it was as if he was mouthing rhetoric from someone else. "The country has got to change. But before it happens, they's lots of people going to be killed. And you might just be one of them."

No, I won't, Ellen thought grimly. Gently she urged him to continue talking.

"The people to be killed will just be picked out," he said. "Just picked out, like—ah, how do you say it—?"

"At random?" she offered. "Picked at random?"

"Yeah, that's it. And it can happen to anybody, at any place. That's the way the world works, see? That's how it be going to happen here. The streets of San Francisco be going to run red with blood before it's over."

The night grew quieter around them. Head rose and took her arm. "Come on."

They walked to a vacant lot a block away. It was overgrown with bushes and weeds. Head led her to a dirt area behind the bushes.

"Lie down on the ground. Pull your dress up and spread your knees apart."

He dropped his trousers, got down between her legs, entered her. She blanked her mind again until he ejaculated.

Later, Head and Ellen left the bushes and he walked with her back to the parking lot to retrieve her coat, purse, briefcase, and panties.

"You going to call the cops after I'm gone?" he asked.

"No, of course not. Why should I? I sympathize with you. I mean, I believe in the things you believe in. Not in murder, of course, but in stopping the oppression of blacks in this country. No, I won't call the police."

"Why don't I just go back to your apartment with you, just to make sure?"

"All right, fine." That did not make any sense, she thought. Unless, of course, he planned to kill her in the apartment. "You've got to promise not to hurt me," she said. "I promise not to call the police, but you've got to promise not to do anything harmful to me."

"I promise," said Head.

They walked to where it had all begun, the front steps of her building. This time he let her unlock the door and went inside with her.

In her apartment, Head seemed to want to talk some more. Ellen again encouraged him. He told her of his disciplined life. "I gets up early every day," he said. "Before dawn. I do it to train my body," he boasted, "and for discipline. A man got to have a lot of discipline."

Head now wanted to kill Ellen Linder so that he would be even with Yellow in their quest for Death Angel wings. But he was afraid to. The words of the man with the Vandyke kept running through his mind: *We are not thieves. Nor are we rapists.*

Suppose he killed her? The cops would surely determine that she had been raped. He had shot a healthy load into her. The papers would probably call it a rape-murder; he would get no credit at all for the kill. Might even be put out of the group for it.

Shit. Fucked up again.

Then he decided that he might as well make the most of a bad situation. He went over and put a strong hand on Ellen Linder's throat. Without gentleness, he forced her into the bedroom. Pushing her onto the bed, he fell on top of her like a great, panting, dark animal.

After he came a second time, Head was through with her. But just for the night; apparently he had designs for the future.

"Give me your phone number," he ordered. She did. "And the one where you work." She gave it to him. "I'm going to call you soon for a date," he promised. Then he pointed his right index finger at her head like a gun. "Remember, if you call the police, I'll come back and kill you, hear? You be long gone."

Head left and Ellen Linder called the police.

At the end of Day Four, there were three victims.

Quita Hague was dead, hacked to death.

Richard Hague was still alive, in serious condition but expected to recover, with more than two hundred stitches in his face and head.

And Ellen Linder had been raped twice, forced to perform fellatio once, and placed in fear of losing her life for more than two hours.

Day 11

The lights had been turned off in the loft and a movie projector was grinding away, throwing a bright picture onto a silvery portable screen. The film was silent, but the man with the Vandyke narrated it from the rear of the room.

"Here you see scenes from the Watts riot," he said. "Note that most of the policemen are white. Also note that not a single arrest is being made in a nonviolent manner; usually there are two white policemen for each black man being arrested, and they are very liberal in the use of their riot clubs."

The film was patchy and broken, lacking any sort of continuity, as if it had been spliced together with selected scenes taken from an assortment of reels of varying quality.

"There was a great deal of publicity about looting," said Vandyke. "It was the excuse that the police department used to justify so many broken black skulls and smashed black faces. But the fact of the matter, as you can see by these scenes, is that our people were only salvaging merchandise that lay in the path of the various fires and would have been burned anyway. Of course, most of the stores in Watts were owned by Jews, and we all know that they'd rather see a TV set or a suit of clothes burn up rather than go to a

59

poor nigger without him paying an inflated retail price plus some outrageous interest rate every month.''

As the men in the loft watched the film, Muslim observers, who had come with Vandyke, walked slowly up and down the sides of the room, studying them. They searched their faces, looking for expressions of hatred and hostility. Such expressions were not hard to find—not in *this* audience. Not in the faces of Head, Yellow, Judo.

The film switched from Watts to the rural South. Sharecropper shacks, forlorn-looking black women, little black children with flour-sack clothes and no shoes.

"This is how poor blacks are forced to live in some parts of America today," said Vandyke. "They are practically in bondage, terribly oppressed, living indebted to white landowners year after year after year. There is, of course, a method to the white man's madness here: the white father keeps the black father under his heel throughout their lifetimes; the black children grow up exactly the way their fathers did; then the cycle completes itself when the black son is grown, and the white son takes over where his father left off.''

There was an undercurrent of grumbling among the dozen men in the loft audience. Vandyke always knew when it was coming. He always paused at appropriate moments to let it come.

The film changed scenes again, this time to a white Establishment confrontation with a black demonstration where fire hoses, then dogs, were turned loose on teenage blacks, on women, on old people.

"These are atrocities," Vandyke intoned in an ice-cold voice. "This sort of evil is the type of thing that could be expected if America was a dictatorship under an Adolf Hitler or a Joseph Stalin. But it is insanity that such things go on today in the finest civilized country in the world. Stop the film, please—''

The projector was turned off, the lights turned on. Vandyke walked to the front of the room. He scanned the set faces of the men before him. "Evil," he pronounced, "must be met with evil. It is no good to try—as the white man teaches—to combat evil with good, for evil is strong and good is weak. But if we *use* evil to *fight* evil, then the evil we use becomes good.''

In the audience, Judo frowned. He was not sure that what he just heard made sense. He swallowed and licked a drop of perspiration off his upper lip. It was hot in the loft, the air beginning to thicken. Judo rubbed his sweaty palms together—then suddenly realized what he was doing and quickly looked to see if the decal on his left palm was still there. It was. The decal was square-shaped and had a number on it: 125. As usual on the afternoon of a meeting, it had been given to Judo to admit him to the loft. Each man attending was given one. It was moistened and pressed into the palm of the left hand, where the black man's skin was light enough for it to show. That imprint on the left palm was his admission to the meeting.

"It is clear to all righteous-thinking black men," Vandyke continued, "that the white devils are out to destroy the black race. Throughout the years they have literally cut open our mothers' bellies to destroy black babies. They are evil and will resort to any atrocity in their efforts to put us under. That is why we must get all the fear out of our hearts and fight back. Fight back in the same way they are fighting us: with evil. Except that our evil, when we use it, becomes good."

Judo glanced at Head and Yellow. Head, as usual, was nodding stupidly. You could tell that motherfucker *anything* and he'd agree with it. Yellow, on the other hand, was nodding *thoughtfully*, as if he actually understood what Vandyke meant. Maybe I'm slow, Judo thought; some of the things that were said in the loft just didn't make sense to him.

Judo was glad when the lecture portion of the meeting was over and the men in the loft had a few minutes to mingle and socialize. He went over to a corkboard set up on a portable easel. On the board were several rows of small, ID-type photos. Some of them had tiny black wings drawn in ink on each side of the subject's neck. Judo looked enviously at them. Next to him, Head and Yellow did the same.

"Death Angel wings, man," Yellow said, his voice quiet with awe.

"That's for me, man," Head said enthusiastically. "I *gots* to get me them wings."

A tall, handsome black came up and stood with them. "What's

61

swinging, brothers?" he asked. "You all daydreaming about becoming Death Angels?"

"Right on, man," said Head. "Ain't you?"

The newcomer smiled a brilliant white smile. "I got higher goals, man," he replied smugly. "I not only want to be a Death Angel, I want to be a *lieutenant* in the Death Angels. I want to *lead*, man."

Judo studied the speaker. He had smooth, even features, with a suggestion of boyishness; a Muhammad Ali face: now pretty, now quietly thoughtful, now mischievous. His shoulders were broad, his carriage graceful, catlike. He had a natural strut. His wiry hair was cut even above his ears and around the back of his head, leaving no sideburns, making him look as if he were wearing a monk's crown.

He was Skullcap.

"How you going to get to be a lieutenant?" Judo asked.

"By standing out in the crowd, man," Skullcap said, snapping his fingers. "By making myself *known*." He flashed his bright smile again. "Just watch me in the days to come, brother: you'll see a star be born."

Skullcap walked away, half-strut, half-swagger: a swashbuckler in a checkered suit.

"Big motherfucking deal," Head said when Skullcap was gone. He turned to Judo and Yellow, eager for their friendship again. "Come on over to Shabazz with me, brothers. I'll get us a box of pastry and we can go to my place and eat it."

Judo and Yellow exchanged glances. Then Judo shrugged. "Why not?"

In Head's kitchenette apartment, he brought up the subject of another kill. "Let's go do us a kill, brothers. Get one for each of us tonight."

Yellow shook his head. "Too soon, man. The pigs is probably still worked up over that cunt's head that I chopped off."

"He's right, man," Judo agreed. "It's too soon."

Head took another bite of cream-filled pastry and thought of Ellen Linder. Too soon, shit. They were just chickenshit. He had already done one sting since then by himself. He could not tell them about it because he had only fucked the white woman, not killed her. Motherfucker, he silently cursed: why hadn't he offed that white bitch? If the papers *had* called it a rape-murder, he could simply have denied to the Death Angels that he had fucked her. He could have said that he had seen her boyfriend leave just before he made the sting. Or that a white pig cop had fucked her after she was dead. Anything. Nobody could have proved him a liar.

I just didn't motherfucking think, he silently chastised himself as he labored to chew a huge mouthful of cream puff. But he knew it was more than that. It had something to do with the girl herself, some feeling he had for her. Something that not only made him walk out without killing her, but also made him telephone her at the office where she worked.

"You know who this is?" he asked when she answered her phone.

Ellen felt a catch in her throat. "Yes," she said as calmly as she could.

"I said I was gonna call you, remember?"

"Yes, I remember."

For several moments, a heavy silence came over the line, as if Head was not quite sure why he called, did not know just what it was he wanted to say.

Finally he said, "You don't sound too happy to hear from me."

"I'm not," Ellen told him. "You had me very frightened the other night."

"You rather I just didn't call you up no more?"

"I think that would be best, yes. You scare me."

"Okay," Head said. It seemed the easiest way out. He did not know why the hell he even bothered to call in the first place.

Anyway, it was too late to be brooding over it. The cunt got lucky and lived. Head would see that it didn't happen again.

"Man, I don't see how you figure it's too early for another sting," he argued with Judo and Yellow. "Been ten days since the one by the railroad tracks."

"Still too soon," Yellow replied.

"Yeah," said Judo. "Anyway, I got something to do tonight."

I guess I know what too, Head thought jealously. You and that new wife of yours. Head could not help wishing that *he* had someone to occupy his time.

"How 'bout you, little brother?" he asked Yellow. "You and me? Go stinging?"

"I got something to do too," said Yellow.

Judo and Yellow finished their pastry and left. Head sat alone in the dingy little kitchenette, looking at the crumbs and crumpled bakery paper where they had eaten. Stayed just long enough to eat my pastry, he thought sullenly. Fine motherfucking friends. He looked at a partially eaten napoleon in front of him, decided he was no longer hungry, and pushed it away. Sighing quietly, he looked around at the shabby furniture, the depressing walls, the aura of utter gloom that seemed to pervade the place when he was there alone. It was like the solitary-confinement hole in the white man's prison—only worse.

Got to get out from this place for a while, he decided anxiously. Don't like it here by myself.

Head got up from the table, stuck a loaded automatic pistol in his belt, and left the apartment.

The University of California Extension campus was only a block from the little apartment where Jesse Lee Cooks lived. Its main entrance ran slightly uphill from Laguna Street, through a large double gate that was closed to traffic after all classes had ended for the night. Just inside the gate, on either side, were trees and shrubs. Often, when Jesse grew lonely at night, when he became blue and moody thinking about his wife and children, he would walk over to the Extension entrance, loiter back away from the gate near those trees and shrubs, and watch the people drive in to attend evening classes.

What puzzled Jesse about the people attending UC Extension was that they did not appear to be college students—as he imagined college students to be. Jesse's impression of a college student was someone white, young, wearing a sweater, the boys having blond hair, the girls with bouncy young breasts and ponytails. Jesse did not know what extension classes were; to him, a college was a college. When he saw middle-aged men and women arriving for evening classes, he assumed them to be teachers. The black middle-aged people he guessed were maintenance and clean-up help. It did not register in his dull mind that the "teachers" far outnumbered the younger "students," or that as many "clean-up help" people entered as did white people.

Often as he stood there watching the gate, Jesse wished that he were smarter, that he knew more, that *he* could drive into the campus and park, get out of the car with a thick, impressive-looking book in his hand, and walk into one of the Extension buildings. Cool, casual, confident. How motherfucking sweet that would be. At times when he felt that way, he secretly, briefly, regretted having wasted all the years he spent in federal prison: years during which, instead of lying idle in lockup, he could have been going to school studying something, studying *anything.*

If the white men who ran the prison would have let him, that is.

Which Jesse Lee doubted.

And even if he had learned a little something, he knew he never would have gone far enough to get into college. Not the kind of college he imagined, anyway. College with white girls with bouncy breasts, wearing sweaters, flashing perfect smiles. Cool, casual, confident girls.

Like the one slowing down at the gate now. . . .

She was twenty-eight but looked younger. Her auburn hair was cut short, a little longer than gamine-length. She wore jeans, a light crew-cut pullover, and over it a bright plaid blouse unbuttoned all the way down. The Mustang she drove was gold with a black vinyl top and had bucket seats. Sharp, sporty. There was an AAA sticker next to the left taillight; this woman was not about to change her own flat.

In the rear window was a decal that read: CAROLINA.

That was in the South, thought Head, as he watched from the shadows of the trees. The South, where little black kids didn't have shoes. And were called niggers.

Head walked over to the Mustang as it slowed almost to a stop to enter the gate and negotiate the hill. He waved a hand to signal the woman to stop. She did. Possibly because she thought he might be an Extension classmate. Or in trouble. Whatever—she stopped.

"Give me a ride," Head said.

There was something about his voice. He was not *asking* for a ride; he was *telling* her to give him one.

She must have frowned and looked at him more closely then. He was approaching the passenger door—

God, it was unlocked!

She probably tried to accelerate, but it was too late. Head could move fast when he wanted to. And at that moment he wanted to. He was not going to make the same mistake with this one that he made with Ellen Linder.

He snatched open the passenger door and drew his automatic.

She must have been filled with sheer terror at the sight of him up close: his eyes wide and wild, lips curled in the insane hatred he felt. She must have seen the gun as he aimed it at her face—

Head shot her four times. The first bullet went all the way through her lower neck and shattered the window in the driver's door. The second entered her upper neck and lodged in the brain area. The third entered her right cheek, tore up her mouth and tongue, and exited. The fourth went into her right side, hit the chest wall and aorta, then coursed down to penetrate her liver and lodge in her left kidney. Mercifully, she died quickly.

Her name in life had been Frances Rose. All she had been doing was trying to get to class on time.

But she had been white.

Everything happened very quickly after that.

Head hurried away, walking north on Laguna and turning the corner at Haight.

John Fishchbach, a university security guard, ran down the hill to the gate. He found Frances Rose slumped forward against the steering wheel. Her head was blood-soaked. Fishchbach ran to summon an ambulance.

Dr. Herb Kressel and an acquaintance, Harris Silverman, were leaving a UC Extension building when someone shouted that a woman had been shot down at the gate. Dr. Kressel and Silverman hurried down to see if they could help.

And across the street from the gate, a woman named Mary Turney left her second-floor apartment and came downstairs to wait for the police to arrive. She had seen the killer from her window; she wanted to describe him to someone while the image was still fresh in her mind.

* * *

Officers Thomas O'Connell and William Kelly were patrolling in a radio car when the first call came in about the shooting at the UC Extension gate.

"That's close," said O'Connell, the senior officer. "let's make it."

They radioed that they were on their way to the scene. The patrol car leaped forward and sped toward the UC Extension gate. Six blocks from the scene, however, Communications advised that another unit had arrived ahead of them. Almost immediately following that notification, a description came on the air which had been obtained at the scene from the witness Mary Turney. The shooting suspect was a Negro male, approximately twenty-five years old, five nine to five ten in height, muscular build, wearing a blue knit watch cap, an olive-drab army jacket, and light trousers.

"Let's take a perimeter drive and see if we can spot him," Kelly suggested.

"Right. Up Haight to Steiner and back around."

The radio car started to prowl. Down Buchanan Street. Nothing. Up Haight Street. Nothing. Around into Steiner Street—

"Over there," said O'Connell, bobbing his chin at the sidewalk. A muscular, bald-headed black man in a dark sweat shirt and khaki trousers was walking down Steiner toward Waller.

"No army jacket," said Kelly.

"Witness could have been mistaken," replied O'Connell.

"Yeah. Or he could have taken it off."

The car was creeping up slowly behind the bald man.

"What do you think?"

"I think we'd better have a look."

The radio car drew alongside the bald man and stopped. O'Connell and Kelly got out.

"Just a minute, please—"

The black man, Jesse Lee Cooks, halted and warily faced the two officers. His right hand moved slightly—perhaps an inch, perhaps reflexively—toward his belt.

"Watch it," said O'Connell. Both officers saw that Cooks had been sweating profusely, as if he had been running. This was no time to take chances; a woman had been shot back there. "Put your hands on top of your head," Kelly ordered.

Cooks glared at them and made no move to obey. His right hand moved again; a twitch, an impulse.

O'Connell and Kelly quickly drew their service revolvers. "Just freeze, mister!" Kelly covered him while O'Connell, his gun reholstered, got Cooks's hands up and patted him down. He found the automatic in Cooks's belt. "Okay, mister, down on the sidewalk," O'Connell ordered. "Spread your arms and legs wide."

While Kelly continued to keep him covered, O'Connell placed Cooks under arrest, knelt beside him and handcuffed him, and began routinely to recite to him his constitutional rights.

"You have the right to remain silent—"

At the end of Day Eleven there were four victims.

Quita Hague, hacked to death.

Richard Hague, surviving, his butchered face beginning its slow, painful healing process.

Ellen Linder, raped, ravaged, threatened with death, trying not to remember her ordeal.

And Frances Rose, her young face blown apart by bullets fired at close range.

Day 37

Anthony Harris left his new wife, Carolyn, after seventeen days. He would later say that it was because he could not stand the way she smelled: that she had an offensive body odor and did not bathe regularly. Carolyn would probably give a different reason for the early termination of their marriage; but whatever the cause, it did end, after less than three weeks, and Anthony moved out.

He moved to the YMCA, then to the Empress Hotel, a neighborhood hotel, off the beaten track. It is not listed in any of the guidebooks. A guest does not have to show a credit card to check in. Most people would call the Empress a flophouse.

On Sunday morning, November 25, 1973, Anthony sat up on the side of his lumpy bed at the Empress and reached for his trousers. He pulled them partway on while sitting, as he had become accustomed to doing in the narrow confines of a prison cell, then stood up and pulled them the rest of the way on and fastened them. There was no window in his room; he had to walk down the hall to look out and see what kind of day it was. On this particular morning, looking out the window at the end of the hall, he saw that it was drizzling rain. Eddy Street, two stories below, was gray and gloomy-looking. "Shit," Anthony muttered. That kind of weather depressed him.

He shuffled back to his room, wondering what time it was. As he passed the hall bathroom, he saw that it was occupied, the door closed. He went into his room and urinated in the sink in the corner. Then ran cold water until the smell went away, and washed his face. Putting on his shirt and shoes, he went down to the lobby and looked at a plug-in Westclox behind the desk. It was quarter of ten. Anthony crossed to a pay phone on the far wall. He called Black Self Help Moving, where he worked, to see if Larry Green was around.

"Black Self Help," a cool, even voice answered.

"Who speaking?" Anthony asked.

"Man, you called here. Who you want?"

"Larry. Is Larry around?"

"No, he's not here. Who's this?"

"This Anthony."

"Anthony, my man," the voice replied cheerfully, "what's shaking? This is J.C."

J.C. was J. C. Simon, a handsome, swaggering black with his hair cut bowl-shape on his head, no sideburns.

"What's happening down there, man?" Anthony asked.

"The place is dead, brother," J.C. replied. "I'm the onliest one around. What you doing?"

"Nothing. I ain't doing nothing."

J.C. lowered his voice. "How'd you like to go out with me for a while?" he asked conspiratorially.

"Out where?"

"Oh, just out," J.C. said vaguely.

"I don't know, man." Anthony was immediately uncomfortable with his answer. He was rapidly running out of excuses not to go out with the men from Black Self Help when he was invited. Too much time had passed for him to continue saying that he was fresh out of prison and adjusting. And to continue to play being a nervous newlywed wouldn't wash anymore, either; it was common knowledge that he and Carolyn had split.

"How about it, brother?" J.C. pressed.

"Sure, man," said Anthony.

"All right!"

"Can you come get me? It's raining out."

"Right on. You still at the Empress?"

"Yeah, right."

"Be down in the lobby in a half hour. I'll be driving the van."

Anthony hung up and went back upstairs to his room. He had no watch so he would have to estimate when half an hour was up. He flopped down on the bed and closed his eyes. It was three days past Thanksgiving, a month until Christmas. He did not know yet what he was going to do at Christmas. He supposed he could go down to Southern California and visit his mother in Santa Ana. Or even his white wife in Monrovia. His most recent wife, Carolyn, might even give him a Christmas dinner if he asked real nice—but she would have to take a bath that morning for him to be able to stand her. He sighed quietly. Christmas was going to be a problem, all right. He did not want to spend it alone.

Shit, he thought moodily. He had thought he would be all settled by now. Have a nice Muslim wife, be working, making a decent life for himself, practicing the Islamic faith. Instead, he was living in a seedy little hotel room all alone, and getting nowhere fast. How the fuck did things get so turned around on him?

Anthony opened his eyes and stared at the ceiling. He thought about the day he was released from San Quentin—

It was a thirty-minute drive from the prison into San Francisco. He was taken to a Halfway House and given a room. He was to remain there until he found approved employment and a suitable place to live. Less than an hour after his parole supervisor left, he had a visitor: a slim, light-skinned Negro, freckle-faced, handsome in a shy, almost boyish way.

"Hey, brother, I'm Larry Green from the mosque. How's it feel to be out?"

"Feels fine. What you want?"

"Came over to welcome you back to the black man's world. And to invite you to join the mosque."

"Why?"

Larry shrugged. "We heard about you from the inside, man. How you a righteous thinker. And how you know judo and all that stuff. We'd like you to teach self-defense to some of our junior and teen members. Maybe a couple afternoons a week."

71

"Man, I got to work," Anthony protested. "I got to get out and find a fucking *approved* job."

"We can fix that," said Larry with all the confidence of a much older person. "We can put you to work at either the Shabazz Bakery or the Black Self Help Moving and Storage Company. Both places are approved for ex-cons coming back into society, because they're connected with religious organizations, see, and the pigs have to be very careful how they fuck with religious freedom. So we can put you to work, and a couple afternoons a week you can take time off to teach at the mosque. What do you say?"

Anthony shrugged. Why not? he thought.

It was on the second floor of the mosque, in a large, heavily matted room, that Anthony began teaching judo and karate to teen and junior Fruit of Islam members. The Fruit of Islam was the Nation of Islam's younger rank: the youth who were being trained for leadership. Anthony worked with another instructor, whom he knew only as Wally 4X. Wally taught general health and body building. They alternated the classes, one teaching the juniors, ages eight to twelve, the other the teens, thirteen to eighteen. They had a good working relationship from the first day, and found that they liked each other in spite of the obvious differences between them.

"Say, I haven't seen you down at Black Self Help, man," Anthony said early on. "Where you work at, the bakery?"

"No, I have an outside job," said Wally. "I work for the city. I'm a civil servant."

"You a spy for us?" Anthony wanted to know.

Wally 4X smiled in tolerant amusement. "No, nothing so exciting. I'm just an ordinary P.E. instructor for the schools. The faith has nothing to do with my job. See, man, I'm not a Separatist like those guys down at Black Self Help. They're Nationalist Muslims; they want a separate state for the Nation of Islam. Me, I'm a *religious* Muslim. Islamism is my faith, not my politics."

"You believe in the Word, don't you, man? The Word that comes to us from New Mecca?"

"I believe in anything that makes sense," Wally replied, "whether it's the Word or whatever. But one thing I don't believe is that Chicago is New Mecca."

"Man, those cats down at Black Self Help would skin your ass if they heard you say that."

"Precisely why I never go down there," Wally said. "I'm a liberal Muslim. Like the Nation of Islam ministers that teach the faith in this mosque, I don't advocate death to the white man. At this point I am firmly convinced that without the white man, the black man would perish. Twenty-five years from now, I may change my mind."

"If you live that long."

"Oh, I'll live that long," Wally said confidently. "If I can keep away from you badass Death Angels, that is."

Anthony laughed. "You crazy, man."

They never discussed politics *or* religion after that, and they got on very well together.

The person Anthony spent the most time with in his early days of freedom was Larry Green. The young man's friendship was a refreshing change after a long association with convicts and street people. He considered Larry to be a basically good kid. He came from a decent home and family, grew up not in a city slum but in Berkeley, and was a high-school basketball star. His extremely light skin—a *café au lait* complexion—caused him frequent consternation, particularly when he was around dark brown or pure black Negroes; and the fact that he was very skinny—over six feet and usually under 150 pounds—was also a source of self-conscious embarrassment to him. Only when he was in action on the basketball court did he feel that what he was doing compensated for his skinny body. And that, unfortunately, only lasted through high school.

From the first day that Larry visited him at the Halfway House, Anthony let the young man hang around with him. It was flattering in a way; none of Anthony's own younger brothers—Kenny, Pinky, Stanley, Jarvis—had ever looked up to him. It was nice to be admired, to be thought of as *someone*.

"Say," Larry asked him early in their relationship, "could you teach me some of that judo so I can take care of myself better?"

"Yeah, I guess so," Anthony said. "You want to join the class at the mosque?"

Larry shrugged. "That's kind of chickenshit stuff that you teach

73

to those kids. I want to learn some of the badass stuff like you taught Jesse Lee in the joint.''

"Jesse Lee Cooks? You know him?''

"Sure. We got him a job at the Shabazz Bakery when he got out of Q. Anyway, that's the kind of stuff I want to learn. That badass stuff.''

"Well, before you learn any *badass* stuff so you can be a *badass* like *badass* Jesse Cooks,'' Anthony mimicked, "you going to have to learn some of the basics, what you call the chickenshit stuff. You got to learn to walk before you can learn to run, understand?''

"Sure, Anthony,'' the younger man answered agreeably. "Whatever you say.''

"If you don't want to join a mosque class, where do you want me to teach you?''

"How about your room at the Halfway House?''

"Yeah, I guess we can use that for some of the simple stuff, long as I don't have to throw you. We'll give it a try.''

Anthony gave him regular lessons, once or twice a day, in the room at Halfway House. He taught him hip throws first, then side kicks, finally open-hand attacks to the eyes, throat, body. Larry was an enthusiastic student; he did not mind repeating a move over and over again until he perfected it; and when Anthony told him to practice a certain technique fifty times, more often than not he would do it a hundred. The young man took to jujitsu as if he had been born for it. Before long, he had progressed past the basics and was into mastering the deadly heart-burst punch, the terrible straight-finger larynx thrust, and the brutal neck breaks. Larry Green was learning to compensate for his skinny body somewhere else besides the basketball court.

The one thing about Larry that sometimes irritated Anthony was the younger man's morbid curiosity about life in prison. He wanted to know even the most minute details.

"Say, brother, tell me about the queers in prison,'' he asked. "What do you do when they cop a feel? Bust their asses?''

Anthony shrugged. "Queers don't usually bother you unless it looks like you want it. Or if you're young and they think you're prime. Then they fight over you or try to buy you. But if you got a rep, a good, solid rep for whipping ass, you get left pretty much alone.''

"How 'bout the Muslims? They stick pretty much together?"

"Oh, yeah. Out at Q, everybody sticks together. See, you got a lot of different gangs that runs together. You got the honkies, you got the spiks, you got them crazy, motherfucking Indians, you got the regular niggers, and then you got the Black Muslims. They the cream, see? Just like the Islamic lessons say. Don't nobody fuck with the Muslims in Q."

"Far out, man," said Larry. "Shit, I wouldn't be scared to go to the joint if I could hang with the Muslims. I wouldn't even *mind* going in."

Anthony grunted quietly. "Like shit you wouldn't mind. It ain't no tea party in there."

"I could cut it, man," Larry said confidently.

Anthony nodded. At the rate the kid was going, he'd probably find out someday. He wanted to learn about all the wrong things.

At his first meeting in the loft, Judo was questioned by the man with the Vandyke and by other Death Angel members who were attending.

"We are always pleased to welcome a new recruit from the San Quentin Mosque," said Vandyke. "It has been our experience that those Muslims who have served in the white man's prison are unusually strong because they have been repressed, and they are usually filled with hostility because they have suffered. For the most part, they become good and reliable Death Angels. But before they do, we have to find out where their hearts are. Now tell me, brother, do you think it would be easier for you personally to kill a white child or a white woman?"

"I don't know," Judo replied.

"A white woman or a white man?"

"I don't know," he said again. He felt distinctly uncomfortable.

"Well, I shall tell you, brother," said Vandyke. "It takes a far better man to kill a child than a woman, and a better man to kill a woman than a man. That is why our quota for heads is lower for children than for women and men. Do you understand?"

"Yes," Judo said. But he did not. It sounded suspiciously like a cop-out to him. Like maybe killing kids was easier than killing men.

"Do you think you would be capable of an act of decapitation?" Vandyke asked.

"Capable of what?"

"Decapitation. Cutting off a white person's head."

"I'm not sure," Judo said.

"We, of course, accept any method of eliminating our white enemies," Vandyke said, "but decapitation is preferred because it is a very vicious way of killing and shows that a man is not afraid of blood. Are you afraid of blood, brother?"

"I don't know," Judo replied. "I don't think so, but I don't know."

"If you ever feel you might be afraid of blood," Vandyke said, "just think back to the days when the white man cut open our mothers' bellies and fed the unborn black fetus to his livestock."

Judo felt ill.

"Does anyone in the audience have a question for our new brother?" Vandyke asked.

A burly black man stood up. "I want to ask the new brother if he would have enough nerve to cut up the dead body of a white devil."

Judo held back the feeling of nausea and forced a half-smile. "You kidding me, man?"

"No, man, I ain't."

Another stood up. "Could you do it or couldn't you?"

This is a joke, Judo thought. "Sure, man, I could do it," he answered.

Later that evening, Judo was shown snapshots of what appeared to be actual executions of white people. There were so many of them, and they were spread out in such a haphazard manner on one of the tables, that their detail all flowed together in a grisly montage of death. One photo did stand out, however: that of a white man tied to a straight chair, with a black man standing in front of him, firing a pistol almost point-blank at his face. Judo could not be sure, because he did not examine the snapshot that closely, but he thought the man firing the gun was a tall, handsome black with a bowl haircut, whom he had seen among the men in the loft.

The one called Skullcap.

On that Sunday morning in November when it was drizzling rain, Judo walked out of his hotel and waited in a doorway until Skullcap drove up in the van. It was the white Dodge van, the one in which he had ridden with Yellow and Head the night Yellow hacked the white woman to death.

"What's happening, brother?" asked Skullcap as Judo got into the van.

"Nothing, man. Nothing." Judo was on edge. He wished he could think of some way to get out of going with Skullcap and still save face. But there did not appear to be a way; none that didn't sound chickenshit anyway.

"You got your piece, man?" Skullcap asked.

"Yeah."

"Good. I need to borrow it."

Judo frowned. "What the fuck for, man? Where's yours?"

"I loaned it to a brother in Oakland. He's still got it."

"Well, shit, man, can't you borrow one from somebody?"

Skullcap turned a flat stare on him. "I am borrowing one, brother. From you."

There was something about Skullcap's voice and eyes that warned Judo not to argue further. Skullcap was by far the most dangerous man he had yet met in the loft meetings. His tall, handsome appearance aside, his brilliant smile and loose strut, his aura of being totally cool, totally hip—all that aside: there was something in the man, something very close to the surface, that was unspeakably terrible, unequivocally deadly. It was something that Judo, with all his kung fu prowess, did not care to challenge.

"You can borrow the gun, man," he said.

Skullcap smiled. "Thanks, brother. Put it in that case there behind the seat, will you?"

Judo picked up an attaché case from the floor of the van and put his gun inside it. He noted that the case was black and matched the black raincoat and black pigskin gloves that Skullcap wore. Skullcap also had on dark glasses despite the absence of sunlight, and a dark gray fedora cocked to one side of his head. He belonged, Judo thought, in a white Caddy convertible instead of an old Dodge van. In spite of the underlying threat of danger about him, Skullcap was one very sharp motherfucker.

"Say, man, where we going?" Judo asked.

"You'll see in a couple of minutes, brother," Skullcap answered. "I got us a devil all picked out."

As he drove along the almost deserted Sunday morning streets,

Skullcap hummed an old Bible hymn he had learned as a child.

When J. C. Simon was three years old, he had pinworms wiggling out of his anus, nostrils, and mouth. They were caused by his touching fecal matter and putting his fingers on his lips and nose. The condition caused the child severe itching and restlessness. At night the female pinworms would constantly be exiting his body and depositing new eggs to grow new worms. The boy was unable to sleep. He became uncontrollably irritable and difficult to handle. The condition became so bad that he was debilitated and unable to walk.

Hazel, his mother, took him to the doctor time after time. "Enterobiasis," the doctor always said, and gave her a prescription for piperazine. "This will clear it up, Mrs. Simon, but it's going to keep coming back until the boy quits touching his anus."

J.C. finally quit the disgusting habit when he was five. But for two years prior to that, he remained in almost constantly horrible physical and mental condition.

J.C.'s father was Samuel Oscar Simon. He worked as a milk deliveryman. After J.C. was born, he moved his family from Opelousas, Louisiana, to Beaumont, Texas. There were three other children, all older than J.C., and eventually there would be born four younger than he. Samuel was thirteen years older than his wife. When J.C. was ten, his parents separated and Samuel moved to Houston.

For a period after his father left the household, J.C. had trouble in school. His teacher summoned Hazel for a conference.

"Something is the matter with the boy's hand," the teacher said. "He can't hold a pencil anymore. I think you'd better take him to a therapist of some kind."

Hazel had J.C. try to hold a pencil. The boy's hand seemed to go limp; the pencil fell to the desk.

"I don't know what I'm going to do," she told the teacher. "I can't afford no doctor bills right now."

"Well, you might as well take him home," the teacher said. "He can't attend school if he can't hold a pencil."

Hazel took her son home.

"J.C., what do you think is the matter with your hand?" she asked him.

"I don't know, Mamma," he said, eyes downcast.

"Does it hurt?"

"No, Mamma."

"Does it feel numb?"

"No, Mamma."

She laid the boy down on his bed and sat beside him. She started massaging his little hand and fingers. J.C. seemed to relax. "Does that feel good, sugar?" his mother asked.

"Yes, Mamma."

Hazel began to massage the boy's hand as a matter of regular routine. Before long he was back in school again, holding a pencil with no difficulty. It had not been physical therapy that J.C. needed; it had been attention in a home that his father had left.

As J.C. grew up, he was very close to his family. His mother was his best friend, his sisters and brothers next. He rarely made any close outside friends; the people he liked best were the ones who lived in his house. J.C. had respect for his family: he was a good boy and stayed out of trouble. Not mischief, but trouble.

When he was old enough, he went to work as a busboy at the Beaumont Country Club. He was an easygoing, likable adolescent who got on well with everyone. At Lincoln High School he made the football team. He would have been a star player but he injured his knee. It never did heal correctly and J.C. grew to manhood with a kneecap that frequently slipped out of place.

His grades in high school were good enough to get accepted at Texas College in Tyler, two hundred miles north of his home. Texas College was an all-black school subsidized by the Baptist Church. With normally some five hundred-plus students in attendance, the college had been in existence since 1894, highly regarded by educators. It was highly regarded by J.C. also, but that did not preclude his having problems there. He was away from home for the first time, away from the "friends" he valued most—his family. He had difficulty adjusting to his new environment, difficulty concentrating on his classes. He dropped out and went home. Hazel, his mother, made him go back.

Over a period of three years, J.C. dropped out several times, and each time his mother made him return. During the periods that he was in attendance, he was at least a fair student, sometimes better than fair. Over three calendar years, he accumulated enough credits to equal four semesters' work—putting him at the halfway mark toward a degree. His studies were in general academic foundation; he was going in the direction of the social sciences.

Then he met Patricia.

They left school and moved down to Houston. J.C. got a job as a food selector in a grocery supply warehouse. They lived modestly but not uncomfortably. In 1970 their daughter was born; they named her Jacqueline Christine, but from the beginning she was called Crissy. She was an ordinary little girl born to ordinary black parents under ordinary circumstances. By all odds, everything about this young family should have remained ordinary. Then J. C. Simon met some men who were members of the Nation of Islam. Black Muslims.

J.C. was impressed by the Muslims. They appeared cool, confident, with it. They dressed sharply, like young businessmen. They were clean-shaven, neatly groomed. They walked with shoulders back, a slight strut, a swagger. Most impressive to J.C., they seemed to know who they were.

J.C. fell in with the Nation of Islam members. He visited the temple there in Houston. He began to feel a part of it. Their doctrines, the policies they preached, all seemed to make sense to him. He himself and his family had never felt particularly oppressed, so he was not attracted to it to escape any hardship; but he could see around him some of the inequities that the Islamic faith was trying to abolish. Before long, J.C. had joined the Houston mosque.

Things began to go badly between J.C. and Patricia. Since he had become a Muslim, the two of them looked at things from entirely different perspectives. Their values began to be at odds, and with them their individual priorities. Soon J.C. left Patricia and went back to Hazel's home in Beaumont.

Beaumont to Houston was only a ninety-minute drive, and J.C. still attended meetings at the Houston mosque. It was in the summer of 1970, after one of those meetings, that he and several friends found themselves in a small group being addressed informally by a dignified black man in a well-tailored business suit who spoke in a quiet but knowledgeable tone.

"Yes, Houston is a marvelous city, a very friendly city, and I have thoroughly enjoyed my short visit here," he told them. "I wish I were able to stay longer, but my schedule simply will not permit it." He looked around at his young audience with a paternal smile. "Ah, how I wish we had young men like you in San Francisco. You know, San Francisco is going to be the very first Muslim-run city in the country. We already have a master plan for the gradual acquisition of various business enterprises. And I don't mean to imply any *illegal* take-over; I mean a strictly legitimate attrition wherein white business owners will sell out to Muslim buyers. Everything strictly aboveboard." A subtle smile came to his lips. "Of course, we may have to—well, *encourage* some of the white folks to move on, but there are plenty ways to do that. My point is: San Francisco is going to be *the* city for all of us Black Muslims. Chicago will still be New Mecca, but San Francisco will be where the opportunity's at—especially for Young Turks like you fellows. Ah, if I could only be your age again. I tell you, wild horses couldn't keep me away from San Francisco."

It was not long after the man's visit that a carload of the "Young Turks"—five of them—left Houston for the two-thousand-mile drive to San Francisco.

J. C. Simon was one of the five.

Skullcap was still humming as he drove the van down Eddy Street and turned into Larkin. Judo saw that they were heading into the Civic Center, where all the city, state, and federal buildings were located.

"Man, where the fuck you going?" he said, more an accusation than a question. "This neighborhood is crawling with pigs."

Skullcap glanced disdainfully at him. "Not on Sunday, man," he said, like a patient teacher reminding a slow student of the obvious.

Skullcap drove down Larkin to the 400 block. He passed the federal building on one side, a bank of stores on the other. On the corner was a bar, Harrington's Irish Club. One door back was Erakat's Grocery.

Skullcap turned at the next corner and drove along a practically deserted street between the federal building on one side and the state building on the other. He completely circled the block and parked on the north side of the federal building. Around the corner and down the block were the grocery and the bar. Skullcap glanced at his watch. It was quarter of eleven.

They waited, watching the street.

Particularly watching the grocery.

At ten minutes to eleven, twenty-one-year-old Randy Clough, a slight man with long sideburns, walked past the Erakat Grocery on his way to Harrington's Irish Club. Clough's father-in-law owned Harrington's; Clough was on his way to work. As he passed the grocery, he glanced inside. Saleem Erakat, the owner, was just getting ready to open.

In the van, Skullcap watched Clough pass the grocery and enter the bar. "Okay," he said, "now that that sucker's out of the way, we're ready." He reached for the attaché case behind the seat. "Here's how we'll work it: you go down this side of the street and stand by that big building right across from the store. I'll go down the side of the street that the store is on and go inside. You keep watch, hear? If anybody comes in, you cross the street and come in after them."

"What the fuck good that gonna do, man?" Judo argued. "I ain't got no piece, you got my piece."

"Won't nobody know that, man," Skullcap said patiently. "Anyway, I been watching this place for a long time; been going in and buying apples from the old fool who owns the place; hardly anybody ever comes in the first hour on Sunday morning. Believe me, I know what I'm doing, brother. Now come on, let's go."

The two men alighted from the van and went their separate ways. Judo watched Skullcap as he walked along the opposite side of the street, strutting: black raincoat, black pigskin gloves, fedora cocked slightly to one side, attaché case swinging in a short arc, long legs carrying him with just a hint of arrogance. The man looked *good*, Judo thought. No fucking question about it.

He moved into place in front of the federal building as Skullcap entered the grocery.

Saleem Hassan Erakat was fifty-three years old. A Jordanian Arab, he had operated Erakat's Grocery at 452 Larkin Street for thirteen years. He had a wife, Somiha, and four children ranging in age from a young teenage girl to a twenty-year-old son. Every member of the family worked in the store, which was open seven days a week. On weekends, most of the grocery's business came from neighborhood apartment residents, but during the week there was a steady flow of civil servants from the nearby government buildings. They came over on their coffee breaks and lunch hours to buy sandwiches, fresh fruit, Hamm's beer. Erakat's Grocery was a popular place in the Civic Center, and Erakat himself was a popular man.

On this rainy Sunday morning, the stocky, thick-haired grocer had just taken the empty cash-register tray into the back room. It was a tiny room, used for quick meals during the long business day. There was a four-burner gas range in one corner, an aluminum sink on legs in another, a round breakfast table, a pair of mismatched chairs, and a variety of pots, pans, dishes, bowls, cups— most of them in a constant state of drying on the wing counter of the aluminum sink.

Erakat put the cash-register tray on the table and started to open the cloth money bag to count out the day's starting change. Just then he heard someone enter the store. He stopped what he was doing and went into the front. A tall black man in a raincoat, carrying an attaché case, had just come in. Erakat recognized him.

"*As-salaam-alaikum*," the black man said, speaking the Muslim greeting.

"*Walaikem as-salaam*," Erakat replied, which translated roughly to, "Peace be with you also." "Did you come in for your apple today?" the grocer asked.

"Not exactly," said the black man.

He opened the attaché case and removed the gun.

From across the street, Judo watched through the store window as Skullcap and Erakat talked. He saw them move toward the rear of the store until they were out of sight.

Judo swallowed nervously; his throat was suddenly dry. He felt very vulnerable standing in front of the huge federal building, whether from the sheer size of it or the fact that it represented authority, he did not know. All he knew was that his bowels were churning. He could not stand still. Glancing apprehensively up and down the street, he started crossing to the opposite sidewalk.

As he did, a retired waiter named Joaquin Calles came around the corner, walking toward the store.

In the back room of the store, Saleem Erakat calmly pointed to the money bag on the table. "There is the money. That is all there is. Take it. I do not resist you."

"I have to tie you up," said Skullcap, "so you won't follow me out or call the police."

"I will not follow you out," the Jordanian said. "I am not so crazy as to follow a man with a gun."

"I said I have to tie you up, motherfucker!" Skullcap snapped. The hand holding the gun was shaking; all of Skullcap's movements were sudden, jerky. Erakat took note of the nervousness.

"Tie me up then," he said calmly. "Do what you have to do."

A necktie belonging to the grocer was draped over one of the mismatched chairs. Skullcap snatched it up. "Turn around," he ordered. "Put your hands behind your back."

Erakat obeyed. Awkwardly holding the gun, Skullcap wound the necktie around Erakat's crossed wrists and managed to double-knot it. He did not do a very good job of it; a strong man like Erakat could have freed himself very quickly had he the chance.

But Saleem Erakat would not have a chance.

"Now go in there," Skullcap said, waving the gun toward a closet-size bathroom.

He followed Erakat into the bathroom, grabbing a quilted lap robe from one of the chairs and wrapping it around the gun.

Judo got to the front door just steps ahead of Joaquin Calles. He stood in the doorway, blocking the entrance. When Calles walked up, Judo said, "Closed, man. The store's closed."

Calles looked pointedly at the OPEN sign hanging in the door. Judo followed his eyes. For an instant it seemed as if the older, retired waiter might challenge Judo. If he had, Judo might have killed him with one or two well-placed blows. As it turned out, Judo

84

merely reached inside the door and flipped the sign around to
CLOSED. Joaquin Calles walked away.

Judo remained in the doorway for another minute, fidgeting,
shifting his weight from one foot to the other, trying to wet his lips
with a dry tongue. Presently the drizzling rain stopped. Judo's eyes
blinked rapidly. Shit, man, lots of peoples liable to come out soon's
they see it's quit raining, he told himself. Better warn the brother—

Anything to get out of that fucking doorway.

Judo hurried into the store.

And from around the corner came another Erakat customer, sev-
enty-four-year-old Nellie White, her dyed red hair a touch of
brightness in the gray, sunless day.

In the rear bathroom, Skullcap made Saleem Erakat sit on the
floor in a corner. The grocer tacitly obeyed; the sooner this thing
was over, the better.

"You remember me coming in here every day for an apple,
huh?" asked Skullcap.

Erakat nodded. "I remember most of my customers," he said
truthfully.

"You won't remember anymore," Skullcap told him.

With the muzzle of the gun barely protruding from the lap robe
he had wrapped around it, Skullcap nudged Erakat forward until
the grocer was looking down at the floor on which he sat.

Then Skullcap squeezed the trigger and shot him once behind the
right ear.

Judo heard the muffled crack of the shot as he was hurrying to
the rear of the store. He went into the back room and in the small
corner bathroom saw Skullcap bending over the grocer. There was
blood on the wall behind the slumped victim, and more blood dripping from his head to a small pool between his spread legs. Judo's
eyes widened in shock.

"Man, what the fuck happened?" he blurted.

"I finished a white devil," Skullcap said with a smirk. Then his
expression hardened. "Get your ass back out to that door, man!"

Judo hurried back through the store. His mind was a turmoil of

85

fear; one apprehensive thought after another raced through his head, vying for recognition. He felt sweat literally pop out on his brow.

Before he reached the front door, he saw Nellie White enter. He dropped to a crouch behind a row of shelves. Got to get that old woman, he thought. If I don't she'll see me, she'll identify me. Blame me for shooting that sucker—

Judo crept down the length of shelves toward Nellie White. She looked pretty old, he thought. Got brittle bones. He could snap her neck easy—

But Judo never quite got to Nellie White. The unsuspecting elderly woman looked in a bin in the front window for some fresh garlic, saw that there was none, and quickly walked back out of the store.

Judo blinked away the rivulets of sweat that were running into his eyes. He watched Nellie leave, then ran back to the rear of the store again. Bounding into the back room, he startled Skullcap, who was at the round table, examining the money bag.

"Man, we got to get the fuck out of here! There's all kinds of people starting to come in here!"

"We going," Skullcap said calmly. He opened the attaché case and put the gun and money bag inside. He noticed Judo glance at the money bag. "Don't get no ideas, motherfucker. This money goes into the Death Angels' treasury." He snapped the case shut. "Come on."

Skullcap started for the front of the store. Judo looked around desperately to see if there was anything in the room worth stealing. There was not. Mustering his courage, he stepped into the tiny bathroom and felt behind the slumped victim for a wallet. As he did, his fingers brushed Erakat's wristwatch. It was low on his wrist, below where Skullcap had tied him. Judo worked it off. Then he felt again for the wallet. He found it and worked it out of Erakat's pocket.

Stuffing the watch and wallet into his own pocket, Judo started after Skullcap. The door leading back into the small rear room had moved almost to a closed position. Judo pulled it open and hurried toward the store.

"Come on, chump, hurry up," said Skullcap. "An' don't be touching nothing, sucker; you don't be wearing gloves."

Judo hesitated. Had he touched the doorknob just before leaving the bathroom? He could not remember. Uncertain, he took a tentative step backward.

"Okay, let's split," Skullcap ordered. He walked briskly toward the front door. Judo, not wanting to be left in the store alone, immediately forgot about the doorknob and hurried after him.

On his way out, Skullcap picked up a Baby Ruth candy bar, unwrapped it, and proceeded to eat it as they walked back to the van.

Five minutes later, Nellie White returned to the store, this time for milk. For the second time, she saw or heard no one on the premises. Yet the door was wide open. Looking around the quiet, still store, Nellie felt a chill in her spine. Involuntarily, she shuddered. Then she hurried out and went next door to Harrington's Irish Club.

Jack Holder, a retired sausage-maker, was sitting at the bar in Harrington's, having his customary Sunday morning drink, when Nellie came up to him. "There's something wrong in Sammy's store," she said. Few people called Erakat by his proper name of Saleem; most called him Sammy.

"What do you mean?" said Holder. "What's wrong?"

"The store's open but nobody's around. Not Sammy or any of the kids or anybody. It's kind of—scary."

"Let's have a look," said Holder.

They went next door. In the back, Holder found Saleem Erakat where his killer had left him.

Officers Dennis McCaffrey and Andrew Citizen responded to the call. Upon arrival at the Erakat Grocery they secured the premises and summoned an emergency ambulance. After the ambulance arrived and the attendant determined that Saleem Erakat was officially and legally dead, the officers requested a watch lieutenant and additional help at the scene. They also notified the Crime Lab, the Photo Lab, and Homicide.

While all this was going on, word began to spread swiftly

through the neighborhood that the popular grocer had been slain. Telephone calls were made, friends were advised, known acquaintances of the dead man were told. Within an hour, a dozen relatives had arrived at the grocery. Men, women, and children, they were crying and wailing in the custom of Jordanian Arabs in mourning. One woman lay facedown on the floor and wailed for an hour; the policemen in the store had to step over and walk around her. Outside, in the steadily drizzling rain that had begun again, a crowd of passersby gathered and stood peering in the store windows, looking curiously at the distraught family.

In the meantime, procedure continued to be followed. A Crime Lab specialist named McCarthy arrived, and a photo man named Clement. Three officers named Ward, Gisler, and Copeland began searching out and questioning possible witnesses.

But most important of all—not only to the crimes already committed, but to the eighteen additional crimes which would *be* committed in the next 142 days—there arrived at the scene two Homicide inspectors to take charge of the Erakat investigation.

Their names were Gus Coreris and John Fotinos.

At the end of Day Thirty-seven, there were five victims.

Quita Hague, hacked to death.

Richard Hague, surviving, his butchered face still painfully healing.

Ellen Linder, raped, ravaged, threatened with death.

Frances Rose, her face blown apart by close-range gunshots.

And Saleem Erakat, tied up and executed with a single shot behind the ear, after greeting his killer with the words, "Peace be with you also."

Day 53

Gus Coreris walked like John Garfield used to walk: a little too fast, cocky, with his arms swinging as if he were on his way to a fight.

His partner, John Fotinos, thicker, stockier, was oddly more graceful, and was able to keep up with Coreris apparently without difficulty.

One got the impression that if they *had* been on their way to a fight, that Coreris's opponent would have had to do battle with a wild, tenacious tiger of a man who would have fought tooth and nail until he either won or was killed. Fotinos, on the other hand, would have fought like a bear: calmly and conservatively, waiting until he got his arms around his opponent. Then he would have broken his back.

They had been partners, working Homicide, for thirteen years. Closer than most brothers, they had few, if any, secrets from each other, and were able to communicate almost silently at times. They knew things about each other that even their respective wives did not know, because in the business of bodies and bloody murder, there are many things a man cannot take home to the family he loves. Those things he shares only with his partner. Or his priest.

Coreris and Fotinos were both forty-eight years old, both native San Franciscans, both Greek Orthodox. Prior to becoming working policemen together, their lives had indirectly crisscrossed and matched many times. Fotinos had known Coreris's wife-to-be, Kathy Picras, most of his life; they had attended grade school, junior high, and high school together. Coreris had played football at Poly High against Fotinos at Mission. Their religious ties in the Greek Orthodox community of San Francisco were mutual. They both went off to World War Two—Fotinos in the Navy, Coreris in the Army Air Corps—and both returned home to marry San Francisco girls: Coreris marrying Kathy, Fotinos marrying a Catholic girl, Barbara Stevens. They became police officers, both rose through the ranks, both made inspector and were eventually assigned to the General Work Detail handling the scut work of the police department: assaults and batteries, sex crimes, surveillances, anything else that turned up. Finally they became Homicide partners.

Over the years they fathered between them four daughters but only one son each. Those sons also became policemen. The two Homicide partners had begun a tradition.

On December 11, 1973, when Saleem Erakat had been dead for sixteen days, Coreris and Fotinos still were not sure what kind of killing they were dealing with. That was what they told their lieutenant when they brought him up to date on the status of the case.

"We know we've got a robbery," said Coreris, "because thirteen hundred bucks was taken. What we aren't sure of is whether the *reason* for the killing was robbery."

"What other reasons are you considering?" the lieutenant asked.

"A couple," said Fotinos. "It could have been a professional hit where the hit man picked up the money because it just happened to be there. The thing has got the M.O. of a hit: victim's hands tied behind his back, a single, small-caliber slug behind the ear, the whole thing appearing to be well thought out in advance."

"The weakness in that theory, of course," said Coreris, "is the black lookout that witnesses saw at the front door. No white hit man is going to use a black for a backup. So if we're talking about a hit man, it's got to be a black hit man. Which in turn means we're eliminating a lot of motives. We're eliminating gambling, loan-sharking, protection: none of those would use a black hit man. If any of those operations had a reason to execute Erakat, they'd import a professional *white* man.''

"We don't think it's that anyway," said Fotinos. "But what it could be is a possible revenge killing." The husky officer leaned forward in his chair. "Maybe a couple of blacks pissed off at Erakat about something. Maybe he wouldn't give them credit, or sell them beer because they were under twenty-one, something like that. A Saturday-night run-in of some kind that they came back and settled first thing Sunday morning."

"Or even a spur-of-the-moment thing," said Coreris. He occasionally brushed his neat black mustache flat as he spoke. "Maybe they were the first customers of the day and Erakat said or did something to offend them. So they decided to teach him a lesson."

The lieutenant sighed quietly. Coreris and Fotinos were creating a dilemma. A self-employed grocer had been shot and killed at his place of business. His store was robbed of thirteen hundred dollars, his person robbed of wallet and watch. Yet the two best Homicide cops in the department were for some reason reluctant to treat it as an ordinary robbery-murder. "What bothers you two about this case?" he asked bluntly.

"The necktie around the wrists," Coreris said without hesitation. "It doesn't fit the pattern of two blacks holding up a grocery store."

"It might *be* a holdup-killing," said Fotinos, "but it's something *else* too. That execution touch has got to put it in a different category."

"Got to," Coreris emphasized. "Either a psycho, a revenge killing, a professional hit—something. But it wasn't just a heist murder."

The lieutenant mulled it over for a couple of moments. Finally he said, "This is a case that the public and the papers are going to watch for a while. Erakat was well-known and he was popular. There were 250 mourners at his funeral. The cortege out to Woodlawn had eighty-five cars in it. In the Middle East there were memorial services by more than a thousand members of the Erakat family still living over there. And the Arab Independent Grocers

Association has put up a five-thousand-dollar reward. I'd like to see the case cleared up as quickly as possible—and as *cleanly* as possible. By the same token, I want it cleared up *right*. What it comes down to, I guess, is that you're going to have to go where it leads you. Let's just get us a killer.''

"Yessir," the two detectives replied in unison.

When they left the lieutenant's office, Fotinos said, "Well, where do you want to start?''

"Let's start with a cup of coffee," Coreris said.

They might as well, Fotinos thought. They sure as hell didn't have any place better to start.

At that moment, at the city jail, Paul Roman Dancik was being released from a short incarceration of less than five days. He had been arrested the previous Friday by Narcotics Inspectors Corrales and Herring in the 300 block of Haight Street. The charge against him was suspicion of violation of Section 11359 of the California Health and Safety Code: possession of marijuana for resale.

Dancik had half a dozen prior arrests for drug-connected offenses: possession of hypodermic needles and syringes, possession of marijuana plants, loitering in areas where known narcotics trade was conducted. He had been a suspected user and/or dealer for at least five years. His favorite place to shoot heroin was in his inner left elbow: that was where most of his needle marks were.

Dancik had just passed his twenty-sixth birthday the previous month. He was a thin young man, as most confirmed drug users are: nearly six feet tall, barely 130 pounds. He usually listed his occupation as an artist. Before San Francisco, he had lived in Monte Rio, a hamlet seventy-five miles north of the Bay Area. But he had lived all over the state—and been in minor scrapes with the law everywhere he lived. In San Bernardino he served five days in jail for failure to obey a posted sign. In Carmel he served another five days for violation of a municipal code prohibiting dogs running loose in the business area. In Santa Ana he was arrested for assault and battery. In Laguna Beach for the same thing. He was no stranger to trouble even before he started using drugs.

When he was released from jail that morning, Dancik had shaggy brown hair and a droopy Zapata mustache. He was wearing denim

Levis, a dark sport coat, and a white shirt. When he left the jail property room, he had plenty of money: included in the personal property returned to him was $345 in U.S. currency and $250 in Mexican pesos.

When Paul Roman Dancik left the jail, he went immediately back to the 300 block of Haight. He had been five days without a fix. He needed to score—bad.

When Anthony Harris finished instructing the teen judo class that Tuesday afternoon, he toweled the sweat from his body, got dressed, and hurried outside to meet Debbie.

"Hi. Sorry you had to wait," he said.

"That's all right, silly," she replied, taking his hand and squeezing it. "I don't mind waiting for you."

Debbie was a short, round-faced black girl, not slim, but not heavy either. She was pleasant, rather docile, an energetic, hard worker, from a decent, honest family. She practiced Islamics as a religion, not a holy war against the white man. Anthony had met her a month earlier at the mosque. He had immediately been smitten by her—and she by him. It was the kind of feeling he had dreamed about during his final days in San Quentin.

As they walked down the street, holding hands, they talked about a wedding they had attended the previous night. Larry Green had married an attractive young girl named Dinah in a Muslim ceremony, and the newlyweds had then driven across the Bay Bridge to the Holiday Inn in Emeryville for a two-day honeymoon.

"I'll bet old Larry is really getting it wet over there in that motel," Anthony said to Debbie. She pinched his hand smartly.

"You know I don't like that kind of vulgar talk, Anthony," she chastised.

"Hey, I'm sorry, baby," Anthony apologized, but he still had a lewd grin on his face.

"Uh-huh," Debbie said knowingly, "you say you sorry for *saying* it, but that look on your face tells me you still *thinking* it."

"Hey, you know me too well, woman," he said, feigning chagrin. "How you get to know me so well in such a short time?"

"I don't know," Debbie replied quietly. She was not playing a game now. "I just did, somehow."

Anthony looked steadily at her and his own voice softened. "Yeah, I guess you did, all right."

They held hands a little more tightly as they walked. Anthony sighed an inaudible sigh. Yes, this *was* what he had dreamed about in San Quentin.

He just wished it had happened before he got involved in all that other shit—

Shortly after noon on the rainy Sunday that Saleem Erakat had been killed, Judo had stood on a street corner and boarded a number 5 McAllister bus. It was uncrowded; he took a seat alone near the rear. As the bus proceeded along its route—starting, stopping, starting again—Judo surreptitiously slipped Erakat's wallet out of his pocket and examined its contents. The money first: $64. Judo quickly put it in his pocket. Then the other contents: credit cards (which frightened him because he did not know how to use them); miscellaneous papers, ID photos, something written in funny symbols, which Judo thought was Chinese but was actually Arabic. Junk, he thought.

He kept the wallet concealed on his lap as the bus halted and two black men got on. They came all the way to the rear of the coach and sat several seats behind him. He pretended to pay no attention to them, but was already formulating a plan that indirectly involved them.

The bus driver, Judo saw, noticed where everyone sat. In his big overhead mirror, he would glance up and watch which seat was chosen by each new passenger. He had done that with Judo; he had also done it with the two black men sitting in the rear seat. That was perfect, Judo thought. With a handkerchief, he carefully wiped his fingerprints off the wallet and its contents.

Judo stayed on the bus until the two black men in the rear got off. Then, when the driver was concentrating on pulling back into traffic, Judo reached behind him and tossed Erakat's wallet onto the rear seat. When the driver found it, he would think the other two men had disposed of it.

Judo rode a few more blocks and got off the bus, feeling very clever and crafty. It did not occur to him that all he had done was indicate that the Erakat killing had been perpetrated by two black men—which, in fact, it had.

The wallet was found by the bus driver, Fred Langlois, when he routinely inspected his vehicle's interior at the end of the line.

Langlois was a suave, cool black man who wore a beard, mod glasses, and one earring. He was independent, hep, tough, definitely his own man. And he was honest.

He turned the wallet over to his supervisor.

For a while, Judo enjoyed wearing Saleem Erakat's gold wristwatch. It was a great convenience simply to glance at one's arm to find out what time it was, instead of constantly having to search for clocks in store windows, or ask total strangers on the street. Judo would have liked to keep the watch.

But he ran out of money.

Roy Wittenberg owned Roy's Jewelry and Loan Company on Sixth Street. Wittenberg waited on Judo when he brought Erakat's watch in to pawn.

"Ten dollars," he said, after examining the watch.

"Come on, man, it's worth more than that," Judo protested.

Wittenberg bobbed his chin at a showcase full of watches. "Not to me, buddy. Ten dollars."

Judo took the ten.

Honky motherfucker, he thought as he left the store.

Paul Roman Dancik was having problems. He had more than $300 cash in his pocket, had been out of jail for six hours, but could not make a drug connection.

Dancik had immediately returned to the general location of his most recent arrest: Haight Street around Buchanan and Webster. That was the site of a large, low-income housing project where in the past Dancik had been able to connect for any kind of drugs he wanted. But on this day, for some reason, every contact he tried he had come up empty. It was crazy. Like he was in a strange city or something.

Around midafternoon he went to the project apartment of a

95

black man known to him as Luther G. Luther was an outrageous-looking individual: he had dyed red hair and a black mandarin mustache, and habitually dressed in tight trousers stuffed into the tops of cowboy boots, Western-style. He had not one but *two* white wives, both of whom he claimed to be legally married to by way of Hindu wedding ceremonies.

Luther G was not a street person; he was simply an eccentric. He did not steal or otherwise hustle. For a living he worked nights as a warehouse watchman. Both his wives also worked, one as a salesclerk, the other as a tour guide on Fisherman's Wharf. Among the three of them, they earned enough to live modestly and satisfy their drug habits. All three were cocaine habitués.

Luther was not pleased to see Paul Dancik when he answered his door that afternoon. He knew Dancik had recently been arrested right there in the projects. And he could see that Dancik had a desperate look in his eyes.

"Man, what the fuck's the story around here?" Dancik asked Luther. "I can't connect."

"Nobody around to connect with," Luther said, not inviting Dancik in. "Too much heat. Ever'body done set up in new locations."

"Can you put me on to some, man? I need to connect."

"I can put you on to some snow. That's all I use."

"I don't want that shit, man. I want something real."

"Sorry," said Luther. He started to close the door.

"Wait a minute, man," Dancik pleaded. He pulled a roll of bills from his pocket. "Listen, it's worth twenty to me just for a lead."

Luther thought about it for a moment. His wives, who were bisexual, had been wanting a double-headed dildo they had seen in a sex shop the previous week. It cost $19.95.

"Okay," said Luther, "you give me the twenty and come back tonight. I'll have a contact for you then."

"Out of sight," said Dancik.

He gave Luther G the twenty and left.

At the mosque, Skullcap was looking for Judo.

"He already left," said the Fruit of Islam sentry at the rear door.

There was a stranger with Skullcap, a big black man the guard had never seen before.

"Where'd he go, you know?" Skullcap asked.

"He met some sister and they headed that way," the sentry told him, bobbing his head down the street.

"Thanks, brother. Come on," he said to the stranger, "let's see can we catch up with him." They hurried off in the direction the sentry had given them.

The stranger with Skullcap was a husky, moonfaced man, six one, 210 pounds, a solid man with barely an ounce of fat on him. When he walked, he appeared unusually burly, as if he had extra muscles that other men lacked. He was clean-shaven, his hair trimmed very short and neat. He wore round, gold, wire-rim eyeglasses that looked incongruous on a man of such obvious strength and power. Against his dark brown complexion, the gold rims looked like ornamentations.

Call this man Rims.

Manuel Leonard Moore never liked white girls. In school they often ridiculed him because of a speech problem he had: he slurred some words, forgot some others, mispronounced some, and frequently interjected a grunting or hawking sound to substitute for a word or phrase he was not sure he could handle.

"Looks like a monkey, talks like a monkey," the white girls would say.

"Aw, go finger-fuck yourself," Manuel told them.

Sometimes a white boy would overhear him and there would be a fight. Manuel was big enough and strong enough to win most of the fights, but that did not matter; after the girls told what he said to them, he was usually expelled anyway. From the time he was fourteen years old, he was suspended from school on a regular basis.

At home, Manuel's father, Raymond Moore, was what is euphemistically described as a strict disciplinarian. That is, when Manuel was suspended, his father beat the hell out of him. Raymond Moore had no time for the psychological approach to childraising. He had nine others besides Manuel, and he broke his back ten and twelve hours a day as a laborer for a paving company to support his large family. As far as he was concerned, there was only one rule that needed to be applied to raising his children: be good—or get a beating for being bad. Regular attendance at the Church of Christ with his wife Viola only reinforced his "spare the rod, spoil the child" conviction.

Attending school was sheer torture for Manuel. He did not learn to read or write—yet, incredibly, he continued to be passed to the next higher grade. Within the framework of the California system of education, Manuel Leonard Moore actually progressed into the tenth grade—*his sophomore year of high school*—without learning to read. He did learn to recognize certain words by the way they looked alone—but not many; and he learned to sign his own name; but he could not identify the individual letters in his name unless they were in the exact sequence in which he had learned them.

Manuel began to steal when he was thirteen. Nothing big, nothing very valuable, just kid-type stealing, shoplifting, petty thefts. The family lived in San Bernardino County then, in Southern California. Most of the time when Manuel was caught, it was by the police in the little town of Fontana. Each time, the Fontana PD handled the violation without going through the formalities of the juvenile court. After all, Manuel was not really a *bad* boy, not a criminal; he was just a local black kid who had a speech problem and was not too bright in school. He would be all right, as soon as he was old enough to go out and get a laborer's job.

There came a time, however, when the Fontana PD was unable to handle Manuel informally, internally. When he was fourteen, he ran away—probably from one of his father's severe beatings—and when he was picked up and returned to the area as a runaway, he had to face the court process. That process committed him to the Verdemont Boys Ranch. They kept him less than a year, then released him to his home on probation. According to their evaluation, he had made "real progress"—they had taught him the alphabet all the way up to H.

Manuel Moore was now one of society's misfits. He could not read or write, he was ridiculed for a speech problem, the schools did not want him, his father knew only one way to handle him, he was too young to hold a job legally, and he had a juvenile police record.

What to do? Manuel wondered. He did not know. He had no direction, no guidance, no goals. A piece of flotsam in the mainstream of life.

Manuel began to break the law with stunning regularity. Before his seventeenth birthday, he was arrested twice for violation of juvenile curfew, and investigated for six burglaries and one car theft. After that, it was anything and everything: suspicion of robbery, battery, burglary, forcible rape, possession of alcohol by a minor, failure to appear on traffic citations, receiving stolen property, possession of marijuana, violation of probation, drunk driving; then more burglaries; and more and more. Occasionally they locked him up: 60 days for petty theft, 15 days for failure to appear on traffic citations, 120 days for receiving stolen property, more failures to pay traffic fines: 7 days, 4 days, 6 days, 5 days—he was in and out of the county jail like it was a transient hotel. The longest term he served was ninety days for petty theft; the shortest, two days for a traffic violation.

In 1969 the State of California apparently got tired of playing games with Manuel. It convicted him of second-degree burglary and sentenced him to serve from six months to fifteen years in prison. He was sent to San Quentin. After two years and three months there, he was paroled. He stayed out thirteen months, then was arrested for two burglaries and returned to prison as a parole violator. This time they only kept him one year. As they had been with parole violator Jesse Lee Cooks, the people who decide these matters were certain that a very short term was adequate to prepare Manuel Moore to reenter society.

One thing was certain: that short term was long enough for Manuel to embrace Muslimism fervently.

As Anthony Harris walked along the street holding hands with Debbie, J. C. Simon and Manuel Moore hurried to catch up with them from behind.

"Hey, brother, wait up," said J.C. "Look who I got with me."

Anthony turned and was surprised to see Manuel. He and Manuel and Jesse Lee Cooks had all belonged to the San Quentin Mosque together. "Well, kiss my ass if it ain't the Man," Anthony said. He was genuinely happy to see Manuel, whom he had always

liked. He looked upon Manuel Moore as a big, muscular, gentle
giant, always affable, always friendly, ready to do anything for a
brother. As Manuel approached, Anthony offered his hand, palm
up. Manuel slapped it down smartly.

"Hey, Ant'ny," said Manuel, smiling widely. "How do you be
making it, man?"

"All right, Big Man. Making it just fine. When you get out?"

"Le's see," Manuel said, frowning, thinking about it, trying to
formulate an accurate answer in his mind. He was unable to do it,
unable to track the days in his slow mind; but it did not embarrass
him with Anthony, who was his friend. He merely grinned and
shrugged, "I ain't be out long," he said.

"He's been at the Halfway House," J.C. said. "But now he's
going to stay at my place. And he's going to work at Black Self
Help."

"All right!" said Anthony. He remembered then that Debbie
was waiting discreetly on the side for him to finish talking. "Oh,
say, this here is Debbie," he said. "Sugar, this is the Man, Manuel
Moore. Him and me done a little time together up in Big Q; ain't
that right, Man?"

"You right." Manuel looked at Debbie. He wished he could be
supercool like J.C., say something like, "How you swinging there,
little mamma?"—but from past experience he knew he could not
handle that kind of talk. He always fucked up when he tried. So he
just smiled and said, "Hi."

"Hello, Manuel," Debbie said, "it's nice to meet you." Debbie
held out her hand and he awkwardly shook it with his own big paw.
"Do you have any people in San Francisco?" she asked.

As Debbie engaged Manuel in conversation, J.C. drew Anthony
aside and spoke to him in a confidential tone. "What you going to
be doing later tonight, brother?"

"Why?" Anthony asked suspiciously.

"I just thought you and me could take Manuel out for a while.
Show him around. You know what I mean?"

Anthony glanced self-consciously at Debbie. She did not like J.
C. Simon and did not approve of Anthony associating with him. "I
ain't sure what I'll be doing tonight," he hedged.

J.C.'s expression did not change but Anthony could see his eyes
harden and turn cold. "Okay," J.C. said, "I just thought since

Manuel was a friend of yours, you might want to help him get started on the right track, you know? I just thought it might look funny to the other guys down at Black Self Help if you didn't try to do nothing for your friend you was in prison with. But maybe you see it a different way."

Anthony was properly chagrined. He looked down at the sidewalk, then over at Debbie again. Both Debbie and Manuel were looking at him. "Okay, man, okay," he said quietly to J.C.

"Hey, good deal, brother!" J.C. replied with a smile. He always smiled when he got his way. "We'll pick you up on the corner over by Alamo Park 'bout nine. Is that cool?"

"Yeah," Anthony grumbled, "that's cool."

After leaving Anthony and Debbie, J. C. Simon took Manuel Moore home with him. J.C. had an apartment on Grove near Fillmore. It was in a modern but modest two-story, multi-unit building set on a narrow but very deep lot. Larry Green and his wife Dinah lived in the same building.

For nearly three months, J.C.'s estranged wife Pat and their little girl Crissy had been living with him. They had come up from Houston the last week in September to try for a reconciliation. It had been at J.C.'s instigation; he wrote Pat how well he was doing, how he had been promoted to assistant manager at Black Self Help, how he had made new friends through the mosque, and how in general he felt that they could make a go of it if she would come to him.

Patricia made the trip to San Francisco. And found that nothing had changed.

In San Francisco, just as he had done in Houston, J.C. still put his Muslim friends first, and her and Crissy second. J.C. still went out nights and left her and Crissy alone. J.C. still talked about four hundred years of oppression by white people, still scorned what he referred to as the "Caucasian intellect," still expected her to adjust her personal philosophy to suit his. And J.C. still brought strange, wild-eyed friends home to sit with in a dimly lit corner and talk in low voices about God knows what.

No, J.C. had not changed. Pat knew it from the first week. But she tried to find a way to work it out, for Crissy's sake. The child worshiped her daddy—and J.C., when he was not busy with some

Black Muslim meeting or whatever else he did with his time, reciprocated. Daddy and daughter together were a sheer delight to see. But the moments were rare.

By the end of the second month, Pat had decided to return to Texas. She was just waiting for the right time, the right excuse. It came the night J.C. brought Manuel Moore home to stay with them.

"J.C., are you crazy?" she asked him in the privacy of their bedroom. "That man can't stay with us. Why, you don't even know anything about him."

"I know he's a brother," J.C. replied. "That's all I have to know."

"Well, it's not all *I* have to know. For God's sake, J.C., I'd be afraid to close my eyes at night with him in the next room, much less let Crissy go to sleep unguarded."

"Woman, that is a lot of shit," J.C. said firmly. "The man is a *brother*. He is just out of prison and he needs help."

"Let him get help at the Halfway House or whatever it is that he was staying at."

"He is finished with the Halfway House. What he needs now is *personal* help, *individual* help. He needs *my* help."

"I think you the one who needs help," she snapped. "Help in the head."

"Whatever I need," he replied coldly, "it ain't advice from you. Now you fix supper for me and the brother, hear? And later on tonight after supper, him and me is going out for a spell, and I don't want to hear no shit about it either. Understand?"

Pat turned and silently left the room. She certainly did understand. All too well.

Judo was waiting on the corner when Skullcap and Rims drove up. He was surprised to see them not in the van but in a black Cadillac several years old. Judo got into the back seat. "Where'd you get the wheels, man?" he asked Skullcap.

"They belong to the boss," Skullcap replied.

Judo nodded. He was not quite sure who Skullcap meant, but he did not pursue the matter. He patted Rims on the shoulder. "How you making it, brother?"

"I be doing all right, just fine," said Rims. He grinned back at Judo. "I gonna get me my first devil tonight."

Judo felt a sudden depression come over him. Shit, he thought. You too? Weren't there any sane people left? Then he grunted silently to himself. You a fine one to wonder, he thought. What the fuck *you* doing here? And with a gun in your belt, too.

Judo tried to tell himself that he thought they were going out on a stickup. But he knew that he should have known better.

"Say, man, you got your piece?" Skullcap asked. Then without waiting for an answer, he said, "Let the brother hold it for a spell. Get him used to handling one."

Motherfucker! Judo thought. Why his gun? Why the fuck didn't Skullcap get his own piece back from whoever the fuck he let borrow it? Else get him another one. Judo did not like other people handling his gun.

Nevertheless he slipped it from under his coat and passed it up to Rims.

The moonfaced black examined the weapon in what he hoped was a respectful, intelligent manner. "Look like a nice piece, man," he commented, even though he would not have known the difference had he been handling a German Luger instead of an ordinary .32-caliber automatic.

"It is, man," said Skullcap with a grin. "I can give witness to that, can't I, brother?" he asked Judo.

"Yeah, sure," Judo said sullenly. He wanted his gun back.

"Just hold on to it for a spell," Skullcap told Rims, as if it were his gun instead of Judo's. "Get the feel of it while we look for us a devil."

The Cadillac moved south on Steiner, toward Haight.

When Paul Dancik returned to Luther G's apartment, the door was barely opened to him—three inches on a security chain. Through the narrow slit, he could see an attractive white girl with a peaches-and-cream complexion, wearing the uniform of a tour guide. One of Luther G's *ménage à trois*, Dancik thought. Not bad either, if a man was interested in sex—which at that moment he was not.

"Is Luther here?" he asked through the slit.

"No, but he left this for you." The girl handed him a scrap of paper with a telephone number on it.

"Is this all? No name or nothing?"

"That's all."

Shit, Dancik thought irritably. "Can I use your phone?"

"We don't have one," the girl said. "The deposit's too high. But there's a pay phone over by the corner of the parking lot."

She shut the door before Dancik could say anything further, leaving him standing there with the scrap of paper in his hand.

Shit, he thought again. He left the apartment building and started across the parking lot toward the pay phone.

"There one," said Rims as the Cadillac, now on Haight, cruised past the parking lot. They were near the pay phone and could see a young white man coming toward it.

"That's just a man," Skullcap said. "We can keep looking and find you a woman or a kid."

Rims shook his head. "I just—" He hesitated, the words faltering, then he blurted it out: "Ijustsoondoitquick."

"Okay, brother, it's your devil. I'll circle the lot and you can come up on him from behind."

"Yeahthat'sgoodthat'sgood."

Skullcap accelerated slightly and rounded the block to the other side of the projects. Now they were in a position to see the white man *going* toward the pay phone, instead of *coming* toward it; his back was to them. Skullcap pulled to the curb and left the engine running. He slapped Rims on the thigh. "Go get that devil," he said in a voice oddly reverent, as if he were sending forth a preacher to spread the gospel.

Rims put the gun under his coat and got out of the car. Skullcap looked in the back seat at Judo. "Be nice if you'd back the brother up," he said pointedly. "Or you just gonna sit back there and watch?"

Judo felt a hot flush of embarrassment. "I could do a lot more, man, if you wouldn't keep taking my piece."

"Shit, man," Skullcap chided, "you don't need a piece. You a fucking black belt, remember? I mean, your fucking *hands* supposed to be deadly weapons, daddy." Skullcap's tone was derisive. It was obvious that the swashbuckler felt he could take the judo fighter.

A moment of heavy silence hung between them: challenging silence such as Judo had uncomfortably experienced with Head. His eyes were locked with Skullcap's eyes, and Judo knew instinctively that Skullcap would die before he averted his eyes first. Knowing that, Judo did not even try to make a contest of it. He looked away.

Skullcap glanced out the car window at Rims lumbering across the parking lot behind the white devil. "Well, brother?" he said pointedly to Judo.

Judo got out of the car and hurried after Rims.

The pay phone in the corner of the projects parking lot stood on a single pole seated in the cement apron. At the top of the phone was an oval pod with an open front, which afforded protection from the elements for the instrument but not the user. A six-foot-long bench seat was mounted on a cement ledge just behind the phone; a thick growth of shrubbery and vines grew between the ledge and the corner of a building a few feet away.

Paul Dancik walked up to the phone, the scrap of paper in one hand, and fished around in his pocket for a dime.

A few yards behind Dancik, automatic held under his coat, a wide-eyed, determined Rims moved ever closer to him.

Behind Rims, Judo walked fast enough to make it look to Skullcap as if he were trying to catch up with Rims, but slowly enough that he would not actually accomplish it.

Just around the corner of the building behind the pay phone, a man named Eduardo Abdi was on his way to use that same phone. Abdi was a small man in his forties, dark, swarthy, wearing a mustache. He had eyes that never stopped darting, shifting, searching, eyes that wanted to see everything, miss nothing. What he saw when he stepped around the corner of the building caught him completely by surprise and caused him to stop dead in his tracks.

Paul Dancik stepped up to the phone pod, dime in one hand, scrap of paper in the other, and reached for the receiver.

Rims stepped up behind Dancik and leveled the automatic. Nervously he wet his lips. "Hey, you—"

Without picking up the receiver, Dancik turned at the sound of the voice. Rims held the gun out straight and shot him three times.

Dancik did not fall. The scrap of paper fluttered to the ground and he put one hand on his chest where the bullets had gone in. He and Rims stared incredulously at each other. Then Dancik began to stagger toward Rims.

Behind his round glasses, Rims's eyes grew wide with fright. He turned and looked pleadingly at Judo, who was poised fearfully nearby. What the fuck do I do now?! his look asked.

Dancik staggered past Rims, staggered twenty feet out to the sidewalk and stood there, eyes wide, probably seeing nothing. A single trickle of blood flowed over the middle of his bottom lip and ran down his chin.

Eight feet away, Eduardo Abdi watched the scene, transfixed.

Rims took a few steps toward Dancik, whose back was now to him. He wondered if he should shoot him again. Deciding he had better, he raised the gun; but before he could fire, Paul Dancik, already dead, fell straight back and lay across the sidewalk like a carefully placed barricade.

Judo rushed to the fallen body and began to go through its pockets. Rims walked over and looked at him in revulsion. "We don't be 'posed to rob no devils," he said, recalling his San Quentin Mosque training.

Judo ignored him. Rims began to blink rapidly, consternation shrouding his moonface.

"Man, I say we don't be 'posed to do that!" he said loudly.

"Shut up, fool!" Judo said. He found a thick wad of currency and shoved it into his pocket. Then he found another. Jesus Christ! Was this fucking guy a bookie's runner or something?

"Man, we gonna get in a lot of shit over this!" Rims said, meaning the robbery, not the killing.

"Will you shut the fuck up!" Judo snapped. He stood up and for a brief moment he and Rims faced each other over the dead man's body.

Standing now about ten feet away, Eduardo Abdi was, incredibly, unobserved by either.

Watching the scene from his apartment across the street, a sixty-five-year-old black man named Albert Cook thought all three men

106

were together. He had heard the shots and run to his living room window. It looked to him as if three men were arguing.

But it was only two: Judo and Rims, caught up in a moment of murder and madness, one killing the devil, one robbing the dead, neither able to understand the motive of the other.

From across the parking lot, an automobile horn sounded. Skullcap. Judo and Rims suddenly remembered where they were, what they were doing, and why the horn was blowing.

Motherfucker, what if he drives off without us!

The two blacks turned and raced across the lot.

Officers James Long and Al Lambert were in a radio car three blocks away when the shooting call was broadcast. They rolled on it at once and were at the scene within one minute. As soon as they arrived, Eduardo Abdi ran up to them.

"I was just gonna call you guys," he said excitedly.

"What happened here?" Long asked.

"We were just standing here," Abdi said, "when two guys came over and opened up on us."

Lambert was checking the victim. "Looks gone," he said.

"You know him?" Long asked Abdi.

"Sure. We were working a case together."

"A case? What kind of case? Are you a police officer?"

"I can't say any more," Abdi told him.

"This guy's gone," said Lambert. "Which way did they go?" he asked Abdi.

"Across the lot."

Lambert cautiously moved onto the lot to check it out. Long was suspicious of Abdi and his remark about "working a case together," but he was also acutely aware that precious seconds were ticking away without a description of the gunmen being on the air. "Give me a quick description of the two men," he told Abdi.

"Well, let's see," said Abdi. "They were both black. The one guy was about five seven or five eight; maybe a hundred forty-five, hundred fifty; had an Afro, but it was a short one. He was wearing a navy-blue pea coat and blue jeans. That's all I remember."

"That's plenty," said Long, impressed. Maybe the guy *was* an officer. "What about the second man?"

"He looked the same," said Abdi.

"The same? You mean exactly?"

"He might have been ten or fifteen pounds lighter. Maybe he had a shorter Afro. But dressed the same way."

"Navy-blue pea coat and blue jeans?"

"Yeah."

"Are you sure you got a real good look at these guys?"

"Yeah. Positive."

Long was skeptical, but at the moment Abdi was all he had. "Wait here, please, while I call this in," he told the witness.

While Long was at the patrol car broadcasting the descriptions he had been given of the gunmen, and Lambert was still checking the edge of the shadowy parking lot, a small crowd began to gather near the body. No one noticed when Eduardo Abdi slipped into that crowd and disappeared.

In the Cadillac, driving south on Buchanan, Rims was completely out of sorts.

"This be my first sting," he said to Judo, "and you done fuck it up. You done make it look like a shitass street robbery by taking that devil's money. Like, we don't be 'posed to steal, man."

"The brother's right," said Skullcap, at the wheel.

"Shit, man, *you* did it," Judo retorted. "Or maybe you done forgot the money bag from that store. 'Member, you said it was going into the Death Angels' treasury?"

"That's different, man." Skullcap defended himself at once. "If you took the money for the treasury, that's different. Is that what you did?"

Judo tried desperately to think of some way to hedge, to evade a direct answer, to keep some of the money for himself. But they were at a stoplight and Skullcap's eyes were riveted on him in the rearview mirror. "Yeah, man, that's what I did," he said reluctantly.

"How much you get?" Skullcap asked.

"Shit, man, I don't know!" Judo snapped. "I didn't stop to count the fucking stuff—" Then he suddenly realized that he *could* salvage some of the money for himself. He had grabbed *two* rolls of bills from that sucker. Unless Rims had seen him take both of them, all he had to do was just hand over one. In the darkness of

108

the back seat, he surreptitiously felt in each coat pocket, trying to determine which roll was the smallest.

When the light changed, Skullcap pulled around the corner on Duboce Avenue and parked. "Let's see the money," he said.

Judo randomly selected one pocket and pulled out the roll of currency it held. He passed it forward to Skullcap, who examined it in the light of the dashboard.

"Pesos!" Skullcap literally spat. A fine spray of spittle landed on Rims's left hand. The big man wiped it off in disgust. "Fucking Mexican pesos!" Skullcap continued in mixed anger and incredulity. "Shit, man, this stuff don't be worth more than twenty dollars in American money."

"What the fuck you mean?" Judo demanded. "You got a whole fucking handful of money there!" As long as he had to give it up, he wanted some decent credit for putting it into the Death Angels' treasury. Twenty dollars would not buy much credit. "Got to be more than twenty bucks there!" he insisted.

"Hey, motherfucker, don't tell *me*," Skullcap said. "I be from Texas, remember? I *know* how much this greaser money is worth. It's worth shit, that's what it's worth."

Son of a bitch, Judo thought. That meant he had another roll of shit in his other pocket. Motherfucker. He had hoped to score good so he could impress his new girlfriend.

"Do this mean I stung a Mesican?" Rims asked almost petulantly. "I don't be get no credit for no sting?"

"Hey, you going to get credit, brother," Skullcap said in as gentle a voice as Judo had ever heard him use. Skullcap obviously liked Rims. "That sucker was white, brother, and I'm going to witness it for you. Nobody going to do you out of that sting."

"Good," Rims said, nodding. "Good. Good." He repeated the word several times, grinning at Skullcap, sorry now that he had been so quick to wipe away his new friend's spit.

Skullcap started the car and pulled away from the curb. "Want to try another one?" he asked. He glanced in the mirror at Judo. "You about ready to get one, brother?"

"Not tonight, man," Judo said. "I ain't in the mood no more. That Mexican money done got me upset." It was the best excuse he could think of.

"Sure it has," Skullcap replied knowingly. He was beginning to understand what Head had said about this man not having the heart to be a true Death Angel.

"Run me up Webster a few blocks and drop me off, man," Judo said. "I got someplace to go." His new girlfriend had an apartment on Webster.

As they drove north again, they all heard the sound of another siren speeding toward the projects parking lot.

At the scene of the shooting, Paul Dancik was still stretched out across the sidewalk, his feet pointing toward the curb. A Central Ambulance unit had responded to the call and a medic named Michaud was bent over the body. When he got up, he said, officially, "Okay, he's dead." Officer Al Lambert logged the time of the pronouncement at 2150 hours—ten minutes before ten. Lieutenant Klapp and Sergeant Racin of the Northern District had arrived to take charge of the physical scene, while Lieutenant Ellis, along with Inspectors Podesta and Schneider, of Homicide, responded to take charge of the investigation itself.

A Photo Lab inspector named Sleadd and a Crime Lab man named Ken Moses went to work as soon as the medic got out of the way. The first thing the Crime Lab man did was draw circles around three brass shell casings that were found on the ground between the pay phone and the point where the victim had staggered and fallen.

"Look like thirty-twos," he said, half to himself.

The Photo Lab man began to flash pictures from all angles. Each flash lighted the scene in stark, deathlike white, for a split instant making the living and the dead look the same.

In the nearby small crowd, Officer James Long looked for Eduardo Abdi. The little witness was nowhere to be found.

Skullcap stopped the car in the middle of a block on Webster. The sound of two more sirens was splitting the night silence. The men could not tell if they were heading toward the projects or not.

"Go on, take off, man," Skullcap said urgently. "You on your own now."

Judo got out of the car and walked quickly away from it. He did not even say good-bye to his friend Rims, whose eyes were darting nervously back and forth as if he expected a battalion of police to descend on him at any second. Nor did Judo think to get his gun back from Rims. He just got away from the car and its two remaining occupants as fast as he could.

Crossing the sidewalk, Judo hurried past a few doors, then ducked into the entrance of a convenient apartment building. He stood just inside the doorway, hiding, until the Cadillac proceeded down the block and around the corner. Then he came back out and started walking toward the apartment of his new girl.

Crazy motherfuckers, he thought, now that he was away from his friends. He had been happy to see Rims when the moonfaced man got out of San Quentin, but now that he saw him in the company of Skullcap, he realized that Rims was as fucked up as the rest of them. I got to find a way to get shed of these mothers, he told himself. Else I be ending up like they be.

He was almost to the corner when he suddenly remembered the other roll of currency he had taken off the white devil. Mexican pesos, he thought. Shit. He wondered where he would be able to trade it for American money. Even if he did only get twenty bucks for it, that was better than nothing. He stopped now in the light of a streetlamp to examine the money. Looking at it, his eyes got very wide.

Motherfucker! It wasn't pesos, it was fucking dollars!

Quickly, trembling, he counted it: 50—100—120—140—160 —200—250—

Judo shoved the money back into his pocket and hurried down the street. He was exhilarated. His face split into a wide grin.

Midway down the block, he paused and gave the finger to the general direction in which the Cadillac had gone.

Back at the death scene, a man named Smith from the San Francisco coroner's office arrived and took charge of the mortal remains of Paul Roman Dancik. He wrote out a receipt for the body and gave it to Officers Long and Lambert. Dancik was loaded into the coroner's panel truck and taken away to the morgue.

At the end of Day Fifty-three, there were six victims.
Quita Hague, hacked to death.

111

Richard Hague, out of the hospital, his butchered face now horribly scarred.

Ellen Linder, raped, ravaged, threatened with death—and soon to have to decide whether to allow her attacker to escape formal punishment for what he had done to her.

Frances Rose, her face blown apart by close-range gunshots.

Saleem Erakat, tied up and executed with a single shot behind the ear.

And Paul Dancik, shot three times in the chest as he attempted to use a public telephone at the edge of a housing project parking lot.

Day 55

Gus Coreris and John Fotinos were concentrating heavily on the Saleem Erakat case. Erakat had been dead for eighteen days. So far they had nothing but suspicions and evidence which they could not correlate with suspects.

"I still say it was Muslims," Fotinos insisted, emphasizing a hunch he had developed early on in the initial investigation. He based it mainly on the description of the black man seen at the front door by Joaquin Calles. "If it had just been some punk stick-up guys, they wouldn't have been so neatly dressed and well-groomed. Got to be Muslims."

"Muslims don't steal," said Coreris.

"Everybody steals," Fotinos retorted.

"Orthodox Greeks don't," said Coreris.

"That's different," Fotinos allowed.

The two detectives were perusing Crime Lab reports on the Erakat case. Coreris scanned the list of physical evidence. It was lengthy—all the items found in close proximity to the victim which might yield fingerprints: a small loaf of bread, four size AA Eveready batteries, a six-pack of Hamm's beer, a can of Franco-American Beef Gravy, a light bulb, a two-ounce jar of Sanka

113

instant coffee, two empty Coke bottles—*ad infinitum.* Plus the
OPEN-CLOSED sign from the door. Miscellaneous papers from the
table in the back room. One expended .32-caliber bullet casing.
And the victim's wallet, which had been turned over to Homicide
by the municipal bus line.

The Erakat death scene had been processed for latent fingerprints, and numerous usable prints had been developed—but so far
none of them had been matched to anyone whose prints were on
file. Fotinos and Coreris were concentrating on a palm print that
had been lifted from the inside doorknob in the tiny bathroom
where the body was found. When they had a hunch who the palm
print might belong to, they filled out a Form 64 and sent it down to
the crime lab. Form 64 was a request for any laboratory examination involving latent prints, firearms, laundry or dry-cleaning
marks, tool marks, documents, blood, hair, semen, paint, or other
matter which was capable of being identified, evaluated, and compared. So far Coreris and Fotinos had sent in a number of Form 64s
on the palm print, with no positive results.

"Harold George came back negative," said Fotinos, tossing the
report onto a pile. "John Hunter, negative." Another toss. "Leroy
Doctor, negative. Earbie Moore, negative." He tossed them all
onto the pile. "At this rate, we'll soon eliminate every creep in the
city."

"I had a lot of hope for the Earbie Moore hunch," said Coreris.
"Who made the report on the print?"

Fotinos looked at the typed name and scrawled signature at the
bottom of the Form 10—Laboratory Results of Examination. The
name was Mitchell L. Luksich.

"Mitch Luksich," said Fotinos. "Why? You think he might
have made a mistake?"

"Shit, no," said Coreris. "Luksich don't make mistakes."

In the basement of the Hall of Justice, in a cubicle barely large
enough for his six-foot-seven-inch, 230-pound frame, Mitch Luksich was bent over a microscope examining the striations on two
spent slugs: the microscopic marks etched into the body of a slug
as it passes through the barrel of a weapon. Infinitesimal, these
marks are as distinctive as human fingerprints: no two are alike.

At twenty-nine, Mitch Luksich was one of the most qualified firearms experts in the business. A biology graduate from San Francisco State College, he had been a crime lab employee for the SFPD for seven years. He was an individualist, wearing cowboy boots and smoking foul-smelling cheroots in urbane San Francisco. Articulate and confident, he could talk for hours about firearms; he had a personal collection worth more than half a million dollars, and spent nearly every weekend traveling to gun shows all over the country to buy, sell, and trade weapons. He made far more money bartering old guns than he did as a civil servant, but his job was as important to him as his hobby, because he was a man of science and nothing gave him greater pleasure than to locate infallible truths through the lenses of a microscope.

As he was doing now.

On a counter beside his microscope was a cellophane envelope marked "Lab. 73-9082" with the name "Dancik" on it. It contained three spent shell casings and two spent slugs which had been removed from the body of Paul Dancik. The third slug taken from his body was under Luksich's microscope. Also under the microscope was another slug from another cellophane envelope, that Luksich was carefully examining, slowly and carefully comparing, slowly and carefully—and patiently, always patiently—matching the minute striations.

When he was finished, and had satisfied himself that he was absolutely, *scientifically* correct, he picked up the phone and called Homicide.

"Gus, Mitch Luksich," he said when Coreris answered. "I just made a match of the slug the coroner took out of Saleem Erakat's head. It was fired from the same gun that killed a fellow named Dancik who was shot on the street night before last."

Luksich had no way of knowing it as he spoke, but his phone call was the first line in a terrible pattern yet to be drawn.

J. C. Simon strutted into a coffee shop on Market Street, a swashbuckler now in work clothes. Manuel Moore lumbered in behind him. They sat in a booth next to the window. J.C. unfolded a *Chronicle*, took out the sports section, and pushed the rest of the paper to Manuel. Self-consciously, Manuel accepted it.

J.C. began to emote on the second Ali-Frazier fight, which was six weeks away. "Ali going to *ruin* that motherfucking Frazier," he predicted. "Ali got Allah behind him. He got the prayers of every Muslim in the world going for him. Frazier's nothing but a white nigger. Muhammad will *de*-stroy him!"

"Frazier awful tough," Manuel said dubiously. "He like a fireplug."

"Don't mean shit," J.C. assured him. "Ali going to hit all over him. Then, after he beat Frazier, he going to go after George Foreman. That be when he win the title back."

"Foreman awful tough," said Manual. "And big."

"Size don't mean nothing to Ali," J.C. said disparagingly.

They ordered milk and doughnuts. While they ate, J.C. continued to scan the sports pages. He noticed that Manuel was not reading the rest of the paper.

"You want the sports, brother?" he asked. "I can read another part."

"No, man, that's okay." Manuel looked out the window, embarrassed.

"What's the matter, brother? Something wrong?"

"No, everything be cool," Manuel said. But there was something in his voice—a strain, a pull—that told J.C. it was not so. He put aside the paper in concern.

"Listen, man," he said quietly, "if you got a problem, you can tell me about it, you dig? I mean, we brothers, see? We got to share things and help each other. I mean, people like us, if we don't got each other, we got nobody. We don't survive. Now what's bothering your ass?"

Manuel sighed quietly. "I can't read," he said.

J.C.'s eyebrows went up. "No shit? I mean, for real? You can't read nothing?"

"Nothing but a few things. Signs and stuff like that. And my name."

"How far did you get in school?"

"Second year high."

"Without *reading?*"

"Yeah. Teachers just kept on passing me."

"Well, kiss my black ass," J.C. said in astonishment. "Second year high school without being able to read." He shook his head. "The fucking white man's educational system. What about the two times you were in the joint? Didn't they try to get you to go to school?"

Manuel shook his head. "One counselor say it be too late for me. Say my learning motor—something like that—done got too. old."

"He's full of shit," J.C. said almost viciously. "Fucking white man just don't *want* no black men educated. Nobody *ever* too old to learn." He leaned forward eagerly and touched Manuel's hand. "Listen, brother, you want to learn to read?"

Manuel blinked rapidly several times. "S-s-sure."

"Then *I'm* gonna teach you how, man. We'll start tonight; lesson number one tonight. Right after we get back."

"Get back from where? Where we going to?"

"We going out tonight," J.C. said.

His face had become a cold mask.

Seven weeks after she had been assaulted and raped by Jesse Lee Cooks, Ellen Linder met with Inspector John T. O'Shea and Assistant District Attorney Robert Podesta in the latter's office in the Hall of Justice. Podesta, one of the rising young attorneys in the DA's office, was not related to Inspector Podesta, of Homicide, who was then working the Dancik killing.

"Miss Linder, as you know," said Podesta, "the man who assaulted you, Jesse Lee Cooks, has been in custody for the past six weeks on a homicide charge. Through his attorney, he has tentatively agreed to plead guilty to first-degree murder if we will agree not to prosecute him on the four charges placed against him for the incident in which you were involved. Those charges are kidnapping, rape, oral copulation, and aggravated assault. We'd like to know if you would agree to this."

"I'm not sure," Ellen Linder said hesitantly. "Are you saying that this man won't be punished at all for what he did to me?"

"Not exactly," said Inspector O'Shea. "He'll receive the same *amount* of punishment no matter how many charges there are against him. The only difference is that this way we'll get him back into prison faster, and it'll cost the taxpayers less to do it."

Ellen studied O'Shea thoughtfully. He was the Sex Detail officer who had investigated her case. A week after her assault, he had been watching television and had seen Jesse Lee Cooks being put into a radio car at the scene of the Frances Rose killing. The description Ellen had given him of her attacker had come at once to the surface of his mind. On a hunch, he had gone downtown at once and secured photographs of Cooks. Ellen had identified them the same night.

Now she was being asked not to prosecute Cooks for what he had done to her. Just let all those hours of terror and anger pass into the forgotten, as if they never happened.

"Let me explain it this way, Miss Linder," said Podesta. "Since there is no longer a death penalty in California, the most severe sentence Cooks can receive for *any* crime is life imprisonment. Since he is a twice-convicted felon who would be pleading guilty to first-degree murder, there is no question that he will get exactly that. Now, even if we tried him on the four charges stemming from your assault, he would still get the same sentence—life."

"Do you think you could convict him for the things that he did to me?" Ellen asked.

"In my opinion, definitely," Podesta said. "I certainly don't want to mislead you in that respect. The chances of a successful conviction on our part are very high. But again I have to point out that even *with* a conviction—a conviction on all charges—the court will still merge the sentence with that given for the murder charge."

Ellen Linder nodded slowly. "So it really doesn't matter what he did to me?"

"In a way, no," said O'Shea. "Not as far as punishment goes. Not after what he did to Frances Rose."

Ellen Linder thought it over.

She finally agreed to it.

"But only on condition that his guilty plea is accepted," she specified. "Only on condition that he goes to prison for the rest of his life."

"There's no question that he will receive a life sentence," Podesta assured her.

When Ellen Linder left Podesta's office that day, she felt

118

satisfied that justice had been done. Although it did not seem quite right that, after what she had gone through, it should all be summarily dismissed like that—as if it never happened; and it did not seem altogether just that even though Cooks was going to receive the maximum sentence allowable, none of it would be for what he had done to *her*; she nevertheless resigned herself to the fact that none of it really mattered, not as long as Cooks would spend the rest of his life in prison.

What she did not realize was that in California there was no such thing as a *firm* life sentence. Sentences in California—even supposed life sentences—tend to be quite flexible. California had a bad habit of letting its convicted killers out to kill again.

Arthur Agnos was a pleasant-looking man of thirty-five, clean-cut, well-groomed, a Greek-American of ambition, intelligence, and very definite upward mobility. He was employed as a consultant—read "troubleshooter"—to the California State Legislature's Joint Commission on Aging. A liberal, he was sincerely dedicated to working with senior citizens, blacks, low-income families, in any blighted or needy area in which he felt he could serve. He was a doer rather than a talker.

On the evening of Thursday, December 13, 1973, he left his home at 637 Connecticut Street and drove in his Volkswagen a short distance to the 900 block on Wisconsin Street. He was to attend a meeting there of residents of a public housing development. The topic of discussion was to be the necessity of having a new health clinic to serve the area. Agnos was strongly in favor of such a clinic. As he drove toward the meeting place, he developed in his mind as many reasons as he could think of to support that position.

The time was 7:00 P.M.

Skullcap and Rims started prowling at eight o'clock. In the borrowed Cadillac again, they drove south on the Bayshore Freeway.

Rims was worried because Judo was not with them. He still had Judo's gun. "Maybe it don't be right for us to use his gun when he don't be along," Rims fretted.

"Don't matter whether he's here or not," Skullcap said. "And it don't matter who the gun *belong* to, long as he's a brother."

119

"Yeah, but what if we sting with it, then when he find out, he be pissed?"

"Let him," Skullcap replied with easy confidence. "Nothing he can do about it."

"He tough," Rims reminded his friend. "He know all that judo shit."

"Shit is right," Skullcap said derisively. "That's about all it is: a lot of shit. Man, I can take him, and I don't know none of that shit."

"You can take him?"

"Bet your sweet ass I can, baby. You probably can too. That motherfucker ain't half as bad as he's got people thinking he is."

"I don't think I want to fuck with him," Rims decided.

"Don't nobody *want* to fuck with him. The dude's a brother, whether anybody likes him or not. He just been slow developing the kind of heart a true Death Angel needs. Which means we got to help him along when we can. Meanwhile, he got no complaint if *you* use *his* piece to develop your own heart. So don't sweat about it, hear?"

Rims sighed a heavy sigh and drummed the thick fingers of one hand on his knee. He would try to take his friend's advice. Clearly, he did not expect it to be easy.

Skullcap got off the freeway at Army Street and doubled back, driving up Kansas Street toward the Potrero Hill district.

Art Agnos left the Potrero Hill health committee meeting with a good feeling. The session had been very friendly and, in his estimation, productive. He had even been asked to run for a position on the board of directors; the people liked him that well.

As he walked toward his car, two women came after him and caught up with him under a streetlight. They were residents whom he had seen at the meeting; both were named Susoeff and they lived in the next block. Agnos, smiling as he usually did, stopped to talk with them.

None of them paid any attention to the black Cadillac as it drove slowly by and pulled to the curb near the corner.

Skullcap got out and walked back toward where the white man and two white women were talking. His mind raced as he planned

120

what to do. He had a chance now to do *three* stings at once—two of them women. That would put him well in the lead for the next Death Angel wings. But he had to do it just right. The women were facing him as he walked toward them; they had already glanced up and noticed him. The man's back was to him, and the man had not turned around, probably did not even know he was coming. The thing to do was get the man first, in the back, before he knew what was happening. Then pick off the two women. Quick and easy.

Nothing to it, he told himself. He slipped Judo's gun from his pocket and held it next to his thigh. Even as he walked toward premeditated murder victims, he still had the slight strut. Going to kill the blue-eyed motherfuckers, he thought.

Skullcap walked directly up to Art Agnos and shot him twice in the back.

Agnos felt as if someone had punched him. He whirled around to face his assailant. What he saw was a handsome black man who was staring blankly at him. The man did not blink. His expression carried no sneer, nothing at all ugly. He appeared to Agnos to be in some kind of state.

Skullcap froze where he stood. Something was wrong: the white devil was not falling. Instead, he had turned around and was staring back at him—

What the fuck was this?

Skullcap felt his bowels churn. Cold sweat popped out along the length of his spine. The two white women were backing away; they appeared to be shrieking, but Skullcap heard no sounds coming from them: his ears suddenly seemed blocked. The smell of burned nitrate from the two bullets he had fired was heavy in his nostrils. Everything around him started to become hazy, cloudy, slow: like a dream sequence in a movie.

And still the motherfucker stood there! Two bullets in him and he would not fall down. Staring at him—

A ball of fear rose in Skullcap's chest. He almost threw the gun away from him, as he would a disgusting bug that had landed in his hand. But he was too frightened even for that.

With a whimper, he turned and ran.

Art Agnos still did not fall. Under his coat, the back of his shirt was slowly being saturated by a widening spot of blood. The dull,

121

punchlike feeling was becoming a burning pain. But he stayed on his feet. Presently he felt supporting hands take hold of his arms. What seemed like a faraway voice was urging, "Bring him over here! Get him inside!"

He was half led, half helped, across the street and into someone's house. It was a relief to feel carpet under his feet; at least now if he fell it would not be on concrete.

And fall he finally did. The people helping him felt his legs go out under him. His body went limp. Gently they laid him on the living room floor while someone called the police and an ambulance. Meanwhile, the members of the black family whose home he was in did what they could to make him comfortable.

In the Cadillac, Skullcap and Rims were on the Bayshore Freeway again, speeding north. Rims was driving this time. Skullcap sat beside him, talking out loud, but more to himself than to Rims.

"Motherfucker *stood* there! Wouldn't fall! Stood there looking at me! Looking at my face! White motherfucking devil!"

"Manjustcalmdownnow," Rims said excitedly, running his words together in a nervous string. He gripped the steering wheel almost desperately. As he drove, he threw quick glances at Skullcap. "Don'tgetsouptightonmeman!" he said. There was a plea in his voice. Rims needed a calming influence, not a strung-out madman.

"Never saw nothing like it," Skullcap said, ignoring Rims as if he had not spoken, was not nervous, did not need his composure to drive the big, unfamiliar car. "Two slugs and the motherfucker did not even go *down.*" Furiously he slammed a fist into the palm of his hand. It made a loud noise—*smack!*—startling Rims. "And I missed getting those two women!" Skullcap suddenly remembered. "Motherfucker!"

"Don'tbeworryingnoneaboutit," Rims spurted like a gush of steam. "Thatsuckergonnadie. Iknowhegonnadie. Youstillgonnagetonestinganyways."

"What make you so sure?" Skullcap asked. "How you know he gonna die?"

"Shitman," said Rims. Then his voice slowed down. "I know that man has *gots* to die. Man don't live with two bullets in him."

Skullcap thought about it. Rims was right; somebody shot twice in the back at close range like that *had* to die. The sucker must have suffered some kind of delayed reaction; maybe he died standing up, then fell. At any rate, Rims had a point: Skullcap would still get credit for one sting. That was not as impressive as three, but it was better than nothing. He reached over and slapped Rims fondly on the knee.

"You right, brother. I'm going to calm down. No sense getting uptight. We out here to just take care of business. I got one for tonight; now we got to go find one for you." Skullcap looked at the next freeway sign: Oak Street. "Get off at the next ramp," he said.

In an apartment at 651 Scott Street, three blocks north of Oak, Marietta DiGirolamo was getting ready to go out. She had been waiting all evening for her boyfriend and sometimes roommate, Paul Wilson; now it was past nine o'clock and she was tired of waiting. She was going to take a walk, maybe get a drink.

Marietta DiGirolamo was thirty-one years old. Five feet one inch tall, she bordered on fleshiness at 125 pounds. But her figure was nicely proportioned and she had good breasts. Her hair was thick and dark, falling well below her shoulders in back. In profile, she looked very much like the actress Ellen Burstyn.

At her bathroom mirror, Marietta applied a touch of coloring to her already dark eyebrows and leaned forward closely to examine the corners of her upper lip. For years she had fought an on-again, off-again battle with dark lip hair, which she blamed on her Mediterranean heritage; but lately she had been more conscientious about keeping it bleached or removed. That was because of her boyfriend, Paul Wilson. Paul liked her face completely clear of all dark hair. He wanted her as smooth and creamy as possible.

Idly Marietta wondered if all black men were like that about white women.

Back in the Potrero Hill area, Art Agnos had been removed by ambulance and taken to Mission Emergency Hospital. Police officers Michael Thompson and Theodore Schlink III, using flashlights, were searching the sidewalk, gutter, and street where the victim had been shot.

123

"Here's one," said Schlink, bending to pick up a spent shell casing. "Matter of fact, here's *two*," he amended, seeing a second one as he reached for the first.

"And here's one of the slugs," said Thompson. He retrieved a spent copper bullet from the curb.

The two officers continued their search for a few minutes, then gave it up. "The other one must still be in him," Schlink guessed.

"Let's get over to Mission and see if he's conscious yet," suggested Thompson.

The two officers drove to the emergency hospital. When they got there, however, they were not permitted to interview Agnos. He had just been wheeled out of the X-ray lab and was being prepped for surgery.

Marietta DiGirolamo walked three blocks south from her apartment, then turned on Haight Street and walked over to Divisadero, thinking she might find her boyfriend in one of the neighborhood bars. As she walked, she turned up the collar of her coat against a chill breeze coming in off the bay.

The black Cadillac was cruising south on Divisadero when Skullcap spotted her. "There's a nice female white devil for you, brother," he said. "Pull over."

Rims pulled to the curb and Skullcap motioned for him to get out. He slipped Judo's gun to the moonfaced black.

"Go get her, baby," he said, sliding into the driver's seat. "I'll pull right around the corner and keep the engine running."

"I'll be get her," Rims said determinedly. "Fucking white bitch gonna die."

Rims crossed the street and walked toward Marietta DiGirolamo. She stopped and looked in a shop window, then she started toward him again. He mentally measured her pace. At the speed they were both walking, they would meet near the middle of the block. Or so he thought. Then Marietta fooled him. Abruptly she turned and started back in the direction from which she had come.

Rims stopped and his mouth dropped open. He blinked rapidly several times. What the fuck she doing? he asked himself. For a brief moment, his entire plan was disrupted by the white woman's sudden change of direction. So slowly did Rims respond to this surprise turn of events that he almost aborted. He actually took a tentative step back toward where the car had been, then he saw Skullcap drive past on his way to the corner. Quickly he hurried after the woman.

Marietta stopped again to look in the same store window. It was a candle shop; the window was filled not only with decorative candles but also displays of incense, teas, herbs, and lotions. After looking in the window a second time, Marietta again reversed her course and resumed walking back toward Rims. You white evil bitch! Rims thought. He was infuriated at the way she kept changing direction. In his simple mind, he took it as something she was doing purposely to distract and confuse him.

They were almost upon one another now: the unsuspecting white woman, drawing her collar closed against the evening air; the bull-bodied young black, eyes now wide and unblinking behind his round, gold glasses. They moved abreast of each other, as if to pass—

Rims suddenly shoved her into the doorway of a barbershop. He stepped in after her and raised the gun. Her face flashed anger at being shoved. "What the hell do you think you're doing?" she snapped.

Rims shot her twice in the chest. Her body jerked with the impact of each bullet. When the second one hit her, she spun around, facing the door. Rims fired again, shooting her once in the back.

Marietta started to fall back out of the doorway.

Rims turned and ran down to the corner.

William Bryan, in the city from Sonoma, fifty-five miles north, was stopped for the light at Haight and Divisadero. He saw Rims and Marietta in the doorway, saw Rims fire the shots and saw Marietta lurch backward out of the doorway and fall to the sidewalk. Rims ran around the corner. A municipal minibus started along the street in the same direction he was running. Bryan saw several people tentatively approach the fallen victim, so he quickly decided to follow the man who had shot her. As soon as the light changed, he made a left turn and pulled as close to the rear of the minibus as he could. He edged out over the center line to look past it. By that time, the running black man had disappeared.

The minibus driver must have seen where he went, Bryan thought. Tooling his car around, he caught up with the bus. He yelled over at the driver.

"Did you see where that guy went?"

"What guy?" asked the driver.

"The guy that was running! He shot a woman back there!"

The driver shrugged. "I didn't see no guy running."

Didn't see no guy running? He must drive that bus with his eyes closed.

"Listen," said Bryan, "a woman was just shot back there. Will you use your radio to call the police?"

The driver shook his head. "There are a lot of pay phones around; you'll have to use one of them." He closed the door of the bus and drove away.

William Bryan stared after him incredulously.

Another person who saw Rims shoot Marietta DiGirolamo was Gerald Bjork. On his way home from the Gold Cane cocktail lounge where he had been drinking beer with a friend, he was walking along Haight Street and had just turned the corner to go down Divisadero when he heard the first shot. He whirled around just in time to see Rims fire the second shot. Then he watched, stunned, as the third shot was fired and the woman fell out of the doorway and pitched backward to the sidewalk.

Bjork watched Rims dash around the corner and run down Haight. He saw the minibus proceed along Haight, saw William Bryan's car make a left turn and pull up behind it. He could see the black man running for perhaps a hundred feet, then Bjork lost sight of him.

Bjork started to cross the street to where the victim was, but changed his mind. This was not his business.

He walked on home instead.

As soon as Officers Lloyd Ritter and Frank Peda arrived at the scene, they summoned a Code Three ambulance and had Marietta DiGirolamo transported to Mission Emergency Hospital. She was unconscious during the entire trip.

After the victim was taken away, the usual routine followed. A lieutenant was called to supervise the crime scene; he was Lieutenant Joseph Lordan, platoon commander of Park Station. The Crime Lab was notified; Inspector Moses responded to the scene. The Photo Lab: Inspector Sleadd. Homicide: Inspectors Podesta and Schneider.

Three spent cartridge casings were found on the sidewalk and turned over to Moses. From a small purple cloth purse Marietta had been carrying, her identification and address were determined.

"Get Sergeant Rivas out here to go with you to the victim's address," Lieutenant Lordan instructed Ritter and Peda.

The officers, along with Rivas, drove to the Scott Street address that Marietta had left barely an hour earlier. No one answered the door to her apartment, number three. They tried number four. A black woman named Stella Burton came out and talked with them. She told them about Marietta's black boyfriend, Paul Wilson, describing him as six two, 180 pounds, short hair, about thirty-five. The officers exchanged glances. William Bryan and other witnesses had described the assailant as six feet to six two, medium build, about thirty years old, wearing a cap. Ritter and Peda almost read each other's thoughts: *Maybe we lucked out on this one.*

Since the door to apartment three was open, the officers entered to look for the name of a next of kin or friend. They did not find a name, but they did find six unpaid traffic warrants issued to Paul Wilson.

"Leave them there," Rivas said. "We'll let the morning shift come back and get him."

At Mission Emergency Hospital, Marietta DiGirolamo was quickly wheeled inside and examined by Dr. Noyes of the night staff. He checked her thoroughly for vital signs. There were none.

"Dead on arrival," he told the ambulance steward.

In another section of the hospital, Arthur Agnos was in a surgical field being operated on by a team of doctors. His spleen had already been removed and the surgeons were now attempting to repair his punctured kidney. They would then turn to his collapsed lung.

At the end of Day Fifty-five, there were eight victims.

Quita Hague, hacked to death.

Richard Hague, his face horribly scarred.

Ellen Linder, raped, ravaged, threatened with death—and her ordeal not even formally charged to the person who did them to her.

Frances Rose, her face blown apart by close-range gunshots.

Saleem Erakat, tied up and executed with a single shot behind the right ear.

Paul Dancik, shot down as he attempted to use a public telephone.

Arthur Agnos, his internal organs—lungs, spleen, kidney—torn apart by two bullets in the back.

And Marietta DiGirolamo, thrown into a doorway and shot to death as she walked down the street.

Day 62

In the Potrero Hill district, fourteen black men were involved in a different kind of meeting.

It was exactly one week after the shooting of Arthur Agnos. The fourteen men were residents of the area. Some were young, some old, some working, some retired or unemployed, some had families, a few did not. Besides being black and living in the same neighborhood, they had one other thing in common: they were all angry.

"Just when we're starting to get something positive going in this area," one of the older men said, "some low-life nigger has to come down here and shoot a white man."

"He wasn't white, he was Greek," a younger man said. It got a few laughs, but drew only rancor from the older man.

"We're not here to make jokes, lad," he said sternly. "We're here to see if we can offset what happened, if we can make up for it in some way so that any help we might have received in support of our neighborhood clinic will not be withheld because we've been made to look like we belong in the jungle. Does anyone have any suggestions?"

"Yeah, I've got one," another of the younger men said, with obvious bitterness. "Let's ask for the clinic on the basis of neighborhood need, and not worry about some black motherfucker who comes down here and shoots somebody. We got no control over that."

"Well, perhaps we should *get* control then," his senior said. "Here's a liberal white man who can be of great help to the betterment of this area for black *and* white. Not only *can* he help, but he *wants* to help. He has a genuine, sincere desire to help minorities—whether they be minorities of color, like us; minorities of age, like our juveniles and our senior citizens; or any other deprived group needing help. So what happens? He comes to one of our meetings and promptly gets shot by some wild-assed nigger with a Saturday night special."

"That kind of stuff is the police's business, not ours," said another of the men.

"Right on! We're not responsible for crime in the goddamned streets!" said another.

"We are when they're *our* streets," the older man said. "And when *our* people are committing the crimes."

"Hey, man, don't start with that 'our people' shit. Just because they're black don't make them *my* people. I don't have nothing in common with junkies, pimps, welfare cheats, Black Muslims, or any other such shit. I work, I support my family, I don't ask for nothing, and I don't *give* nothing."

"You still can't paint your face white, man. And every time a nigger does something violent to a white, you gonna pay for it— one way or another."

"I'll be goddamned if that's so!"

"And *I'll* be goddamned if it *isn't*. Let me ask you a question. Has anything been done about the neighborhood health clinic since last week's meeting? Has any of the action we proposed been carried out? Anything at all?" The speaker looked around the room, his eyes flicking from face to face. No one answered him. "No, it hasn't," he answered himself. "Nothing has been done—and nothing will be done. The meeting might as well have not been held, because the second that insane nigger pulled the trigger, everything we had accomplished for us and for our neighborhood up to that point went into limbo."

"Well, what the fuck do you want us to do about it, man? Patrol the streets with our own Saturday night specials?"

"I wish to Christ we could. But it would never be permitted. Still, we have to do something. We must show *our* whites—the whites that we have to live and work with—that we as blacks are not to be classed with these street killers."

"Do you have any suggestions?"

"I have one. I propose that we form a bodyguard detail, and that on the night of our meetings we assign blacks to protect the whites that attend."

"Shit, man, that would just be wasted effort," another of the older men said. "Chances are, whoever shot Art Agnos won't ever come back around here again."

"That doesn't matter. Point is, it would *look* good. And the whites—*our* whites—would automatically disassociate us from any of the street violence."

"Won't it seem kind of peculiar to the other blacks?" a man in the corner asked. "Like maybe we're siding with white *against* them?"

"To a few I'm sure it will. But eventually they'll realize that it's for the good of the neighborhood as a whole—black *and* white." He looked around for more comments. There were none. "Shall we take a vote on it?"

There was a show of hands. It was unanimous: blacks would guard whites in the Potrero Hill district.

"Maybe it won't be for long," said one of the men after the meeting. "Maybe the cops will catch the crazy motherfuckers that did it."

The police, as usual, were trying. Methodically, relentlessly, they had been following up every lead they had for a week.

At two o'clock in the morning following Marietta DiGirolamo's death, Sergeant Roger Maher and Officer Ronald Morehen had her apartment building staked out waiting for her black boyfriend, Paul Wilson, to show up. He arrived shortly after two. They followed him into the lobby and caught up with him at the top of the stairs. They were cautious; his description was too close to the killer's for comfort. As they approached him, he heard them and turned.

"I'm E. D. Moore," he said. "I understand the police are looking for me."

"Mr. Moore," said Sergeant Maher, "do you also use the name Paul Wilson?"

"Yes, I do. I understand that my wife has been shot."

"A Marietta DiGirolamo has been shot, Mr. Wilson. We'd like you to come down to Park Station with us regarding that matter."

"Am I under arrest?"

"No, sir, not at this time. But we are going to request that you allow us to search your person for weapons only, nothing else."

Moore permitted a quick pat-down with no objection. Then Maher and Morehen escorted him to Park Station. They turned him over to Schneider and Podesta of Homicide. The two homicide inspectors questioned him at length. Upon verification of what he told them, they satisfied themselves that he was not the killer. They subsequently turned him back over to the uniformed officers.

"You are under arrest now, Mr. Moore—or Mr. Wilson, whichever is correct. There are twelve outstanding traffic warrants against you."

Marietta DiGirolamo's boyfriend was booked and held in lieu of more than $300 in fines.

Mitch Luksich was at his microscope again, this time with six new specimens to examine: the three spent shell casings found at the scene of the Marietta DiGirolamo killing, and the single spent slug and two shell casings picked up where Art Agnos had been shot.

As Luksich worked, he occasionally made an audible but unintelligible sound: a low, modified grunt, or a not-quite-silent intake of breath. Each time he did so, Gus Coreris and John Fotinos, waiting just outside his cubicle, looked over expectantly, thinking that he might be ready to speak. When he continued to work without even looking at them, they exchanged impatient glances and resumed their vigil. Coreris had a strained look on his face that said, *Goddamn it, why does everything take so long?* Fotinos, just as impatient but showing it far less, simply shook his head once, then tried to think of something else. Something pleasant. Like his youngest daughter, Teresa, now eleven, who had come along after he and Barbara thought they had all the family they would ever have. Three fine kids: Elizabeth, thirteen; Christine, eleven; Anthony eight—then surprise! Another one. Twelve more years of parochial school tuition that he had not planned on. But the first time he had looked at the new baby, he had known—as he had with the others—that she would be worth it. In the Fotinos household, family pride and love were not measured monetarily.

In the cubicle, Luksich continued to work. He matched the ejector marks on each case. Not satisfied with just that, he compared a series of fine, very minute machining cut impressions made by the firing pin. Also the amount of "bulging" or expansion common to each of the cases, and a slight protrusion of the primer out of its pocket on each one—both of which characteristics indicated to Luksich's ultratrained eye that there was excessive headspace in the pistol. In layman's language, this meant that the breech of the weapon was just a touch larger than it needed to be for the size ammunition for which it was designed. A shade more quality control should have been present in the manufacturing stage, Luksich thought.

When Luksich finally sat back from the microscope, he used a thumb and forefinger to smooth down the mustache that curved around the corners of his mouth. "Same gun, gentlemen," he announced.

Fotinos and Coreris appeared in the doorway as if by magic.

"All four?" asked Fotinos, as if it were too good to be true.

"All four," Luksich confirmed. "Erakat, Dancik, DiGirolamo, and Agnos. Same gun."

"I'll be goddamned," said Coreris. He looked hard at his partner. "Young, well-groomed, nice-looking blacks."

"Muslims, like I told you," said Fotinos.

"All using the same gun," Luksich interjected.

"Shooting only white victims," said Coreris.

The three men all looked at each other. A heavy silence fell over them for a moment. Finally Luksich stood up, towering over the two detectives.

"I've got a feeling it's going to be a long winter, gentlemen," he said quietly.

* * *

On the advice of a friend, Gerald Bjork, who had witnessed the killing of Marietta DiGirolamo, called the police and told them about it. He was interviewed and then taken to headquarters where he went through a series of mug shots of blacks who had a police record and fit the description of the DiGirolamo killer. After going through numerous photos, Bjork selected one which he said he felt was the man he had seen do the shooting.

The man whose photo Bjork selected was one Jasper Childs.* He was known to be a practicing Black Muslim and was employed at the Black Self Help Moving and Storage Company.

Two days after identifying Childs, Gerald Bjork was transported in a surveillance vehicle to a parking place near Black Self Help. The vehicle was a camper with curtained windows. Under the direction of homicide inspectors, Bjork used binoculars to observe the activities of Black Self Help employees. Among the individuals observed by Bjork was the same Jasper Childs whom he had identified by photograph. Bjork saw Childs come and go several times during the course of the surveillance. Each time he seemed to become less and less certain that Childs was positively the man he had seen kill Marietta DiGirolamo. Finally, because the detectives could not act on anything less than a 100 percent identification, the surveillance was terminated.

Gerald Bjork observed numerous employees of Black Self Help during the surveillance. He identified none of them positively.

Four of the men who worked for Black Self Help were visibly upset on the afternoon of December 14, 1973. They had just received word that earlier that same day, Jesse Lee Cooks had been sentenced to life in prison. They had been very upset when Jesse had been caught; now they were doubly upset because they had just learned that Cooks had pled guilty to first-degree murder.

"Dumb son of a bitch," said J.C. "He *knows* he wasn't *ever* supposed to plead guilty."

"That's right, he wasn't!" Manuel Moore said, agitated. "The laws of the mosque don't be allow that."

"He wasn't being tried by the laws of the mosque," Anthony

*This person's name has been changed because he was never positively identified by the witness.

Harris said dryly. Sometimes he had the feeling that Manuel was not playing with a full deck.

"It don't matter what law they tried him under," Larry Green said. "He's still *bound* to obey the laws of the mosque. And those laws say don't *never* admit no guilt in the white man's court."

"Right on," said J.C.

"What the hell was he supposed to do?" Anthony asked impatiently. "I mean, man, they caught him with the fucking gun sticking in his belt. It wasn't exactly circumstantial evidence."

The other three looked at him with flat, fixed stares that bordered on hostility. Even Larry, who had been his "little brother" friend since the day Anthony got out of San Quentin, seemed now to be somehow looking at him through different eyes. There were times when he felt like a stranger among them. And that disturbed him— because if he could not feel accepted with these men who were his own color, his own faith, then where on Allah's earth *could* he be at home?

"Sometimes I wonder about you, man," J.C. said in a glacial voice. The cool, handsome black was studying Anthony. His piercing eyes looked as if they wanted to strip off Anthony's skin and see right into the pit of him, actually examine his core. "I really wonder, man," he repeated.

"Well, don't sweat none about it, sport," Anthony said evenly. "I still got a right to my own opinion. Ain't *no* motherfucker going to tell me what to think." There, it was said. If J.C. wanted to call him out, the door was open. It seemed to Anthony that Simon had been looking to pick a fight with him for a long time. Now he had his chance. And if Mr. Cool took it, Anthony was going to break his fucking back.

But J.C. did not take the bait. He merely stared Anthony down: riveted his eyes to Anthony's, until finally Anthony just said, "Shit," and looked away. Kid stuff, he thought. Yet he could not help wondering *why* J.C. had not accepted the challenge. Instinctively he knew that J.C. was not afraid of him. J.C. was not afraid of *anything*. If Jesse Lee Cooks had been the most dangerous man Anthony had ever met, then certainly J.C. Simon was the most fearless.

Whatever the reason, J.C. and Anthony, each firmly believing he could take the other, did not physically clash that night. But each felt inside that it was only a matter of time.

"I'm tired of being alone," Anthony told Debbie that night. "I need to *be* with someone."

"You are with someone, sugar," she told him. "You're with me, almost every night."

"I don't mean just be with for a few hours. I mean have somebody to stay with, to be close to all the time, when I'm—" His voice trailed off.

"When you're what, sugar?"

Anthony swallowed and looked away. They were sitting on the couch in her apartment. Gently she took his chin and pulled his head around to face her.

"When you're what, sugar?" she asked again.

"When I'm scared," he said quietly.

Debbie drew his face down to her bosom and held it there. She rocked him a little and stroked his forehead. At that moment, she was very much in love with Anthony Harris.

"Are you saying that you want to move in with me, Anthony?" she asked.

"I'd like to," he said. As he spoke, his lips moved against her breast.

"You're still married to Carolyn, aren't you?"

"Yes." And, he thought, as far as he knew, he was not divorced from his first, white, wife. Unless she had divorced him without his knowledge. "That thing with Carolyn wasn't really a marriage, you know that," he said. "I only was with her a couple of weeks."

"It's still a true marriage," Debbie countered. "You did exchange vows."

Anthony sighed a heavy, soul-weary sigh. "I'm sorry I got into that. I don't know why I did it. I was just out of prison and didn't have nobody; I guess I was lonesome to have somebody and someplace to call mine." He shook his head against her breast. "Shit, I can't never seem to do nothing right."

She held his head a little tighter and rocked him a bit more, as she would do to soothe a child of its hurt. That's what Anthony was, really, in many ways: a child. Lost. Uncertain. Tired and wanting to sleep.

"There, there, sugar," she cooed. "Everything's going to be all right. You can move in and stay with me if you want to. I'll take good care of you. You can be my sugar baby, all right?"

With his face still against her breast, Anthony nodded.

Maybe with her he could straighten out everything that was so fucked up, he thought.

Before it was too late.

In the apartment on Grove Street, J. C. Simon's wife was packing to go back to Texas. J. C. prowled the room, trying to talk her out of it.

"You're just not used to San Francisco yet, baby," he said. "Give yourself a little more time. It's a fine city; pretty soon you'll love it just like I do."

"It's not the city," said Pat. "You know it's not the city."

"What is it, then?" he asked. "Is it the apartment? You want to move to a different place?"

"It's not the apartment, J. C." Pat kept her voice nicely under control. She did not want to get into another of those arguments that neither of them ever won.

"Well, what is it then?" J. C. asked in agitation. "What do you want out of me?"

"I don't want anything out of you, J. C. Not anything at all." Methodically, she continued packing, folding Crissy's clothes and putting them on top of her own.

J. C. paced. He shoved his hands into his pockets. He sighed dramatically. Pat ignored him. She had seen him act before. Finally J. C. glanced into the other room and saw Crissy playing on the floor.

"It's not fair for you to take that baby away from her daddy and not even give me a reason," he accused.

Pat faced him directly. "Now you listen to me, J. C. Simon," she said with an edge. "If you cared as much about that baby as you care about all your friends, you'd be coming back to Houston with us. Back where you belong. Instead of staying up here where you're going to find nothing but grief."

J. C. smiled his tolerant smile. "What you talking about, grief?" He chose to ignore the comment about his friends. That was an old thorn between them, and it stuck both ways.

"You know what I mean," Pat said. Her pretty young face turned sad. "This isn't the place for you, J. C. These aren't your kind of people. If you stay up here, you'll be all alone. I know you think you've got a lot of friends, and I know you think they all care about you; but they don't, J. C. They don't at all. You'll find that out someday. When you get into bad trouble and need them, they won't be nowhere around."

"You're talking scare talk," J. C. said. "You're talking like you got a Caucasian mentality, woman."

Pat shook her head. Caucasian mentality. How often lately had he come up with that phrase, or one just like it? She used to think that he was simply verbalizing, that he did not really know what he was saying. It was the mosque speaking; something he had picked up in a pamphlet. But lately she was not too sure. Lately he seemed more and more to *know* what he was saying. And, even more frightening to her, to *believe* it.

"You just won't listen, will you?" she said. "Won't listen to anyone. You just think you know it all."

J.C. stared at her without responding. His gaze was flat, penetrating. Unmoving. And unmoved.

Sighing quietly, Pat resumed packing.

Two nights later, in the Bay View district, Ilario Bertuccio was finishing his last chore of the night at the 7-Up bottling plant where he worked: he was sweeping down the loading dock with a horsehair push broom.

Bertuccio was eighty-one years old. A small man—five three, 135 pounds—he could have retired on his pension and Social Security. But he was a healthy old man, alert and agile, and no one—not friend, not relative—could convince him to stay home and take it easy. Ilario had worked all his life. He enjoyed work, firmly believed that it was healthy. That was why he had the job at 7-Up. It did not pay that well, the hours were not very good, the duties certainly not challenging. But it was work.

When he finished sweeping, he returned the horsehair broom to the plant's utility closet and washed up in the men's room. He ran a pocket comb through his thick white hair and let it fall into place. Then he put on his Windbreaker and zipped it up against the night coolness. He went into the bottling room, slipped his nightly free

138

bottle of 7-Up into a paper bag, and left by the employee door. He lived about a mile away, on Goettingen Street on the other side of the freeway. It made a nice walk for him every night after work.

As he headed home, Bertuccio hummed an old Italian folk song and with a half-smile thought of the friends and relatives who constantly advised him to retire. They meant well, he knew, but they did not understand him. Work was good for him. It was healthy.

Ilario Bertuccio had long ago made up his mind that he would never quit work. He would work until he died.

A white Dodge Dart, borrowed from Yellow, turned off the Bayshore Freeway and drove south on San Bruno to Bacon. It turned left on Bacon to Bay Shore Boulevard, then doubled back to Phelps. It cruised along Phelps.

Skullcap was at the wheel, scanning the street on the left. Rims was in the passenger seat, doing the same on the right.

"Fucking streets are dead," Skullcap muttered, as much to himself as to Rims.

"Yeah, dead," Rims echoed. He had Judo's pistol between his legs; his fingertips rubbed gently over it, as if he were petting a puppy. From time to time he would glance at his friend behind the wheel, trying to think of new things to say that might cheer him up. For days now, Skullcap had been out of sorts: depressed, irritable, edgy. The reason for it, Rims thought, was the white devil who had not died. The one that had not even fallen down after Skullcap shot him twice in the back. Skullcap was still upset about it; he had not received credit for a sting.

Rims hated to see his new friend upset like that; he kept trying to say things that would make him feel better. "We ought to see can we get us a couple of sisters when we be through tonight," he said now. "We could go over to the mosque to the community hall and see could we find a couple."

"Yeah, maybe," said Skullcap. He said it in hopes of making Rims shut up. The last thing he wanted—or needed—just then was a woman. They were more fucking trouble than they were worth.

"You feel better with a new sister," Rims said. "Man always feel better with a sister, specially when she be a new one. We find one gonna do right for you."

"Yeah, right," Skullcap said.

139

But he knew that no sister was going to make him feel better. His needs were not that simple. The only thing that was going to purge his low-down feeling was to destroy a blue-eyed devil. Destroy one of the evil beings that had persecuted his race for so long. Blow the life out of a grafted snake, that's what he had to do.

And preferably a female snake.

"There one now," said Rims as they approached the intersection on Bancroft and Phelps.

Skullcap looked at the devil Rims was talking about. It was a white-haired old man carrying a paper bag under one arm. Probably a fucking old white wino, Skullcap thought.

"You sting him," Skullcap said. "I'll do the next one."

He would see that the next one was a woman.

Across the city, in the Lincoln Park district, a twenty-year-old college student named Angela Roselli* was attending a Christmas party at the apartment of some friends. She had been at the party for about an hour and, after three drinks, was beginning to feel mellow. Sitting in a corner with several other people, she was sharing her first joint of the evening with the young man next to her.

Angela was a pretty girl with very long, very dark hair and a Candice Bergen mouth complete with an occasional hint of a lisp. Her face had a natural glow to it, and outwardly she seemed vibrant and full of life. The fact that she cared little about what went on around her was betrayed only by her eyes: they had a hollowness to them that reflected a total disinterest in anything difficult, anything requiring more than token effort, anything physically or mentally challenging. People who knew her could not ever remember seeing her excited about anything. She was an escapist, a noncontributor; if the world had started to sink, she would not have bothered to tread water.

At the party there was a lot of liquor, a lot of pot, perhaps even some harder stuff not being shared openly; but Angela stayed away from hard drugs, preferring the pleasant mellowness of substances she knew she could handle—mostly wine and marijuana.

---

*The name and identity of this person have been altered at her request.

"This is good shit," said the young man next to her, passing the joint. "Best I've had in a while."

"Me too," said Angela. She sucked in a deep drag and handed the joint back to him.

Somewhere in the apartment a stereo was playing "O come, all ye faithful."

Skullcap pulled the Dart to the curb and turned off the headlights. In the rearview mirror he could see the little old white man approaching the corner where he would cross the street. Skullcap looked over at Rims.

"Sting the devil," he said softly.

Rims swallowed dryly. His eyes under the round gold frames grew wide. An almost idiotic grin spread over his lips. "R-r-right on!" he stuttered emphatically.

With Judo's gun in hand, Rims got out of the car and walked toward the little white-haired man. As he walked, he held the gun close to his thigh, allowing him to swing only one arm, causing him to pitch his right shoulder forward to compensate for it, creating an overall effect of a sailor trying to use his sea legs on land.

Walking toward Rims, Ilario Bertuccio probably felt no anxiety at all. He liked most people, trusted most people, considered no one—acquaintance or stranger—suspect. He had lived his entire life that way. At eighty-one, he probably could not have changed even if he had wanted to.

But he would never have a chance to want to.

When Rims drew abreast of Bertuccio, he raised the pistol and started firing. The first bullet entered Bertuccio's right shoulder, hit a bone, detoured across his chest, and exited his left armpit. The second drilled through his right chest and back. The third did the same. The fourth entered his left chest and exited his back.

Bertuccio fell. In seconds his upper front torso was saturated with blood. He died almost instantly.

Angela Roselli left the Christmas party at nine thirty. She was feeling good, very mellow, and it was a fun party, but she had grown tired and decided to call it a night. The effects of the drinks she had consumed earlier had now worn off; she was still up from the pot, but not so much that it would impede her driving.

She got her coat, said good-bye, and left. Her 1965 Ford was parked nearby. She got into the car and drove off.

Fifteen minutes later she was looking for a parking place near Grove and Central, a block from her apartment.

Skullcap and Rims were driving down Grove Street, going home. Skullcap was in a worse mood now than he had been earlier. They had been driving around for ninety minutes looking for a devil for him to sting, and had not found one. Skullcap wanted to sting a woman; he refused to settle for a man. They had been unable to find a woman out alone in an uncrowded situation; they were either with someone or there were too many people around. They had seen several good male candidates, but Skullcap would not settle for them.

"It's got to be a woman devil or nothing," he told Rims emphatically. "I'm tired fucking around. I want my Death Angel wings, man!"

"Sure, okay, man, okay," Rims replied, not a little fearfully. He did not want to mess with Skullcap; the man was too dangerous. Besides, Rims liked him and wanted to keep him for a friend. He had never had a friend as smart as Skullcap before; just being with him made Rims feel smarter. "We just keep trying," he had said earlier to placate Skullcap. "We look all night if we has to."

They had been looking for an hour and a half, and now Skullcap was thoroughly irritated and ready to call it all off. "Fuck it," he said angrily. "Fuck the Death Angels! I don't need this kind of shit!"

"Don't say that now, man," Rims implored. "You be okay. We go out again tomorrow night and find you a woman devil. Why, we even find you *two!* Come on now, man, don't be so pissed. Come on. It be all right. Tomorrow night it be all right."

At that moment they approached the intersection of Grove and Central, and Skullcap saw the young white girl looking for a parking place.

"Wait a minute," he said, looking up and down the deserted street. "Maybe it'll be all right tonight still."

In a Cadillac borrowed from a friend, Yellow and Judo were cruising Grove Street looking for Skullcap and Rims.

142

"The motherfucker promised to have my car back by nine," Yellow said sullenly.

Judo grunted derisively. "You be lucky you *ever* get the sucker back," he said. "He done have my piece for over three weeks now. Every time I ax him for it, he say he left it at home or some other excuse. I'm getting tired of it, man."

"Wait a minute," Yellow said, peering down Central. "Ain't that my car double-parked up there?"

Judo squinted. "Look like it is."

Yellow swung into the 600 block of Central.

Skullcap had got out of the Dart and let Rims take the wheel. He had walked in the shadows along the sidewalk, scanning the block, while Rims drove along Central and double-parked to wait for him. Now, as the young white girl in the '65 Ford negotiated her parking place, Skullcap walked over to the Dart and checked with Rims.

"Everything look okay to you, brother?"

"Look fine," Rims said, wide-eyed again.

Skullcap gave the block a final cursory look and started across the street. A pair of headlights swung around the corner and came toward him. He paused a beat, considered turning back. Then he recognized the car. He watched it pull into a driveway at 617 Central, just behind where the white girl had parked. In the light of the streetlamp, Skullcap could see that Yellow was driving the Cadillac, and that Judo was sitting next to him. He smiled inwardly. Keep your eyes on me, brothers, he thought. You'll see a star be born.

Angela Roselli saw the black man walking toward her. She decided that he was about to hit on her, try to pick her up, make out with her. Either that or he was going to hassle her because she was a white girl in a predominantly black neighborhood. She and her roommate constantly had to endure dirty looks, muttered comments, even outright open hostility from the black residents who did not appreciate their presence in the neighborhood. They had expected it when they moved in, but due to financial and location considerations, had moved in anyway. After all, it was a free country. They simply rolled with the verbal punches whenever necessary.

Angela was preparing to do just that when the black man in the white Superfly hat and suit walked up to her. She glanced at him, frowned at the zombie look on his face, the fixed, staring eyes as if he were in a trance. When he was several feet from her, he raised a pistol from next to his leg and began shooting at her.

Angela was not immediately aware that she was being shot. The first two reports sounded like firecrackers exploding. The bullets hit her side, her rib cage, her stomach. The third one nicked her spine and her legs gave out. She fell. The fourth bullet, aimed at her head, missed as she dropped; it shattered the window on the driver's side of her car. As she pitched to the ground, she began screaming.

As soon as the girl started screaming, Skullcap turned and ran. He wanted to shoot her two or three more times to make certain she would die, but her screams frightened him. He hurried over to the Dart and got in. Rims stamped the accelerator and the car shot forward.

"I got her three times, man," Skullcap said anxiously. "You think she'll die?"

"Yeah, brother, three times, she gots to die," said Rims.

But as the car sped away, both of them could still hear the girl's screams.

In the Cadillac, Yellow and Judo had watched in morbid fascination as Skullcap walked up and shot the girl. Then, as he turned and hurried away, they had looked at each other incredulously.

"Shit, man!" said Judo. "Let's get the fuck out of here!"

Yellow continued to stare at him, transfixed. Judo punched him on the muscle.

"Come *on*, man! Move it! Get us the fuck out of here!"

Finally Yellow responded. He shifted the Cadillac into reverse and gunned it backward out of the driveway. The tires screeched and as Yellow cut the wheels the body of the car lurched sideways on its shocks. Yellow quickly cut the wheels and jammed the gas pedal again. The car jerked forward.

Angela Roselli was facedown in the street next to her parked car, trying to raise her gunshot body off the ground. She had stopped screaming and managed to get up on her elbows when she became aware of the big car backing out of a driveway. She saw two Negro faces in the front seat. Then the car turned and its headlights swept over her. The car started directly for her.

My God, they're trying to run over me!

Exerting all the willpower in her body, Angela threw herself sideways and rolled under her parked car to relative safety.

The Cadillac sped past her and in seconds was gone.

Back at Bancroft and Phelps, Officers Allen Duncan and Patrick White had secured the death scene of Ilario Bertuccio. They had recovered four spent .32-caliber shell casings and turned them over to a man from the Crime Lab. A Photo Lab man was moving around the body shooting flash shots. Captain John McSweeney of Operations had arrived to take charge of the crime scene. Inspectors McKenna, Podesta, and Nelson were there from Homicide. All three winced when they heard that the four shell casings were .32s.

A Mission Ambulance Service steward named Van Steen was standing near his vehicle, patiently waiting for the police work to be completed. Van Steen had already pronounced Bertuccio dead. As soon as the picture-taking and evidence-gathering was over, the coroner's representative, Schultz, who was over talking to an officer, would issue a receipt for the corpse and Van Steen would take it to the morgue. Meanwhile, there was nothing to do but wait. And think about how cold San Francisco was at night in December.

In another ambulance, Angela Roselli was being rushed to San Francisco General.

"Am I going to die?" she asked the ambulance steward.

"You'll probably have to have surgery right away," the steward answered noncommittally.

A police officer named Foster was in the ambulance with her. "Can you tell me what happened?" he asked.

She shook her head. Tears ran out of the corners of her eyes and down her temples. At first Foster thought she was not going to answer him, then he heard her say, "A black man walked up to me. Without saying a word he started shooting me."

145

Foster leaned close to the steward. "*Is* she going to die?" he asked quietly.

The steward shrugged. "Hard to say," he whispered. "She took two bullets in the chest, one in the stomach."

When the ambulance backed up to the emergency door, a resident on duty jerked open the ambulance door. "What have you got?"

"Gunshot wounds, multiple."

The resident snapped his fingers at two orderlies. "Trauma unit!" he ordered.

As the orderlies moved Angela from the ambulance and into the hospital, Officer Foster heard something drop to the floor. He bent and retrieved the object.

It was a .32-caliber bullet that had fallen out of Angela Roselli's body.

At the end of Day Sixty-two, there were ten victims.

Quita Hague, hacked to death.

Richard Hague, his face butchered.

Ellen Linder, raped, ravaged, threatened with death.

Frances Rose, her face blown apart by close-range gunshots.

Saleem Erakat, tied up and executed with a single shot behind the right ear.

Paul Dancik, shot down as he attempted to use a public telephone.

Arthur Agnos, surviving after having his lungs, spleen, and kidney ripped apart by bullets.

Marietta DiGirolamo, thrown into a doorway and shot to death as she walked down the street.

Ilario Bertuccio, gunned down in the street as he walked home from work with a bottle of 7-Up under his arm.

And Angela Roselli, also shot down in the street as she was returning home from a Christmas party.

Day 64

Judo and Yellow were walking down Franklin Street on their way to a loft meeting. Judo was again fuming about his gun, which Skullcap still had.

"This is it tonight, man," he said angrily. "Either he gives me back the piece or him and me are gonna go at it."

"You better be careful with him, brother," said Yellow. "I mean, like I know you know kung fu and all that, but you talking about one mean sucker now."

"Shit, I can take him. I can take him easy."

Yellow glanced dubiously at him. "Hey, man, can't nobody take him *easy*. I'm telling you, he *mean*."

"We'll see how mean he is if he don't have that piece for me," Judo promised.

As they walked along the street, Judo sensed that Yellow was *up*: he was hyper, charged, ready to take on something heavy. "You taking anything?" Judo asked suspiciously.

Yellow looked aghast. "You crazy, man? I don't *take* nothing. I'm a Black Muslim, brother, not some nigger pimp. My spirit comes from Allah, not from some shit in my arm."

"You acting pretty high," Judo said.

"I *am* high, brother!" Yellow exclaimed. "High with the Word! Ready to take up my sword for Allah again!"

"Listen, brother," Judo said urgently, "you done proved yourself a man once already. Don't make no sense for you to do it again. Listen, why don't you and me just forget about this Death Angels' shit and go on and just practice our religion without no more killing? We don't have to be Death Angels, man."

"The blue-eyed devils must be killed," Yellow said. "The grafted snakes must be destroyed."

"They don't have to be destroyed by *us*," Judo argued. "Let those others do the killings; they're all crazy motherfuckers anyway. But we're not crazy, man. You and me, we're all right in the head, you know what I mean?"

"You not talking from the heart, brother," Yellow said.

"Yeah, I am, man." Judo took Yellow's arm and stopped him. "Look, man, you and me, we not like these other dudes, you know? We don't need to all the time be killing white folks—"

"White devils," Yellow corrected.

"Whatever. But what I'm saying is, I don't think there's any reason to do any more killing. Either one of us."

Yellow's eyebrows rose. "Either one of us? The way I see it, you hadn't done *any* yet. 'Less there's some I don't know about."

"I haven't done it because I'm not sure it's right, man," Judo said quietly. His eyes met Yellow's and held. Judo was sincerely fond of his younger friend; he felt closer to him than he had ever felt toward any other male, even his own brothers. If only he could find a way to get inside Yellow's head and sweep out all the shit the Death Angels' meetings had put there.

"I don't believe you mean any of this," Yellow said resolutely. "You having a moment of weakness, of doubt. It'll pass and your heart will be strong once more." He started walking again; Judo fell in step beside him.

"Look, man," Judo pleaded, "if you'll just think about it, you'll see there ain't no sense to it at all—"

"Quiet!" Yellow hissed a caution, bobbing his chin up the street. There was a white man approaching.

Judo stopped talking. The white man was in his thirties, lean, not too tall. He looked ordinary.

"Watch this," Yellow whispered when the man drew near.

Before Judo knew what was happening, Yellow had stepped in front of the white man and struck him a crushing hand slash to the larynx. The unsuspecting man's eyes bulged and he clutched at his throat. Yellow kicked his feet out from under him and he pitched to the ground. Blood ran from each corner of his mouth.

"Let's go!" Yellow said, stepping over the fallen man. He took off running. Judo, overcoming his surprise, sucked in a breath and ran after him.

Judo looked at Yellow running in front of him: green raincoat flapping, knit ball bouncing at the crown of his ski cap, tennis shoes slapping against the pavement. Then it came to him. He's crazy, he thought. Yellow was crazy. Just like the others.

They were all crazy.

Maybe *he* was crazy too.

In the loft, Judo went up to Skullcap, ready to fight. "I want my piece back, man. And I want it *now.*"

"Why, sure, brother," Skullcap said pleasantly. He slipped Judo's .32 automatic from under his coat and handed it to him, grip first. "Sorry I kept it so long, man. But you can be sure it was put to very good use. Am I right, brother?" he said to Rims, standing beside him.

Rims grinned what looked to Judo like an imbecilic grin. "You right!" he confirmed.

"I done made arrangements to get me a new piece very shortly," Skullcap said. "The brother over in Oakland had to go underground, so I let him keep my old one. Brothers have to look out for brothers, dig?"

"Yeah, sure," Judo said. He was examining his gun, making sure it was not damaged in any way.

Yellow walked up and slapped Rims playfully on the muscle. "Hey, brother, I been hearing good things about you. You really on your way!"

Rims grinned again, pleased. "I be doing all right," he said. He had one female and two male devils to his credit, and was ahead of all of them.

"Man, that is *fine!*" said Yellow. He nudged Skullcap. "Ain't that fine, brother?"

"Right on," Skullcap replied. There was a tinge of jealousy in

149

his voice. He thought of the two devils who lived after he stung them: the man talking to the two women in Potrero Hill, and the girl parking her car the other night. As close as he had been to them, they had still lived. It was piss-poor luck. If they hadn't lived, Yellow would be congratulating *him*.

As if Judo could read Skullcap's mind, he said, "You not been doing too well lately, have you?"

"Still better than you, motherfucker," Skullcap replied coldly. "Least I got the heart to *try*."

Before Judo could say anything further, someone clapped his hands for attention. "You all sit down now," a voice instructed. "The man be coming up."

Presently the well-groomed man with the Vandyke entered the room, accompanied as usual by his bodyguards. The men in the loft all took seats. Judo and Yellow sat on an old daybed against the back wall. All the lights in the room were turned off except for an overhead bulb above Vandyke. When the room was quiet, he opened a zippered leather binder and began to read.

"Allah has said, 'Behold, I have set before you the way of life and the way of death.' The Messenger of Allah, in the person of the Honorable Elijah Muhammad, teaches us that the devil's way of life is one of sport and play. He tells us that there are two people: one a people of foolishness and mischief, who are the enemy of Allah from the time they are made, and are appointed for destruction. This is the white race. The other people are of the family of Allah, and to them Allah will restore the rulership of the earth. These are the people of the black nation. Science has already proved that the white race has never fully developed physically or mentally. They are still a race of inquisitive children. Their whole civilization is one of play; even their statesmanship and their scientific experiments are another form of play. The white race intends to die laughing; there can be no other reason for making themselves and those who follow them the laughingstock of every civilized black nation on earth. The Messenger teaches us that we—the blacks—are the father of races. We will no longer follow an irresponsible child-race in the way of death. We follow Elijah Muhammad, a man who leads us in the way of life!"

In the back of the room, Judo leaned close to Yellow and whispered, "Be right back, man. Got to take a piss."

Quietly he stood up and slipped out the nearest door. Yellow stared curiously after him. Never before had Judo—or anyone, for that matter—left the room during a meeting. Yellow frowned. What was going on with him? The way he had been talking earlier, and now leaving a meeting—

Yellow glanced around the room. Everyone was watching and listening intently to the speaker. Even the two bodyguards, who were supposed to watch all movement in the audience, were caught up by the lecture and not paying proper attention to their duties.

Intrigued by what Judo might be up to, Yellow decided to slip out also—or try to. He waited until Vandyke took a few steps at the front of the room, when all eyes were on him, following his movements; then he slid off the daybed, dropped into a crouch, and duck walked out the rear door.

Yellow went as quietly as possible down the steep wooden stairs that led to the loft. When he got to the bottom, he stopped and listened. Hearing nothing, he wondered if Judo had gone home. He walked softly to the building's office, looked in, saw no one. Going to the rear door, he peered through its small window and looked out back. Nothing.

Just as he was about to give up and go back upstairs, Yellow heard a sound from the direction of the first-floor bathroom. He frowned again, at himself this time. Maybe Judo *had* gone to take a piss. Yellow tiptoed to a doorway and inched one eye around the edge to see the bathroom door. It was open. Judo was inside. But he was not taking a piss. Instead, he was using a fingernail clipper to tighten the bolts of a small air vent above the toilet.

What the fuck could he be doing? Yellow wondered. Then it came to him. Judo was either taking something out of the vent, or putting something in. The vent was a hiding place.

As Yellow was grinning in delight at his own cleverness, Judo finished with the vent and got down off the toilet seat where he had been standing. Yellow jerked his head back and hurried away from the door. One of his shoes hit the leg of a folding chair and moved it noisily. Judo, wiping his hands on his trouser legs, froze at the sound and looked up anxiously. He stepped out of the bathroom and picked up a hammer from a nearby crate. Holding the hammer up to strike, he moved to the doorway and stepped quickly through it. No one.

Yellow was back at the stairs by then, climbing them on all fours. Halfway up, one of the steps creaked loudly under his weight.

Again Judo heard the noise. Again he followed it with the hammer raised. But when he got to the bottom step and looked up—nothing.

Judo finally put the hammer down and went quietly back upstairs. When he slipped back into his place beside Yellow, his young friend glanced at him, nodded, and resumed giving his full attention to Vandyke. Judo stared at Yellow for a long moment, studying him suspiciously, looking for some outward sign of guilt or conscience. Yellow just kept listening intently to Vandyke and watching the speaker's movements. Judo finally looked away and stopped staring.

Out of the corner of his eye, Yellow saw him turn away. Yellow expelled a silent breath of relief.

After dinner on Saturday night, in the apartment they now shared, Anthony Harris and Debbie Turner sat on the couch to watch television.

"What time is it?" Anthony asked, opening the newspaper to the TV listings.

"Anthony, I have to talk to you about something," Debbie said.

"Yeah? What is it?"

"I'm pregnant."

Anthony put the paper down and looked at her. His mind worked rapidly, tallying the weeks, the days. He did not think they had been together long enough for her to know she was pregnant. Not if the baby was his.

"Is the baby mine?" he asked. Then before Debbie could answer, he raised his hand and said, "Never mind, don't say nothing to that. I don't want to know."

For a few minutes, neither of them said anything. Anthony resumed reading the television listings, finished them, but made no move to turn on the set. Debbie moved to a chair across from him. She picked at her fingernails and smoothed wrinkles out of her skirt, glancing at him now and then to see if he was looking at her. Finally she asked, "Why don't you want to know, Anthony?"

"I don't need no more worries," he said quietly. "I got enough already."

"What kind of worries you got?" she wanted to know.

Anthony's expression became sardonic, then it changed to half sardonic and half helplessness, then it became all helplessness. "I'm not sure I could explain it even if I wanted to," he said.

"You don't want to try?"

He shook his head. "Not now. I gots to figure it out some more. Then maybe I can explain it."

Debbie came over and sat next to him again. "What about the baby, Anthony?" she asked. "What must I do about it?"

Anthony put his arm around her and pulled her head to his shoulder. "We'll have it," he said. "We'll have the baby. It'll be ours."

Debbie had hoped against hope that he would say something like that. Now that he had, she cried silently against his shoulder.

It was commonly believed throughout the San Francisco Police Department that Chief of Inspectors Charles Barca had a photographic memory. No one could remember his ever forgetting anything. Occasionally a subordinate would test his memory by deliberately failing to carry out a minor or insignificant instruction from Barca, thinking it would slip the chief's mind. Invariably, just as soon as the slacker thought he was safe, Barca would fall on him like the proverbial ton of bricks. It was considered a never-to-be-forgotten experience to be reamed out by Charley Barca. Few men ever tested him a second time.

Barca joined the police department during the Depression. He became the youngest officer ever to make sergeant, one of the first Italian-Americans to rise to the rank of captain on the civil service rolls, and *the* first man of Italian descent to become the chief of inspectors. None of which surprised anyone who knew him. From his days at St. Ignatius High School where he played softball and ran the mile, Barca was considered a fierce competitor and a sure bet to get ahead in life. In appearance he was strictly soft-sell: average height, medium build, well-groomed, a face pleasant enough to belong to a monsignor. It was *under* the surface that the high voltage was hidden: the unlimited energy, the relentless determination, the incredible memory, and above all the total dedication to law and order.

It was the dedication to his job that prompted him to convene, on Saturday, December 22, 1973, a pre-Christmas, weekend meeting with all the lieutenants of the various police bureaus, as well as Gus Coreris, John Fotinos, and several other homicide inspectors. On the desk before him were all the Incident Reports of all the cases thus far connected to the .32-caliber automatic pistol to which Mitch Luksich had matched all the recovered shell casings and slugs. One by one, Barca went over them in his mind.

"Erakat, Dancik, DiGirolamo, Bertuccio—all murders," he said aloud. "Agnos and Roselli, attempted murders. By the way, how is the Roselli girl?"

"Not good, Chief," a homicide inspector answered. "One of the slugs nicked her spine. And she's got a collapsed lung."

Barca's expression darkened slightly. Random violence disturbed him to the very core. Domestic quarrels, murders for hire, killings during robberies—there was some pattern, some logic, to such crimes. But the four murders and two attempts with which he was faced here were without rhyme or reason. They were mindless.

"All right," he said, "I want a special unit formed to get this killer—or killers—as the case may be. I want it to be a hunt-and-prevent unit, and I want it on duty from dusk until dawn. Select the men from both the uniformed and plainclothes ranks; have them work in civilian dress and unmarked autos. I want this operation given top priority. These killings are wanton, vicious, and unprovoked. I want them stopped."

At the back of the room, Fotinos and Coreris exchanged glances. They knew the look on Charley Barca's face. It meant sixteen-hour days and lots of black coffee.

Just hours after the Barca meeting, Yellow returned alone to the building where the loft meetings were held. He slipped unnoticed into the employee rest room on the first floor, locked the door behind him, and stepped up onto the toilet seat. From his hip pocket he produced a small screwdriver and quickly loosened the screws of the air vent he had seen Judo tightening. With the faceplate re-

154

moved, he peered inside the vent. There, just inches inside, was Judo's automatic pistol.

Yellow grinned in delight, then he suddenly had to go to the bathroom. Stepping off the toilet, he urinated. Without bothering to flush the toilet, he stepped back up, got the gun, and hung the faceplate back in place.

Minutes later, the fully loaded automatic in his waistband, Yellow left the building and walked out into the streets of the city.

Donald Crum, a twenty-four-year-old longshoreman, waited at the corner of Twelfth and Market to cross the street. He had just finished dinner in a Market Street diner and, walking home, lighted his first after-dinner cigarette. There was a breeze coming in from the bay; Crum patted his neatly styled hair to keep it in place. Not too many longshoremen had styled hair, but that did not matter to Crum. He had worked on the San Francisco docks for two years and was grappling-hook tough; no one ever kidded him about *his* styled hair.

When there was a break in traffic, Crum crossed the street and walked south on Market, toward the Civic Center Hotel where he had been living for five months. He noticed a man a few years younger than himself come out of a bar on the corner. They shared a yard of sidewalk until Crum, longer-legged, walked on ahead. He noticed that the young man was carrying a brown paper bag with a stuffed Teddy bear in it. To each his own, Crum thought.

The man with the bag containing the Teddy bear was Neal Moynihan. Nineteen years old, he was a fifth-generation San Francisco Irishman—on both sides. His grandfathers were Cornelius Moynihan and Michael Minihan. The daughter of Michael Minihan had been his mother. She was dead now and his father, Cornelius J. Moynihan, had remarried. The Teddy bear that young Neal carried was a Christmas present for his sister, Christine, who was ten.

Neal was a slim young man with a baby face and thick black hair growing far back on a very high forehead. He wore old denims and motorcycle boots, and as he walked he whistled a new rock tune to which he had not yet learned the words.

As Neal Moynihan walked south on Twelfth Street, with Donald

Crum a few feet ahead of him, Yellow came around the corner from McCoppin and walked toward them.

Two blocks away, Mildred Hosler, age fifty, trudged along Gough Street toward Otis. She had two blocks to go to her bus stop at Otis and Van Ness. The bus ride would take ten minutes. Then, when she got off at Ellis, she had a little more than three blocks to walk until she was home. Mildred was a quite heavy woman; she had difficulty breathing if she walked too far or too fast. That was why she measured every trip in terms of how many blocks she would be on foot.

What a blessed relief it would be, she thought, when she never had to do any extensive walking again.

Walking toward the two white men, Yellow felt his nostrils flare. His eyes were wide and unblinking. A small amount of white, foamy spittle had collected at the corners of his mouth.

I will slay these grafted snakes for Allah, he thought.

His eyes darted from one man to the other. The taller one, with the styled hair, was closest to him. He would die first. Then the shorter one carrying the paper bag. Two devils for Allah—

But even as Yellow was planning it in his mind, the first white man turned off the sidewalk and entered the Civic Center Hotel. For a terrible moment, Yellow thought the second man was going to do the same. Like Rims had felt that night on Divisadero when Marietta DiGirolamo kept changing direction, Yellow could see his plan for murder being foiled at the last moment.

But Allah remained with him: the second man kept walking.

Yellow slipped the gun from his belt and held it at his side.

Neal Moynihan glanced up at the light-skinned Negro approaching him on the sidewalk. Automatically he switched the bag containing the Teddy bear to his other hand, the one farthest from the young black. Being that close to Christmas, there were a lot of purse snatchers and parcel snatchers on the streets, lightning-fast young hoodlums who could grab what a person was carrying and be gone before the victim could even yell. As far as Moynihan could tell in the night light of the street, this one walking toward him looked harmless enough; but he was still black, and you never could tell about those people.

Moynihan was on the outside of the sidewalk as they started to pass each other. From the corner of his eye, he saw the black man's hand begin to move. Instinctively he took a step toward the curb. The black man was backing up toward the closest building, a furniture store, its triple window filled with tables, chairs, and other odd pieces of furniture. Moynihan half turned to see what the black man was doing. As he did, an explosion in red suddenly engulfed his head.

The first bullet hit him on the right side of his face, coursed down, and exited his neck. The second hit him in the left side of the neck, coursed down into his chest cavity, and lodged in his left lung. The third penetrated his heart, went all the way through, and exited his back.

Neal Moynihan was dead when he hit the sidewalk.

Donald Crum was a few feet inside the lobby of the Civic Center Hotel, warming his hands at a radiator, when he heard the shots. He ran out to the sidewalk to see what was happening. To his surprise, the young man with the Teddy bear was lying spread-eagled in the middle of the sidewalk, his face a patch of blood. The bag with the Teddy bear was lying next to him on the left, close to his body, as if he had let go of it with great reluctance.

Crum dashed to the body and knelt beside it. "Hey, man, can you hear me?" he said. "Hey, bud, can you hear my voice?"

Moynihan did not respond. As Crum knelt there, he heard the sound of running footsteps—not coming closer but going off into the distance. He rose and stepped over to the mouth of Stevenson Street, a narrow, alleylike lane that jutted one way off Twelfth Street. A figure was running away down the lane.

Crum looked back toward the hotel. The desk clerk was standing out front.

"Hey, call the cops, man," Crum said. He glanced over at Neal Moynihan. "And an ambulance," he said hopefully.

Yellow ran as fast as he could down Stevenson. He cut through a trailer-rental lot and around a couple of buildings. He got to Brady

Street. Down Brady he ran to Otis. He turned right on Otis and ran half a block farther—to a wide but quiet tricorner intersection where McCoppin, Gough, and Otis all came together.

Yellow knew exactly where he was running to; he knew the neighborhood very well. By turning right at the tricorner and heading up Gough Street, he could, in a matter of seconds, be on Market Street, and there lose himself in the pedestrian traffic of that busy street.

That was what he had in mind when he ran up to the tricorner intersection and stood there for a moment to rest. He had an odd little smile on his face, and he was thinking: *Another white devil has been given up to Allah.* Yellow felt a surge of exhilaration, a tickle that flowed from his testicles to his throat. It was not as powerful as the feeling he had the night he cut off the white female devil's head—but it was a tremendous high nevertheless. Allah be praised! he thought. I am a good and worthy servant of the Master!

Yellow laughed aloud.

Then the laughter broke and died as he looked over at the opposite corner and saw an older, heavyset woman staring curiously at him.

An older, heavyset, *white* woman.

Mildred Hosler did not know what to do. She was at the edge of the rounded corner, where Gough flowed around into McCoppin. To her left was a stop sign to halt any traffic coming down Gough. To her right on McCoppin was a bus stop. Behind her, an empty flagpole in the tiny corner yard of a small public building. Directly in front of her was a marked pedestrian crossing: two bold white lines creating a path over to the Otis Street side of the tricorner. Halfway across—because Gough was a six-lane street—was a narrow safety island.

Ordinarily Mildred would have simply walked across and continued down Otis to her own bus stop at Van Ness. But she had seen the young Negro run up to the corner, seen him acting peculiarly and laughing out loud. She was afraid he was drunk or on drugs; she did not want to walk past him. Perhaps if she just waited at the corner for a moment, he would go on his way—

But that was not to be. He had looked over and seen her. Seen her and stopped laughing. And stood there staring at her.

Mildred thought briefly of turning off to her left and walking up Gough, to Market. It was not an immediate desirable alternative to her because, for one thing, it meant an extra two blocks to get to her bus stop, and for another, Gough ran slightly uphill, which made for more difficult walking. Still, it would be better than having to walk past a drunk—or whatever he was.

She made up her mind and starting walking up Gough. As soon as she did, the young Negro started across the street toward her. Because of her size and weight, Mildred could not move too fast, especially on an incline. So she knew she had no chance of getting away from him. Glancing sideways, she saw him walking briskly on an angle to intercept her. He reached the narrow safety island, stepped over it, kept coming.

Mildred knew she was helpless, now at the mercy of whatever this strange young black man decided to do to her. She probably tried to remember how much money she had in her purse. She must have said a silent prayer that he would not hit her or molest her when he took her purse away—

And he did not.

Instead he walked up and shot her four times.

All four bullets hit Mildred Hosler in the left anterior chest area. They formed a pattern partway around her left breast: one at seven o'clock, one very close at seven thirty, one at eleven, one at twelve o'clock, high.

Unlike Neal Moynihan, six minutes earlier and two blocks away, Mildred Hosler, because she was a much heavier person, did not die before she fell.

After he killed the white woman who had been watching him— and there was never any doubt in Yellow's mind that he *had* killed his victims; none of them had ever survived yet, unlike the unlucky Skullcap—Yellow ran back across Gough and up to Market. He fell in with the pedestrian traffic on Market, merging into the ebb and flow of people that seemed always to populate that major crosstown artery on Saturday night. Walking along, he could hear the sirens heading toward Twelfth Street, toward the first devil he had destroyed. Soon there would be even more sirens when someone called about the woman devil on Gough. Yellow grinned and giggled. He was elated, felt almost as he did when he ejaculated,

159

tickled throughout his body. Allah had been good to him tonight, he thought. Praise be to Allah!

Up ahead, near Rose Street, he saw a uniformed policeman talking to a flower vendor on the corner. Yellow suddenly remembered that he had Judo's gun still stuck in his belt. The barrel was warm against his stomach.

Got to get this piece back in that vent, he thought. He walked as nonchalantly as he knew how past the policeman and the flower vendor. When he thought he was past the point of being noticed, he hurried a little faster down the street. He headed for the building where the loft meetings were held.

"Two people were shot down in the street within two blocks of each other just minutes ago," the television commentator said on the 9:00 P.M. newsbreak. "Neal Moynihan, nineteen, died in a fusillade of gunfire from an unknown assailant near the intersection of Twelfth Street and Stevenson, at approximately eight fifteen. Less than ten minutes later, at McCoppin and Gough, a scant two blocks away, Mildred Hosler, fifty, was also cut down by an unknown gunman—"

Judo stared at the TV picture as if transfixed. Live remote pictures of both victims were shown, while the commentator continued to talk.

"Witnesses at both scenes described the gunman as a light-skinned Negro, five eight to five ten in height, one hundred thirty to one hundred fifty pounds. He escaped on foot after each incident. Police at both scenes have recovered similar bullet housings which they say were possibly fired from the same gun, believed to be a thirty-two-caliber automatic pistol—"

Judo felt his mouth go dry. He got up, put on his jacket, and left the apartment.

At the crime scenes, it was confusion compounded.

The responding patrol officers were Douglas Dumas and James Selby in radio car Three-Bravo-Four. They arrived at the Moynihan scene at 8:15 P.M., approximately five minutes after the shooting. They were met there by Inspectors Sullivan and Kennealy of the Sex Crime Detail, who had been nearby. Lieutenant Syme and

Sergeant Bragg were on their way to take charge of the physical scene. Up to that point, everything was proceeding smoothly.

Then the second call came.

Another shooting, less than two blocks away. Dumas and Selby quickly left the Moynihan scene and rushed to the Hosler scene. Despite their close proximity, another policeman, Blackwell in Car 3F-94, beat them there. He was already talking to a witness, Carlos Paniagua, who had observed the shooting of Mildred Hosler from a window at 26 Gough Street.

Inspectors Sanders and Gilford, of Homicide, arrived at the Moynihan scene. They were advised of the second shooting by Lieutenant Syme, who, with Sergeant Bragg, then hurried to the Hosler scene to take charge of that area.

Sleadd, of the Photo Lab, and Tedesco, of the Crime Lab, arrived at the Moynihan scene. Three spent shell casings were located, circled with chalk, and photographed.

A Central Ambulance unit, commanded by Steward Haynes, had also arrived at the Moynihan scene. Haynes officially pronounced Neal Moynihan dead at 8:23 P.M. Deputy Coroner Schultz arrived to take charge of the body.

When they had completed all of their preliminary work at the Moynihan scene, Homicide Inspectors Sanders and Gilford rushed to the Hosler scene. Another Central Ambulance unit was already there; a steward named Holbrook could not determine, because of her weight, whether Mildred Hosler was dead or not. Taking no chances, he rushed her to Mission Emergency Hospital.

Sleadd arrived to photograph the scene, Tedesco to collect any physical evidence. The Crime Lab, Tedesco thought solemnly, was getting quite a collection of .32 caliber slugs and casings.

At both scenes, officers were managing to round up witnesses. Besides Donald Crum, one other person had seen the killer of Neal Moynihan: one Eugene Tracey had heard the shots, looked out his second-floor window, and seen the gunman running down Stevenson Street. At the Hosler scene, four additional witnesses had been located, although none of them, except the original witness, Carlos Paniagua, had seen the killer.

Meanwhile, at Mission Emergency Hospital, Dr. John Eugene officially pronounced Mildred Hosler dead.

* * *

Without being seen by any of the night employees, Judo entered the building where the loft meetings were held and went directly to the first-floor washroom. He locked the door and stepped onto the toilet seat. Using his nail clippers again, he removed the screws and lifted off the faceplate of the air vent. He looked inside. The gun was still there.

Judo took it out and looked at it. He felt it carefully. It was not warm, did not look any different. Then he smelled the barrel. And he knew. It had been fired.

He slipped the magazine out of the handle. Checked it for load. There was only one bullet left in it. When Judo had put it in the vent, the magazine had contained eight rounds.

Judo's jaw clenched and his mouth pulled into a tight line. His nostrils flared in anger, as Yellow's had earlier in excitement. Bastards! he thought. Motherfucking bastards!

It had to be one of the men from the loft meeting. One of the eleven or twelve besides himself who had attended that last meeting. Somebody who had come in late, maybe, and seen him hide the gun there. One of the men he did not know too well—

Angry as he was, Judo tried very hard not to let himself think that it was Yellow who had taken the gun. He hated like hell to think that Yellow would have done that to him, deceived him like that. Yet he had been suspicious of his young friend the very night he had hidden the gun there; he had suspected even then that Yellow had followed him down from the loft and spied on him while he hid the gun.

Wasn't there *nobody* he could trust? he wondered.

Then he made up his mind about something: This was the *last* time anyone was going to use the gun. He had hidden it in that vent in the first place because he did not want to take it home. He did not want his woman to see it. Besides, Muslim rules forbade keeping a gun in the house. Always hide weapons *outside* the home, the lessons taught. Outside the home—but close and convenient enough to retrieve quickly.

But Judo did not *want* to retrieve the gun anymore. He was sick and tired of the gun, did not want the responsibility for it anymore. There was no telling how many people the fucking thing had killed:

162

the old man in the store, that guy using the telephone, the woman on Divisadero, the old man on Bancroft, these two tonight—

No more, he thought grimly. As far as this gun is concerned, *it is over.*

Judo stuck the gun in his belt and replaced the vent plate. He slipped out of the building just as he had slipped in: unobserved.

One hour later, in a borrowed car, Judo drove to the middle of the Golden Gate Bridge and hurled the pistol into the bay.

At the end of Day Sixty-four there were twelve victims.

Quita Hague, hacked to death.

Richard Hague, his face butchered.

Ellen Linder, raped, ravaged, threatened with death.

Frances Rose, her face blown apart by close-range gunshots.

Saleem Erakat, tied up and executed with a single shot behind the ear.

Paul Dancik, shot down as he attempted to use a public telephone.

Arthur Agnos, surviving after having his lungs, spleen, and kidney ripped apart by bullets.

Marietta DiGirolamo, thrown into a doorway and shot to death as she walked down the street.

Ilario Bertuccio, gunned down in the street as he walked home from work with a bottle of 7-Up under his arm.

Angela Roselli, surviving but seriously injured after being shot down in the street as she was returning home from a Christmas party.

Neal Moynihan, shot down in the street on his way home with a Teddy bear for his little sister.

And Mildred Hosler, shot down in the street as she walked toward her bus stop.

Day 65

Judo answered the phone on the first ring. It was Yellow.

"How you doing, brother?" the younger man asked.

"Not bad," Judo replied in a cool tone. He did not bother to ask Yellow how *he* was doing.

"I called to invite you to a little Christmas party down at the loft," Yellow said.

Judo sighed quietly. It was Sunday, the day before Christmas Eve. Judo had purposely stayed away from the loft all weekend because he did not want to be around Yellow, Skullcap, Rims, or any of the other Death Angel candidates.

"I'm busy, man," he lied. "I got some shopping to do."

"The party ain't until tonight, after the stores close," Yellow said. "It won't get in the way of your shopping."

Judo remained silent. Yellow waited what seemed like a long time. Judo still did not speak.

"Something wrong, brother?" Yellow asked.

"Yeah," Judo snapped. "I'm pissed, that's what wrong." He was about to accuse Yellow of taking the gun, but Yellow beat him to it.

"You pissed 'cause I borrowed your gun, man?"

"Fucking right I am!" Judo became twice as angry because Yellow had admitted it so quickly.

"Hey, man, I know I should have asked first," Yellow said contritely, "but I just didn't think, you know what I mean? Allah moved me, brother, and I just acted. Allah directed me to two devils and I destroyed them."

"Yeah, with *my* gun," Judo muttered.

"I was going to tell you about it, man," Yellow said. "That's one of the reasons I'm calling. That and to ask you to come down to the loft for this special Christmas party."

"What's special about it?" Judo asked.

"We going to fix up a special turkey for the white devils," said Yellow.

"What kind of turkey?"

"You'll see when you get there," Yellow teased. "We already got the fixings, though. And the festivities gonna be starting 'bout seven o'clock. Can we count on you to be there?"

Judo did not answer. He tried to think of an excuse to decline, but his mind simply could not conjure up anything believable. Just say no, man! one part of his brain screamed at him. But he could not do it. Whether out of fear or embarrassment or just plain weakness, he could not say no.

"How about it, brother?" Yellow pressed. "Most everybody gonna be there. The others, they'll be expecting you."

"I'll be there," Judo said finally. He could have bitten his tongue off for saying it.

"Hey, good, brother!" said Yellow, his tone sounding genuinely pleased. "Now, listen, tell me what I can do for you to make up for borrowing your piece like I did. I want us to mend our break, hear?"

"You don't have to do nothing, man."

"I don't want you pissed at me, brother."

"I ain't pissed at you." Judo sighed quietly. Just leave me alone for a while, man, he thought.

"You sure, brother?"

"I'm sure," Judo assured him.

"Hey, out of sight, brother! Listen, we'll all see you tonight, man. Dig?"

"Dig," said Judo.

The white man they had kidnapped off the street twelve hours earlier was absolutely terrified. They had him stripped naked and bound hand and foot to a straight-back wooden chair. The chair, in turn, was securely tied to a loft pillar so that he could not move it around or tip it over. A dirty cloth had been stuffed into his mouth and strips of adhesive tape stretched over it. He could breathe, but that was all.

The man was young: about twenty-five. Average: five ten, 140 pounds. He had been selected the previous night while watching a group of street entertainers in Ghirardelli Square, the modern shopping and dining complex at the edge of Fisherman's Wharf. Four blacks followed him out of the complex and caught up with him on a lonely block of North Point Street. They literally surrounded him, one of them pushing the barrel of a gun against his ribs.

"Be cool, motherfucker," he was told with a smile. "Cause us any trouble and you die here and now."

Since they had tied him to the chair, he had wished a hundred times that he *had* caused them trouble, that he *had* made a scene, that he *had* tried to get away. A quick death on the street seemed more desirable with every hour that passed. God only knew what they planned to do to him.

His clothes had been taken away and were lying in a pile in the corner. His wallet, money, and other personal belongings were on a chair next to the pile. His kidnappers had seemed particularly pleased when they examined his identification. "This sucker ain't even from around here, man," one of them said. "He probably won't even be reported missing here."

For the most part he had been left alone in the loft. From time to time one or two blacks who had not been among the abductors would come up to have a look at him. Occasionally they made comments.

"Don't see why the mothers couldn't have grabbed a woman," one of them said. "We could have had a dick-sucking party then."

"You still can, baby," replied his friend. "He look about like your type." The friend laughed all the way back down the stairs.

Another one who came up, alone, glared at him for several long minutes. "You white motherfucking devil," he muttered. "You evil white grafted-snake motherfucking devil."

Still another smiled coldly at him and said, "I got something for you, honky." He took out his penis and urinated all over the bound man's stomach and crotch.

As the day wore on, the captive's body began to ache from the ordeal of being tied in one position; his stomach growled in anger from hunger; he grew stiff, sore, cold. But all of his physical discomfort was insignificant compared to the terrible mental terror he felt. The men who had him were obviously mad, insane. And the things they might do to him—unspeakable.

Although he did not know exactly what those things were, he was certain that his worst fears would be realized. He would gladly have taken his own life than face the coming night hours.

The Crime Lab was deserted that Sunday except for Mitch Luksich and the duty man on call. Mitch was in his cubicle surrounded by two of the things he loved most: guns and microscopes. The guns were a selection of .32-caliber automatics he had been examining in an attempt to isolate the particular make of weapon that had fired the large collection of .32 slugs and shell casings the lab now had. Those shells and casings were spread out in neat groups on Luksich's work counter. There were eight groups, marked *Erakat, Dancik, DiGirolamo, Agnos, Bertuccio, Roselli, Moynihan,* and *Hosler.* In all, Luksich now had twenty-four shell casings and thirteen bullets.

For more than an hour, Luksich had been reexamining and reclassifying each of the casings and each of the slugs, at the same time matching them individually to makes of weapons from which it was possible that they might or might not have been fired. Luksich was a meticulously careful scientist. Once he had microscopically determined that all the slugs had been fired from the same gun, he could have taken them as a group and eliminated various weapons that could not have fired them. But Luksich preferred to eliminate them individually, one at a time, slowly and precisely, in order to double-check his previous findings as he went along. That was why he was working alone on the Sunday before Christmas Eve.

He was almost finished now. The last four slugs and casings

were from the group marked 73-9359—Hosler. The casings had been retrieved at the McCoppin and Gough crime scene; the slugs had been removed from Mildred Hosler's body at the autopsy. One by one, Luksich put them under the scope. Slowly and with great care, as if he had never seen them before, he checked them again, from the beginning: the caliber, the manufacturer, the headstamp, type of fire, primer type, presence of residue, mutilation of case, bullet weight, breech impressions, ejector marks, extractor marks, chamber marks, anything else that the eye of the microscope could show him.

Finally he was finished. Finished and scientifically satisfied. He went to a nearby desk, lowered his big, tired frame into a chair, and reached for a Dictaphone mike. He began dictating.

"Subject: Characteristics of Evidence Bullets and Cartridge Cases. Laboratory Numbers: 8580, 9082, 9151, 9152, 9322, 9323, 9357, and 9358. Evidence to Date: Twenty-four thirty two-caliber Automatic Colt Pistol cases and thirteen bullets.

"Paragraph. Body of Report: The twenty-four thirty-two-caliber ACP cartridge cases are largely of Remington-Peters manufacture. This is standard ammunition and quite common. Only four of them are not Remington; these are of Winchester-Western manufacture and are marked W-W. This is also a standard cartridge and quite common.

"Paragraph. The ejector mark left on these cases is readily identifiable in its characteristic appearance. There is also present a mark just below this ejector mark which appears to have been made by the ejector cut in the breech face.

"Paragraph. The firing pin impression on these cartridge cases is also readily identifiable and indicates that the firing pin is round with a number of concentric machining cuts. One of these concentric cuts exhibits a bulge which would indicate a chatter mark or pit at the tip of the firing pin.

"Paragraph. There are two factors present which indicate excessive headspace in this pistol: the expansion or bulging of all twenty-four cases in a similar fashion, and the slight protrusion of the primer out of its pocket.

"Paragraph. The thirteen bullets all match microscopically and exhibit six lands and grooves with a right-hand twist. Special characteristics exhibited are a land width of .046 inches, and an indication of fairly deep rifling. Several high spots left on some of the lands indicate less than high-quality manufacture.

"Paragraph. The characteristics listed: ejector markings, excessive headspace, rough firing pin and less than high-quality manufacture, as well as barrel characteristics, are common to a large percentage of thirty-two-caliber automatics.

"Paragraph. Inclusion or elimination of some certain models is not possible because of vagaries of manufacture. Example: normally high-quality pistols of German and Czech manufacture were turned out rather crudely during war years, and some of these models, in particular the CZ Model 27, exhibit characteristics similar to our evidence cases and bullets; however, another CZ Model 27 made under occupation does not.

"Paragraph. A large number of the current crop of inexpensive imported automatics also exhibit characteristics similar to our evidence cases. The few guns that can be eliminated are: all Colts, all Remingtons, all Hungarian Frommes, the Langerhan, the Dreyse, and Stock. End of report."

Luksich fished a cheroot from his pocket and lighted it. A cloud of offensive gray smoke rose to the ceiling. Luksich yawned and stretched. That was all he could do for the present.

He rose, got his coat, and left the office to enjoy what little was left of his weekend.

In Homicide, Fotinos and Coreris were also putting in extra time. They already knew, through an earlier phone call to Mitch Luksich, that the slugs and casings from the two latest killings matched those from the previous six shootings. Even though officially only one of those previous cases—Erakat—was theirs, they were nevertheless looking over all the facts of the other five cases, plus the two newest ones.

"What turned up on that little spik who was standing there when Dancik was shot?" Coreris asked across their facing desks.

"Zilch," said Fotinos. "Practically zilch anyway. They found a woman named Thelma-something in an apartment on Frederick Street. She says the guy's name is Eduardo Abdi. Says he claims to be a traveling missionary who goes around preaching to fruit pickers in the fields."

Coreris rolled his eyes. "Christ, just what we need."

169

Fotinos shrugged. "Well, hell, maybe he'll give the case a little color."

Coreris grunted. "We already got all the *color* we need."

"That's for sure," said Fotinos. He bobbed his head at the reports that Coreris had. "Did anybody check out the acquaintances of that black boyfriend of the DiGirolamo girl? Maybe he had a Muslim buddy who didn't like him living with a white woman."

"I don't think they went any farther than the guy himself," Coreris said. "He was clean all the way around except for some lousy traffic warrants."

"I'm gonna make a note of it," Fotinos said. "If all else fails, I'm gonna check the guy out. Get the names of some of his friends. You never can tell with these blacks."

Coreris shrugged. "Might as well. What the hell."

"Right. What the hell."

"Look in the Agnos file and see if there's been a follow-up call to have him look at mug shots again."

Fotinos rummaged through his own stack of reports and pulled out the one for Art Agnos. "No follow-up," he said. "He claims he can't identify the guy."

Coreris snorted. "He looked right into the bastard's face, for Christ's sake!"

"He's a Greek," Fotinos said. "He don't remember so good, maybe. Besides, they all look alike, you know. Especially under a streetlight holding a gun."

The phone rang. Fotinos picked it up.

"Homicide, Inspector Fotinos." He smiled. "Hello, Kathy," he said to the wife of Gus Coreris. "No, I don't know where he is, Kathy. Last time I saw him he was trying to get some blonde in Records to go have a drink with him—"

Coreris picked up the line. "Don't pay any attention to him, sweetheart. He's drunk again. What did you want?"

"Just to remind you that it's the Christmas Eve weekend, Gus. And that we *do* have children. They may be grown, but they still like to celebrate holiday weekends as a family."

"I know, sweetheart, I know. We're wrapping up right now. I'll be home in an hour."

"Promise?"

"I promise."

After Coreris hung up, he stared out the window at the twilit city for a moment, thinking of his dark-haired, vivacious wife, the mother of his two grown kids. Two grown kids! God, that was hard to believe. Especially when he looked at her. To him she was still the same young beauty he had been smitten by so long ago. What a wonderful thing it was, he reflected, to remain in love with the same woman for so many years.

Coreris sighed and looked down at his hands. Then he frowned. They did not look like his hands at all; they looked like his father's hands. That's because you're going to be forty-nine years old next month, he told himself. He shook his head wryly. I wonder, he thought, why Kathy isn't getting any older?

"Want to call it a day?" Fotinos asked. His own family would be waiting for him also.

"Let's go over a few more things first," Coreris answered.

There were still monsters loose in the city. Sometimes the women did not understand that.

In another part of the city, other men were also concerned with catching the killer. Three executive directors of Arab organizations in the Bay Area, and an Arab attorney, met at the home of a wealthy Arab businessman.

"Our brother Saleem Erakat has been dead for one month," the businessman said. "We must do something more in an effort to apprehend his murderer." He looked at the lawyer. "Do you think it would help if we doubled the reward?"

"Possibly," the attorney said. "It certainly can't hurt."

"The police: are you satisfied that they are doing everything they should be doing?"

"Absolutely," the attorney assured him. On the coffee table before them was the morning edition of the *Examiner*. It was open to page 5, where there was a one-column story headed:

TWO SATURDAY
MURDERS TIED
TO OTHERS

171

The item, released by the police department's public information section, stated that the Moynihan and Hosler killings in the Mission District had definitely been linked to at least three other shootings during the month: Paul Dancik on December 11, and Marietta DiGirolamo and Arthur Agnos on December 13. The attorney knew, through a source he had at the Hall of Justice, that more than just those three shootings had been connected by the department; he knew that a total of eight shootings, six of them fatal, had definitely been committed with the same gun. And he knew that one of those victims was Saleem Erakat.

Why the police had decided not to link all of the incidents, the Arab attorney did not know. Probably, he guessed, to give them a reserve supply of information to use as checks and balances on future leads or informant tips. Whatever the reason, *he* was certainly not going to divulge anything he knew. Yet he felt he had to do a little more to help these good gentlemen who were so troubled about their friend's death.

"I have a thought," he told them. "It is all well and good to double the reward, and I think you should do it. Increase it to ten thousand, by all means. But I believe you can go one step further in possibly helping to apprehend these killers. I think if you are willing to establish a legal defense fund for any informant who comes forward that it might encourage a response."

Several eyebrows raised. "A legal defense fund? You mean for one of the killers?"

"Yes. I realize that it is a rather unorthodox suggestion. But it occurs to me that the chances of an *un*involved informant coming forth would seem to be very slim. With blacks such as these, I think a much better chance exists that one of the actual participants would come forward."

The eyebrows were lowered now and thoughtful expressions set in. This was something the Arabs could understand. "A traitor, yes," one of them said, and the others nodded.

"Exactly," said the attorney, "a traitor. Someone who knows what happened but may be afraid to come forward because of his own involvement. I think we might very well encourage this sort of treachery if we word an announcement to the papers just right."

"How would that be?" he was asked.

172

The attorney thought for a moment, then said, "Something like this: 'We will provide a defense fund for anyone with information about the killing who fears going to the police because of'—let's see—'because of their own problems with the law.' I think that's broad enough to cover a multitude of sins, as the Christians say, yet it definitely gets the point across. What do you think, gentlemen?"

The others unanimously agreed.

The attorney was given the task of preparing a joint press release which doubled the reward and established the defense fund. It was to be sent to the papers that very day.

This was the first indication from any area that an *involved* party to the killings might receive a less-than-hostile reception if he came forward to inform on his accomplices.

In the loft, the white man tied to the chair was trying to shrivel up inside himself. His eyes were wide with terror and his pale, naked body trembled both from fear and exposure. For an hour now the blacks had been coming upstairs in twos and threes, and just standing in front of him, looking at him, studying him. And smiling, forever smiling: wide, bright smiles: pearly-white teeth in dark faces with eyes that seldom blinked.

He knew the time was near because there was an electricity among them, an underlying tension and excitement, a nervousness, like the aura in a contender's dressing room minutes before a title shot. What the bound man did not know was the *reason* for the feeling. Something was going to happen; he just did not know *what.*

They're going to sexually attack me, he thought. Like he had heard they did to new men in prison. That must be why his clothes had been taken away and he had been left naked. They planned to hold him down and use him sexually, force him to serve them sexually.

And then, pray God, when they were finished with him, they would throw him in an alley somewhere and it would be all over. God, it would be all over—

But even as he thought it, he knew he was deluding himself. He knew that it was not going to be like that. A terrible, putrid sick-

173

ness deep in the pit of him told him that he was living his last minutes of life. This loft—this shabby, seedy loft with its heavy, musty smell—was the last thing he would ever see.

They were going to kill him.

When nighttime came and the loft grew dark, he heard them filing up the stairs, laughing and joking and making fun out of everything, like rowdy kids on a playground. Then the lights went on and the doorway to the stairwell was carefully closed and bolted. They came over to him and stood around him in a semicircle, the first time all of them were there at once. There were no smiles, no grins, now that the time had come. This was going to be serious business, done purposefully and determinedly. There was, their faces said, a *reason* for what they were about to do.

One of the men went to a closet and came back with a topless cardboard box containing a collection of knives, meat cleavers, metal cutters, and machetes. "Everybody take one," he said.

The men filed up to the box; each one selected a single instrument.

"Now line up."

The men formed a single column.

"We'll take turns. I go first."

The man stepped next to the bound, gagged prisoner. He paused a beat, then suddenly, viciously, cut off the man's left ear.

The next one in line opened a pair of metal cutters and snipped off a thumb.

The next used a meat cleaver to chop off three toes.

The victim's screams were choked back by the gag in his mouth. Only muffled, horrible, animal grunts could be heard in the room. Mercifully, the bound man soon lost consciousness.

The carnage continued nevertheless.

Methodically, the men in the line butchered their prisoner like a hog in a slaughterhouse.

Judo arrived at the loft after it was all over. "You too late, man," Yellow told him. "All the fun done through."

Judo frowned. Yellow had a curiously wasted expression on his face. Looking around the loft, Judo noticed that of the men who were still there, most of them looked the same way: as if they were

174

very weary from long hours of labor. A line of perspiration even lay across Yellow's boyish upper lip, and he did not bother to lick it off as he usually did.

The man who had passed out the weapons came up to Judo. "Since you weren't here to help with the main work, brother, we gots a little special job you can do. You don't mind helping us out, do you, brother?"

"No," Judo said. He had to force the word out.

Judo was led to the back of the loft. There, on a rolled-out tarpaulin, was a bundle that closely resembled a huge frozen turkey. It was identical in shape to a turkey: wrapped in white opaque plastic and bound with yellow plastic rope. The rope had even been fashioned into a net, just like the turkeys in the freezer at the supermarket.

"We got a dead animal we gots to get rid of, brother," said the man. " 'Preciate it if you'd throw it in the bay for us."

Judo swallowed dryly. "I don't have no car, man."

"The van's downstairs," said Yellow. "You can take that."

Judo wet his lips. Several of the men in the loft were looking at him. "Right on," he said with no enthusiasm at all. He looked at Yellow. "Give me a hand downstairs, brother," he said.

Judo and Yellow each took two corners of the tarp and lifted. The bundle rolled sideways and lay still. They carried it downstairs and out to the van. With some difficulty, they got it into the back of the van.

"That sucker be heavy," Judo said. "Come on with me and help me out, man."

"Man, I can't do it," Yellow said. "I'm late for somewhere I got to be."

"Come on, man," Judo insisted. "You owe me one for that gun shit."

Yellow's expression tightened. "Listen, brother, let me tell you something," he said with an edge, "after tonight I don't owe you a fucking thing. I been sticking up for you a lot lately, and tonight when you wasn't here on time, I put my fucking head on the block and stuck up for you against *everybody*. For a long time now I been taking your part when some of the others been putting you down. You not the most popular dude around here right now, you know what I mean? Some of the others say you think you too good for the rest of us; say you think being a Death Angel is shit. But I stick up for you, see? I say, hey, this brother, he just be *slower* than the rest of us. That's why he ain't done no stings yet. That's why his *attitude* don't seem right. That's why he wasn't here on time tonight to take part in the party." Yellow put a stiff forefinger against Judo's chest. "I been sticking up plenty for you lately, brother. And I'm the *onliest* one been doing it too. So I don't figure I owe you shit, man—for the gun or anything else!"

Yellow slammed one of the rear doors of the van and stalked away. He got into his own car and drove off the lot.

Judo stood there alone for a few minutes, staring into the darkness. *Take off, man!* his mind screamed at him. *Go on! Run! Disappear and don't never come back!*

Can't, he answered. *They know where you live, where your woman is.*

Forget her! Leave her behind.

Can't. Can't do that.

Why not?

Because I care for her.

Shit, his conscience said. Then: *Okay, baby, it's your funeral.*

Turning, Judo rolled the turkeylike bundle into a corner of the van and flipped the tarp over it. Closing the other rear door, he got into the van and drove off.

Larry Green drove away from the rear of Black Self Help and cut over to Haight Street, heading west. As he passed Octavia, a car came around the corner and began following him. The car was being driven by a black man; another black man sat beside him.

Five blocks farther along, Larry glanced in the rearview mirror and noticed the car. He kept checking it several times every block; it did not take him long to determine that it was following him.

A mile up the street, at Masonic, the black driver of the car doing the following set a portable red flasher on the dashboard and switched it on. Larry saw it at once and pulled to the curb. He got out of the car and stood by the driver's door as the two men approached him. One man remained on the passenger side of the car; the other man came up to Larry. He showed Larry an ID card.

"I'm Inspector Gilford of the police department," he said. "May I see some identification, please?"

"Yes, *sir!*" Larry produced a driver's license and a Social Security card. Gilford studied them and compared the license photo with Larry's face. He noted Larry's dress: gray sweat shirt, khaki trousers, heavy shoes. There was a yellow hard hat on the dashboard. Gilford, who had worked both the Moynihan and Hosler killings, was struck by the similarity between Larry Green and the description given of the Moynihan-Hosler killer: light-skinned Negro, about twenty-five, medium height, 135 pounds, light-colored trousers, darker shirt or jacket.

"Mr. Green, we're investigating two homicides that took place in the area just west of Market and Van Ness on Saturday night."

"Yes, *sir.* I heard about those," Larry said. He emphasized the "sir" just enough for it to be offensive.

"Do you frequent that general area?"

"Yes, *sir.* Five, sometimes six days a week. I work down there. At the Black Self Help Moving and Storage. It's over on—"

"I know where it is," Gilford said. "Mr. Green, were you in the Market–Van Ness area on Saturday night?"

Larry shook his head. "No, *sir.* Nowhere around there."

"Could you prove that?"

"If I has to."

Gilford handed Larry's ID back to him. "Mr. Green, do you consider yourself a law-abiding citizen, who cooperates with police authorities?"

"Yes, *sir,*" Larry replied.

"Would you consent to letting my partner, Inspector Sanders, and me search your vehicle?"

Larry's eyes narrowed. "If I say no, you can't do it?"

"That's correct. But then that would be very uncooperative, wouldn't it? And make us very suspicious of you."

Larry studied the expressions of the two officers. There was no warmth or humor in either face. These men were black, both of them, but they were not his kind of black. Larry decided to play it loose.

"I'm a good citizen," he said cockily. "Search it."

Gilford and Sanders conducted a thorough search of Larry

Green's automobile. They found nothing incriminating: no gun, no dope, no bloodstains, nothing. Gilford, who had a nagging suspicion about Larry, was disappointed. So was Sanders, who almost *smelled* murder on the young Muslim. Something told them both that this light-skinned kid was dirty. Neither of them knew *how* he was dirty—but he *was* dirty.

There was no way to prove it that night, however.

"Okay, Mr. Green, you're free to go," Sanders said when the search was over. "Sorry to have troubled you. Thank you for your cooperation."

"Yes, *sir*," Larry said one final time. Both officers felt like slapping the "sir" right out of his mouth.

Larry got back into his car and drove away.

As Sanders and Gilford watched him go, their nagging suspicion about him seemed to increase. As if perhaps they had turned a poisonous reptile loose.

Judo drove out to the edge of Sutro Heights and parked facing the ocean. It was late now and very cold this close to the sea. Judo shivered as he sat in the dark van and looked around fearfully for anyone who might be watching him. He could see no one—but, he guessed, he really should not expect to; anyone with even half-sense would be inside where it was warm, doing last-minute things getting ready for Christmas. Not sitting up on an ocean bluff in the cold with a bundle of—

Judo shivered almost spastically as he thought of the *thing* on the cargo deck behind him. God only knew what it was: parts of a man, a woman, a couple of kids—

It suddenly occurred to him that he had just thought the word "God" instead of Allah. And a moment earlier he had thought about Christmas. Both the deity and the day and everything they represented were Christian; as a Muslim he had no business thinking about either. But in times of stress, his mind and thoughts always seemed to revert to what came naturally. And that was God, not Allah.

Judo took a deep breath. Got to get my shit together, he thought. *I am a Muslim*. I may not be a fucking *Death Angel*, but I *am* a Muslim. And I got to start *acting* like one. I gots to be strong and

178

resolute, like the Prophet Elijah say to be. Got to get my head right and my heart right. I know I can straighten out if I can just take that first big step—

First big step *you* better take, asshole, is to get that bundle taken care of, he told himself rudely. Some honky cop liable to come up on you any minute just sitting here like this.

Right. Judo turned up his collar and got out of the van. He opened the rear doors and dragged the bundle over to him. It was a heavy sucker, he realized as he lifted it by himself for the first time, a lot heavier than he thought it was the first time he had commented on its weight. That time, standing with Yellow back on the lot, he had said it mainly to try and get Yellow to come with him to dispose of it. Now he was finding out just how heavy it really was.

He rolled it slightly to pull loose the corners of the tarp. With the four corners pulled up tautly, Judo twisted them together. Then he turned around and edged one shoulder under it. He bent over and lifted, feeling the bundle come off the cargo deck and fall against his back. He grunted as the full weight of it pulled on his shoulder. *Heavy sucker—*

Mustering all his strength, Judo carried the bundle out past the safety barrier to a section of cliff that dropped precipitously to the water below. By the time he got to the edge, he was perspiring heavily and the cold wind from the sea was giving him a threatening chill. *Just a few more steps,* he told himself.

When he was at a place he considered suitable, Judo turned so that the bundle was toward the sea. All he had to do now was release two corners of the tarp and the turkey-looking package would roll down a slight embankment and fall directly into the sea.

But it did not work out that way.

As Judo tried to let go of two corners, he felt all four of them slipping from his grip. The weight of the bundle—easily in excess of a hundred pounds—dragged over his shoulder like an anvil, almost as if it were trying to pull him into the sea with it. Judo let out a terrified gasp as he momentarily lost his balance and thought he was going to go over the embankment backward. It was during the split second that it took him to regain his equilibrium that he let go of the bundle entirely. It dropped to the embankment, rolled down—taking the tarpaulin with it, rolling itself up in it as it gained momentum—and finally pitched over the edge and fell into the sea.

Over, Judo thought, panting. *Over and done with. Won't nobody ever find the sucker now—*

Ten hours later, on Christmas Eve morning, two miles south of where Judo let the bundle fall into the sea, two young women, Dorene Racouillat and Sara Scott, were walking Dorene's dog on the beach at the foot of Pacheco Street. They found the bundle washed up on the beach. The yellow twine, fashioned into a net, had held during the bundle's roll down the embankment, subsequent plunge into the sea, and tumultuous journey down two miles of rocky, sandy coastline; but the tarpaulin had folded away in places and there were tears and rips in the plastic. One such rip was triangular, about four inches in length along each side. Through the hole, the two young women could see the unmistakable sight of hairy human flesh with a streak of matted blood across it.

The police were called. Officers John Hanifin and Max Schenk responded. As soon as they saw what the bundle contained, they summoned the various persons who were required at the scene: Lieutenant Mikulik and Sergeant O'Connor, to take charge of the physical area; Hicks of the Photo Lab to take the gory pictures; Jackson of the Crime Lab to look for physical evidence; Armstrong and McKenna of Homicide; and Dr. Jindrich of the coroner's office to pronounce the victim dead. The latter was only a formality.

The bundle was eventually moved downtown to the coroner's office. More gory photographs were taken. Then the morgue attendants began the worst job of all: the unwrapping of the bundle. What they found was ghastly.

The body was without head, hands, or feet. The head had been severed at the base of the neck, the hands just above the wristbone, the feet just above the ankles. Both arms were held in place at the sides of the torso by wire. The knees had been drawn up to the chest and also bound in place by wire. The lower abdomen had been cut open from hipbone to hipbone; intestines and other internal organs had spilled forth from the gaping wound. It was a sight that even the most hardened morgue attendant would remember for a long time to come.

There was no way to identify the body: no marks,scars, tattoos, or anything else that might offer a clue. And of course no latent prints, dental work, or anything of that nature—not unless the other parts of the body were found. Or unless a missing persons report turned up, or someone came forward who would recognize what there was of the remains.

In the interim, the body was listed as John Doe #169.

At the end of Day Sixty-five, there were thirteen victims.

Quita Hague, hacked to death.

Richard Hague, his face butchered.

Ellen Linder, raped, ravaged, threatened with death.

Frances Rose, shot in the face at close range.

Saleem Erakat, tied up and executed.

Paul Dancik, shot down as he attempted to use a public telephone.

Arthur Agnos, surviving, after having his lungs, spleen, and kidney ripped apart by bullets.

Marietta DiGirolamo, thrown into a doorway and shot to death as she walked down the street.

Ilario Bertuccio, gunned down in the street as he walked home from work with a bottle of 7-Up under his arm.

Angela Roselli, surviving but seriously injured after being shot down in the street as she was returning home from a Christmas party.

Neal Moynihan, shot down in the street on his way home with a Teddy bear for his little sister.

Mildred Hosler, shot down in the street as she walked toward her bus stop.

And John Doe #169, kidnapped, horribly tortured, decapitated, his hands and feet butchered off, bundled up like a turkey, and thrown into the sea.

Day 101

Between Christmas and New Year's, victim number seven visited victim number ten in the hospital.

Angela Roselli was lying in her hospital bed, bored to distraction. For a person who had as little interest in a full and active life as Angela appeared to have, one would have thought that confinement to a hospital room would have suited her just fine. It did not. The mainstay of hospital patients was daytime TV and reading. Angela did not care for the former and detested the latter. She had been raised in a Catholic household and attended parochial schools where the nuns insisted on students maintaining a high level of reading proficiency. Angela had grown to hate reading at a very early age. When she grew to adulthood, she chose almost never to read. Most times it would not have mattered to her whether she even knew *how* to read. If she had been able to transfer her reading ability to, say, Manuel Moore, she probably would not have missed it at all.

From her hospital bed, she looked up to see a smiling, olive-complexioned man in the doorway. "Are you Angela Roselli?" he asked.

"Yes. Who are you?"

He came in, smiling more broadly, walking as if he might have a sprained ankle or a hernia. "I'm Art Agnos," he said. "I understand that we belong to the same club."

Angela frowned. "I don't understand."

"According to the police, we were both shot with the same gun. Maybe even by the same guy."

"Oh, yeah," she said in sudden comprehension. "You're the fellow who was shot in the Potrero Hill district a few weeks ago."

"That's me. How are you getting along?"

Her expression did not change. "Not too hot," she replied in the same neutral tone she used whether talking of friend or foe, right or wrong, life or death. "My spine is damaged. They think I will be able to walk again, but nobody will say how long it will take. I'll have to have a couple of operations first, I guess. How are you?"

"Surprisingly well, considering. They removed my spleen, but everything else is in place and functioning. Kidneys seem to be okay. And they got the bullet out of my lung."

"I had a lung wound too," Angela said. "In fact, I had a collapsed lung."

"That's always an experience," Agnos said wryly. "Much pain?"

"Not as long as they kept the morphine coming."

"How about now: you have pain anywhere else?"

"Oh, sure. Knife-slicing pains in my legs all the time. I'm still on the morphine."

"Have they told you how long you'll be in here?"

"I'm going to be transferred to Kaiser Hospital pretty soon. I don't know how long I'll be there. Quite a while, probably."

Agnos nodded. "Well, it could be worse, I guess. We could both be dead."

"That's right. I guess we belong to a second club too. A pretty exclusive one. The survivors' club."

"That's for sure."

A silence came over them for a moment as they both thought of the people they knew of who had not been as lucky as they. Their eyes met and held. They could not help wondering how many others would become members of the two clubs.

How many more victims?
How many more survivors?

At the state capital in Sacramento, plans were being made in the Division of Law Enforcement, California Department of Justice, to conduct an interpolice department meeting as early as possible for the purpose of establishing a task force to investigate an ongoing series of execution-type killings throughout the state. For the purpose of obtaining budgetary approval of the plan, a presentation was being made to department heads by Richard Walley from the Intelligence Analysis Unit, a group whose purpose was to correlate and cross-reference all known criminal activity throughout the state.

"Gentlemen," said Walley, "as of last Friday there have been sixty-four execution-type murders in California during the past three calendar years. That figure is up forty-two percent since the last quarter, when the total was forty-five—an indication that the incidents are rapidly increasing. All of the victims of these incidents have been killed by shooting at close range, or by hacking with a machete or meat cleaver. The incidents have occurred primarily in San Francisco and the East Bay area of Oakland and Berkeley, as well as in the Los Angeles and Long Beach areas in the southern part of the state. They are not exclusively limited to these metropolitan areas, however; there have also been incidents in the counties of Ventura, Santa Barbara, and San Diego. The victims in these crimes have been exclusively white. The suspects, as described and identified by witnesses and survivors, have been exclusively black.

"A large majority of the known suspects identified in these homicides have been found to be Black Muslims. There is widespread speculation among law enforcement personnel—including black police officers—that the homicides were committed as an initiation to a select group of Muslims. There is also a considerable depth of feeling that the homicides are sparked by teachings in the Muslim religion which are presented in such a manner as to incite hatred against Caucasians. The feeling is that mentally deranged or inferior blacks, upon being taught these doctrines, then go out and act them out in real life.

"It is being proposed that this bureau establish a central repository for all information pertaining to homicides with the following *modus operandi*: hackings, unprovoked street attacks, hitchhike kidnappings; all unexplained homicides of a similar nature, and all black-perpetrator/white-victim homicides.

"In addition, it is proposed that a meeting be held with representatives of all involved law enforcement agencies to discuss the formation of a task force for mutual investigation and cooperation in the termination of this statewide criminal activity."

At the end of the presentation, several questions were asked and answered. After brief discussion, the budgetary item was approved.

The meeting, which was to involve twenty-five police and sheriffs' departments, was scheduled to take place in Oakland, one of the cities most affected by the type of homicide being studied.

The sometimes slow, but always methodical, gears of the criminal justice system had begun to grind.

On January 2, 1974, in a posh private club on the South Side of Chicago, five black men met for lunch. Well-dressed, affluent-looking, quiet and mannerly, they sat at a round table laid with crisp linen, shining silver, sparkling crystal. The table was in a room to itself. After the main course was served, the waiter closed the door behind him as he left; he would return only when signaled to do so by one of the men opening the door from within. The five men were always accorded such privacy; it was understood that the topics they discussed over their meals required it.

"I received word this morning that a problem may be developing at Temple Number Twenty-six in San Francisco," said one of the men, who was an attorney.

"What sort of problem?" asked another, who was an administrator.

"I'm not sure exactly. There have been a number of random street killings there recently—all white victims. The suspects have all been black—"

"Naturally," a third man interjected. He was a public relations man.

The lawyer smiled briefly. "In this case, the suspicions seem to

185

be well-founded. Apparently a number of survivors and witnesses have described the assailants, and in every case it was a black man."

"Have they caught anyone yet?" asked a fourth man at the table, an accountant.

"No. But apparently the police have determined that all or most of the killings have been done with the same gun."

"What has this to do with Temple Number Twenty-six?" the administrator asked.

"They inquired about stopping what they term unnecessary police patrols in the immediate neighborhood of the mosque. From what I gather, the police have put extra units on the streets between dusk and dawn, and some of the executives of the mosque feel that this is harassment of some kind, that it may be discouraging members from attending services and meetings."

"Are the police engaging in actual surveillance of the temple?" the public relations man asked. "Because if they are, we can put a stop to that, can't we?"

"Yes, we could definitely put a stop to it—if we could prove they were doing it. Putting a place of religious worship under police surveillance is a serious matter, constitutionally speaking. In this case, however, I don't think they are. We have three men in the San Francisco Police Department—practicing Muslims—who cooperate with us when they can without compromising their jobs. One of them checked into this for us and couldn't find any formal surveilling going on around the mosque. I would imagine that the elders of Temple Number Twenty-six are just running scared."

"Do we have any idea who these street killers are?" asked the accountant in a morbidly curious voice. The thought of blacks killing whites obviously intrigued him.

The lawyer shrugged. "Not really. There's a great deal of speculation at the mosque, of course. Some of the board seem to think that they may be maverick Fruit of Islam members."

"That's a bit farfetched," the public relations man said derisively. "The Fruit of Islam keeps a very tight check on its people. We've worked for years to overcome their ex-convict, gun-carrying, robotlike image. I can't see them letting it all go down the tubes at the hands of a few dissident members. I think they'd put a stop to it themselves."

"I agree," said the administrator. "Besides, Fruit of Islam men would concentrate on policemen, bill collectors, loan sharks, white tricks out looking for black women—that sort of thing. Didn't you say these were random killings?"

"Yes."

The public relations man shook his head slowly. "Probably some poor, insecure misfits heard one of our more fiery sermons, misinterpreted it, and went out to do what he thought was Allah's work."

"Or heard one of our more fiery sermons and did *not* misinterpret it," the accountant said. "Some of our sermons have been known to be pretty specific in calling the white man a grafted snake. We all know that some of the things said from our pulpits can be pretty, ah—stimulating, shall we say."

"We also know," said the public relations man, "that some of these poor black fools who resort to violence are encouraged from other quarters as well."

All heads turned and looked at the fifth man at the table. He had said nothing throughout the entire conversation, merely listened, nodded, raised his eyebrows occasionally, and continued eating. Now he paused in his meal and used a linen napkin to wipe the neat Vandyke that surrounded his mouth. He smiled tolerantly as he addressed himself to the public relations man's pointed comment.

"We all have our own way of accomplishing our goals for Allah, my brother," he said firmly but without rancor. "Who is to say which of us is right and which of us is wrong? Only Allah Himself, I think."

"That is a very narrow view," the public relations man replied with an edge. "The Nation's purpose is to *raise* the lot of American blacks, not reduce them to jungle animals."

"A child must crawl before it can walk upright," said Vandyke.

"Very sage, I'm sure. But hardly an excuse for murder."

The accountant interjected a quick, "Right on," and added, "I couldn't agree more. It's time we realized that this is a business, not a terrorist group."

"I'll second that," said the lawyer. "Let's start emphasizing respect for the law, whether it's the white man's law or El Allah's law. Criminal disobedience won't get us anywhere."

"Neither will subservience," countered Vandyke.

"All right, all right," said the administrator with a chuckle. "Let's not beat a dead horse, gentlemen. We all know that it isn't for us to decide anyway. Policy is the Master's prerogative." He patted his ample belly. "Someone open the door so we can order dessert."

Arnold George Lucas* went into a combination bar-poolroom on Seventh Street and slid onto a stool. "Gimme a Coke and some sugar, Max," he said to the bartender.

Max, a burly black ex-wrestler, put a Coca-Cola and a shaker of sugar on the bar. Arnold laid down a fifty-cent piece.

"Keep the change," he said.

"Gee, a whole fifteen cents," said Max. "Maybe I'll take the afternoon off."

Smartass, thought Arnold as Max moved down the bar. If there's one thing I don't need today, it's a smartass.

Arnold drank a third of the Coke, then poured an ample amount of sugar into it. Holding his thumb over the top, he shook it up, then drank about half of it.

Arnold was a twenty-one-year-old black man, tall, with a natural Afro, an engaging personality, and an eighty-dollar-a-day heroin habit. He was drinking sugar and Coke to give him a much needed blast of energy to go out and pull his daily burglaries to support his habit. Normally in a better frame of mind, he was depressed this particular morning because it was cloudy and looked like rain. Arnold did not like rain.

"Hey, baby," said one of the black pool players. "I see where City High lost another fucking game last night. Don't those boys know they supposed to throw the ball *through* the hoop? Not just hit the rim? They ain't had no team at all since you graduated."

"You got that right," Arnold said. He had been all-city his last two years of high school. All-city, and in the running for half a dozen college scholarships, and maybe—just maybe—a future shot at pro basketball.

Then for kicks one night he tried heroin.

---

*This individual's name and identity have been altered. To identify him accurately could possibly jeopardize his life.

Now Arnold was a street thief and burglar, supporting a monkey that ate nearly twenty-five hundred dollars' worth of shit every month.

Arnold had been arrested the first time at the age of nineteen. The charge was trespass. He had been casing a house he intended to burglarize, but had not begun an entry. At the time he was caught, he had a stolen car parked nearby with a set of burglar tools in the trunk.

In the two years following that incident, Arnold had subsequent arrests for auto theft, burglary and auto theft combined, and burglary alone. He was in and out of jail in San Francisco almost as frequently as Manuel Moore had been in San Bernardino. His life was a vicious, merciless circle revolving around his need for heroin. Even at that moment he was facing a burglary charge for which he was out on bond. His trial was set for the following month.

Finishing his Coke and sugar, Arnold waved at Max, who did not wave back, and walked out into the dull, cloudy day. Looking up at the sky, he hoped it would not rain. He hated climbing in and out of windows when the sills were wet.

Skullcap paced the apartment, his face a mask of inner torment and frustration. Why, why, *why* did everything have to go wrong in his life? Why did *nothing* ever conclude the way he thought it would, the way it was projected, predicted? He had been a party to six stings—*six!* Yet he had only one—Saleem Erakat—to his credit. Rims had been on only five, and he had *three* stings to his credit: two male devils, one female. Even Yellow was ahead of him. Yellow had been on three stings and had credit for three: two female devils, one male. All told, including Head's sting, their little group had eight—and he personally had only *one* of those.

And I'm the one who wanted to be a Death Angels' lieutenant, he thought bitterly. Shit. Some lieutenant. Can't even keep up with the privates. The only person he was ahead of in stings was that motherfucker Judo—and that was only because Judo had *nothing* to *his* credit. That was the most galling realization of all: he shared the bottom of the ladder with a man who had no heart.

Allah, Allah, Allah, where have I gone wrong? he asked—not as

189

much directing his question to a deity as to himself. Skullcap was really not that religious; he just wanted to *be* somebody, *in* something: he wanted respect, attention, approval, even envy if he could inspire it. He cared little which group he used to achieve his status; had he been white, he probably would have joined the Ku Klux Klan. So when he used the word "Allah" he did not use it as Yellow did, fervently, frantically; rather he used it as he did "man" or "motherfucker." As a figure of speech only.

Still, Skullcap was superstitious enough about religion to hope for some divine intervention, whether luck or whatever, to put him on the right path to the fame and glory he so yearned for. He desperately wanted a *sign* of some kind, something to show him which way to go next.

He thought he found that sign one day early in January of 1974 when, frustrated and depressed about the lack of progress in his life, he opened a letter he received in the mail and found it to be a contribution solicitation from the main mosque in New Mecca. Skullcap read it briefly; he had no intention of sending them any money. But there was something about the solicitation that intrigued him: the picture of the Chicago mosque on the pamphlet enclosed with the letter.

He sat and stared at that picture for a long time. New Mecca, he thought. Where it was *at*. Where everything was done, planned, approved, made to happen. Where the Muslim newspaper, *Muhammad Speaks*, was written, printed, distributed. Where the great Muslim ministers made pilgrimages to see the face of Elijah Muhammad and hear the voice of Allah spoken through his holy mouth.

New Mecca. Where, Skullcap thought craftily, if a man played his cards just right, saw the right man, made himself known in just the right way, he might *still* work his way into something.

But was it worth the gamble? he wondered. Worth the time, the expense? He would be taking a big chance, maybe all for nothing.

Putting the letter down, Skullcap crossed the room and looked at himself in a mirror. He kept his face cool, hard, unsmiling. He studied his countenance. After a moment, he nodded.

No question about it: he *looked* like a Death Angels' lieutenant.

That made up his mind.

He would go to New Mecca.

* * *

On a Monday night in mid-January, Arthur Agnos returned to the Potrero Hill district. He came back to attend a meeting to elect board members of the group attempting to obtain a new neighborhood health clinic.

When Agnos parked his car down the block from the meeting place, he noticed four husky blacks standing in front of a nearby building. Easy now, he told himself. What happened before was a once-in-a-lifetime experience. Just because a black shit you, doesn't mean that every black in San Francisco is out to get you. Just relax.

As casually as possible, Agnos got out of his car, locked it, and started up the block. As he did, the four blacks came across the street toward him. Agnos felt a sudden urge to run—but he quickly put it down. He was a reasonable man; he told himself that such an urge was foolish. But he could not help remembering the punchlike feeling of the bullets entering his back, could not help remembering the pain of the ensuing weeks as his damaged body healed.

Even with those memories, however, Agnos knew he would not run.

He stopped and waited for the four blacks to walk up to him.

"Mr. Agnos," one of them said, "we're your escort."

"My escort?"

"That's right. We're going to walk around with you tonight. We want to show anybody who's looking that when you come into this neighborhood, you come as a friend. And that nobody better *ever* mess with you again. That okay with you?"

Agnos shrugged. "If you think it's necessary."

"We think it is," the black man said. "The hate has got to stop someplace. Maybe this will be the place."

Agnos nodded slowly. "Maybe it will."

The white man and his four black friends walked down the street together.

Skullcap felt like a million dollars as he strutted down the concourse to board the big TWA jet for Chicago. He had never flown before but he was not in the least nervous. This was *living*. He had on his best suit, cleaned and pressed; his shoes were shined; he was wearing a new shirt and tie: in all, he looked as good—or—better than any of the Fruit of Islam members who were supposed to be such hot shit. Add to it that he was carrying a brand-new vinyl briefcase, and he guessed that he really must look good.

"Hello," said the stewardess as she took his boarding pass and tore off the seating stub for him. "Seat 17-B," she added, then turned to the next passenger.

Skullcap followed the other passengers down the aisle. He went too far and another stewardess had to direct him back to the proper row. Then he sat in the wrong seat, the window seat, and had to be asked to move into the middle.

It took a moment for Skullcap to realize that he was going to be sitting between two white men for the entire flight. He had not known that the seating configuration was three and three, and it had not even occurred to him to consider who his seating companion—or companions—might be. All he had been able to think about was that at last he was on his way to New Mecca, on his way to *being* somebody. He had been given a sign and he was on his way. It did not matter that he was going uninvited and would arrive unexpected, that it was costing him all of the little money he had saved and all he could borrow, that, basically, he was going to the main mosque to try and get credit—and a position of authority—for the collective accomplishments of others. It did not even matter that he was not a devout believer in the Nation of Islam, that almost any group or organization could have substituted for it. All that mattered was that he was *going.*

And if he had to sit squeezed between two white devils for the entire flight, so be it. Skullcap smiled to himself. There was one amusing consolation to it. The two white devils would certainly be shocked if they could see the contents of his briefcase. It contained color photographs of white devils who had been stung.

In the San Francisco area that January of 1974, five diverse people, none of whom knew each other, were carrying on their respective lives.

Tana Smith, age thirty-two, was living alone in her neat little apartment at 2908 California Street, and working as a secretary in the Scientific Development Division of the Bechtel Corporation. Tana—who pronounced her name Tay-na—had been feeling extra good lately. For a long time she had been plagued with a weight problem; extra desserts, an extra drink now and then, had taken their toll on her naturally *un*slim young figure, and before she knew it she was far too heavy and felt unattractive, dumpy. But a concentrated effort on her part over some long, difficult months had brought her to the point where she could skip that dessert and decline not only the extra drink but the first one also. She had slimmed down almost to her normal weight again and was feeling good, looking good. It was a pleasure these mornings to look at herself in the mirror and not think: Oh, God! Now, as she parted her brown hair in the middle and brushed a shine to it, she often saw a smile on her pert, pixielike face.

Now that she was not brooding about her weight any longer, Tana was making happy plans. She was going to plan a visit to see her mother and stepfather in Florida. She was going to moonlight again as an usherette at the Opera House; she dearly loved the opera. She was going to buy some material and start making clothes again; she was a marvelous seamstress and thoroughly enjoyed sewing.

In short, Tana Smith intended to start enjoying life again. Enjoying it with zest and vigor.

Fifteen city blocks away from Tana Smith, at 709 Scott Street, lived Vincent Wollin. A craggy-faced, amiable man of sixty-eight, Wollin was a retired Coast Guardsman and, later, cabinetmaker. He lived in a small, private boardinghouse with six other men and one woman. His pleasures in life were simple: every day he rode the bus to St. Vincent de Paul's recreation room, where he played dominoes and shot pool with anyone who happened to be around. Later, he would go have coffee and doughnuts somewhere. Except for the evening meal at the boardinghouse, Wollin practically lived on coffee and doughnuts, a diet he not only was very fond of, but which fit very nicely into his retirement budget. After he ate, Wollin often walked over to City Hall and sat for a while feeding the pigeons.

As far as Vincent Wollin was concerned, he had a good life. He was a solitary man but not lonely, lived modestly but not uncomfortably, and, as he approached his sixty-ninth birthday later in the month, was healthy, active, spry, and full of the capacity to enjoy life thoroughly in his retirement years. He had known some men who were almost driven crazy by the relative inactivity of retirement. But not he. Vincent Wollin liked it. He hoped he lived twenty more years.

Two miles from where Vincent Wollin lived, a man fifteen years his senior had a small room. His name was John Bambic and he lived alone in a lower-class, semicommercial neighborhood. He was a toothless old man with tufts of wispy white hair growing far back on his head. He had the watery, rheumy eyes and dottering lower jaw of the very old, but he was an unusually strong man for his age, and he appeared husky in the layers of clothes he wore—undershirt, shirt, sweater, coat, overcoat—so that none of the punks who hung out on South Ninth Street ever bothered him.

Bambic was strictly a loner. As with so many San Franciscans, no one knew where he came from, what he had been earlier in life, or what, if anything, he was hiding from. He kept totally to himself, spoke to no one unless spoken to first, and never engaged in personal discussions of any kind. He dressed shabbily in clothes that looked as worn as his aged face, and supplemented his Social Security income by prowling in trash bins for anything of meager worth that might bring him twenty-five or fifty cents: a stack of discarded but still current magazines, empty bottles that had deposits on them, still serviceable wearing apparel that some wino might buy, anything. A lot of people considered John Bambic a derelict and would have nothing to do with him. But he had something most people did not: complete independence and freedom. Which he obviously valued very highly.

Another person in San Francisco at that time who valued independence was a woman named Jane Holly. At the age of forty-five, Jane had worked long and hard, with her husband George, to reach a plateau in life where they owed nothing to anyone. One of fourteen children born to a St. Louis family during the Depression, Jane could well remember when times were hard: when money was short, food was rationed to the plate, clothes were mended and remended. In a family that large, it was a case of constantly making do.

But that was all past for Jane Holly. She had worked for Wells Fargo Bank for fifteen years; George had been a Gray Line tour guide for the same length of time. They were not burdened with a large family: their one son, Stephen, was grown and gone: at twenty-three, he was in the army, stationed at Fort Sill, Oklahoma, married to a lovely girl named Paula Louise. What Jane and George earned now, they could spend on themselves exclusively.

Jane Holly looked forward to her middle years, looked forward to the comfort they would bring. She delighted in making plans for the future: things to do, things to buy, places to go. Her joy when she shared those plans with someone was total—and always emphasized by a bright, infectious smile. In January she was already making plans for the celebration of their twenty-fifth wedding anniversary. It was not until April 3, more than two months away, but that did not matter to Jane. The earlier she started planning, the more fun it was.

The last of the five people was a young woman named Roxanne McMillian. A quite pretty Sally Struthers type, twenty-three years old, Roxanne was one of eleven children born to the Schumacher family, formerly of South Dakota. She was married to Alan John McMillian and they were the parents of a new baby boy, Leon, born three months earlier. For a while they had been buying a small home in Cupertino, some fifty miles south of San Francisco, but recently they had found a purchaser for it and were in the final stages of selling it. John, as Roxanne called her husband, had found a job as a shoe salesman and the little family was moving up to the city. They did not have a place to live yet, but John was looking for one every day.

Roxanne hoped that her husband would find a nice place for them to live. She had liked the little home they owned in Cupertino; it was a shame they could not keep it. But there were no employment opportunities for John that far away from the city, and it took too long and was too expensive to commute. Anyway, they would be better off without a big mortgage payment hanging over their heads. In an apartment, they would not have the upkeep of a house and all the attendant expenses. They would be able to budget themselves better, which was important now that they had a baby.

Still, Roxanne hoped that John would find them a nice place. It was not going to be easy adjusting to life in the city. A pleasant apartment could make all the difference in the world.

So Roxanne McMillian waited to see what the end of January would bring. And life went on for her, and for Jane Holly, for John Bambic, for Vincent Wollin, and for Tana Smith.

Five diverse people, scattered about the Bay Area like trees in a big forest, with nothing in common *except* the forest, and nothing to draw the paths of their lives together except fate and tragedy.

At the mosque in Chicago, Skullcap was being shuttled from one person to the next because no one could figure out exactly who or what he wanted, and Skullcap was not about to come right out and say—not unless he was certain he was talking to the proper person.

"Perhaps if you could tell me who in our San Francisco Mosque sent you?" one of the male secretaries asked.

"I told you, *nobody* sent me," Skullcap replied impatiently. "I have come on my own to see the person in charge of promotions."

"What kind of promotions?"

"Promotions to lieutenant."

The secretary frowned. He was a very light young Negro, lighter even than Yellow. "Lieutenant of *what*?" he asked in growing irritation. Skullcap did not answer. The secretary rolled his eyes toward the ceiling. "Look, I cannot keep sending you to every executive in the place," he warned. "You've already been to our membership director and to our special organizations director. Both of them sent you back to me because they couldn't figure out what you were talking about or what you wanted. I can't figure it out either. Now I'm afraid if you can't state *specifically* what your business is, you'll just have to leave."

"Let me see the Honorable Elijah Muhammad then," Skullcap demanded.

"That is quite impossible," the secretary replied, aghast. "His Excellency grants audiences only on very special occasions."

"This *is* a special occasion," said Skullcap.

"Oh? And what precisely is special about it?"

Skullcap leaned across the desk and lowered his voice. "It involves the deaths of a number of grafted snakes."

The secretary looked at Skullcap as if he were insane. He shook his head emphatically. "I'm sorry, but I'm afraid I couldn't possibly request an audience for you. Perhaps if you wrote us a letter—"

"Letter! Letter! I come all this way and you tell me to write a letter!" He began to tremble in anger, and pointed a threatening finger at the light-skinned young Negro. "You will be sorry for this! Hear me? You will be *sorry!*"

Skullcap turned and stalked away from the desk and out of the building. Without regard to traffic—fortunately there was none— he strode across the street and whirled back around to glare at the mosque from the opposite sidewalk. He did not know how long he stood there before he heard a familiar voice.

"Having some trouble, are you?"

Skullcap looked around and saw the man with the Vandyke beard.

"There's a coffee shop up the street," Vandyke said. "Come along and I'll buy you something to eat. We can talk."

Two hours later, Skullcap was on a city bus riding back to O'Hare. His briefcase was on his knees, empty. His plane ticket was in his pocket, a return reservation confirmed by Vandyke from the pay phone in the coffee shop. There was an expression of confusion and disappointment on Skullcap's dark face. He was returning to San Francisco with the same status he had when he left: simply a candidate for Death Angel wings—no more, no less.

"I certainly admire your spirit in making the long journey to New Mecca on your own initiative," Vandyke had told him. They had been sitting in a quiet, isolated rear booth. "I must say, however, that I wish you had waited until my next visit to your area and had consulted me about it. I could have counseled you there in San Francisco; after all, that is my job. We could have saved you the plane fare and the trouble of, ah—*borrowing* these photographs. Incidentally, I want you to leave these with me, if you don't mind. Since no one knows you borrowed them, it won't matter, will it? No, of course it won't.

"Now, then, about this proposal of yours that you be promoted to the rank of lieutenant among the Death Angels' candidates— well, I'm afraid it simply cannot be done. In the first place, no such rank exists; all Death Angel candidates have equal status until their respective wings are earned. Secondly, I'm sure you realize that if such a rank *did* exist, it would have to be awarded to the brother among the candidates who was at the forefront of the others: the brother who was setting the best example, who was leading the way: the brother who was serving as an inspiration to the others. That brother, I'm afraid, would not be you, my boy. From what you've told me, you appear to personally have had very bad luck in your quest for Death Angels' wings. I know how great your desire is to lead, and I commend you for it: to want to lead is a noble ambition. But for now I would have to counsel you to first achieve your wings; first show everyone that you can do what is *basically* required of you. *Then* show that you can move to the forefront as a leader.'' Vandyke had looked down at the photographs and accompanying newspaper clippings. ''This is simply not enough, my boy,'' he added quietly. ''More will have to be done. Much, much more.''

On the bus going back to the airport, Skullcap reheard the words over and over in his head. *More will have to be done.* Sitting in the back of the bus, the empty briefcase on his knees, his expression gradually changed from confusion and disappointment to depression, and then—as he reviewed Vandyke's counsel—to anger. *More will have to be done.*

All right, he finally told himself. If that is how it must be, then that is how it *will* be. More *will* be done.

Grimly, he stared into space. And he thought: The streets of San Francisco be soon run with blood.

Arnold Lucas sat slumped down behind the wheel of an old jalopy on the parking lot of the Hall of Justice. He had the rearview mirror adjusted to that he could see any car that pulled onto the lot, and the sideview mirror adjusted so that he could see anyone approaching his car on foot. His junkie eyes kept darting from mirror to mirror. He was waiting for two dudes who wanted to buy some guns.

Arnold frequently sold burglarized merchandise from his car to people whom he had meet him on the Hall of Justice parking lot. That particular place was as safe as any he had ever found. Hundreds of creepy, suspicious-looking people paraded there every day: to go to court, to visit the jail, to give statements to the police, to meet lawyers or bail bondsmen. Hundreds of people—all of them weird in one way or another. No one was likely to notice a few more weird ones.

198

Besides, Arnold never stayed on the lot very long. Because he had a heavy drug habit—he shot four dime bags of heroin, at ten dollars a bag, twice every twenty-four hours—he rarely had the time or the patience to haggle about price. If it was four o'clock and he had to connect for his shit and fix himself by five, he would take fifty dollars for a color TV when he might have been able to get a hundred.

Most people who bought from Arnold knew about his eighty-dollar-a-day habit and thought he was an asshole. They cheated him any way they could. It was a common joke in the South of Mission District that Arnold would have sold his sister any afternoon for fifty bucks, but if you wanted to wait until evening when he was in a hurry, you could get her for ten.

Sitting on the lot now, his eyes darting from mirror to mirror, he mentally inventoried the guns he had for sale. There were two Saturday night specials, neat, little, chrome-plated .22-caliber revolvers; one .25-caliber automatic; and two .38 snub-nosed pieces that the street people called "bulldogs." And one he almost forgot about: a .32 Beretta automatic. Most of the weapons he had stolen in various apartment and store burglaries; the Beretta he had bought from a guy for thirty bucks, knowing he could turn a fair profit on it.

Arnold's eyes flicked to the rearview mirror as a black Cadillac pulled onto the lot. It parked nearby and two black men got out and walked toward him. One of them had droopy eyes and was wearing a scarred brown-and-yellow warm-up jacket whose school colors Arnold vaguely remembered. Arnold had known Droopy Eyes for a number of years; in the past six months he had sold him three .32-caliber pistols, one .38, and one .357 Magnum.

Arnold did not recognize the second man; he was tall and lean, and he walked with a slight swagger, a hint of a strut. His expression was ordinary enough, but there was something distinctly dangerous about his eyes. A bad dude, Arnold thought.

"Greetings, brother," his friend said as the two men walked up to the car.

"What you in the market for?" Arnold asked without preliminary. He did not go for that "Greetings, brother" shit. As far as he was concerned, the fucking Muslims were all crazy. Didn't smoke pot, didn't shoot H, didn't bang white cunt. Crazy.

"We want to buy a lightweight piece," his friend said.

"I got a couple of twenty-twos, a twenty-five, and a thirty-two," Arnold told him.

"Are the twenty-twos automatics?"

Arnold shook his head. "Revolvers. The twenty-five and the thirty-two are automatics."

"Let's see them."

Arnold opened the trunk and let the two men examine the pistols while he kept a close watch on any movement on the lot.

"How much for the thirty-two?" his friend asked.

That was the one Arnold had bought from a guy for thirty dollars. "Fifty-five," he said without hesitation. "It's a nice cold piece; couldn't be traced in a million years."

The friend looked at the other man with him. The other man shrugged, embarrassed. "All's I got is forty."

"I'll lend you the other fifteen, brother. You want the piece?"

"Yeah, man."

"Then I'll lend you the other fifteen."

"Hey, thanks, brother. I won't forget it."

"We'll take the thirty-two," Arnold's friend said to him.

The money and the gun changed hands, and the two buyers walked quickly back to the black Cadillac. Arnold put the fifty-five dollars with forty-five more he already had, making an even hundred. He drove off the lot, figuring five dollars for a meal, five dollars toward his past due rent, and eighty dollars for his fixes. That left him with a ten-dollar head start toward tomorrow's fix.

And that was about as close as Arnold George Lucas ever came to getting ahead of life.

On the night of January 28, 1974, J. C. Simon led a strutting group of black friends to the Winterland Auditorium to watch a closed circuit telecast of the second Muhammad Ali–Joe Frazier heavyweight fight. This was a return match from a bout Ali had lost in March 1971, nearly three years earlier, when he had returned to the ring after his long layoff for refusing to be drafted into the army. Joe Frazier had become champion during that time, and Ali tried to wrest the crown from him. It was a losing effort; Frazier, strong and tough, dropped him in round fifteen and won a unanimous decision. Now Frazier had lost his title to big George Foreman, and he and Ali were matched in a twelve-round return bout billed for the American Heavyweight Title. The winner would likely get a shot at Foreman for the world title.

With J.C. that night, among others, were Manuel Moore and Anthony Harris. Anthony, who had not been anywhere with his co-workers from Black Self Help since Christmas, was along this particular evening only because everyone had gone directly from work to the auditorium; the fight was starting early on the West Coast because of the three-hour time difference from Madison Square Garden, where it was taking place.

At Winterland, the group of blacks found Larry Green and several others selling the Muslim newspaper, *Muhammad Speaks*, outside the auditorium. "You brothers grab a handful and start selling," Larry said, pointing to a stack of papers up against the building.

"Sure thing," replied the affable Manuel Moore, always eager to help anyone do anything.

"No, come on, man, we going to the fight," J.C. said irritably.

"Yeah, we not down here to sell papers," said Anthony. It was one of the few times he and J.C. had ever agreed about anything.

"We're *all* going to the fight, brother," Larry replied coolly. "That don't mean we can't sell some papers for the Nation first." Larry's jaw was set, his eyes fixed. Sometimes, for one so young, he could be fiercely determined. The difference between Larry's devotion to Islam, and the devotion of J.C., Manuel, and Anthony, was clear: J.C. ran hot and cold, depending on the circumstance; Manuel was led into the faith without really understanding it; and Anthony merely *used* it, for security, friendship, acceptance; but Larry's dedication was total, fanatical, inflexible: Larry *believed*.

"Islam comes first," he said now, flatly, unyielding. "The fight comes second."

J.C. and Anthony reluctantly took a few papers and started moving through the arriving crowd, hawking. Every third or fourth black man bought a copy, maybe every tenth or twelfth white man. A lot of people—of both colors—tossed them into wastebins once they got inside.

After a few minutes, J.C. and Anthony went back to Larry and protested any further sales effort. "Come on, man, we gots to get inside. These seats ain't reserved, you know. It's catch-as-catch-can. All the good seats gonna be gone if we don't be getting in there."

Larry finally conceded. The leftover papers were locked in the trunk of somebody's car and the group of young black men hurried inside to see their idol, Muhammad Ali, adopted son of the Master, Elijah Muhammad, fight the only man who had ever beaten him. They were unanimous in their belief that Allah would guide Ali to victory.

And revenge.

Elsewhere in the city, other people were unconcerned about the Ali-Frazier fight.

Tana Smith, feeling good about her lost weight, had decided to begin making some new clothes. She told her girlfriend, Nancy Lobaugh, about her plans when she talked to her on the phone.

"I'm going to a fabric shop tonight and get some material to make a few blouses. Maybe some skirts too."

Nancy was happy for her friend; she knew about her personal problems, knew what she had gone through to get herself in shape again. She had known Tana for fourteen years, since they were college freshmen together in Kentucky. It had been Tana's fervent love of and praise for San Francisco that had convinced Nancy to move to the West Coast. Both young women had been there ever since.

After Tana finished talking to Nancy on the phone, as she was getting ready to go out she recalled a conversation that day with a co-worker.

"Aren't you afraid to go out alone at night, Tana?" the co-worker asked. "The way those niggers have been shooting white people on the street?"

"Of course not," Tana had replied in a cool tone. "And I really don't appreciate the use of the word 'nigger.' If you mean 'Negro,' please pronounce it properly."

The co-worker had been piqued at Tana. After all, Tana *was* a Southerner. But Tana Smith could not have cared less about the woman's pique. Tana was her own person. She had believed in and spoken out for the civil rights of blacks long before it became fashionable to do so. If anyone wanted to discuss blacks with her, they would do it in proper, acceptable terms. "Nigger" was not such a term.

For Vincent Wollin, January 28 had been a good day. It was his sixty-ninth birthday and he had stayed out all day to celebrate it. He had left his boardinghouse, wearing his favorite old knit watch cap from his Coast Guard days, at 9:30 that morning, and all day long he had done just exactly what he wanted to do. He had stopped for coffee and doughnuts not once but *three* times, in three different places. He had walked around downtown and looked in all the store windows. He had sat in the sunshine in Union Square and watched the people coming and going. Shot some pool with a total stranger in a pool hall south of Mission—and felt sorry for all the winos and derelicts he saw on the street down there. Thank God he wasn't in a predicament like that; thank God for his service pension and Social Security. It might not be much, but it kept him from wearing rags and sleeping in doorways at night.

As the day progressed, Vincent ambled over to St. Vincent de Paul's, as was his almost daily custom. He played dominoes with another old-timer who frequented the rec room. When he grew tired of that, he went down to City Hall to feed the pigeons. Vincent deluded himself that he could recognize certain individual birds in the flock, and that they depended on him for daily food. A few of them he called by name—names he had given them, names of men who had been his friends long ago at sea: Sam, Harry, Dutch, Cookie.

When it got on toward time for the Civic Center workers to quit for the day, Vincent caught a Van Ness bus and rode to the Wharf. He walked down to Aquatic Park and sat on a bench looking out at the bay. The winter water was sparkling from the last rays of the sun shooting under the superstructure of the regal Golden Gate Bridge. Vincent put on the tan raincoat he had carried all day, and turned up the collar against the evening chill. It had been a fine day, this sixty-ninth birthday of his. It really was not as bad growing old as some people thought. Idly, Vincent wondered how much longer he would live.

* * *

Old John Bambic started making his rounds of the trash bins about six o'clock in the evening. Most everything had been dumped by then and the winos had not yet begun their scavenging. Bambic had learned early on in the game of survival that if a man wanted to pick up anything at all of value in the area south of Mission, he had to beat the winos to the trash bins. Particularly in the wintertime, when the evenings got cool early.

Bambic usually started on Seventh around Minna or Natoma streets and worked his way up and down: up the street, down the alley, over a block, then start again at the next corner. He carried a cardboard box with him, the sturdiest one he could find early in the evening. On this particular evening it was a beer carton which had previously held twenty-four twelve-ounce bottles of Coors.

Bambic concentrated mostly on the trash bins behind buildings that had rooms or apartments above the stores. The larger bins used by cocktail lounges and liquor stores were cleaner to rummage through, but there was seldom much to be found in them; people in stores did not often discard anything of value. But people who lived on the upstairs floors, that was a different story. They would throw away anything that they did not want to be bothered with: bottles with deposits on them; small articles of wearing apparel that only needed mending to be serviceable again; larger items of clothing that did not fit any longer; practically new magazines and paperback books; an occasional clock or toaster that needed only minor repairs; shoes that would be like new with half soles and heels; and dozens of other items that to one person were worthless, but to another had the potential of at least meager value and profit.

There were secondhand dealers in every kind of merchandise imaginable all over the South of Mission District, and John Bambic knew them all. Nightly he prowled the streets and alleys, collecting booty to be recycled into the skid row economy.

He was eighty-four years old, born a decade and a half before the turn of the century; he had been sixteen when San Francisco had been destroyed by the great earthquake; he had lived through the Spanish-American War, World War One, World War Two, Korea, Vietnam. Seen the coming of electricity and the automobile, and watched America grow from adolescence to adulthood.

All to scavenge for junk in the trash bins of San Francisco in his twilight years.

At the Holly residence, George had gone to his Masonic lodge meeting, and his wife Jane was sorting laundry. Jane usually did the laundry at the Lightning Coin Launderette, a block away on Silver Avenue. She tried to do it when George had something else planned, so they could both be out at the same time. There was no sense in either of them having to stay home alone if it was not necessary.

As Jane Holly separated the clothes into two small piles—whites and coloreds—she thought about her son Steve, in the army in Oklahoma. He was a tall, good-looking young man, wearing a mustache like her husband did; in fact, strongly resembling George in every way, with none of her features at all. One would think there would have been a *little* of her in him, somewhere. Oh, well. Maybe the grandchildren, she resigned herself.

When Jane finished with the laundry, she checked the time. George would not be home until around ten. That gave her plenty of time to walk over and get the laundry done. She put the two bundles of clothes into a net laundry bag. There was not too much to do this week; in fact, there was never much to do anymore, now that she and George were alone.

Putting on her coat and picking up the evening paper, Jane Holly left the house carrying the net laundry bag and walked over to Silver Avenue. The Laundromat was brightly lighted as always; it never closed, and there were nearly always customers in the place. On this night there were a dozen people there when Jane arrived. Most of them were women; all of them were black. Not too many whites walked over from her side of Silver Avenue to do their clothes there; most of them preferred to go farther away and patronize an establishment that was not almost exclusively black. But Jane Holly had no qualms about going to the Lightning. She treated everyone decently, be they white or black, and all she asked from anyone was to be treated decently in return.

Jane put her laundry into two machines, fed change into them, and started the wash cycle. Then she got a can of grape soda from a vending machine and sat down at one of the tables to wait. She opened the paper and began to read a section.

Presently a stocky black man wearing glasses came over and sat across from her. "May I?" he asked politely, indicating the part of the paper that Jane was not reading.

"Help yourself," said Jane.

Together, the white woman and the black man read the evening news.

Two miles down Silver Avenue was Edinburgh Street. A block over from Silver, on the corner of Peru, was 102 Edinburgh. It was into this building that Roxanne McMillian, her husband Alan John, and their four-month-old son Leon were moving.

The building was disappointing. It was nowhere near as nice as Roxanne had hoped it would be. An older, two-story shingle structure, it was in a generally run-down condition. Some of the shingles were broken off at the corners or pulled loose entirely; the two front doors, standing side by side, one leading upstairs to number 100 Edinburgh, the other leading into the first-floor flat, number 102, were scratched and scarred; five concrete steps leading up to the front stoop, and the slab railing of the stoop itself, had new stains upon old stains from unidentified spills; and the public sidewalk for the entire width of the building was covered with spray-paint graffiti: "Bebop," "Robles," "Anna," others. It was a long way from the neat rows of homes in Cupertino.

But Roxanne was a spunky young woman. She could adjust to just about anything to keep her little family together and make everyone happy. Everyone being primarily John.

The flat, she decided with her customary optimism, was not too bad. Not really. There was nothing she could do about the outside of the building or the neighborhood, but the flat she could definitely fix up. It would take a *lot* of fixing up—but it could be done. With a little paint, a little wallpaper, and lots of soap and elbow grease, she would transform the dingy, depressing little place into a cute, cozy home that would be their peaceful sanctuary from the squalid area around them.

With those positive thoughts firmly planted in her mind, Roxanne McMillian began moving into the flat at 102 Edinburgh.

The fight on closed-circuit TV at Winterland went the full twelve rounds. Muhammad Ali won it by a unanimous decision. He was

too much for Smokin' Joe Frazier that night. In the second round
he had Frazier reeling and in trouble; the fight might have been
over right then but Referee Tony Perez thought he heard the bell
and halted the action twenty seconds early. Ali was unable to get
Frazier that close to a knockout again, but he nevertheless won a
clear victory. And gave Muslims around the world cause to celebrate.

"He did it!" Skullcap said jubilantly as he strutted out of the auditorium with Rims and Judo. "My main man did it! He whipped
that white nigger good!"

"I thought Frazier be tougher than that," said Rims. "He didn't
look too tough tonight."

"He's tough," Judo said. "He just had an off night."

"What kind of shit you talking, man?" Skullcap asked. "You
supposed to be for Ali, man; he's a brother. What you talking up
that white nigger Frazier for?"

"I ain't *talking up* nobody," Judo said with an edge. "And I was
for Ali, same as you. I just ain't putting down Joe Frazier, is all. He
is still a tough fighter."

"He's a chump," Skullcap said.

"If he be a chump," Rims asked thoughtfully, "then that mean
Ali didn't beat nobody good, don't it?"

Judo smiled and Skullcap looked at Rims in surprise. Rims was
not supposed to be smart enough to figure that out. Skullcap wanted Frazier to be a nothing, but he wanted the win to be a great victory for Ali. Even someone as slow as Rims knew he could not
have it both ways.

Judo patted Rims on his burly back. "You getting smart, brother," he said. "I'm glad to see you starting to think for yourself."

"What's that supposed to mean?" Skullcap asked flatly.

"It mean just what it say," Judo replied. "Seem to me there's
too much of one person doing the thinking for another around here
lately. I think things be a lot better if everybody think for hisself."

Skullcap stared coldly at Judo but said nothing. They got back to
where the borrowed Cadillac was parked. "You drive," Skullcap
said to Rims. Skullcap got in the front seat on the passenger side;
Judo slid into the middle of the back seat.

"So you think each man should do his own thinking, huh?"
Skullcap said over his shoulder. "Okay. That sounds like a good

deal to me. I'll think only for myself tonight. Let me see now: I think I shall go out and sting some devils for Allah. What about you?'' he asked Rims. ''Think for yourself now,'' he cautioned.

Wiseass motherfucker, Judo thought. But Rims had already taken the bait.

''I'll sting some too,'' Rims said eagerly.

Skullcap looked around and locked eyes with Judo. ''How about you, brother? Thinking strictly for yourself, of course.''

''We can't go stinging,'' Judo said. ''I lost my gun.''

''Well, now, that just don't matter none,'' Skullcap said with one of his cold, brilliant smiles. He opened the glove compartment and took out a .32-caliber Beretta identical to the one Judo had thrown into the bay. ''We can use my artillery tonight,'' Skullcap said, holding up the gun. He fell silent and stared at Judo for a long moment. Then, in an almost threatening tone, he issued the final challenge: ''You have yet to accomplish a single sting, brother. Are you with the Death Angels or against them?''

Judo had no way out.

''I'm with them,'' he said.

''Drive down Geary Boulevard,'' Skullcap said to Rims, a satisfied smirk on his dark face.

They cruised Geary. As they approached Divisadero, Skullcap saw a pretty white woman walking along the street.

''Let me out,'' he said. Tonight, *he* would lead.

He got out of the car, the words *More will have to be done* reverberating in his head. He felt good. The gun in his hand, held close to his thigh, was *his*. The night was *his*. The moment was *his*.

Tana Smith, six blocks from home, was on her way to the fabric shop. Her thoughts were probably on the type of material she planned to buy and the pattern of blouse she would make. There were so many nice styles she could wear now that she had slimmed down—

Skullcap walked up behind her, raised the gun, and shot her twice in the back.

Tana hit the sidewalk hard. Skullcap paused and peered down at her, crouching slightly, the gun smoking in his hand. Just then a station wagon came by. The driver slowed down and looked at him.

Skullcap straightened and ran.

The man in the station wagon, David Bienvineste, was a florist. He had just delivered flowers to a patient at Mount Zion Medical Center, two blocks away. Now, as he realized what was happening, he was momentarily stunned. He stared at the crouching black man with the hat cocked to one side, revealing a shaved hairline that left no sideburns. Then the man saw him and ran away.

Bienvineste gathered his senses and swung the car in a quick U-turn. He screeched to the curb and ran over to Tana. She was clutching her lower abdomen and moaning, "Oh—oh—I'm hurt—I'm hurting—"

"Jesus," Bienvineste muttered, more a prayer than an oath. He tentatively touched Tana's shoulder. "Listen, I'll get help," he said nervously. "I'll get help."

The only thing he could think of was that Mount Zion Medical Center was two blocks away. He started for it, running as fast as he could. He had completely forgotten that he had a car.

The Cadillac moved south on Divisadero for a few blocks. Then Skullcap said, "There's too much traffic on this street, man. Cut over to a side street."

"Right, brother," said Rims. He made a left turn and drove one block to Scott Street.

"Okay, who's next?" Skullcap asked, twirling the Beretta on one finger like a movie cowboy.

"Be careful with that fucking thing, man," said Judo.

"The safety's on," Skullcap told him disdainfully. "Now who's next?"

"Me! I be next!" Rims said gleefully.

"I kind of figured you might," Skullcap said, in an obvious dig at Judo. "Go on, pick your devil."

"There one!" Rims said almost at once. He pointed out the window at a short, stocky white man walking jauntily along Scott Street.

"Get him then," Skullcap said. "I'll slide over and drive."

Rims stopped the Cadillac and got out. Skullcap handed him the Beretta.

Across the street, Vincent Wollin was whistling softly as he headed for home. It had been a very nice day, this sixty-ninth birthday of his. He was happy but very tired. He would certainly sleep well tonight—

Rims hurried up behind him, held the gun very close to his back, and shot him.

Vincent turned around, wide-eyed. He knew exactly what had happened. "You—you—shot me—" he said incredulously.

"Yougotthatrightmotherfucker," Rims said.

Vincent turned back around to walk away and Rims shot him again.

David Bienvineste burst through the emergency entrance of Mount Zion Medical Center and rushed to the desk. "A woman's been shot!" he said frantically.

"Does she have insurance?" the admitting clerk asked.

Bienvineste stared at her. "What?"

"Insurance. Does she have insurance?"

"You don't understand! A woman has been shot!"

"We can't admit anybody who doesn't have insurance," the clerk said. "Hospital regulations."

Bienvineste could not believe his ears. "The woman needs help!" he shouted.

"I'll call a city ambulance," the clerk said. "That's the best I can do. It'll be here in five or ten minutes."

Bienvineste stared incredulously at her. Five or ten minutes? The woman was *seconds* away. She could be *carried* to the hospital on a stretcher.

The clerk asked exactly where the woman was and began making the call. Bienvineste shook his head in disbelief. Then he hurried out and ran back down the street to see what he could do to help the woman until the ambulance came.

Which, he guessed, would be five or ten minutes.

Where Tana lay, there were already several other people around. A black man had found her on the sidewalk and put his rolled-up coat under her head in an effort to make her more comfortable. A Japanese woman, who had been standing in a doorway six feet from the attack, remained where she was, staring at the scene. And a very nervous, mustached young man, who was on his way to a nearby store to buy cigarettes, paced back and forth around the fallen woman as if unsure exactly what to do.

Someone knelt beside Tana and tried to close her coat collar around her throat. "Don't—" Tana said thickly. "Don't—" The least little movement wracked her with pain. "Take—me—to—San Francisco General—" Her friend Nancy Lobaugh had been seriously injured in an automobile accident and had received superb treatment at San Francisco General.

"What did she say?" one of the bystanders asked the nervous man with the mustache.

"She said don't take her to San Francisco General," he answered unhesitatingly.

More people were gathering now and a siren could be heard in the distance. Before the siren got any closer, a police unit arrived. Officers Ronald Morehen and William Fox hurried to the victim. David Bienvineste ran back up and told them the hospital had summoned an ambulance. To be on the safe side, Officer Fox ordered another one, Code Three, through Communications. Across the street, a gold Cadillac parked and one of two black men got out and came over to the small crowd. "I suppose this is something else going to be blamed on the crazy black people," he said sarcastically when he found out what had happened. No one paid any attention to him.

Presently the ambulance arrived. "I'm hurting so bad," Tana said as they lifted her onto the gurney.

"The poor thing," a woman in the crowd muttered.

"I wonder if she has any children," another said.

"If she does, I hope she gets to see them one more time."

"Oh, I hurt—I hurt—" Tana said. The attendants slid the gurney into the ambulance. Seconds later it was speeding toward San Francisco General.

"I saw the whole thing, Officer," said the black man from the gold Cadillac. "It was a white man done the shooting."

The officers were busy looking for shell casings and securing the scene. Before they could respond to the black man, he stalked across the street, got into the gold Cadillac, and drove away.

211

The officers found two spent casings. "Thirty-twos," one of them said pointedly. By now every policeman in San Francisco knew the *modus operandi* of the street killers.

The nervous man with the mustache continued to pace. Things seemed to be moving too fast for him. This thing that had happened was very important. He was a *witness*. He seemed to think he should be *doing* something—but he did not know what. Everything gushed into his head at once: the woman not wanting to be taken to San Francisco General, the man in the gold Cadillac who had seen a white man do the shooting, the woman wanting to see her children one more time. He must try to remember all of it, he told himself.

He continued to pace nervously.

The Cadillac, with Skullcap at the wheel, drove east on Fulton to the Opera House, then cruised randomly around the Civic Center.

Rims turned in the seat and looked back at Judo. "You next now, brother," he said innocently, as if it were Judo's turn at some simple game they were playing.

"Maybe he *still* ain't ready yet," Skullcap said, feigning the same tone of innocence with which Rims spoke. "Maybe his heart *still* ain't strong enough."

"My heart strong as anybody's," Judo retorted, somewhat less than enthusiastically.

"Good!" Skullcap said, seizing the statement. "You ready then!" He guided the car out of the Civic Center. "I'll just cruise until you see a devil you want. Say when, brother."

Skullcap drove slowly down Tenth Street.

The police had arrived at the scene of the Scott Street shooting. Officers Herman Popp and Vincent Neeson found Vincent Wollin lying facedown on the sidewalk. There were two bullet holes in the back of his raincoat; each was surrounded by powder burns. The officers summoned an ambulance.

Lulu Badger, a middle-aged black woman, hurried across the street to the officers. "I seen it all, Officers, I seen it all!" she exclaimed. "It was awful! I was waiting over there on my front porch for a ride to take me to church. I goes to the Saint Andrew's Bap-

tist Church and my ride usually come about eight o'clock. I likes to
always be ready and waiting so I don't delay nobody, you know. I
believe when people is nice enough to give you a ride, you ought to
be considerate enough to be ready when they gets here—"

"Can you describe the man who did the shooting, ma'am?"
Officer Popp interrupted. "We want to get it on the radio as quickly
as possible."

Lulu Badger described a black man about twenty-five years old,
wearing a turtleneck sweater and dark trousers. While she was giving her description, Officer Neeson searched the scene. He found
two .32-caliber shell casings.

When the ambulance arrived, the steward determined that Vincent Wollin was still alive. He was removed from the sidewalk and
rushed to San Francisco General.

"Well, what about it, man?" Skullcap said impatiently. "You
ready or not? You *got* the heart or *not* got the heart?"

"I got the heart, man, but I'm just taking my own good time,"
Judo said, playing a delaying game.

"He gonna do it," Rims said supportively. "He be okay."

Skullcap grunted softly. "He's hedging."

"Like hell I am!" Judo snapped.

"You are," Skullcap said easily, in a finely controlled voice.

"Man, I said I'm not!"

"You are." A calm, precise statement. Purposeful. Infuriating.

"*I am not!*" Enraged. Insulted. Frustration mushrooming inside
him.

"Then prove it," Skullcap said evenly. "Prove you got the
heart, just like we done proved that we got it."

Judo's expression was contorted: his eyes wide, nostrils flared,
thick lips puffed out in an angry pout. "Give me the motherfucking
gun!" he snapped at Rims. When Rims held the gun out to him,
Judo snatched it from his hand. "Go up that street there!" he ordered, indicating Ninth Street. He was breathing in short bursts
now, like a man having a mild asthma attack. I got as much heart as
anybody, he thought angrily. Ain't *no* motherfucker gonna say I
got no heart! No way! I am a *man!*

Looking out the window, Judo saw what looked to be an old

white derelict approaching a trash bin next to a place called Phillips' Bar and Grille. "Stop," he said to Skullcap. "Right here." The car stopped and Judo got out. He walked toward the white derelict.

At the big trash bin, old John Bambic, holding his Coors carton under one arm, rummaged through the loose papers and other junk, looking for something of value. He hoped he would find something. It was getting late and, at eighty-four, Bambic was tired. He wanted very badly to lie down, close his old eyes, and rest—

Judo walked directly up to the old man and shot him once in the back. Bambic pitched forward against the trash bin. Judo shot him again. Bambic's body jerked and turned around.

Then the old man reached out with both hands and grabbed Judo around the neck.

Judo's eyes got as big and round as silver dollars. "What the fuck you doing, man?" he said, surprised. He tried to pull the old man's hands away from his throat, but Bambic held on tenaciously. "Leave go, man!" Judo snapped. "Leave go my neck!"

In a room overlooking the street from the second floor, Charles Archeletta was lying on his bed watching a TV documentary about the Rosenberg atomic spy trial. When he heard the two shots, he rushed to the window and looked down at the struggling men.

"Ahrrr—" The sound came from old John Bambic's throat like a cry of vengeance.

"Leave go!" Judo still demanded, the features of his face now twisted in fear.

Walking down the street toward the struggling men was a city warehouseman named Richard Williams. He had heard the noise of the gunshot while still farther down the street and had thought they were firecrackers. Now, seeing the two men wrestling, he was not so sure.

Judo was still holding the gun but for some reason—surprise, fear, panic—did not have the faculties required to shoot Bambic again. It did not even occur to him to strike Bambic in the head or face with the gun. All he could think about was getting Bambic's viselike fingers from around his throat—and to accomplish that he could think of no tactic except to pull at the old man's wrists.

214

"Ahrrrr—" came the blood-chilling rattle from Bambic's throat. The wrinkled, toothless old face was but inches from Judo's, and Judo could feel and smell Bambic's warm, sour breath gushing out at him with every gasp the old man took.

From the bar on the corner, two customers came out onto the sidewalk and looked to see what the commotion was all about. They stood cautiously near the lighted bar entrance and peered into the darkness alongside the building.

"*Leave—me—go—!*" Judo said for the last time. Then he felt the strength draining from the old man's hands, literally felt the cablelike fingers becoming weaker by degrees, and he knew that momentarily the desperate grip would fail and he would be free.

When it happened, when at last the incredibly strong old hands slowly dropped away from his neck, Judo took an extra split second to glare hatefully at his victim-attacker, and to curse him.

"You old white motherfucker!" he hissed.

Then he ran back to the car.

Behind him, gallant old John Bambic lost consciousness and slumped to the sidewalk.

At San Francisco General, Vincent Wollin, the second person to be shot as the night of terror began, was the first to die. He expired just three hours before his sixty-ninth birthday would have been over.

In another part of the big hospital's trauma unit, a team of doctors was laboring to keep Tana Smith alive. One of the bullets had perforated her liver. The prognosis for her survival was not good.

Officers Douglas Dumas and James Selby were on patrol in Unit Three Bravo-Four when the call came in on the Bambic shooting. They rolled on the call at once. It was to be their third response in the series of street killings: they had also been the first officers on the scene at the Neal Moynihan killing, and the first team at the Mildred Hosler scene, both thirty-seven days earlier.

The two officers were already aware of the Tana Smith and Vincent Wollin shootings. They both had a hunch that the black killers with the .32-caliber automatic were on a spree again.

They were right.

* * *

In the Cadillac, Rims was the personification of delight. He was
bouncing up and down on the seat and grinning from ear to ear.
"You did it, brother!" he shouted joyfully. "You destroyed a
white devil!" He reached back and slapped Judo smartly on the
knee. "I told you it be easy! Didn't I tell you! I knew you could do
it, brother!"

In the back seat, Judo, trembling, was rubbing his neck. "That
crazy old motherfucker like to choke me to death," he muttered.

"Next time, don't get so close to the devil," Skullcap said.

"Tha's right," Rims agreed. "The grafted snake be dangerous
sometime, maybe."

Skullcap was still driving, watching traffic carefully. They were
on the freeway, heading south. Oddly enough, they were just passing San Francisco General, off to their right.

"Where to now?" Skullcap asked for suggestions.

"I be want a female devil tonight too!" Rims said excitedly.

Skullcap glanced at him. He heard Vandyke's words again:
Much more will have to be done.

"Why not, brother?" he said easily. He smiled a cold, terrible
smile. "We rolling, so let's *keep* rolling."

In the back seat, still holding the murder gun, Judo felt sick to his
stomach.

Back on Ninth Street, Central Ambulance number 81 had
reached the scene of the Bambic shooting. Ambulance steward
Nitschke was slowly, patiently examining the fallen man for vital
signs. He was being very careful: with a man as old as the victim
obviously was, a mistake was easy to make.

Dumas and Selby had secured the scene and already found the
two .32-caliber casings from the bullets that had hit the victim.
They gave them to Ken Moses of the crime lab.

"Let me guess," said Moses. "Thirty-twos, right?"

"The man's brilliant," said Dumas.

"A genius," agreed Selby.

Within minutes, the shooting scene was crawling with police
brass. Lieutenant Syme arrived from Southern Station, along with
Sergeant Bragg. Two other district sergeants, Rider and Syming-

ton, also showed up. A full captain, named Keel, arrived. Inspectors Gilford and Sanders were on the scene at once, as was Charles Ellis, the lieutenant in charge of Homicide.

Coreris and Fotinos were there too, but they were not concerning themselves with the crime scene. They had a city map partly spread open between them and were trying to project where the killers would strike next.

"Okay, starting at Geary and Divisadero, where the woman was shot," said Fotinos, "it's just about a mile south to Scott and McAllister, where the old guy got it."

"Right," said Coreris. He opened another fold of the map and traced an imaginary line down to where they were now. "And it's two more miles down to here."

"Where next?" Fotinos wondered.

"Well, the bastards are heading south, that's obvious," said Coreris. "First they jump down one mile, then two miles."

"Maybe next time three miles," said Fotinos.

"Maybe."

They traced another imaginary line south along the freeway. "Figure somewhere around Army Street or a little past," Fotinos guessed.

"It's worth a chance," Coreris said. "Let's go."

As the two homicide detectives slipped unnoticed away from the scene, Steward Nitschke officially pronounced John Bambic dead. The third one shot, he was the second to die that night.

Four miles south, the black Cadillac cruised Silver Avenue. Skullcap was still driving. Rims, unusually elated, was scanning the street, looking for the next suitable devil. They passed slowly by the Lightning Coin Launderette. Rims saw a lone white woman among all the black customers.

"There a devil in there, right in the midst of all them sisters. I'll destroy her."

Skullcap threw him a cursory glance. "Too many people in there," he said. He drove on by.

"They be black peoples," Rims argued. "They won't care if I be kill a grafted snake among them."

"Fucking man is insane," Judo muttered to himself.

"It's too risky, brother," Skullcap protested.

"Risk don't bother me none when it's for Allah," Rims declared. "I be led to this white devil by Allah, to destroy her from among our black brothers and sisters. Take me back there."

Skullcap shook his head. "Brother, I don't think you should—"

Rims reached into the back seat and took the gun from Judo. "Take me back!" he insisted.

Skullcap looked at his face, at the fixed eyes, the grim line of mouth. And at the gun Rims was holding. "Okay, brother," he said quietly, "hang loose. We going back."

He guided the car around the block and pulled to the curb near the corner of Silver and Brussells. Rims, looking almost as if he were in a trance, got out and walked to the Laundromat entrance.

Inside the Laundromat were six black women and two black men.

And Jane Holly.

Jane got up from the table where she was sharing her newspaper with the black man, and went over to dryer number ten. She removed some of her clothes and transferred them to a folding table. Then she returned to the dryer and reached in for the rest.

Rims walked through the front door, went directly up to Jane Holly, and shot her twice in the back.

The black customers on the premises froze. The man who was reading Jane Holly's newspaper rose to a half crouch, then he too froze. Jane Holly did not fall; she staggered sideways along the row of shiny stainless-steel dryers.

Rims turned and hurried out the front door. As soon as he was gone, the crouching black man rushed to Jane Holly, put his arms around her, and eased her to the floor. When she was all the way down on her back, the man said, "Somebody watch her while I call the police."

Fotinos and Coreris were cruising within a mile of the scene, scanning the streets, when the shooting call was broadcast.

"Son of a bitch," said Fotinos. "A few more blocks and we could have caught them in the act." He punched down on the accelerator and shot the unmarked police car forward.

Officers Paul Maniscalco and Robert Van Dis, in Unit 3C-2, beat them to the scene. They cordoned off the scene and held all witnesses for interrogation.

"Two shell casings over by the dryers, Inspector," said Van Dis. "Look like thirty-twos."

"I'll eat them if they aren't," Coreris said.

"You got crime and photo labs coming?" asked Fotinos.

"Yessir," said Maniscalco.

An ambulance arrived at the same time as a captain named Conroy, a lieutenant named Smith, a sergeant named Fursley, and another patrol unit carrying Officers Gretton and Cardinale. Jane Holly, still alive, was removed from the scene and rushed to Mission Emergency Hospital. Crime Lab Inspector Walt Ihle also arrived. Earlier he had worked the Tana Smith shooting scene. He went immediately to the shell casings, which were being carefully guarded on the floor by one of the uniformed officers.

"Thirty-twos?" he asked Fotinos, who was standing between him and the casings.

"Nothing but," Fotinos replied. "That makes two murders and two attempts so far tonight."

"Three murders," Ihle corrected. "They lost the Smith woman on the operating table a few minutes ago."

Tana Smith, the first to be shot, was the third to die that night.

And still the black Cadillac cruised.

"We are *rolling!*" Skullcap said, exhilarated. He was now feeling as high as Rims felt. The last shooting had done it for him. It had been magnificent! Rims just walked into a Laundromat full of people, killed a white devil, and walked right back out again. Nobody had touched him, nobody had tried to interfere with him in any way. It was like he was a god, a soldier of Allah, come down to slay the grafted snake. Maybe we *are* blessed, Skullcap thought. *Something* was sure watching over them tonight.

"Whose turn now?" Rims asked, eyes wide and wild, again fondling the Beretta as if it were a puppy.

"Mine!" Skullcap said, riding the crest of his enthusiasm as if it were a great wave and he a master surfer. "My turn again!"

Skullcap's eyes darted from sidewalk to sidewalk as he guided the car west on Felton Street for a mile and a half, moving slowly

219

through the short residential blocks, pausing at every corner to look up and down the cross streets for potential victims out alone.

A female devil, Skullcap thought. I gots to get me another female devil. Tonight I be making up for all the misses I had, all the blue-eyed devils that didn't die like they was supposed to do after I shot them. Tonight I get enough to earn my Death Angel wings! Gots to get all females. Or kids, if any be out.

They turned into Avalon Avenue, then started searching the smaller streets: up Vienna, down Naples, up Edinburgh—where the young white woman was moving boxes into her new apartment.

"Ooooo-weee! Look what I see!" Skullcap said, jive-talking. "A white female devil just begging to be *de*-stroyed by Allah's mos' handsomest dude, yours truly."

Rims grinned idiotically at him, while from the back seat, Judo, just now beginning to feel the full emotional weight of what he himself had done, closed his eyes and held his hands over his ears, trying to block out all sight and sound of what was happening.

Skullcap guided the car slowly around the corner on Peru and pulled to the curb. He took the gun from Rims and slid out from under the wheel. "You take over the driving, brother," he said with a smile—a genuinely happy smile. "I be right back. It only take me seconds to snuff out this grafted snake."

Skullcap strutted back to the corner, the gun at his side. He felt *good*. Felt *right*. Felt *with it*. With the Beretta in his hand, he was— at last—*somebody*. With the power of life and death. The entire feeling translated into his strut, his swagger. The swashbuckler in the Superfly hat was about to strike again. All for Allah.

Roxanne McMillian removed a box of towels and dishcloths from the car, crossed the sidewalk in front of Skullcap, and started up the five outside steps to her door. She saw Skullcap coming but tried not to pay too much attention to him. Living in the city, she was going to have to get used to all kinds of people—

"Hi," Skullcap said pleasantly as he passed by the steps.

"Hi," Roxanne returned his greeting.

Then he raised the gun and shot her twice, once in the back and once in the side as she was turning to speak to him.

Carol Matison, a sixteen-year-old white girl, was watching television in her home half a block away, at the corner of Peru and Madrid. She heard the two shots, thought—as so many had—that they were the sounds of firecrackers, and got up to look out the window. As she peered out into the darkness, she heard heavy, running footsteps—clomp! clomp! clomp!—like shoes with big wooden heels. Then she saw Skullcap run up to a Cadillac with high tail fins and jump into the passenger side. The car lurched away from the curb and screeched around the next corner, turning south on Lisbon.

As the car sped down Lisbon, Judo, in the back seat, did not look out the windows. Even if he had, the street and its houses would have meant nothing to him. He had no way of knowing that in the 100 block of Lisbon lived the Stewart family. The same Stewart family to which Frankie and Marie Stewart belonged. The Frankie and Marie Stewart whom Judo, along with Head and Yellow, had attempted to kidnap in the van fourteen weeks earlier.

Alan John McMillian ran to a neighbor's house to call an ambulance. The neighbors did not know him and would not open the door. He ran to another house. Again they would not let him in. Finally a lady across the street yelled at him from her window and said she had called the police for him.

John had been inside the apartment when he heard the shots, immediately followed by Roxanne's screams. He rushed to the front door and found her lying on her side on the steps, blood forming a pool under her. Her assailant had already fled the scene. John picked up his wife and carried her into the hallway. Then he ran out to seek help. Now, as he hurried back to Roxanne, he could already hear the siren indicating that help was on the way.

As soon as the next 217 call came in, police began responding from all quarters. A 217 is an unknown shooting call.

Lieutenant Ellis, of Homicide, was still at the Laundromat with Coreris, Fotinos, and a dozen other men. A patrol officer came in to tell him about the latest incident, less than two miles away. Ellis turned to Coreris. "We've got another one, Gus. Over at Edinburgh and Peru. You and John want to take it?"

Coreris thought about it for a moment. He glanced at Lonnie

Green, the black man who had shared Jane Holly's newspaper. Green was a petty officer in the Navy, on shore leave from the ammunition ship U.S.S. *Maua Kea* docked at Concord. To date, he was the best witness yet to turn up at any of the shootings. In addition to him, there were half a dozen other eyeball witnesses who had seen the gunman—for the first time—close up and in the light. Coreris did not want to let that kind of evidence get cold.

"Why don't you let Sanders and Gilford take it?" he said. "John and I are already ass-deep in these witnesses."

Ellis gave the assignment to Sanders and Gilford, the two black inspectors who had worked the Moynihan and Hosler shootings, and who had subsequently stopped Larry Green for investigation. Along with them he sent Inspectors Podesta and Schneider, two other Homicide detectives.

Walt Ihle from the Crime Lab went also, handling still another one that night. He was not surprised when he got to the scene to find two .32-caliber shell casings being guarded on the sidewalk by Officer William Sowell who, with his partner Robert Hoch, were the first officers to arrive.

In another part of the city, Chief of Inspectors Charles Barca summoned his driver to pick him up. Barca had been notified of the shooting spree that had now taken three lives, might yet be responsible for two others—or even more, for who knew if it had stopped or not?

"Goddamn madmen," he muttered to himself as he waited for his car. When it arrived he slid in beside his driver and said, "Head for Edinburgh and Peru. That's where they were last."

Meanwhile, the ambulance arrived at 102 Edinburgh and removed Roxanne from the hallway. "Let's hustle," the steward said quietly to his helper. "This girl's bleeding by the pint."

The ambulance sped off toward San Francisco General, its siren shattering the night.

In the black Cadillac, laughter abounded.

"You should have seen it!" Skullcap said. "I be walk up and say, 'Hi.' And she turn around friendly-like and say, 'Hi' "—he made his voice rise to mimic Roxanne—"then I aim the gun and pow! pow! I lets her have it! Man, she drop like a wet rope!

222

"Good, good!" Rims gloated, his eyes and smile sparkling. "That be good!"

"Brother, we rolling tonight!" Skullcap said. "We *moving!*"

"Whose turn it be?" asked Rims.

Skullcap smiled widely. "Ain't mine, brother. And it ain't yours. So who do that leave?"

"Hey, brother, it be your turn," Rims said over his shoulder as he drove. "Where you want to go to?" He turned off Lisbon into Brazil and doubled back up Mission Street, heading north. "Where to now?" he asked again when Judo did not answer.

Skullcap looked back at Judo, who still had his head down, eyes closed, ears covered. "Man, will you look at this shit," Skullcap said. "This cat is flipping out." He reached back and pulled one of Judo's hands away from his ear. "Say, man! We got to know where you want to go. It's your turn to sting."

Judo looked out the window until he saw a street sign that told him they were on Mission. He saw the numbers decreasing in the direction in which they were traveling, so he knew they were heading back toward the heart of the city. "Just keep going," he said listlessly. "Keep going."

The distance between them and the last shooting piled up block by block: Thirtieth Street, Twenty-fifth Street, Nineteenth—

"Hang a left and cut over to Guerrero," Skullcap said after a while. "Else we be right back where he got that first dude."

"You mean first devil," Rims corrected righteously.

"Yeah, devil."

Rims drove up to Market, where Guerrero ended, and made a quick left and right to get onto Laguna. They headed north on Laguna. At one point they passed directly by the spot where Head had shot and killed Frances Rose. None of them recognized the place because none of them had been with Head that night. All they knew was that he had killed a white female devil; they did not know where. Or care.

"Somebody gots to tell me where to go," Rims said nervously. He did not like to drive without directions.

"Pull over and park," Skullcap ordered. Rims obeyed. Skullcap twisted in the seat and faced Judo. "It's your turn, *brother,*" he said evenly. "You going to look for a sting to make or not?"

"Not," Judo said, shaking his head. "I don't feel so good, man. That old bastard choking me like that done got me all fucked up—"

"You fucked up, all right," Skullcap said, "but it ain't because of that old man. You supposed to be a fucking black belt: why didn't you break that old man's arms when he grabbed you?"

"I couldn't think—I didn't expect it—the motherfucker had two bullets in him, he wasn't supposed to grab me like that—"

"You a fake, man," Skullcap said coldly. "You a motherfucking phony and you don't have no business being with Death Angels. Get your ass out from this car."

Judo stared steadily at Skullcap. The man's eyes were cold and dangerous, their pupils dilated almost to the circumference of the irises. The face around those eyes was a dark death-mask, an evil countenance of flesh and blood and bone, a terrible animal incarnate. There was nothing of the human being in him at that moment.

And, Judo knew, Skullcap still held the Beretta in his lap.

"I'm going," he said quietly, almost ashamedly. He opened the car door and stepped onto the sidewalk.

"Good riddance," Skullcap said. Then to Rims: "Drive on."

The black Cadillac moved away into the night.

In the trauma unit at Mission Emergency, a surgical team prepared to work on Roxanne McMillian. She had a single wound to her anterior and lateral right chest, and another of the midback. The former had resulted in a bullet being lodged near her heart, the latter in a bullet being lodged near her spine.

"Great," said a surgeon studying the X rays. "We can go for the one near the heart while the other one possibly cripples her, or we can go for the one near the spine while the first one possibly kills her. Is it okay to check 'None of the above'?"

"Only in politics, not in surgery," another doctor answered.

"We're either going to paralyze or kill this gal, you know that, don't you?"

"No, somebody else already did that with the bullets. We're going to try to *un*do what that prick *did*. Come on, Doctor, let's go to work."

As Roxanne McMillian was being operated on at Mission Emergency, Jane Holly was expiring at San Francisco General. Her cause of death was exsanguination due to two gunshot wounds. In laymen's terms, that meant she literally bled to death.

Jane Holly, the fourth one shot, was also the fourth to die.

At ten thirty, George Holly walked over to the Lightning Laundromat. A uniformed policeman met him at the door.

"I'm looking for my wife," Holly said. "She's late getting home. What's going on?"

"What's your name, sir?" the officer asked. Holly told him. Also the name of his wife. "Do you have a picture of your wife, sir?"

"Yes, I think so," Holly said, taking out his wallet. "Can't you tell me what's going on?"

"Yessir, we will in a minute. May we look at the picture first?"

Holly handed over a wallet-size snapshot of Jane. The officer took it over to Gus Coreris, who was interviewing a witness. Coreris looked at it, then over at George Holly in the doorway. His shoulders sagged. Jesus, he thought. Why me? It was bad enough having to all the time look at the dead without also having to break the news to the living.

"Okay," he said quietly to the officer. He smoothed down his dark mustache and went over to the man in the doorway. "Mr. Holly, will you come in and sit down, please? I have something to tell you."

At the end of Day One Hundred One, there were eighteen victims.

Quita Hague, hacked to death.

Richard Hague, his face butchered.

Ellen Linder, raped, ravaged, threatened with death.

Frances Rose, her face blown apart by close-range gunshots.

Saleem Erakat, tied up and executed with a single shot.

Paul Dancik, shot down as he attempted to use a public telephone.

Arthur Agnos, a survivor, after having his lungs, spleen, and kidney ripped apart by bullets.

Marietta DiGirolamo, thrown into a doorway and shot to death as she walked down the street.

225

Ilario Bertuccio, gunned down in the street as he walked home from work with a bottle of 7-Up under his arm.

Angela Roselli, surviving but seriously injured after being shot down in the street as she was returning home from a Christmas party.

Neal Moynihan, shot down in the street on his way home with a Teddy bear for his little sister.

Mildred Hosler, shot down in the street as she walked toward her bus stop.

John Doe #169, kidnapped, horribly tortured, decapitated, his hands and feet butchered off, bundled up like a turkey, and thrown into the sea.

Tana Smith, shot down in the street on her way to buy material to make a new blouse.

Vincent Wollin, shot down in the street on his sixty-ninth birthday.

John Bambic, shot down in the street while rummaging in a trash bin.

Jane Holly, murdered in a public Laundromat while removing her clothes from a dryer.

And Roxanne McMillian, shot down as she was moving a box into her new apartment, by a man who first said "Hi" to her.

Day 164

Between Day One Hundred One and Day One Hundred Sixty-four exactly nine weeks passed.

They were the most unusual nine weeks in the history of San Francisco.

On the morning after Day One Hundred One, newspaper headlines screamed terrible announcements to the city:

A NIGHT OF KILLING IN S.F.
—4 SLAIN ON CITY STREETS

PAIR OF 'MADMEN' SLAY FOUR ON CITY STREETS

S.F. KILLING SPREE—
5 SHOT ON STREETS

TWO-HOUR 'DEATH DRIVE'

MASSIVE MANHUNT
FOR TWO SUSPECTS

Calls requesting information about the purchase of personal firearms started coming into the police department even before the day shift began.

"I want to find out about buying a gun," the call usually went. "Do I have to get a permit?"

"What kind of gun, sir?"

"I don't know. A thirty-eight, something like that."

"To purchase a handgun, sir, you must fill out an application at the store where you pick out the gun. Your application will then be processed by the police department. If approved, you will be notified when to pick up your gun."

"How long's it take?"

"A week to ten days, usually. We have to be sure an applicant isn't an ex-convict or an alien, doesn't use alcohol to excess, is not a drug addict—things like that."

"How do I get a permit to carry it?"

"Permits to carry a firearm on the person are not normally issued in California, sir, unless the party requesting it is an *ex officio* police officer of some kind, or is a licensed private investigator."

"How about for protection?" the caller asked indignantly. "Can't a man carry a gun for protection?"

"No, sir. Protecting the public is the police department's job."

The caller grunted derisively. "You sure as hell aren't doing a very good job of it, Mac." And hung up.

The next call was already waiting on the line. "Hello, I want to find out about how to go about buying a gun—"

When Chief of Inspectors Charles Barca walked into the Hall of Justice, he was besieged by reporters.

"Chief! Do you have any suspects in the case?" asked the one who got to him first.

"No definite suspects," he said. But already his steel-trap mind had dredged up half a dozen street hoodlums he was going to have checked out—just on the off chance that one of them was involved. Police officers throughout the department would be doing the same thing all day long. A lot of crimes were solved on hunches.

"Chief!" another reporter called as Barca walked toward the elevator. "Was the gun last night the same one used in the other recent killings?"

"Same caliber gun," said Barca. "But the ballistics report isn't back on the slugs yet." Something in the back of his mind, some long in-bred cop instinct, told him to wait for that report before commenting on the gun.

"Chief, is it true that you have some close eyewitnesses for the first time?"

"Yes. The killing in the Laundromat was done under bright lights in front of half a dozen people."

"Can any of them identify the killer?"

"Don't know yet. We hope so, of course."

"Any word on the fifth victim, Chief? She still alive?"

"She was an hour ago. In serious condition, but still hanging on." Barca pushed the elevator button and waited. More reporters surrounded him.

"Chief, is the department going to take any special steps to stop these killings, or will they be handled as part of the normal routine?"

"Special steps, very definitely. There'll be a formal statement for you from Chief Scott's office later today." Chief Scott was Donald M. Scott, the San Francisco chief of police.

"Chief, there's a hot rumor going around that—"

"I don't comment on rumors," Barca interrupted.

The elevator came. Chief of Inspectors Barca stepped aboard and was gone.

The rumors of which the reporter had tried to speak were rampant throughout the Hall of Justice. There was now no question in the minds of many that the shootings were racial in motivation. In the beginning there had been room for doubt. San Francisco was a melting pot of ethnic communities; it was not unusual for there to be numerous reported crimes involving mixed subjects: not only Negro/Caucasian and Caucasian/Negro, but also Chinese, Chicano, Arab, Indian, and others. People who dealt with crime in San Francisco were accustomed to considerable ethnic variety in their Incident Reports.

But it was now generally agreed that the recent street shootings fell outside what was normal and accepted coincidence. Within common knowledge around the Hall of Justice was the fact that there were now fourteen shooting victims. Eleven of them dead. All of them white. And all of them shot by black men.

It was even clearer to those in the Hall's inner circle: those who had *all* of the facts. Such as the Hague kidnapping and murder, the Linder rape, and the John Doe #169 butchering. There was a terrible pattern to it all.

"It's some kind of fanatical black group," the rumors went.

"It's a black revenge gang," said another. "Getting even for some of their people who got shot in a robbery or something."

"Bunch of crazy niggers is all," said another. "Nothing unusual about 'em. All spades are crazy; these guys are just *more* crazy."

Gus Coreris and John Fotinos were bombarded with questions wherever they went. Even in the men's room.

"Hey, Gus, what do you figure on this one? Black terrorists?"

Coreris shook his head, feigning uncertainty. "I'm not even close to figuring this one yet," he lied.

"Hey, John, what do you think? Symbionese Liberation Army, maybe?"

Fotinos shrugged. "Hell, it could be anything. Your guess is as good as mine."

But privately they knew.

"Got to be the goddamned Muslims," Coreris said.

"Got to be," Fotinos agreed. "I knew it from the beginning. The sons of bitches are trying to wipe out whitey."

Elsewhere in the Hall of Justice, the old-timers engaged in bloody reminiscences. "Worse night in San Francisco's history," said one of the old jail custodians. "Worse night since that Chinaman went berserk with the ax over on Bush Street back in thirty-nine. Remember? Eddie O'Toole, God rest his soul, was just a rookie cop at the time. Brought him down with a single slug right between his slanted eyes. Damn fine shot."

"Yeah, but there was a night w'ust than that," an elderly Negro porter argued. "I 'members a night when a cabby name of Buck Kelly went crazy and shot five people. Killed ever' one of them. That was in 1927. Or maybe 'twenty-eight."

And so it went. People talked of nothing else.

* * *

230

On the streets it was the same. Dexter Waugh, an *Examiner* reporter, accompanied by photographer Walt Lynott, cruised the various districts of the city and stopped people on the street to interview them. One of those Waugh spoke with was Mrs. Sue Walizer.

"How do you feel about the shootings?" he asked. "Are you frightened?"

"I sure am," she replied. "Why wouldn't I be? I mean, these men harm innocent people. I'd like to know why too. I mean, we didn't do anything. Like the woman in the Laundromat—why her? I just don't understand."

Next Waugh interviewed Mike Donlon. "Will you continue to go out at night?"

Donlon shrugged. "Yeah, I guess so. I'm not sure."

"Are you afraid?"

"I'm a little bit shaky," he admitted.

Waugh stopped Joan Field, a pretty, long-haired lab technician. "Do you go out alone at night?" he asked her. Joan shook her head emphatically.

"Not on a bet."

"Never?"

"Never. I moved to San Francisco two years ago and have made a practice of *never* going out alone at night. I either stay home or go out with friends."

On Irving Street, at a coffee shop called Three Mills Creamery, Waugh spoke with the proprietor, Charles Prongo, who had been in business there for forty years. "Have the shootings made any difference to your business?"

"Not much," Prongo answered. "I get a lot of elderly customers, you know. They all talk about being sure they get home before dark. But they've always been like that. Only difference now is that they talk about it."

"Do you stay open at night?"

Prongo's eyebrows raised. "Are you kidding? I close six o'clock on the nose."

Others were calmer. Edna Leong, an attractive Oriental woman who operated a drugstore, said she did not go out alone at night because it was not necessary for her to do so. "But my daughters go out all the time," she said. "They think nothing of it. Of course, we are Oriental, and all the victims have been whites."

"Do you feel that the streets where you work and where you live are safe at night?"

"I think so. My store is at California and Fillmore, and I live across from the University of San Francisco. I think both areas are pretty safe."

Waugh did not tell her that the location of her store was only nine blocks from where Tana Smith had been killed, and that her home was less than a mile from where Angela Roselli had been shot.

Cornelius O'Leary was very fatalistic when Waugh interviewed him. A Jimmy Connors look-alike, he said, "I take my chances. There's no need to worry about something going to happen. Like that woman shot in the Laundromat: it was fate that she was there."

The blacks who were interviewed had a somewhat more relaxed attitude. "I go out all the time," said Charles DeLoach, an elderly, white-haired, white-mustached Negro.

"It doesn't make me nervous at all," said Ben Foster, another black. "All the people killed was white. I think it was a backlash thing, from unemployment, people getting laid off, people getting depressed."

"The only time I get extremely nervous," said J. J. White, "is when black people are getting killed."

After a half day of interviewing, Dexter Waugh came to the conclusion that the degree of fear was dictated by the individual's color. The shootings had definitely evolved into a racial issue.

Early in the afternoon, a police spokesman gave a large group of newsmen and wire service reporters a formal statement from the department.

"This department today has mounted the largest manhunt in the city's history in an effort to apprehend at least two men who shot and killed four persons and left a fifth critically wounded in random attacks last night.

"The pattern of these murders is strikingly similar to the wave of senseless shootings that began in late November and accounted for at least six deaths and two persons wounded in less than a month. The department is convinced that those slayings, and the more recent ones last night, were the work of the same men. The weapon used in the killings in previous weeks was a thirty-two-caliber automatic—as was the weapon used last night. A complete ballistics examination is being made now to verify that the same gun was used in all the incidents.

"All of the earlier killings were, according to witnesses, perpetrated by black men. All of the victims were white. The same was true of the incidents last night.

"Descriptions of the killers have varied, but it is believed that at least two, possibly more, men were involved. Likewise with the automobiles they are using; there are apparently two or more vehicles involved. One of them has been described as a 1969 Cadillac, black in color.

"A special task force unit, which was put on the streets approximately a month ago, is immediately being increased in size and assigned its own wavelength on the police radio to handle nothing but investigations which appear to be connected with this particular case."

One of the reporters raised his hand. "Which wavelength are they on?"

The spokesman referred to his notes. "Z," he said, "for Zebra."

Zebra, the reporter thought. Operation Zebra. How appropriate. The zebra was black and white.

Sometime during the afternoon, fire department units from various stations, on orders from the mayor's office, quietly drove to Geary and Divisadero, to the 800 block of Scott Street, and to Phillips' Bar and Grille on Ninth Street. At each location, firemen hosed down the street and sidewalk to remove bloodstains which had been attracting the morbidly curious all day.

Someone had already cleaned up the floor of the Lightning Laundromat and the front steps of 102 Edinburgh Street.

When it got dark that evening, Coreris and Fotinos decided to go out and get some supper. They had been working continuously since eight o'clock the previous morning—more than thirty hours.

"Christ, I feel like I was born in these clothes," Coreris complained as they crossed the big basement garage toward their unmarked car.

"I know what you mean," said Fotinos. "I keep thinking I smell a goat, and it turns out to be me."

"Is that what that is?"

"That's it. Want to sit close to me in the car?"

They left the Hall and headed for a quiet little restaurant they knew of on the other side of a residential district. As they drove, both men silently looked out at the streets. They were practically deserted.

"Jesus," Fotinos said, more to himself than to his partner.

"Did you ever see anything like it?" Coreris asked quietly.

Fotinos shook his head. "It's like the city died."

"Or like it closed down as a wake for the four who got it last night."

There was a spookiness about the neighborhood as they cruised through it. Shades were drawn on most of the windows. Doors were closed and still, as if announcing that they were double-locked or barred. Vehicular traffic was sparse; pedestrian traffic was practically nonexistent. There were not even any cats or dogs on the prowl.

"I wonder where they are right now," Coreris said. "The killers."

"Yeah. So do I." It had not been necessary for Coreris to say who "they" were; Fotinos would have known exactly who he was talking about. "They" were constantly in their minds.

They drove a little farther, the gloom of the still city settling even more heavily around them. They both felt alternately depressed and angry. This was *their* city, goddamn it! They were San Francisco born, San Francisco raised. They had fought in the goddamn *war* to preserve this city. They had an *interest* in this city. Nobody had the right to go around killing people in it. Sure, they were homicide cops, and homicide cops handled homicides. But it was different when a husband killed his wife, or a woman murdered her boyfriend, or a hood blew away some longshoreman for not paying back his loan, or a punk stabbed another punk in a street rumble. Those were homicides with a *reason*, homicides that could be *understood*. These—hell, these were ridiculous, they were ludicrous, they were insane. There was no excuse for them.

They had to be stopped.

"We may have to play a little dirty on this one," Coreris said.

Fotinos sighed quietly and said nothing. He knew.

In his cubicle, his barrel-like shoulders bent over the microscope, Mitch Luksich focused sharply on the single slug taken from Tana Smith's body. He examined every minute millimeter of its surface, every scratch, every shading, every pit. Then he slammed his hand down on the counter.

"Goddamn it!" he swore to no one in particular. "Goddamn son of a bitch!"

He had been over all the bullets and casings three times. There were one slug and two casings from the Tana Smith incident, no slugs and two casings from Vincent Wollin, two casings from the John Bambic scene and one slug found in his body by the coroner, two casings from the Jane Holly scene and one slug recovered by the coroner, and two casings from the Roxanne McMillian scene and one slug returned from the hospital. A total of four slugs and all ten casings from the ten shots fired. Four of them—the two that killed Tana Smith and the two that killed Vincent Wollin—were from Winchester-Western cartridges; the other six, that killed John Bambic and Jane Holly, and wounded Roxanne McMillian, were of Remington-Peters manufacture. Like the earlier specimens recovered from the Erakat, Dancik, DiGirolamo, Bertuccio, Moynihan, and Hosler killings, and the Agnos and Roselli shootings, they were .32-caliber automatic pistol cartridges with rifling of six lands and grooves, a right-hand twist, and an extractor-ejector separation of approximately 180 degrees.

The only thing wrong was that they had not been fired from the same gun.

Luksich dragged the phone over to him and dialed Homicide. Fotinos and Coreris had just come back from their eerie drive through the deserted streets to eat supper. Fotinos answered Luksich's call.

"John, I've got some news for you that's both good and bad," said the criminalist. "Those five people last night were shot with a different gun."

"You're kidding," Fotinos said. He covered the mouthpiece and said to Coreris across the facing desks, "Pick up. It's Mitch." Then to Luksich, when Coreris was on the line, "Tell me that again. A different gun was used last night?"

"Right. Same size and type of ammo, probably even the same model and make of gun. But it's not the same one that shot the people back in November and December. Definitely not. That's why I said the news was good *and* bad."

The two homicide inspectors locked eyes for a moment. Both knew what Luksich meant by news that was good as well as bad. In this case, it was a toss-up. Two guns meant twice as much chance of tracing at least one of them. But only half as much chance of connecting *all* the shootings—unless both weapons were found. Six of one, half a dozen of another.

"There's always the possibility," Luksich added, "that we're talking about the same pistol with a different barrel, too. Of course, that would indicate some knowledge of handgun stripping and ballistics."

"These bastards aren't that smart," Coreris said at once.

"All they know to do is load the goddamn thing and pull the trigger," Fotinos agreed. "They probably don't even clean the piece after it's used."

"We're talking about two guns then," Luksich concluded.

On the morning of January 30, two days after the five shootings, the *San Francisco Examiner* carried on its front page, above the paper's masthead, an eight-column box with a telephone number printed twice—page left and page right—in 32-point headline type. The identical numbers—553-9111—stood out boldly, demanding attention. Between them was a plea:

The police need your help.

If you have any information about Monday night's horrifying series of wanton murders—any information at all—call this number: 553-9111.

Ask for Homicide or Operations. Call at any time.

Call even though you may think your evidence is insignificant. Combined with other bits and pieces, it may well be the clue that will lead police to the killers.

Witnesses have provided sketchy descriptions of the gunmen. Read them on Page 16.

On page 16, descriptions of the killers were broken down according to victims. Tana Smith's assailant was described as twenty-five years old, six one, 165 pounds. John Bambic's murderer was reported to be six feet tall, 180 pounds. Jane Holly's killer was said to be about twenty-five, six one, slender. The person who shot Roxanne McMillian was believed to be about twenty-two, five feet ten, 180 pounds. All were identified as blacks. No description was given of Vincent Wollin's killer; the police had held back Lulu Badger's description of the black man in the gray turtleneck sweater, five feet seven, 160 pounds, age twenty-five. They were trying to find witnesses at the other scenes who might remember the gray turtleneck.

In the meantime, Coreris and Fotinos were piecing together a picture of the killers on their own. They had taken all the descriptions from every crime scene since the shootings began and were working up a composite.

"I don't know how many of these bastards there are," Coreris said, "but from these descriptions I'll lay you odds that at least two of them are very close in appearance." He peered across the facing desks at his partner. "What have you got for height?"

"Just a second," said Fotinos, working out some calculations by hand. "Let's see, we've got ten estimates of height, and when we add them together in inches they give us seven hundred twenty-eight inches. Divided by the ten estimates gives us seventy-two-point-eight-eight inches. That makes him six feet, three-quarters of an inch tall. Just a shade under six one." He looked up. "What'd you get for weight?"

"Seven estimates totaling eleven hundred ninety-five pounds. Divided out, it comes to a hundred seventy-one pounds."

"Okay. And we've got nine estimates of age that come to two hundred forty-eight years, and divided out make him twenty-seven years, six months old."

Coreris drew a sheet of paper in front of him and made several figures. "That's it, then. Twenty-seven, six feet to six one, a hundred seventy-one pounds, short hair cropped close to his head with no sideburns, and wears a variety of hats: a Little Caesar hat at the Dancik scene, a snap-brim at Agnos, a Navy watch cap at DiGirolamo, a white knit hat with a white ball at Roselli, and a dark Superfly hat with red band at Smith."

"Snappy dresser," Fotinos said flatly.

"Yeah. A real cool dude, as they say."

"He won't be so cool when we catch the son of a bitch," said Fotinos.

The two detectives gathered up their notes and returned to the streets.

At the California Department of Justice in Sacramento, Richard Walley of the Intelligence Analysis Unit, who had made the presentation to arrange the intrastate law enforcement meeting, was now correlating the latest information on the statewide pattern of black-white execution-type crimes. Since he had made the presentation, three more killings had occurred, and one attempt. The attempt was at Emeryville, just north of Oakland. A young white man, Thomas Bates, from Massachusetts, was hitchhiking near the freeway leading to the Bay Bridge. A dark, older model Cadillac pulled over, ostensibly to give him a ride. Two black men were in the front seat of the car. As Bates hurried over, the passenger window rolled down and one of the men smiled at him. "Hello, devil," he said. Then he stuck a gun through the window and shot Bates three times. The victim was hit in the hip, stomach, and right arm. He staggered to a nearby Holiday Inn and was given aid.

Thomas Bates had survived, but three others had not, and the statewide total had increased to sixty-seven. Then the information from San Francisco's night of terror came in and the figure went up to seventy-one.

Dick Walley called his contact at the California Department of Motor Vehicles.

"I know why you're calling," said DMV. "It's already being done. We're making a printout of every 1969 Cadillac registered in the San Francisco area. A cop named Coreris ordered it this morning. I take it you want a copy?"

"My request is a little more involved than that," said Walley. "I want a printout of the entire state—every 1969 Caddy registered. Then I want the driver's license photo checked against the registered owners. If the photo shows a black man, I want a copy of the picture."

DMV whistled. "You're going to have a lot of pictures. Mind telling me what you're going to do with them?"

"I'm going to sort them out according to height, weight, complexion, and hairstyle, then see if I can circulate them on mug-shot pages to surviving victims and witnesses through law enforcement agencies in the communities where these shootings have taken place. Maybe somebody will recognize one of them."

"Pretty long odds," DMV said skeptically.

"I've got a file here with the names of seventy-one dead people in it," Walley said. "And it keeps growing. I've *got* to play long odds. Can you give me the photos?"

"It'll take a while," said DMV, "but you'll get them."

In his private office at the Hall of Justice, Chief of Police Donald M. Scott was preparing to meet the press. With his coat and tie off, sleeves rolled up, he splashed cold water on his face and with wet palms brushed down his steel-gray hair. The cold water turned his already ruddy face florid for a minute as he dried with one of his plain white handball towels. Scott was fifty-seven, a tall, husky man who was forever fighting the battle of the pastry cart. His one uncontrollable weakness in life was chocolate cake—the richer and creamier the better. He played golf for recreation and handball for blood. To lose a handball match was a traumatic experience for him, one of the few things—outside of crime—that could bring a frown to his pleasant, robust face.

Don Scott had been a San Francisco policeman nearly all of his adult life. Aside from four years spent at the University of California, and a hitch in the Navy during World War Two, he had devoted himself almost entirely to law enforcement. There was virtually no type of police work he had not done, no type duty he had not at one time performed. He climbed the police ladder from bottom rung to top, achieving through the competitive civil service system every attainable rank up to captain of police; then, finally, was appointed by Mayor Joe Alioto to the position of chief.

As Scott was reknotting his tie, the intercom buzzed on his desk and he went out to answer it. "Captain Barca is here, Chief," his secretary said.

"Send him in, please."

Scott was putting on his uniform coat, with the gold stars on the shoulders and the heavy, glittering badge that said CHIEF—SAN FRANCISCO POLICE, when Captain Charles Barca, his chief of inspectors, came in. "What have we got for the press today, Charley?" Scott asked.

"Not much, I'm afraid," Barca answered. He put a typed sheet in the middle of Scott's desk. "Here's a rundown on our progress—if you can call it that."

"What's the story on this black initiation rite theory?"

"Nothing solid, just speculation. Coreris and Fotinos are convinced that the killers are Muslims, but they haven't hit on a motive yet."

"Coreris and Fotinos aren't often wrong," Scott commented as he read the progress report. When he finished reading and had the contents of the page clearly in his mind, he left the paper on his desk and said, "Okay, let's get it over with."

The two men went to a large room where press conferences and other gatherings were held. The press were already assembled. As soon as Scott reached the podium, the questions came at him like machine-gun fire.

"Chief, do you have any suspects at all?"

"Not at this time," Scott said.

"Have you questioned anyone other than witnesses?"

"Numerous people around the city who resemble the described suspects have been stopped and questioned, yes. That's routine procedure in a manhunt."

"Is there any truth to the rumor that the killings are some kind of initiation rite to a secret black sect?"

"There is no evidence to support that theory at the present time."

"Chief, a department spokesman said yesterday that this is one of the biggest manhunts in the city's history. Yet in cruising the districts, we don't see any more radio units on the streets than we normally would. Can you explain that?"

"Certainly. Scores of personal cars are being used, by hundreds of officers in plainclothes. I assure you that, despite appearances, this department is fully mobilized. The largest police task force in the city's history is on the job."

"Sir, is it true that the case was given the code name 'Zebra' because the zebra is black and white, and this case appears to be blacks against whites?"

"Not true at all," Scott said patiently. "The Z-for-Zebra channel happened to be the only frequency available for exclusive use."

"Chief, are you expecting the killers to strike again soon?"

Don Scott sighed quietly. "I wish I knew," he said in the softest voice the reporters had ever heard him use.

Across town, a drawn, grieving George Holly quietly left his and Jane's apartment, which was filled to overflowing with sympathetic friends and neighbors, and walked to a nearby flower shop.

"I'd like some flowers for someone in the hospital," he told the clerk.

Holly was led to a refrigerator display case and shown what was available. He made his selection and asked that they be delivered.

"What's the name of the patient and the hospital, sir?"

"Roxanne McMillian," Holly said. "San Francisco General."

Even in his personal grief, George Holly found time to think about the young woman he had read about in the papers. The one who, unlike his dear wife Jane, had survived the night of terror.

At the end of the second day following the five shootings, the city's headlines were again grim:

NO PROGRESS, ONLY SLIM LEADS
IN HUNT FOR STREET KILLERS

241

Clark Howard

None of the headlines, or the stories under them, offered any reassurance at all to the frightened citizens of San Francisco.

Joseph Alioto, mayor of the city of San Francisco, made his first formal statement regarding the street killings on Thursday. Formerly a practicing attorney, from a prominent Bay Area family, Alioto was a big-chested, balding man who had about him an inbred stateliness and an undeniable charisma. Joe Alioto dearly loved his city. His anguish over what the street killers were doing to it showed clearly in his face.

"I want to first assure the citizens of San Francisco that a maximum police effort is being made to apprehend the persons responsible for the recent series of street slayings," he said at the beginning of his statement. "I can assure them that a maximum effort is being made to protect residents of this city. Literally every police unit is involved in the investigation and the protection of the public.

"Both Police Chief Donald Scott and myself would like to thank the citizens who are coming forward with information useful to this investigation. Cooperation with police is increasing.

"I would like people to be understanding of some police efforts, such as halting people on the streets and requiring identification. I am certain San Franciscans will realize it is necessary under the circumstances. I assure them they will be treated with courtesy, their rights will be protected, and police officers will act within constitutional limits."

At the same time Alioto was issuing his formal statement, Lieutenant William O'Connor, the police department's public affairs officer, was conducting a press conference at the Hall of Justice. For the first time in San Francisco's history, the department officially warned citizens not to venture outdoors after dark.

242

"If people must go outdoors after dark," O'Connor said, "the department strongly recommends that they go in pairs or groups."

"Are there any clues at all to the identity of the two black gunmen?" a reporter asked.

O'Connor shook his head. "None at all."

"Who is in charge of the investigation?"

"Captain Charles Barca has personally taken charge."

"Is the department officially calling it the 'Zebra' case now?"

"There's nothing official about the name. But it has caught on," he admitted. "I haven't heard it referred to by any other name."

"Have you definitely determined the make of car the killers used?"

"Not yet. We have it narrowed down to a Cadillac or possibly a Chrysler."

"Are you stopping persons driving both makes?"

"We're stopping anyone we see in large, black cars of 1969 manufacture or thereabouts."

"Anyone?" a black reporter asked. "Or just blacks?"

"Anyone," O'Connor repeated. "Numerous whites were stopped last night. At nighttime it's difficult to tell the color of a driver. In the daytime we are naturally concentrating on cars being driven by black men. We have no choice in the matter. To pursue any other course would be foolish."

"What about this warning to stay off the streets?" another asked. "Can you elaborate on that a bit?"

"I think the warning speaks for itself," O'Connor said. "All we're asking people to do is use caution and common sense. Avoid isolated areas, dark side-streets, alleys. If you see something or somebody suspicious, don't hesitate to turn around and walk the other way. Don't feel that it's cowardly to be careful."

"Can you comment at all on the rumored existence of a fanatical black sect that is supposedly responsible for some fifty or sixty murders in the state during the past several years?"

"I have no information on such a sect," O'Connor said.

"The attorney general's office is supposed to have a complete file on it."

"Ask the attorney general then," the police lieutenant said without rancor. "I can't help you."

"If you aren't going on the theory that a black sect is responsible for the killings," another reporter asked, "then what are you attributing the crimes to?"

"Psychotics," O'Connor replied quietly. "Crazy men."

In the afternoon, the *Examiner* had another reporter-photographer team on the street, this time interviewing blacks exclusively.

"How do you feel about Operation Zebra?" reporter Hollis Wagstaff asked Richard Matthews, a mustached young black who was attending the postal service academy.

"I don't feel comfortable with all the police around," Matthews said. "But then I never have felt safe around them."

Esta Moran, a long-haired, attractive black housewife, said, "I'm really glad that the police are concerned for a change. I just wonder if they'd be as *much* concerned if it were black people getting killed."

John Dearman, a bearded black attorney, said when interviewed, "I commend the police for their beefing up of the force, but I hope it's not just directed at blacks. I hope blacks aren't being harassed."

Julian Richardson, a bookstore operator, said, "These incidents are the consequence of violent propaganda thrown at us daily by the news and entertainment media."

Other people made other comments as reporter Wagstaff roamed the streets that day. Although they were responding only to a question about Operation Zebra, it was curious that none of the blacks interviewed took the occasion to condemn the unknown street killers or expressed sympathy for the victims.

In the same edition carrying Mayor Alioto's statement, the *Examiner* offered its own reward for the killers. Without fanfare, the newspaper printed a simple statement of its intent, which read:

The *Examiner* today offered a reward of $5000 for information leading to the arrest and conviction of the men who killed four persons on the streets of San Francisco Monday night.

Informants should call 781-2424 and ask for the City Desk. They may, when calling, give their names or other identification. If they wish to remain anonymous, they should give a code name or identifying number which they can use later to establish their claim to the reward.

First the Arab community, now the city's leading newspaper. It was being made easier and easier for someone to come forth with information.

There was some concern at this point among certain groups that the San Francisco Police Department might not be reacting as efficiently as it could to the sudden wave of killings that was terrorizing the city. The *Examiner* decided to check it out. A reporter was sent to the Communications Room of SFPD. Captain Jeremiah Taylor secured the tapes of the previous Monday evening's calls and played them for him.

The tapes indicated that the first report of the Tana Smith shooting at Geary and Divisadero was received at 7:51:50 P.M.—fifty-one minutes and fifty seconds after seven. The call went out ten seconds later, at 7:52. A radio car arrived at the scene at 7:54, two minutes later.

The report of the Vincent Wollin shooting at Fulton and Scott was received at 8:00 P.M., dispatched at 8:00:11 P.M. —eleven seconds later—and a patrol car was at the scene by 8:02, one minute forty-nine seconds later.

The John Bambic shooting incident was first reported at 9:17 P.M., the call dispatched seven seconds later, and the unit on the scene at 9:19. Under two minutes again.

By the time the Jane Holly shooting report came in, at 9:52 P.M., Communications was so inundated with shooting-related reports and requests of an emergency nature that the field call did not go out for forty seconds. A radio car was nevertheless there in one minute twenty seconds.

With the Roxanne McMillian shooting, all records were broken: the report was received at 9:57:02, the call was dispatched at 9:57:05—a mere three seconds later—and in fifty seconds a unit was at the scene.

"The average time factors for the five calls," said Captain Taylor, "is fourteen seconds to get the call on the air to a unit, and one minute thirty-five seconds for a team of men to arrive at the scene. I'd say that was pretty good time."

The *Examiner* reporter agreed. The paper duly reported to its reading public that the police force, as usual, was on its toes.

Examiner reporter Bob Hayes, in an effort to isolate the type of black individuals who were committing the crimes, arranged to interview Dr. Price Cobb, a noted black psychiatrist and author of *Black Rage*, a book dealing with black-related frustrations. Dr. Cobb had no difficulty in classifying the killers for Hayes.

"Bad niggers," he said simply. He smiled at Hayes's look of surprise and explained. "One of the constant themes in black folklore is the 'bad nigger.' It seems that every community has had one or was afraid of having one. They were feared as much by blacks as by whites."

And exactly what was a "bad nigger"? He was a man who seemed "at one moment meek and compromised, and in the next a terrifying killer."

After a lengthy interview with Dr. Cobb, Hayes returned to the paper to do his story, convinced that violence created by a "bad nigger" outside the black community posed a peculiar problem for both black and white. He wrote:

> When violence occurs in the black community, blacks always note that police investigation is usually cursory. Black killing black seldom, if ever, makes page one of the newspapers.

> However, as blacks see it, when black violence strikes the white community, police reaction is swift and overwhelming. The black community becomes a hunting ground. Helmeted, shotgun-bearing officers cruise through their neighborhoods. Whether they know it or not, they only add to the growing hostility between themselves and the community.

> The faces that stare at each other are less than friendly. The black is reminded that if his description resembles that of the suspect, he might end up on the wrong side of a cell door.

Hayes concluded his article by stating that blacks believed that

multiple killers existed in every race. He quoted one black as saying, "The madness that drives black men to kill innocent people . . . involves a sickness that is as American as apple pie."

While Hayes was writing his analysis for the *Examiner,* a reporter from the *Chronicle,* trying to tie in the street killings with the rumored rash of hackings throughout the state, went back through
the newspaper files and came onto the clipping about the Hague
case. He managed to locate Richard Hague, the survivor of the
horrible kidnap-hacking the previous October.

"I know my name has been in the papers before," Hague said,
"but that was back when it first happened. I don't want it used now
if I'm going to talk about the people who did it."

Hague was granted anonymity, and proceeded to give the *Chronicle* reporter an engrossing story of a secret mass murder sect.

The detectives assigned to his late wife's hacking murder, he
said, were Homicide Inspectors Bill Armstrong and Dave Tochi.
Tochi had been sent to a meeting in Oakland which was attended
by a number of representatives from law enforcement agencies all
over the state. The purpose of the meeting was to compare and exchange information on at least forty hacking deaths which had tak-
en place throughout the state. Tochi, Hague said, came away from
the meeting with information of the existence of a black extremist
group that the combined police agencies knew about, but on which
they could not secure evidence through any member, nor penetrate
with an informant.

"It's difficult to place informants into the group because of their
strict screening procedures, and because of the heavy demands
made on members," Hague said Tochi had told him. Tochi and the
other officers who attended the meeting found that the group comprised "a very terrifying form of terrorism, because of the character of the people involved." Some of them "have no criminal record, have never crossed swords with the police. They are involved
in a killing (that is) entirely random and there is no connection with
the victims." Sometimes, after they completed their initiation and
were accepted as members of the sect, they became "clean living
and never got into any trouble with the police again."

The *Chronicle* reporter, substituting the name "Smith" for Hague, wrote the piece for the next edition of his paper and head-lined it:

POLICE BLAME 'SECT'
S.F. VICTIM SAYS

It was the first public indication that members of the San Francisco Police Department unofficially believed that some unholy black rite was behind the rash of street killings.

That night, the third night after the four killings, Janet Lang,* a twenty-four-year-old white woman, was waiting to cross the street at Grant and Vallejo, seven blocks from where Richard and Quita Hague had been abducted. As she stood on the corner, she suddenly felt a sharp point touch her side.

"Stand very still, bitch, or I'll cut you," a voice next to her said quietly.

Janet froze, petrified. The man had seemed to come out of nowhere: one second she had been alone on the corner, the next he was there with the—whatever it was—sticking in her side.

"Walk down the street with me," the man ordered. "If you try to get away, I'll cut you good."

He guided her to a nearby alley. Parked a short distance down the alley was a black Cadillac. Janet had read about a black Cadillac in the paper just that day. She felt her entire body go cold. Oh, my God—

Apparently the man sensed her terrible fear. "Don't worry," he said, "I'm not one of the ones doing all the killing here. But if you don't cooperate, I'll take care of you good with this." He showed her what was sticking against her side: a ten-inch, silver-handled hunting knife.

Janet was forced into the rear of the car and made to lie on the back seat. The man with the knife got in with her and knelt on the floorboard. He pushed her skirt up around her hips and pulled her panty hose down to her ankles. As he rubbed his hand between her

*The name of this individual has been changed to protect her identity in light of the nature of the crime committed against her.

legs, she was able to study his face in the gray illumination from a streetlight near the mouth of the alley. He was a black man with a short Afro; his face was pockmarked and he wore silver, wire-rimmed glasses with lightly tinted lenses.

He must be one of them, Janet thought. She closed her eyes and silently said the Act of Contrition. At that moment, she was absolutely certain that she was going to be killed.

When she was involuntarily moist enough to suit the black man, he dropped his trousers, pulled her right leg up onto his left shoulder, and raped her. All the while, she continued to pray silently for forgiveness for past sins.

When he had climaxed and was through with her, the black man wiped himself off on the hem of her dress and pulled his trousers back up. He took her purse, rummaged through it in the dark until he found what little money she had, and pulled her out of the car. Not even allowing her time to pull up her panty hose, he shoved her roughly toward the street.

"You can beat it now, bitch," he said. "You done served your purpose tonight."

Before Janet reached the end of the alley, the man was in his car and gone the opposite way.

As she stumbled toward safety, Janet Lang continued to pray. Only now she was offering thanks for still being alive. She could scarcely believe her good fortune. He had not been a Zebra killer after all.

Vandyke was not in town, but the men held a formal meeting in the loft anyway. They had to decide what to do. They held an open, round-table discussion in which everyone participated. Everyone except Judo, who was not there.

"I know some of you are very close to getting your Death Angel wings," the droopy-eyed man in the brown-and-yellow warm-up jacket said. "So I hate to be the one to say that we'd better cool it for a while. But that's exactly how I feel about it. This city is *hot* right now. Don't none of us want to do anything that might get us busted."

"Nobody's been caught yet," Skullcap said contrarily. "We got the cops running in circles."

"Somebody *has* been caught," Yellow contradicted. "We got a brother doing life up in Folsom right now." He was talking about Head.

"Yeah," Skullcap replied with a sneer, "a brother who copped out to it. Anybody do that *deserves* life."

"That's not really the point," said Droopy Eyes. "Point is, somebody *did* get caught—and somebody *could* get caught again. I think we're all agreed that we want to avoid that."

"M-m-man, I sure do," Rims interjected emphatically. "I don't want to go back to the joint."

"Amen to that, brother," said another of the men who had also done time.

"If it was just a case of one brother getting caught again and taking the fall alone, we wouldn't have so much cause to worry," Droopy Eyes said. "But there's always the chance that if they catch one more of us, they'll be able to catch us all. And we not just talking about the shit in San Francisco, we talking about a lot more. You brothers from Santa Clara and Marin counties got to be careful too; the cops is still hot up there about that hitchhiker that was cut up and dumped on the boulevard, and that devil on the Stanford campus that was stabbed fourteen times. Then there's that other hitchhiker that got shot on the freeway over in Emeryville the other night. I mean, there's a lot of recent shit could get stirred up for everybody if we not careful."

"So what you saying we gots to do?" Skullcap asked. "Just quit?"

"For the time being. Until everything is cool again. I talked to the brothers in Oakland today; they feel the same way. There's a lot of heavy heat over there because of some devils that have been shot, and one female devil that was hacked and dumped behind the Coliseum. The brothers in Oakland realize that this is a very poor time for hunting grafted snakes."

"Yeah, but what about the ones like me who are *moving?*" Skullcap argued. "What about the ones who are so *close* to getting the wings? It's not fair to make us stop now that we be so close."

"You'll still get your wings, brother. It'll just take a little longer, is all." Droopy Eyes looked at Yellow and Rims. "You two are closer to wings than anybody else. How do you feel about cooling it for a while?"

"I don'twanttogobacktothejoint," Rims said edgily.

"I'll do whatever's best for *all* the brothers," Yellow said. "I know my wings will come to me when it's Allah's will."

Shit, Skullcap thought, there goes that argument.

"Anyone want to argue against cooling it?" Droopy Eyes asked, looking directly at Skullcap. He waited several seconds for a reply. There was none. "Okay, that's it, I guess. Let's cool it for sixty days. No devils are to be destroyed for sixty days. That cool with everybody?"

There was a chorus of agreement as the men nodded and approved the two-month moratorium on murder. There was actually relief in some of their faces, as if a heavy burden had been lifted from their shoulders. For no matter how demanding the reason for it, systematic murder takes its toll emotionally, even on the fanatic. The men in the loft this day were glad to be taking a vacation from death.

All except Skullcap.

And Judo, who was not there.

Herb Caen, respected longtime columnist for the *Chronicle,* arrived at the newspaper at his customary time on Friday morning. Sitting down at his desk, he unfolded a sheaf of notes he had in his pocket and started to sort them out. Almost at once his phone rang.

"Herb Caen," he answered.

"Five white people are dead, right?" a voice asked.

"Who is this, please?" Caen inquired.

"Never mind who it is. I just want you to know that tonight some of us are going out and get ten blacks in trade."

"That's not very smart, is it?" Caen said calmly.

"Smart or not," the caller said, "we're going to do it. Two for one is about right, don't you think?"

Before Caen could say anything further, the caller hung up.

Caen made a note of what was said so that he could pass it on to the police. Then he sighed quietly and shook his head. He had a feeling it was going to be one of those days.

The person who called Herb Caen apparently only read headlines, for as almost everyone else in San Francisco knew, there were four dead in the most recent shootings, not five.

Victim number five, Roxanne McMillian, lay in bed in a San Francisco General Hospital ward, paralyzed from the waist down. Her pretty face was pale and drawn, both from the shock of her experience, the trauma of surgery, and the almost constant pain she felt. For even though Roxanne could not move her legs, she could still *feel* them—and what she felt, hurt.

Her bed was near the door, and with her head turned slightly she could see everyone who came in, and many persons who were just passing in the corridor. She watched the door very closely whenever she was awake, because she was terribly afraid to be lying there helpless like that. It was a fear that, no matter how much she lectured and reasoned with herself, would not go away. Every time a young black man—orderly or visitor—passed in the corridor, she shuddered; every time one entered the ward, she cringed inside. Try as she did, Roxanne could not get it out of her head that she had somehow offended the black men by surviving. They had shot five people on Monday night; four of them had died. She was the only one who had lived.

Now she lay on a hospital bed, unable to walk, and inside her was the dread fear that the black men would somehow come back and finish the job.

It was sheer torture for her every time a young black orderly or doctor passed her bed and said, "Hi." She kept expecting the greeting to be followed by gunshots.

In another hospital, Kaiser, south of San Francisco, Zebra victim number ten, Angela Roselli, was being helped to stand up while a doctor measured the distance from her closed fist to the floor. Angela, whose shooting was now forty-three days old, was being fitted for a cane.

She had undergone surgery twice by now: the first time on the night she was shot, the second after her transfer to Kaiser, where her student insurance would take care of the medical expenses. The spine damage had been corrected enough for her to try to begin walking again—as soon as her cane was ready. She had mixed emotions about using her legs again: she dearly wanted to resume walking, to be able to get around again as she had in the past, and not be bound to a wheelchair; but her legs continued to hurt so constantly, the pain going through them in rushes, like terrible waves, that she was afraid that the exertion of using them again would increase her agony. She had hurt so much, so very much, during the past six weeks, particularly since they had tapered her off the morphine, that she did not think she could *stand* to have it increase.

But stand it she would apparently have to, if it happened, because that was the only way she would be able to walk again.

Angela gritted her teeth as a nurse and an aide held her upright. Her mind was clear of everything except the discomfort she felt; unlike Roxanne McMillian, she had no psychological hang-up about her assailant returning to finish the job. As far as she was concerned, the attack was over: she and the black man who shot her had crossed lives briefly one terrible night, then gone separate ways. Angela had put him out of her mind entirely; she did not even want her name associated with the Zebra crimes, as they were now being called.

All she wanted to do was walk again, get out of the damned hospital, and return to her friends and the noninvolved life-style she had chosen for herself.

Just let the world leave her alone and she would be happy.

In San Francisco, atop Nob Hill, a reservations clerk in one of the city's several elegant-class hotels went glumly into the resident manager's office. "Another one just came in," she told him.

The resident manager rolled his eyes up in exasperation. "Where's this one from?"

"Indianapolis, Indiana. Newlyweds planning to spend five days here on their honeymoon. They canceled through their travel agent."

"Any reason given?"

"The usual: a change of plans."

The resident manager grunted softly. "Sure. A change of plans to avoid a city where it isn't safe to walk the streets at night." He sat back and shook his head. "This is beginning to hurt."

"I know it's no consolation," the reservations clerk told him, "but we aren't the only ones. I spoke with the Saint Francis, the Clift, the Stanford Court—they're all experiencing the same problem: cancellations coming in almost hourly."

The resident manager pondered the situation for a moment, then said decisively, "Keep me posted on this for the rest of the day. If they keep coming in, drastic steps will have to be taken."

"What will you do?" the woman asked.

He pursed his lips in thought for a moment longer, then said, "I'll call the Chamber of Commerce, that's what I'll do. It's their responsibility to make sure the city has a favorable image. Obviously they haven't been doing their job."

The reservations clerk went back to her desk, relieved that the resident manager was going to take care of the problem.

At noon that day, Dr. Washington Garner, a prominent black physician who also served as president of the San Francisco Police Commission, held a press conference to slap the wrist of the black community. The reason for the press conference, he stated beforehand, was that he was not satisfied that black citizens were cooperating as well as they could in the biggest criminal investigation in the city's history.

"As an example of this hesitancy to cooperate," he said, "eight black women witnessed the slaying in a self-service laundry of the fourth victim in the recent shooting spree. Although the women have talked with investigators, police feel that some could supply better physical descriptions than they have.

"On the whole," Dr. Garner observed, "the black community is behind the police department and wants the murderers stopped. But," he added, "they are afraid to come forward."

Asked if he believed the slayings were the work of an antiwhite sect, Garner said he did not. "I definitely do not buy the initiation theory," he stated emphatically. "There is no evidence or reason to believe it's an organized group. If a white person killed a number of blacks, he would simply be classified as a psychopath. I am convinced that these are simply psychopaths committing these murders."

Garner concluded the press conference with a plea for help in hunting down the killers. "I urge anyone in the black community who can give us a definite description of these madmen to come forward," he said. "We promise to keep your identity secret. There are even ways to get around court appearances and that sort of thing. All we want to do is catch these murderers."

So for the third time there was a more than subtle implication that a traitor among the killers might be protected if he came forward as an informant.

Elsewhere, three San Francisco women—Monica Halloran, Margot Hambly, and Roxanne Gudebrod—sought a solution to the problem in another way. They began a campaign protesting the use of their city as a locale for television and motion-picture crime movies.

"Is San Francisco to achieve the reputation of the crime mecca of the nation?" they asked in a letter to Jack Valenti, president of the Motion Picture Association of America. Sending copies of the letter to Mayor Alioto, United States Senators Alan Cranston and John Tunney, and to all the San Francisco news media, the women cited three motion pictures and two television series as prime examples of shows depicting the city as a jungle of violence. *Dirty Harry, Magnum Force,* and *The Laughing Policeman* were the movies; *Ironside* and *The Streets of San Francisco* the TV shows.

"We cannot but feel that the mindless violence of Monday night's chain shooting had its origin in the fictional exploits shown consistently in the productions mentioned," the women said. "Although entertainment producers always claim only to be giving the public what it wants, there is a limit to the degree to which they should be allowed to appeal to the public's baser instincts."

The ladies concluded by saying that an atmosphere of violence was being created and fostered by consistent and detailed exploitation. The image of San Francisco, they said, was being degraded in the process.

There was no response to the women's position from Valenti, Alioto, Cranston, or Tunney.

Still another approach was taken by County Supervisor Alfred J. Nelder, himself a former San Francisco chief of police. Supervisor Nelder, in a telegram to the state capital, asked Governor Ronald Reagan to post an additional $10,000 reward for information leading to the arrest and conviction of the murderers.

Nelder pointed out to the governor that he, Reagan, had the authority to offer the reward under a section of the California Penal Code.

"I feel that it is imperative," Nelder told the press, "that as much money as possible be offered as a reward for these killers. The only way we are going to be able to apprehend them is if someone comes forward with information. Otherwise, it is a hopeless situation. When you have a case of stranger killing stranger, there is almost no way at all of connecting the killer with the victim. You can talk to witnesses until you are blue in the face, match slugs and shell casings until you've got a barrel full of them, and stop and identify people on the street until doomsday comes, and you still won't find the criminals in the case without an informant. A stool pigeon, a snitch, a fink: that's what will solve Zebra. But it takes money—lots of money—to get such an informer. That's why I'm asking the governor to sweeten the pot with what's already been offered by the Arab community and the *Examiner*. I sincerely hope he will do it."

Alfred Nelder did not get his wish. Ronald Reagan never replied to the telegram.

At the Hall of Justice, a young staff assistant from the Department of Motor Vehicles entered the Homicide Department carrying a package containing a 191-page printout from the DMV computer.

"Inspector Coreris?" the messenger asked.

"Over here," Gus Coreris said, waving from his desk.

The staff assistant gave him the envelope. "These are the names of the registered owners of 1969 Cadillacs in San Francisco County, sir," he said.

"Good, good," said Coreris, smiling. "How many names are there?"

"Four thousand, seven hundred and fifty-three," the young man said.

Coreris's smile dissolved. "Jesus H. Christ," he said quietly.

At his own desk, John Fotinos ruefully shook his head. "We better start on them right away," he said, "so we can finish them before we retire from the department."

Coreris opened the package and unfolded several of the attached, perforated IBM sheets. The pages were printed in precise, machinelike lines, each line containing a name and an address, nothing more.

"My supervisor said to tell you that they aren't alphabetized because we've never had a reason to alphabetize registered owners of specific makes and models of cars," the staff assistant said.

"I understand," Coreris said glumly.

"Also, there's no date of birth or physical description because that information is contained only on drivers' licenses."

Coreris nodded wearily. "Sure."

"But he did say that in case you're interested, there's a man named Richard Walley up at the Criminal Investigation and Identification office in Sacramento who's having these same names matched with driver's license photos and descriptions. In fact, he's having it done for every sixty-nine Caddy in the entire state."

Fotinos grunted loudly. "What year do they expect to have that job finished?"

"It's an involved assignment, all right," the young DMV man said. "But we're moving right along on it."

"Thank your supervisor for me," said Coreris. "We appreciate the cooperation."

After the young man left, Fotinos came around the facing desks and stood next to his partner. "Four thousand, seven hundred and fifty-three," he said. "And we don't even know which ones are black." He sighed quietly. "I wonder if I'm too old to transfer to the fire department."

In his apartment, Judo sat staring at the television. A live press conference was being televised. It involved Mayor Joseph Alioto, Chief of Police Donald Scott, and Chief of Inspectors Charles Barca. Chief Scott was responding to a question about the department's progress on the case.

"Progress has been slow, as we expected it to be," he admitted. "This is not a case where we have the usual areas of investigation such as a clear motive, a traceable relationship between the killer and the victim, or witnesses who can provide positive identifications. This is a case where we must fall back on methodical routine and investigative repetition, in the hope that some clue, some evidence, that did not turn up previously, will turn up now. The public, gentlemen, will be our best detectives in this case."

Judo wet his lips, then wiped them dry with the back of one hand. The public, he thought. That meant *everybody*.

"Mr. Mayor," a reporter asked, "do you believe that an informant will eventually come forward to help the police solve this case?"

"I certainly would hope so," Alioto said. "I want to make a public appeal right now for any witnesses or other informants who have knowledge of these vicious crimes to contact Chief Scott here, or Captain Barca, or *any* police officer. And I want to emphasize that we will accept information from *anyone.*"

"Even someone who might be involved, sir?"

"*Anyone,*" Alioto reiterated.

Judo swallowed down a dry throat. Anyone. Skullcap. Rims. Yellow. Head, even if he *was* in prison. Or any of the others who had attended a loft meeting.

Anyone. That covered quite a few people.

"Captain Barca," a reporter asked, "do you think there's any way this case can be solved *without* an informant coming forward?"

"Of course," Charley Barca said confidently. "*Eventually* it will definitely be solved. One of these killers will make a mistake that can be traced to him, or he'll be caught in the act by one of the hundreds of officers we have assigned to the Zebra detail around the clock, or *something* will happen to trip them up. Point is, we don't know *when* such an occurrence will take place. We don't know how *long* the killings will go on in the meantime. That's why we must rely on the public to help us *now.* As the mayor said, we need help from the citizens of San Francisco, and we need it urgently."

Everything that the officials said was reverberating in Judo's mind like a pinball machine gone wild. Threatening catchphrases surfaced, submerged, resurfaced, taunted: *a mistake that could be traced; caught in the act; help from the citizens; information from anyone—anyone—anyone—*

Judo reached over and turned off the set. He had had enough. Of everything. He went to the kitchen door and looked in at the woman washing dishes.

"Start packing," he said. "We leaving San Francisco."

When the press conference was over, Alioto, Scott, and Barca sat down in private to discuss an official chain of command for the Zebra case.

"As I understand it, Chief," said Alioto, "Captain Barca here, who is your chief of inspectors, is to personally have charge of the case. Is that correct?"

"Yes, sir," Don Scott replied. "He will give top priority to Zebra above all other duties."

Alioto looked at Barca. "And at the Homicide Department level? Who will have primary responsibility there?"

"Lieutenant Charles Ellis is in charge there, Mr. Mayor," said Barca. "But of course he has primary responsibility for *all* homicides. We have to assign someone to Zebra exclusively."

"Who will that be?"

"We don't know yet," said Barca. "We'll have to confer with Ellis on it."

"Let's get him over here then," Alioto said. "We might as well settle it right now."

Lieutenant Charles Ellis was summoned to the meeting. The question was put to him without preliminary: who among his cadre of homicide inspectors was best suited to take over Zebra? Ellis answered without hesitation.

"Coreris," and Fotinos, he said. "Gus Coreris and John Fotinos."

"We mean take it over and go all the way with it," said Alioto.

"Coreris and Fotinos," Ellis repeated.

"Work night and day," said Scott. "Stick with it until the killers are caught, tried, convicted, and put away. If it takes ten years."

Ellis nodded. "Coreris and Fotinos."

"Do you agree, Captain Barca?" the mayor asked.

"Completely," said Barca.

"All right. Coreris and Fotinos it is, then."

Later that day, Coreris came out of Lieutenant Ellis's office with an odd expression on his face.

"What's up?" asked Fotinos. He had just come back from the Crime Lab.

"They just gave us Zebra," Coreris said. His voice was a mixture of incredulity, pride, anxiety, and confidence, all toned together almost to a whisper. "They gave us Zebra."

"Holy Christ," said Fotinos. A charge of excitement shot through him. "What did they say?" he asked Coreris.

"Just that it was our baby from now on. You and I don't work anything else. We get *carte blanche* throughout the department: anything we need. And we get to pick two more guys to work with us."

"Two more from Homicide?"

"From anywhere. I told you: *carte blanche.*"

"Who are we going to get?"

"I'm not sure. I'll think about it later. Right now I want to get the whole thing organized. Let's collect every report from every shooting and get them in chronological order so that we can review them. Also, let's get a complete list of every witness to every incident; I want all of them reinterviewed. Let's get together with Mitch Luksich too and see if he's got any new ideas about tracking down the gun—or rather, the *two* guns—that are being used." Coreris suddenly snapped his fingers. "There's somebody else I want to meet with too: that guy from CII that the kid from the motor vehicles department told us about: the one who's having the sixty-nine Caddy registrations matched with driver's license photos. What was his name?"

Fotinos thought for a moment. "Wally something. No, Richard Walley, that was it. Funny you should mention him, because I've been thinking about him too. Even if he *is* covering the whole state, he's still doing one very important thing that can help us: he's separating the white registered owners from the black."

"Exactly," said Coreris. "He might be able to help us in other ways too, depending on what kind of guy he is." Coreris rubbed his hands together briskly. "Okay, partner, let's go to work and catch these sons of bitches."

"Let's," said Fotinos.

A week later, Coreris and Fotinos were driving down to Stanford University, thirty miles south of the city.

"You're sure this guy will talk to us?" Coreris asked.

"I told you, I called him on the phone," Fotinos said. "I explained everything we had to him. And I had a patrol unit take him an envelope with copies of all the Incident Reports. He'll talk to us. It'll be off the record, but what the hell. At least we'll have a little insight."

The person they were discussing was one of the foremost criminal psychologists in the country. He was in California to lecture at Stanford. His insistence that his identity be kept anonymous and his remarks off the record was because he preferred not to become involved in the Zebra case to the extent that he could be subpoenaed to a subsequent trial. Had he gone on record and done a complete and thorough analysis of Zebra up to that point, he might have legitimately billed the city of San Francisco ten thousand dollars. He was that good in his field. As it was, Fotinos had read in the newspaper of his visit and had taken a chance that he could interest him with a telephone call. He had.

"You've got a lot of guts, John," Gus said as they drove south.

Fotinos shrugged. "It worked, didn't it?"

"This guy probably makes more money for a two-hour lecture than you and I together make in a whole month."

"Doesn't matter how much a guy makes. If he's a good guy, he'll try to help you out. If he's a prick, he won't. This doc sounded like a good guy."

When they arrived at the university, a campus security officer directed them to the visitors' quarters. The doctor, a small, dignified-looking gentleman with an almost electric presence, invited them in. "Which one of you called?" he asked with one eyebrow raised curiously.

"I did, sir," Fotinos said, a touch sheepishly.

"Most resourceful," he said, with the slightest hint of irritation. "You go right for the weak spots, don't you? Oh, well. Please sit down, gentlemen."

They sat on a small couch in front of a burning fireplace. The doctor, with all the material on the case spread before him on a coffee table, took a club chair facing them.

"At this point," he said, "based on what information you have thus far, I'm afraid there really is not much I can tell you, at least not much in the way of substantial facts that might help you isolate suspects. You don't need a criminal psychologist to tell you, for instance, that you are dealing with very neat, physically clean individuals; their manner of dress and personal grooming as described by various witnesses has told you that. You don't need me to tell you that they are either very clever or very lucky; their *mo*-

261

dus operandi has shown that. Personally, I would opt for the latter conclusion if it were up to me. I think they have been *very* lucky, and if I had to guess, I would say that their cleverness, their cunning, is quite limited. I don't think you're dealing with very smart people here, gentlemen. Not very smart at all."

The doctor removed a cigar from a leather case and lighted it. Thick smoke reminiscent of Mitch Luksich rose to the ceiling.

"What I *can* tell you, and tell you definitely," he continued, "is that you're dealing with some very latent cowards in this case." He saw Coreris and Fotinos exchange puzzled looks. "Yes, I know that sounds quite farfetched to you. How can people who murder so promiscuously on public streets be cowards? Surely such acts must take a great deal of courage and nerve. Not so, however."

The doctor reached for a sheet of paper on the table. He perused it for a moment while puffing vigorously on a cigar.

"Let us examine the circumstances of the shootings, gentlemen. First of all, fully one half of the victims are women. Each and every one of them was alone at the time she was shot, on a dark street at night, except for the woman in the Laundromat—and because she was the only *white* person in the place, in their *minds* she also was alone.

"Now take the men. Most of them were alone, most of them also on a dark street at night. Most of them were smaller men of less than average height. Half of them were older men, well past sixty or more. The ones who weren't old and small of stature, were young, very slight men, thinner than usual, with outward appearances which perhaps gave the impression of weakness or frailty.

"In short, gentlemen, we have here two or more men who are cowards to the very core. They do not attack police officers, servicemen, or other males from whom there is a possibility of retaliation. They do not attack younger, larger, muscular men—seamen from the docks, burly truck driver types, that sort—from whom they might reasonably expect some kind of physical resistance. They do not attack women who are accompanied by someone, who are in or near a group, who are anywhere that might produce a defense of any kind.

"Instead, they select—whether consciously or subconsciously—the elderly, the helpless, the weak, the alone. In a way they are

262

very much like jackals. The jackal is a predator that preys only on smaller game: rabbits, squirrels, prairie mice: prey over which it is certain that it can achieve victory and escape unharmed. Your killers, gentlemen, fall into the same class. They are almost totally devoid of personal courage. Cowards to the core."

The doctor sat back and puffed on his cigar, studying his two guests. He could see the disappointment in their faces.

"I'm sorry," he said, without actually being apologetic. "You obviously expected more."

Fotinos shrugged. "We'd read how you came up with some pretty solid leads in cases in New York and Boston, places like that. Leads where you were actually able to pinpoint the kind of work a killer did, the neighborhood he probably lived in, things like that."

"Those were cases dealing with *one* murderer, one individual around whom *all* the evidence gradually accumulated. Here we are dealing with two or three persons, possibly even more. Their combined *modus operandi* is affected by idiosyncratic input from each of them. All of their fears, for instance, are mixed into the overall impression they create; all of their respective values, their fantasies, hopes, illusions about themselves: all of it is one big confusing personality stew from which the various ingredients simply cannot be separated—not at this stage, anyway."

Coreris leaned forward. "Doctor, can you tell us anything at all—*concretely*—that might be of some help?"

"Two things," the doctor said confidently. "One is that there's a reasonably good chance that one of the killers will eventually turn on the others. The end result of latent cowardice is always self-preservation. One of them will ultimately feel so threatened that he will inform on the others to save himself.

"The second thing I can tell you is that when the time comes to arrest them, when you know who they are and are actually ready to take them into custody, they will offer no resistance of any kind. They aren't the type to go out in a blaze of gunfire, to go down shooting. They'll give up as meekly as would a middle-aged child molester."

A moment of silence followed, then Fotinos said, "That's it, then?"

"I wish there were more," the doctor said.

The detectives rose to leave. "Doctor, we can't tell you how much we appreciate your time," Coreris said, shaking hands. "One thing you've done: you've made us realize even more what a bitch of a case we've got on our hands."

"Yeah," said Fotinos. "And we hope you're right about that informant theory. It would sure be nice if one of the bastards turned fink before they kill half the population of San Francisco."

On their way back to the city, Coreris and Fotinos drove in silence for a while, each reviewing in his own mind what the doctor had told them. Finally, when they were halfway back, Coreris grunted softly.

"What?" asked Fotinos.

"I've got a lot of respect for that doctor and his conclusions," Coreris said. "And this is no reflection at all on him. But when we *do* go out to bust these bastards, I'm going to carry a shotgun. Just in case."

"That makes two of us, partner," said Fotinos.

Gus Coreris and Dick Walley met later in the week.

Coreris was aware of the independent investigation of statewide killings being conducted by Walley's department at the State Bureau of Criminal Investigation, and Walley in turn knew that Coreris was working solely on the Zebra case in San Francisco.

"It's about time we met," Walley said. "I think what you're working on in San Francisco and what I'm working on around the state is basically the same thing."

"What's that?" Coreris asked. He was cautious with this state cop. Let him be the one to say it first, he decided.

"I think we've got a small network of Black Muslims systematically murdering white people," Walley said bluntly.

Coreris put aside his caution. "I think you're right, Dick," he said.

From that moment on, neither man held anything back from the other.

"I've had suspicions about the Muslims since 1972," Walley told him. "There was just too much coincidence *not* to tie them in. Similar murders, all either unprovoked street shootings or hackings, *had* to be connected; patterns like that just don't happen coincidentally. And then there were the descriptions of witnesses and survivors: neatly groomed young black men dressed in suits and ties, with nothing at all sinister or threatening about their appearances. They just *sounded* like Muslims. You know how they're expected to dress carefully; it's part of their thing.''

Coreris nodded. "My partner, John Fotinos, picked up on that a long time ago. He said the San Francisco killings were Muslims from the very first case we handled—Saleem Erakat, the grocer.''

"You've got a smart partner.''

"The smartest," Coreris told him. "But we're dead-ending on this Zebra thing. The mayor and everybody keep yelling for citizens to come forward and help the police; but even if citizens do come forward, there's a good chance we won't even have any pictures for them to identify. From what we've been able to learn, about half of the men they recruit—in San Francisco, anyway—are clean: no criminal record at all; some of them are straight out of high school; others are being *raised* as Muslims, with after-school classes in physical education, self-defense, that sort of thing—much in the same way of the old Hitler Youth Corps in Germany. The other half of the recruits come right out of San Quentin and Folsom, and on those punks we *do* have pictures. But if these Zebra killers are from the half with no police record, why, hell, they could go on killing indefinitely—no matter how many willing citizens come forward.''

"That's a problem, all right," Walley allowed. "Do you have any ideas about solving it?''

"Just one," said Coreris. "I'd like to put the San Francisco Mosque under photographic surveillance. I'd like to get a picture of every man entering or leaving that place.''

Walley shrugged. "So do it.''

"Can't," said Coreris. "It's a place of worship. The official position of the city of San Francisco is that it would be a violation of the U.S. Constitution to put a place of worship under surveillance. The minute I made an attempt to set up anything like that, there'd be pressure brought from some quarter and I'd probably get taken off the case.''

"And you don't want that?''

"No, I don't, Dick. I want to stay on Zebra until these dirty sons of bitches are in the second-best place for them: prison.''

"What's the first place?''

"Hell."

Dick Walley rubbed his chin and studied Coreris for a long moment. "I like you, Gus," he said at last. "I like the way you think. Would you be offended if I offered you some help?"

"Not at all. What kind of help?"

"Putting that mosque under surveillance. With *state* equipment."

Coreris sat back in surprise. He had not expected such an offer. Walley would be sticking his neck way out. "You're not joking, are you?"

"I never joke about cold-blooded murder, Gus," he replied.

So it was that on February 17, 1974, after the total of random killings of white citizens in California had reached seventy-one, and the number in San Francisco had reached thirteen dead and five seriously wounded, that equipment and personnel of the California Department of Justice began a photographic surveillance of the Nation of Islam mosque known as Muhammad's Temple # 26, located at 1805 Geary Street in San Francisco. The surveillance was done from an apartment directly across the street. Cooperating in the surveillance was an agent of the state's Bureau of Investigation and a homicide inspector from the San Francisco Police Department.

During the course of their surveillance, they secured approximately four hundred photos of black males entering and leaving the mosque. The photos were sorted into groups and still another lengthy process of methodical police work began: that of showing each group of photos to every witness in every shooting.

And with that effort, February passed. A month had gone by without any further killings.

At Black Self Help Moving and Storage, J.C., Manuel, and Larry were unloading a truck of furniture that had been picked up for storage. Like everyone else in San Francisco, they were talking about Zebra.

"The pigs got an answer for everything," Larry said. "Some reporter ask if it true that they call it 'Zebra' because it's blacks hitting on whites, and the pigs they say, 'Oh, no, man, that's not the reason!' They say the reason is some radio channel with a Z number or something. They expect people to believe that shit?"

"Man, you can't tell *what* whites is going to believe," J.C. said. "The Caucasian intellect has evolved over the years into such a fucked-up mess that they believe anything. You know what the mos' important thing in the world is to a white woman? This right here," he said, patting a large, double-door Harvest Gold refrigerator. "Give a white woman the biggest, fanciest, mos' expensive refrigerator on the market, so she can show it to all her friends, and she be happy as a hog in shit."

Manuel grunted as he moved the refrigerator toward the tailgate of the truck. "I wish she be happy with something that don't weigh so much," he said.

"And you know what makes a white *man* happiest of all?" J.C. asked his audience. "Two things: being on the bowling team where he work at, and daydreaming 'bout getting some pussy on the side. Thinking 'bout those two things take up about seventy-five percent of his time. Tha's why the average white man never rises above a certain level in life. And tha's why his woman don't push him no harder: she happy with that fucking refrigerator. Caucasian intellect, man. It's something else."

The men shuffled the refrigerator off the truck and tilted it onto a dolly. "Run it on inside, man," J.C. said to Manuel. Moore was the biggest, strongest, and least intelligent; the others did not hesitate to take advantage of it to make him do the most work. Easygoing, affable Manuel Moore knew it, but it did not bother him. These were his friends, his brothers; he did not mind helping them out.

When Manuel pushed the refrigerator inside, J.C. asked Larry, "You been stopped by the pigs anymore?"

Larry shook his head. "Not since that one time."

J.C. looked around the back area of Black Self Help. His eyes scanned, searched. "You think they watching this place?"

"They watching *every*place," Larry said. "Wherever there a black face, they watching."

"Well, they wasting their time watching around here," J.C. snorted.

"They don't know that," Larry pointed out.

The two of them hopped up into the back of the truck and carried a gas range back to the tailgate. It was much lighter than the refrigerator, easier to move. J.C. remained silent for several moments,

267

but he was studying Larry whenever he got the chance. Finally he said, "Say, you ever hear from Harris?"

Larry shook his head. "I ain't heard from Anthony for a month. Him and Debbie moved out of their apartment."

"You don't got no idea where they gone to?"

Larry shook his head again. "No idea at all, man."

Anthony Harris and Debbie were living across the bay in Oakland. They had moved over there without telling anyone when they were leaving or where they were going. Debbie's baby had been born: a boy whom she and Anthony named Anthony, Jr. Because Debbie was unmarried, she qualified for and received state welfare. Anthony had found a job as a helper in a fish market down on the docks. At night, after he got home from work, he and Debbie, like Anthony's friends at Black Self Help, also talked about Zebra.

"It's only a question of time before the police catch those men," Debbie said as Anthony washed the fish smell from his body. "Men just can't go on killing like that forever and get away with it."

Anthony nodded. "You right," he said listlessly. Personally he was sick and tired of all the Zebra talk. That was all he heard everywhere he went: on the bus going to work, on the docks unloading the fish, at the barrels slitting and scaling the fish, sitting around eating lunch, coming back home on the bus at night, and now in his own house where he expected peace and quiet. He would have liked to tell Debbie to shut up and talk about something else, but he was afraid it would make her suspicious. She had already told him on several occasions that she did not think J.C., Manuel, and Larry were the type of associates he should have. It would not have surprised him at all if she already suspected them of the San Francisco killings; therefore, the least little thing he said on the subject might tie him in with those suspicions. So he just listened, commenting only when he had to.

"What really upsets me about the whole thing, Anthony," she said, "are the insinuations that these killings might have something to do with the Nation of Islam, or with Muhammad's Temple. As if Allah's ministers would preach killing and death like that. The bad part of the whole thing is that most white people don't know anything about Islam; they're liable to believe anything the newspapers say or any rumors they hear. Don't you think that's so, Anthony?''

"Yeah, that so. Supper near ready?''

"In a few minutes. I'll tell you one thing, I'm glad we left there when we did. I'll bet it is really miserable for our people over there right now. What do you think it's like, Anthony?''

"Pretty bad, I guess," he replied disinterestedly. "Listen, I'm going in the bedroom and play with the baby. Call me when supper's ready.''

In the bedroom he saw that the baby was fast asleep. Rather than wake him and have him fidgety all through supper, Anthony just stretched out on the bed and lay there quietly and rested. The bed felt good under his back. He had not been sleeping well lately: he kept dreaming of all the talk he heard about Zebra. Everywhere he went, that was all there was to listen to: Zebra, Zebra, Zebra.

Allah only knew how much he hated that word and all it represented.

The letter was addressed simply:

Chief of Police
San Francisco Police Department
Courthouse
San Francisco, California

It was mailed in a letter-size envelope and stamped with a colorful Expo '74 ten-cent stamp. Eventually a clerk pulled it out of the courthouse mail, crossed out "Courthouse," and scribbled in "Hall of Justice." The letter was then sent over the Chief Don Scott's office. He read it and sent it down to Chief of Inspectors Barca. Barca read it and forwarded it to Lieutenant Charles Ellis in Homicide. Ellis passed it on to Gus Coreris. Coreris and Fotinos read it together. The letter, neatly typed, single-spaced, said:

Dear Sir:

I was once a Muslim and I know for a fact that the Muslims do advocate the killing of whites. In fact, they preach the extermination of the entire white race.

269

Please understand that the information I am about to give you comes from several years of being a Muslim where I too advocated the killing of white children and taught a doctrine of hate. If any member of the group should find that I have given out information my life will be in danger. I am withholding my name for that reason but I cannot go on that my holding back on information could contribute to the brutal killing of more innocent people.

Perhaps an understanding of some of the basis for the white race hatred would make it easier to understand how a Muslim can kill without the slightest feeling of guilt. It is believed and taught that every black person is born with a black and a brown gene. At one time, long ago, a Muslim scientist kept extracting the brown gene until he came up with a yellow person and finally a white person who was the epitome of everything bad. The purpose of this, so says the myth, is for the perfection of the black man. Through looking at the evil of the "white devil" and struggling with him could he in turn perfect himself.

The Muslim ministers teach that the "hereafter" is not going to be heaven but rather the earth after the "white devil" has been overcome.

It is very easy to hate enough to kill if you are a Muslim. When you go to the Temple you are told how the white devil raped your grandmother and how she was made to pull the plow with her body while the white devil's animals rested. You are worked up into a religious fervor, a fervor of hate. You feel that it is your sacred duty to avenge the injustices that have been done to your ancestors. The ministers tell you that you should kill white babies, that no white man should survive on earth, that the black race must overcome the devil. Many times I became so angry that I wanted to run out and hack up a white person. I would have felt justified in doing it.

The Muslims take no responsibility for the reactions to their teachings. The killing of whites is no new thing. Every month I was there someone had gone out and killed someone. Check the police records for the motiveless, brutal killings of whites in the streets in the past few years and you will see that this is true. The Muslims have a built-in protection whereby if you get into trouble with the police you are no longer a Muslim. It is not that no Muslim ever does anything wrong but rather that he is disowned by the group if he gets caught.

The Muslims indoctrinate their members in three ways. The first is the teaching of race hatred and of the superiority of the black race.

The second means is through symbology. Symbols of the cross, the flag, and then the sword are placed on pictures or blackboards in the Temples and you are constantly reminded that the white religion, the white nation, and the white race should come to a violent end. The third means is through the military-like drilling of the Fruit of Islam (FOI—Muslim men's group). Here you are made to march, to respond to commands without thinking, to react without judgment. A command need only be whispered and you are so well trained that you react before you even realize to what you have reacted.

I have heard a Muslim minister speak of the killing of whites in San Francisco, the killing of white police officers, and the killing of white public officials. I have heard talk of "offing" you in that you supposedly have not been sensitive enough to the needs of the group. In fact it was at this point that I began thinking for myself and decided to get out before the real trouble began.

Please do something if you can to stop this hatred campaign before more people get hurt. Of course, I too want our people to be free but these killings are just going to cause trouble for everyone.

I feel sick when I think back to times when other Muslims and I would describe to each other how we would kill whites and what we would do to white women before we killed them, and how we would enjoy seeing white guts smeared across the streets. I am talking straight to you now. You can't imagine the guilt that I feel knowing that I have contributed to the hatred that has led to all these killings. And I am sure that there will be more.

Everything in this letter can be verified and if you have the means to do so please check it out. Understand where I am coming from when I say I can't sign. Please help if you can.

When they were finished reading the letter, Fotinos grunted loudly. "'Please help if you can,'" he quoted. "Why the hell doesn't *he* help if he's feeling so goddamned guilty?"

Coreris tossed the letter onto his desk. "The son of a bitch could probably name every black street killer in the city. So he just sits on the information. Bastard."

"Maybe a garbage truck will run over him," Fotinos said.

"Let's hope it's soon."

The two detectives fell silent for a moment and their eyes met. Their thoughts coincided, and they both knew it.

"Jesus, listen to us," said Fotinos. "Talk about Jumping the gun."

Coreris agreed. "Yeah. It *could* be a crank letter."

"It could even be a *white* crank letter."

Without actually saying it, they were telling each other to stay steady and straight and not to let the case get to them.

It was good advise, and they both knew it.

Besides the letter from the guilt-ridden Muslim, and numerous other crank-type letters and telephone calls, Coreris and Fotinos also had to cope with informants who offered information for pay. An example was Junior Clipper,* a black pimp referred to Fotinos by a fellow officer on the vice squad. Fotinos tried to pin Clipper down at once.

"Do you know anything or don't you, Junior?" he asked bluntly. "Because if you don't, I don't want you wasting my time."

"Man, it ain't exactly what I *knows*," Junior explained, "it's what I might be able to find out, you dig?"

"Find out how? From who?"

"I don't know from who yet, but I can tell you how. See, I gots a few foxes on the street doing for me, you know what I mean?"

"Hooking."

"Yeah, doing for me. Now, every once in a while one of them smartass Muslim cats from the temple decides he wants a *real* piece of ass, see, not one of them religious fucks, but the whole shot, see, sixty-nine and all. When that happen, they usually come to one of my women, see. I mean, my women is the *best*, see, man, and those dudes *know* it. My women is white, see, gots blond hair, shaved pussies, the whole shot, see."

"Get to the point, Junior."

"Yeah, right. I was thinking, if it was worthwhile to you, maybe I could like instruct my women to see could they get any information for you."

"Come on, Junior," Fotinos said dubiously. "You don't really think any of those Fruit of Islam jokers are going to tell anything to a white hooker, do you?"

---

*This person's name has been changed. He is currently serving time in a California prison and to identify him could possibly jeopardize his safety.

Junior smirked. "Hey, man, you be surprised some of the things gets told to my women. When a black cat is about to stick it to a white cunt, he trying to *impress* her, you know what I mean? He trying to be a big man, a hotshot. Shit, he liable to say anything."

Fotinos talked it over with Coreris and they decided that maybe Junior had a point. They went to Lieutenant Ellis, told him the story, and got a hundred dollars out of the informant slush fund.

"We're going to lay a hundred on you, Junior," Fotinos told the pimp. "That's for openers. If you come up with anything, there could be more—much more. But if you rip us off, we'll tell Vice and they'll lean on you every chance they get. Understand?"

"I dig it, man, yeah."

Fotinos and Coreris never got anything from Junior, or from a score of other would-be informants who contacted them as the days and weeks passed. From the slush fund they drew fifty dollars here, twenty there, an occasional hundred if the possibility looked promising. They even chipped in out of their own pockets from time to time when the slush fund ran dry. For the most part they were 90 percent sure that they were being taken, but with thirteen bodies and five near-misses behind them, it was almost impossible not to gamble on the longshot odds of the 10 percent coming through.

Coreris and Fotinos were grimly determined about Zebra. There was not much they would not do to catch the killers.

To work full time for them on Zebra, Coreris and Fotinos had selected two detectives from the Robbery detail. Carl Klotz and Jeffrey Brosch were both in their mid-thirties and had been police officers for a dozen years. Klotz was a big, stocky man with an easy grin; Brosch was smaller, mustached, an ex-army combat engineer.

They chose two burglary men over homicide detectives because they wanted assistants with a fresh approach, fresh contacts not common to Homicide, fresh ideas on handling witnesses and following up leads. They felt that they themselves had enough background between them to satisfy any homicide aspects the case would require, and that two outsiders like Brosch and Klotz would give them a broader experience base from which to work.

The work of the inner core of the Zebra team—Coreris and the immediate crew—continued to be the slow, methodical, tedious police routine that is indigenous to very difficult cases. Witnesses had to be interviewed and reinterviewed; anonymous tips had to be checked out; newly developed leads, however skimpy, had to be followed up; reports had to be reread, reanalyzed, reevaluated; informants—those who did not come forward seeking money—had to be discreetly contacted; photos of new suspects had to be shown; and hundreds—or so it seemed at times—of tiny details had to be attended to in order to stay on top of the daily routine.

Some of the new photos that had to be shown to witnesses were pictures obtained during the mosque surveillance. The frontal shots of black men leaving the temple were enlarged, then the head and shoulders cropped into a second print that resembled a police mug shot. A great deal of caution had to be exercised in dealing with these particular photographs. Both Coreris and Dick Walley knew the official repercussions that would rain down on them if what they were doing became general knowledge. Still, to them, the risk was worth it. Maniacs were loose; they had to be caught.

And the police officers were working against the calendar. All of them knew that the next killing—or killings—could occur any day.

Yellow was restless.

It had been nearly eight weeks since the last stings were made— and *thirteen* weeks since he himself had made a sting. Everyone else had gone ahead of him in the quest for Death Angel wings; or nearly everyone, at any rate. Even Rims, who had only been out of prison a few months, already had five stings to his credit: three male white devils and two female. He himself only had three: one male, two female. True, one of the females was a hacking, and the Death Angels looked with particular favor on hackings; but it still only counted as *one* sting.

It was time for him to get started again, he thought, as he walked aimlessly up Webster Street toward Geary. At Webster and Geary was one end of Japan Center, a modern complex of shops and Japanese businesses. Yellow often wandered around the neighborhood there. With his *café au lait* complexion, he found that he felt oddly comfortable among the yellow-skinned Japanese, sometimes more comfortable than he did in the company of a group of blacks, particularly *pure* blacks without a trace of brown in them.

When he reached Geary Street, Yellow crossed to a large Mayfair supermarket on the northwest corner. He went inside and found the candy section. Much as a child would do, he spent a long time carefully looking over the variety from which he had to choose. After careful consideration, he selected a pack of grape-flavored bubble gum. He paid for it at the checkout counter and went back outside.

Standing on the supermarket parking lot, Yellow chewed two sticks of gum at once and idly watched the people coming and going. He had been standing there several minutes when a trio of young white people, two boys and a girl, dressed in some kind of uniforms, attracted his attention. They crossed Webster and went into the same market he had just left. Because he was curious about their uniforms, Yellow sat down on the concrete base of a light standard and waited for them to come back out. He had often thought that young Muslims like himself should have some kind of distinctive uniform to wear, some mode of dress that would set them apart from other blacks and let the world know that they were special. It was all well and good to practice good grooming with neat haircuts and no facial hair, and to wear nicely pressed suits and neckties like Master Elijah Muhammad insisted they do when attending temple and socializing and selling *Muhammad Speaks* on the street corners, but there was really nothing distinctive about such attire. For all anyone knew who saw them walking down the street, they might be bank clerks or shoe salesmen, anything. They needed, Yellow thought, something special—some kind of coat or hat—something instantly recognizable that, when seen would strike fear into the hearts of white devils and nonbelieving blacks alike.

Someday, he told himself, when he was a powerful and influential leader in the Nation of Islam, he would design such a uniform for the young Muslims who came after him.

The trio of uniformed whites came out of the market and started back up Geary Street. Yellow, putting a third stick of bubble gum in his mouth, got up and leisurely followed them. They proceeded up the long block, across from Japan Center, to Laguna, where they crossed the street and entered a neat, three-story building on the corner. The building was the Salvation Army Training School. The trio of young whites were Salvation Army cadets.

275

Satisfied that he now knew what they were, Yellow walked back toward the market, popping his gum as he went.

Some thirty miles north of San Francisco, in a rehabilitation center in the town of Vallejo, Roxanne McMillian, the lone survivor of the January 28 night of terror, was trying to learn how to use her now handicapped body to best advantage.

Roxie, as her family and close friends called her, had undergone surgery twice at San Francisco General Hospital in the days immediately following her shooting. Then she had been transferred some eighty miles south to Kaiser Hospital in Santa Clara for recuperation. At the end of a month there, they had sent her to Vallejo.

Roxie did not like the rehab center. It was not strictly a therapy school for people such as herself who had to learn to use braces and wheelchairs and other apparatus to compensate for damaged limbs; it was also a rehabilitation center for the elderly and senile, for the retarded and dysfunctional, the spastic and seriously epileptic. They all shared therapy classes together, which was economical but not, Roxanne felt, very practical. With her typical spunkiness, she approached with grim determination this latest challenge in her young life: learning to function as a handicapped person. But she did not feel that the people at the Vallejo center were given the proper treatment. Putting her in classes with very old and infirm, with mental retards, with preteen spastics, was not fair to her or to them. None of them received the individual attention that each of them appeared to need so direly. Roxie left her daily sessions as they did, feeling unfulfilled, dissatisfied, dejected—and even more handicapped than when she started, because for the most part the classes only served to emphasize what she now could *not* do.

Nights at Vallejo were worst of all. Nights were the times when she would lie in bed and involuntarily think about life as it once had been: life when she could do all manner of marvelous things. Like walk. Stand. Drive a car. Play with her baby. Be a wife to her husband.

A lot of things she had once been able to do, they told her at Vallejo that she could learn to do again, in different ways. There were cars with special hand brakes that she could drive. There were many activities in which she could enjoy her little boy as he grew older. She might even learn to stand wearing heavy leg braces.

But there were some things she had to resign herself to not ever thinking about doing again. Some things that had been taken away permanently by the black man who said "Hi" to her that night.

Some things she would never enjoy again.

Anthony Harris had been away from San Francisco, living in Oakland, for six weeks, when he decided to make a quick trip across the bay to see what was going on. During the six weeks in Oakland, he had begun suffering from insomnia and had lost some weight. He told a concerned Debbie that it was just the new job: he could not get used to it and the fish smell stayed in his nostrils even at night. The real reason was that he was worried about whether J.C., Manuel, Larry, and others from the mosque were looking for him. He knew that once a man became a Muslim and joined a mosque, the other members did not look favorably on his leaving, unless he moved away and transferred to a new mosque in another city, which Anthony had not done: he and Debbie had not gone to temple since arriving in Oakland. He had thought several times about calling Larry on the telephone to see what was happening over there, but had finally decided against it: if they were *not* looking for him, a phone call might put the idea in their heads to do so. Better to lay back and wait, he told himself. Better not to make any sudden moves. Even Debbie, religious as she was, agreed with that.

She knew that a man could get into trouble for leaving the mosque.

But after six weeks his curiosity and the semisleepless nights got the best of him, and he made up his mind to go over. He did not tell Debbie what he intended to do; she would have worried and carried on too much, thinking that he was going to start running around with J.C. again, and the others she disliked so intensely. Instead he said that he had learned from one of his co-workers at the fish market that a cousin of his from Santa Ana had just moved up to Oakland.

"I don't know exactly the address where he living," he told Debbie, "but this guy told me where the neighborhood is. After supper

I'm going to go over there and ask around. Maybe I can locate him."

"If you do," replied the unsuspecting Debbie, "invite him over on Sunday. I'll make fried chicken."

Anthony had chosen a Monday night for his trip; he knew that on Monday nights, J.C. and the others, instead of going to temple, had what they called their "social" meeting. Therefore there would be little chance of his running into them at the mosque. What he hoped to do was see someone he knew more or less casually, act as if he had not moved away at all, and see what kind of reception he got. If J.C. and the others *were* looking for him, he would be able to tell by the person's reaction to his presence.

Anthony rode the Bay Area Rapid Transit train through the underwater tube across the bay, and got off at the BART station in the Civic Center. He then took a city bus to within a few blocks of the mosque and walked the rest of the way. It was dark and he proceeded cautiously, a cap pulled low on his head to shadow his face further. To avoid having to identify himself to the Fruit of Islam sentry at the side or rear doors, Anthony squared his shoulders, stuck out his chin a bit, and walked through the front door with several evening worshipers. There were two FOI sentries on guard there also—clean-cut, well-groomed, neatly dressed young men with cold eyes and unsmiling faces—but they did not give Anthony a second glance.

Once inside, Anthony stood on the dimly lighted side aisle of the mosque area and looked at the people whose faces he could see. There was no one there whom he knew. He waited as a few new arrivals came in, but still saw no one familiar. As he was standing there, however, he did notice several young Muslim girls come in and walk toward the stairs which led up to the second floor. Then he remembered: Wally 4X, whom he had known when he taught judo classes there, conducted a gymnastics class on Monday nights. Abandoning his position on the side aisle, Anthony slipped quickly over to the stairs and up to the second floor.

He found Wally 4X in a small room that the instructors used to change clothes. Wally's eyes widened slightly when he saw Anthony. "Man, what are you doing around here?" he asked with a hint of nervousness.

"Why?" Anthony asked. "Some reason why I shouldn't be?"

Wally 4X shrugged. "Guess not," he said. He hung his street shirt on a hook and pulled a sweat shirt over his head.

"Somebody been looking for me?" Anthony asked.

"Not exactly."

"Not exactly? What the fuck does that mean, man?"

Wally 4X's expression tightened. "Say, man, let's watch that mouth, hear? You're not down at Black Self Help now; this is the *temple*. This is where we *worship*. This is where Allah dwells. You want to use gutter talk, go on out to the gutter."

Anthony drew a deep, sighing breath and sat down heavily on a battered straight chair in the corner. "Look, man, I'm sorry, hear? I'm a little edgy; nervous, you know? I didn't mean to say that." He rubbed sweaty palms on his trouser legs. "Can you tell me if somebody's been looking for me?"

"A couple of guys from Black Self Help have been asking about you now and again," Wally said. "Nothing real heavy, understand; just like, 'Say, brother, you seen Anthony around lately?' And one of the lay ministers passed the word around that if anybody saw you, to let him know right away."

"Nobody didn't say what it was about?"

Wally shook his head. "Some of the people kind of figure maybe you owe some money."

"Some of the people, huh? But not you?"

Wally did not answer. He turned away and resumed changing into his gym clothes. Anthony got up to leave.

"Listen, thanks for telling me, man," he said.

Wally looked at him and shrugged again. "Good luck," he said. But he did not call Anthony "brother."

For some reason, Yellow fell into the habit of walking up to the area around Geary and Webster streets, and positioning himself someplace where he could loiter and watch the Salvation Army cadets as they walked from their school down to the big Mayfair market. He had found that nearly every night a dozen or more of them, usually in pairs or small groups, walked the long, long block—it was actually two blocks but was uninterrupted by a cross street—down to Mayfair for a snack of some kind. Yellow normally

watched them from a tree-edged parking lot in front of the St.
Francis Square Apartments, a large complex which set back off
Geary some thirty feet, leaving room for tenants to park their cars
in front of the buildings. There were trees along both sides of the
public sidewalk for practically the entire length of the long block:
city-owned trees on the outside, near the curb, and trees belonging
to the apartment buildings on the inside, edging the parking lots. It
was easy for Yellow to sit on a car fender or under a tree and watch
the cadets as they strolled down from the school every evening.
Yellow was fascinated by the young cadets.

Man, they look *good,* he thought. They look *right.* Not cool, not
even particularly sharp, but *right.* They are *con-*fident. Man, it
would be out of sight if the Death Angels could be that confident.
As it was, the Death Angels *never* seemed confident. Everything
they did was done *right now.* No planning, no preparation: just go
out and do it, sucker, and hope it turns out all right.

That always seemed to be the way lately, he thought. Everything
half-assed. Always a couple of pieces that didn't fit. Just like him: a
piece that didn't fit.

Wonder why that is? he asked himself with a sigh. Wonder *why*
he didn't fit? Whites always seemed to fit with other whites.
Blacks—the pure blacks—fit well with other blacks. Even the lighter ones, the browns, fit with other browns as well as with blacks.
Why was it that it was only *him* that did not seem to fit? Him—with
his skin almost yellow, with freckles across his face, hair that was
halfway between kinky and straight. Damn his mother and father,
he often thought vehemently, for bringing him into the world as
such a fucking freak. Better almost to be a white devil than the
kind of misfit he was—

No, I take that back, he thought quickly. Allah, I didn't mean to
think that. I wouldn't want to be a white devil under any circumstances. Better to have just one drop of black blood in his body
than to be pure white—because Muslim law stated that a single
drop of black blood made a black man. So please forgive me, Great
Allah. I am thankful for the black blood that I have, and I curse the
white blood that has diluted it.

Without black blood, he thought, he would not have found Allah and been given Allah's strength to serve. He would not have known how it felt to have a heart so strong that he could kill the blue-eyed devil with no remorse at all—

Except, Yellow thought, it was not quite true that Allah had given him the heart to kill.

Yellow had tried to kill before the spirit of Allah moved him. . . .

It had been in the middle of summer, July, but the city was still very cool at night. Yellow, wearing a light raincoat and soft-soled moccasins, walked down Scott Street looking for a number. In the light of a streetlamp he found it. He went to the door and rang the bell. A forty-year-old white man, the building manager, came to the door. "Yes, what can I do for you?" he asked in an effeminate voice.

"Do you have an apartment for rent?" Yellow asked.

The manager's eyes flicked up and down Yellow's body, which was obviously slim even under the raincoat; then the eyes rested on his light, youthful face with its sensuous lips and sad but pretty eyes. "Yes, I have one vacancy," he said. "Follow me, please."

Yellow followed the manager up to the third floor. When they got inside the vacant apartment, the manager made a point of closing the door behind them.

"Some friends of mine told me you like to have sex with young black men," Yellow said.

"Well, yes," the manager replied, "but you're not exactly black. Still, you *are* attractive. Would you *like* to have sex with me?"

Yellow nodded.

The white man took off all his clothes and knelt on the couch, bracing his hands on the wall, his back to Yellow. "All right, dear, put the fucking thing in me," he said.

Yellow, still fully dressed, was surprised to find that he had an erection. He had expected to be revolted by the sight of the naked white man. But he was not. Far from it. He actually felt desire coursing through him.

Opening his raincoat and trousers, Yellow released his erect pe-

281

nis and worked it into the white man's ass. Son of a bitch, this is *good!* he thought. He pumped a few times—only a few, for he was very quick—and ejaculated in a sweet burst.

"Ahhhh—" the white man said, feeling good.

But Yellow quickly changed that. In one coordinated motion, Yellow drew himself out of the man's rectum and, pulling a ten-inch butcher knife from his belt, stabbed him in the middle of his back.

The white man groaned and slumped forward on the couch. Yellow zipped up his trousers, used the flap of his raincoat to wipe off the wooden handle of the knife sticking out of the man's back, then went quickly through the pockets of the man's nearby trousers. He found a thick roll of currency, nearly four hundred dollars.

"All right!" he said aloud to himself.

Shoving the money into his raincoat pocket, he quickly fled.

It was one thirty in the morning and Gus Coreris was on his way home, a place he had left at seven thirty the previous morning, exactly eighteen hours earlier. He had a stubble of beard and his mouth felt as though it had a throw rug in it from too many cigarettes. But in a way he also felt relieved: another night had passed without a killing—the fifty-eighth night that the Zebra killers had not struck. Every night, along about eleven or eleven thirty, Coreris and John Fotinos would start to feel the tension easing out of them. Midnight was the magic hour; no Zebra crime had ever occurred after midnight.

"That's because they're good, clean-living, American black boys," Fotinos had said. "They practice early-to-bed, early-to-rise."

"I thought maybe at midnight they turned into pumpkins," Coreris replied.

Their kidding aside, when midnight came they both relaxed. They were all right, then, until five thirty or six that evening, when they would start to tense up again. After six o'clock, every time the Homicide phone rang, their stomachs did simultaneous flip-flops.

Now, after fifty-eight days, they had begun talking in optimistic terms.

"Maybe the bastards died," Fotinos said hopefully. "Maybe they had a fight and killed each other."

"I'd settle for them having left town and gone somewhere far away," said Coreris.

But even as they said things like that, both detectives knew down in the deepest part of them, down in the part that made them the good cops that they were, that it was only wishful thinking. There would be more killings. It was just a question of time.

But at least there won't be any tonight, Coreris thought as he drove home. The rotten bastards, whoever they were, probably were tucked in for the night and sleeping like babies.

Coreris was driving up Geary Street. He always made it a point to drive past the Black Muslim temple whenever he was anywhere near it. He liked to look at it in passing; it somehow made him feel close to the Zebra killers. If only it were possible to get a man—a black policeman—inside that mosque, he thought wistfully. But it would be an impossible task. The Muslims were too careful, too strict about background, to allow a stranger into their ranks unvouched for. Coreris grunted. Damned shame the Muslims didn't have the same problem. It was a known fact that *they* had several members in the San Francisco Police Department. After all, you can't exclude a man from being a cop because of his religious preference; that would be unconstitutional. Next thing you know, Coreris grumbled silently to himself, there'll be American Nazi party members wearing badges and carrying guns. Sometimes he got a funny feeling that somewhere along the line the inmates had taken over the asylum.

Tonight as he drove past the darkened mosque, Coreris saw a figure hurry down the street. As he passed under a streetlight, Coreris recognized him. His name was Willie Fields and he was an armed robber and statutory rapist whom Coreris and Fotinos had once sent to prison. As he walked briskly down the street, Coreris saw that he was carrying a package of some kind under his arm.

I wonder what that son of a bitch is up to? Coreris thought. Slowly he pulled to the curb, trying to stay behind Fields so that he would not notice him. But Willie's criminal instincts were too alert; he saw the shadow of the moving car and swung his head around to scrutinize it. In the glow of a streetlight, he recognized Coreris. His eyes grew wide and he bolted down the sidewalk toward an areaway between buildings.

Coreris leaped from the car and went after him. He saw Willie dash into the areaway. Pumping his legs, he plunged in after him. Coreris was not afraid that Fields might be waiting to ambush him; he knew that Willie was a gutless coward when it came down to one-on-one. He also knew that he had little chance of catching the younger man. Coreris was bone-tired after his eighteen-hour shift, and frankly could not run as fast as he had been able to at twenty-five or even thirty-five. But even if he could not catch Willie, he would throw a goddamned good scare into him.

At the end of the areaway, Willie cleanly vaulted a back fence. End of chase, Coreris thought. Then there was a thud on the other side, and he heard Willie curse. He hurried ahead, his chest heaving, legs growing warm. Reaching the fence, he peered over it in time to see Willie frantically gathering up some sheafs of paper he had dropped.

"Freeze, Willie!" Coreris ordered.

Instead of obeying, Willie clutched the papers he had retrieved and darted away again. In seconds he had disappeared into the shadows.

"I'll get you, Willie!" Coreris shouted after him. Run, you night-crawling scum, he thought. He shook his head in disgust at the rob-ber-rapist. They just keep letting the bastards back out, he thought.

Coreris had started to turn away from the fence when he noticed a manila envelope lying where Willie had stumbled. The asshole left something, he thought. Laboriously, he climbed the fence and got the envelope.

Coreris made his way back to the car. Inside, with the doors locked and his gun on the seat beside him, he shined the tiny beam of a penlight on the contents of the envelope. There was a stack of perhaps ninety or a hundred pages of standard 8 1/2-by-11-inch pa-per. Coreris flipped through some of the pages at random. As he skimmed, certain phrases and passages registered in his mind:

". . . Why must a Muslim murder the devil? Because he is one hundred percent wicked and his ways are like a snake. . . . All Muslims will murder the devil . . . is required to bring four devils, and his reward shall be transportation to the Holy City Mecca. . . . Good believers say, Islam comes first and family second. . . . You see us pulling the wagon filled with the dead. Help us and Allah will bless you. . . . We believe that the destruction of the devil will take place in America. . . . If we divide ourselves into groups and each one wants an independent leader, this is the work of the devil (white race) . . . this dividing of the black man one against the other is the basis of the rule of the white man . . . the white race is always referred to as the devil, due to the wickedness of the people. . . . Devil means a totally wicked people . . . the enemies of Allah are known as the white race or European race, who are the sole people responsible for misleading nine-tenths of the total population of the black nation . . . love your brother believers as yourself . . . kill no one whom Allah has ordered not to be killed. . . . How long has the devil white man to rule and when is his time up? The exact day is known only to Allah. . . . Islam is the only religion that will survive the final war between Allah and the devil. Islam will put the black man of America on top of all civilization. . . ."

Gus Coreris sat staring incredulously at the stack of papers in his hand. God in heaven, he thought, can this stuff be real? Is this madness actually being taught to people? Are black youngsters and little children being exposed to this—this—*venom?*

He put the papers back into the envelope. Shuddering once, he pulled his gun closer to him on the seat, started the car's engine, and drove away from the mosque area.

Yellow sat on the fender of a car on one of the apartment parking lots on Geary Street, watching an occasional pair or trio of cadets walk down the street from the Salvation Army Training School. It was almost nine o'clock; he had been sitting there for an hour. The evening was cool but Yellow was dressed warmly: lightweight raincoat, wool knit cap, tennis shoes with heavy socks.

Under his raincoat, Yellow had Skullcap's .32-caliber automatic. He had borrowed it earlier that evening, stopping in at Skullcap's apartment after leaving his own. At first, Skullcap had been reluctant to let him have the gun.

"Man, don't you think you ought to wait until after we have

285

another meeting?'' Skullcap asked. ''Until everybody decides that enough time has passed for us to start again?''

''Nine weeks has passed,'' Yellow said. ''That's time enough. Anyway, I don't have to wait for no vote; Allah has moved me: Allah has told me which white devils to kill and when to do it.'' His young face was tight with determination. ''If you don't want to lend me your gun, I'll attack the devils with a machete, a knife, a broken bottle—anything.''

''Hey, brother, I didn't be saying I didn't want to lend you my piece,'' Skullcap corrected him. ''You can use my gun anytime you want to. Alls I was saying is that maybe it's too soon after the big night for *any* of us to start again.''

''I don't have no choice,'' Yellow said resolutely. ''I told you: Allah has pointed my way.''

Skullcap looked over at Rims, who had been in the apartment with him when Yellow arrived. ''What do you think, man?''

Rims shrugged. ''The brother say he moved by Allah. It ain't for us to decide.''

Skullcap sighed quietly. There did not seem to be any way out of it for him. He did not really think it was too soon; if it had been up to him, they never would have *stopped*. What concerned him was that *he* wanted to be the one to start it again; *he* wanted to get the jump on everyone else with another big night like the one nine weeks ago; a night that would set the city on its ass again. In another week or so he himself would have proposed resuming their stings. Now it was too late; Yellow had beaten him to it. There was no way he could get out of lending him the gun. If he refused, every brother in the mosque would know about it the very next day. All Skullcap could do now was act magnanimous. He laid a hand on Yellow's shoulder.

''The gun is yours for the night, brother,'' he said. Going to his bed, he reached under his mattress and got the pistol. Trying to look professional, he checked the magazine to see that the weapon was loaded, then handed it to Yellow. ''Go and do Allah's work in safety,'' he said in his most reverent tone.

Yellow had taken the gun and left.

Now he sat on the fender of a car next to a Geary Street sidewalk and watched Salvation Army cadets stroll down to Mayfair Mar-

286

ket. As he sat there, a white man walked by who reminded him of the homosexual he had stabbed and robbed the previous year. The man had somehow survived. But these devils tonight—they would not survive.

He looked up the sidewalk and saw a young white couple walking toward him.

The Salvation Army Officer Training School at 1450 Laguna was one of four such facilities in the United States. This particular one, a well-kept three-story building overshadowed by a high-rise directly next to it, was on April 1, 1974, accommodating sixty-six cadets from the thirteen westernmost states. Two of those cadets, Thomas Rainwater and Linda Story, both first-year students who had entered the school the previous September and were a month away from completing their first of two years, had attended a night study class from seven until nine, and then left the school together. They had ninety minutes of free time until the ten-thirty curfew and had decided to walk down to Mayfair market for a snack.

Thomas Rainwater was a husky, dark-haired young man of nineteen who had come to the Salvation Army school after attending Bethany Bible College in Santa Cruz, California, for one year. He was a native Californian, born in Monrovia, whose parents and fourteen-year-old sister were then living in the desert community of Ojai, where his father, Arthur Rainwater, with the help of his wife, operated a rest home for the elderly and convalescent. Thomas had last visited his family three months earlier, over the Christmas holiday.

Linda Story was twenty-one. An attractive brunette, she had a complexion that required no makeup. She usually wore her hair parted in the middle and pulled straight back into a bun. This gave her a rather severe look to some, merely serious, studious, to others. There was nothing at all pretentious about her and most people considered her a sweet, likable person. One of five children, from Hayward, California, she had attended Peralta Community College for Non-Traditional Study in nearby Oakland before entering the Salvation Army's cadet program.

Just after the evening study class ended at nine, Thomas and Linda met on the stairs and together signed out of the building, logging Mayfair market as their destination. They noticed that several other students had signed out earlier for the same place and were still out, so they expected to meet some of their classmates either there or en route. They left the school, crossed Laguna, and started down Geary. Neither of them was in uniform. Thomas wore dark slacks, a long-sleeved striped shirt over a crew-neck tee shirt, and deck shoes. Linda wore a skirt and blouse under a light coat.

"Aren't you cold without a coat or anything?" Linda asked.

Thomas smiled his easy, gentle smile. "No, I'm fine. Maybe I've still got some of that good Arizona warm weather in me."

Just days before, Thomas had returned from a two-week evangelism campaign in Arizona. In a group consisting of Captain Alfred Van Cleef and seven other cadets, they had toured the state addressing various religious congregations. Thomas himself had spoken before congregations in Phoenix and Tucson. His topic, which clearly expressed his feeling toward mankind in general and his own special goals in particular, was "One Life to Live, One Life to Give."

"That was such a beautiful theme," Linda told him now when she was reminded of his trip. "You're very lucky to know exactly what you want to do in life. So many are still trying to decide."

"I guess I am lucky," Thomas said. "I want to do orphanage work. That's all I've ever wanted to do, since the day I decided on this kind of career."

Linda smiled. She felt good being with Thomas. He was such a good, solid young man; not so solid that he was solemn, as she herself was sometimes thought of, but solid in that he was not flashy or loud or offensive in any way. And he had a good sense of humor, which she felt was important in a religious life.

They walked along slowly, with Thomas on the wrong side of her on the sidewalk, talking quietly, neither of them noticing the light-skinned young Negro sitting on the car fender watching them.

Half a block away and across the street, at the Miyako Hotel in Japan Center, two vice detail detectives, Dennis O'Connell and Daniel O'Brien, had just parked their car at Geary and Laguna and were on their way to the hotel on a vice investigation. Each of them carried a decoy suitcase of clothing as they entered the hotel by the garage entrance. They were using the garage instead of the lobby entrance because they were working undercover: they were part of a trap being laid that night in an effort to apprehend several prostitutes who had been stealing from Japanese businessmen staying in the hotel.

Down the street, on the same side on which Linda and Thomas were walking, a woman named Elizabeth Ann Lee was in the bedroom of her apartment, the window of which looked down on the parking lot where Yellow sat. Mrs. Lee had a stereo set playing and was taping the sound track of a Broadway musical.

A few doors down from Mrs. Lee, a man named Frank Richardson was in a bedroom in his apartment, next to a window which also looked down on the same long parking lot.

While Officers O'Connell and O'Brien were entering the hotel garage, and Mrs. Lee and Mr. Richardson were busy in their respective bedrooms, Thomas Rainwater and Linda Story walked past the trees that partially concealed the car where Yellow was sitting.

Yellow saw them and got down off the car fender.

Allah is with me, he thought.

Yellow's young face was again a mask of murder. His eyes were fixed, lips parted slightly, tiny bubbles of saliva accumulating at each corner of his mouth. And, as usual, he had an overwhelming urge to urinate.

He slipped Skullcap's gun from under his raincoat and put it into his coat pocket, keeping his hand on it. Pushing quietly through the trees, he stepped from the parking lot onto the sidewalk and fell in behind the two Salvation Army cadets.

They're white, he kept thinking. Pure white. Not like me. Not all mixed up with black and brown and yellow. They are *all* white.

Guide me, Allah. Use my hand to strike down the white devils. Be with me, Allah—

Yellow raised the gun to shoot the young white couple in the back. Then he changed his mind. I want to see the faces of the white devils when they die, he thought. And I want them to see Allah in *my* face.

He hurried along the sidewalk, overtook the couple, and passed

289

them. Going on ahead, he continued walking until he judged himself to be a dozen feet in front of them. Then he turned, raising the
gun.

Linda Story and Thomas Rainwater froze. Their eyes widened in
surprise and fear at the sight of the murderous yellow face in front
of them, and the gun leveled directly at them. For a split instant
they remained petrified, then, as if they were one, they turned and
tried to flee.

Yellow was cool. The white devils, he thought contemptuously,
were cowards. And he would not be blessed with seeing their faces
when they died. But it made no difference.

He shot Thomas first, twice, low in the back. Then he shot Linda, also twice, also in the back.

Linda fell as soon as she was hit, and lay in the gutter without
losing consciousness. Thomas, as had so many male Zebra victims,
did not fall at once; he began staggering forward, lumbering heavy-
footed like a drunken man. In the gutter, Linda started to scream.

"No! Oh, no! No!"

Thomas kept moving forward: twenty feet, thirty, fifty. Finally,
at the driveway to the St. Francis Square Apartments parking lot,
he collapsed. He fell into the driveway on his back, right arm flung
out above his head, left bent grotesquely under him, eyes open but
seeing only darkness.

Behind him, Linda Story continued to scream.

Yellow had stood watching in fascination as the white devil staggered away from him. The woman in the gutter had started to
scream. He glanced at her, then ignored her. The white devil walking away had to fall, he thought. If he fell, Yellow was sure he
would die. Allah would make him fall.

He watched, waiting. The screams from the woman continued.
Again Yellow flicked his glance toward her, irritably now. If she
did not shut up he was going to stick the gun in her mouth and pull
the trigger.

The male devil was a good distance down the sidewalk now,
though only seconds had passed. Die, beast, Yellow prayed. Allah,
make the beast die.

The woman's screams penetrated his consciousness again.

Bitch, he thought. He pointed the gun toward where she lay and fired a fifth shot. It missed her by several feet and buried itself in the ground next to the gutter. At that point the pistol jammed and failed to eject the shell casing all the way. Although Yellow did not know it, he would not be able to fire the weapon again until it was unjammed.

Finally the male devil fell. Allah be praised! Yellow thought.

Then he saw two men running toward him on the opposite side of the street. Plunging through the trees onto the parking lot, he ran from the scene of his holy carnage.

The two men running toward the scene were O'Connell and O'Brien, the vice detectives who had been entering the Miyako Hotel with their decoy suitcases. As soon as they heard the shots, they immediately abandoned the luggage, then ran toward the sound of the gunfire. They did not see Yellow because he was in the shadows of the trees. But they did see Thomas Rainwater in the driveway and Linda Story in the gutter. O'Brien stopped where Rainwater had fallen; O'Connell ran up to where Linda Story lay. She was facedown in the gutter.

"Where are you hurt, miss?" he asked, kneeling beside her.

"My—back," she said. "My back—burns—"

"Who shot you?"

"I don't—know—"

O'Brien hurried up. "The guy's dead," he whispered. He peered down at Linda. "You get an ambulance. I'll look around for the shooter."

O'Brien drew his gun and stepped through the trees onto the parking lot.

Frank Richardson had gone to the bedroom window as soon as he heard the shots. He was looking out as Yellow plunged through the trees from the sidewalk onto the lot. He saw Yellow trip on something, stumble forward, and break his fall by putting one hand on the trunk of a parked car. Quickly steadying himself, Yellow then ran down the length of the lot.

Frowning, Richardson noted that the car Yellow had touched was a white Plymouth with license plate number DAD 368.

* * *

Elizabeth Lee was also looking out a bedroom window. She had heard the five gunshots and now she heard screams. The screams were a woman's and sounded terrible and desperate. Elizabeth opened the bedroom window. Just as she did, Yellow ran past her apartment.

"What happened up there?" she called to him.

Yellow, surprised, paused and looked up at her. For a split second, he locked eyes with the woman. Then he resumed running.

Elizabeth Lee watched him run to the east end of the building and disappear from sight.

On the street, the first two police units had arrived and radioed for an ambulance. Officers Michael Pedrini and Ronald Parenti, searching the scene, found the four .32-caliber shell casings that had ejected from the pistol. Officers in other units, arriving at the scene, began to spread out both in radio cars and on foot in an attempt to pick up the trail of the gunman. Gus Coreris arrived with Chief of Inspectors Barca to take over the Homicide investigation.

"Those casings thirty-twos?" he asked Pedrini. "As if I didn't already know."

"Yessir," the patrol officer answered.

Ken Moses of the Crime Lab came over to take possession of the casings.

"Call Mitch Luksich at home," Coreris told him. "See if he can come downtown and give us a definite make on these tonight."

Park Ambulance number 82 arrived to take Linda Story to Mission Emergency Hospital. "Looks like another spine-damage victim," one of the attendants said quietly. "She's not moving her legs much."

The other attendant nodded. "The dirty pricks that are doing all this shooting are either damn good shots or else the people they're picking on are all very unlucky. Spine shots nearly every time."

Two captains, two lieutenants, and a dozen more units arrived on the scene, and a dragnet of fifty searching men had soon sealed off a large area around the shooting scene. They searched for several hours, talking to witnesses, trying to trace the killer's movements in and around the several large apartment complexes that lined Geary Street. But they turned up nothing.

"If he had just run the other way," Vice Officer Dennis O'Connell said later that night.

"Yeah," his partner, Dan O'Brien agreed. "He would have run right into us."

But again a Zebra killer had been lucky.

Yellow had escaped.

At the end of Day One Hundred Sixty-four, there were twenty victims.

Quita Hague, hacked to death.

Richard Hague, his face butchered.

Ellen Linder, raped, ravaged, threatened with death.

Frances Rose, her face blown apart by close-range gunshots.

Saleem Erakat, tied up and executed with a single shot.

Paul Dancik, shot down as he attempted to use a public telephone.

Arthur Agnos, surviving after his insides were ripped up by bullets.

Marietta DiGirolamo, thrown into a doorway and shot to death.

Ilario Bertuccio, killed while walking home from work.

Angela Roselli, surviving with nerve damage in her back.

Neal Moynihan, shot down taking a Teddy bear to his little sister.

Mildred Hosler, shot down as she walked toward her bus stop.

John Doe No. 169, kidnapped, tortured, decapitated.

Tana Smith, murdered on her way to buy blouse material.

Vincent Wollin, murdered on his sixty-ninth birthday.

John Bambic, murdered while rummaging in a trash bin.

Jane Holly, murdered in a public Laundromat.

Roxanne McMillian, surviving but paralyzed from the waist down.

And Thomas Rainwater and Linda Story, the former dead, the latter surviving but critical, shot down on the street as they walked to a market for a snack.

Day 177

Coreris and Fotinos had worked through the night after Thomas Rainwater was killed and Linda Story wounded. They were at the shooting scene interviewing witnesses; at the Crime Lab where Luksich was working to match the shell casings found at the scene; at the coroner's office to retrieve the two bullets from Rainwater's body; at San Francisco General trying to talk to Linda Story, and retrieving the single bullet that had been removed from her in surgery; and back at their desks as the sun came up, wearily but methodically going over what little information they had.

"Tennis shoes again," Coreris said, reading the descriptions compiled from witnesses. "This was the same little bastard that did Moynihan and Hosler back in December."

"Different gun," Fotinos reminded him.

"I don't care about the goddamned gun," Coreris said stubbornly. "This is the same shooter. And I'll tell you something else: this is a *third* guy. This isn't one of the bastards that was out on the night of the five shootings. This is the one that fits the oddball description we keep getting every now and then. This punk is younger, skinnier, and a lot lighter colored than the other two or three or however many more there are. And he dresses like a kid: tennis

294

shoes, army jackets, ski caps. The others are sharper: they dress like cool dudes, not high-school kids.''

"Sounds logical," Fotinos allowed. "But the two guns worry me. I can't figure that angle. Unless it's a sect of some kind that keeps its guns in one place and allows any of the members to use them. What really bugs me, though, is what in the hell has happened to the *first* gun. It hasn't been used in over three months. The last seven victims have been hit with this second gun. You know, if these bastards are smart enough to shoot half a dozen people with one gun, then dispose of it where it can never be found, and do the same thing with a second gun and a third gun, et cetera, et cetera, we may just end up with a case that never makes it to trial. Even if we catch them and stop them, we may not be able to convict them.''

"At this point, I think I'd settle for that," Coreris said wearily. "I think I'd settle for anything just to stop the killings.''

"Yeah. Well, we had a nice long intermission," Fotinos said. "Exactly nine weeks. But I've got a feeling we aren't going to be so lucky this time. I've got a feeling that another rampage is about to start.''

Coreris stared at his partner. He had long ago learned to respect the "feelings" of John Fotinos. "How long do you figure until the next one?''

"By Easter," said Fotinos.

Coreris looked at his calendar. Easter was two weeks away.

Anthony Harris was watching television in Oakland when the program was interrupted with a bulletin about the Rainwater-Story shootings. Anthony tensed and glanced over at Debbie. She was dozing at the other end of the couch, her legs curled up under her pink chenille robe, unaware of the bulletin.

Man, I am glad I got out of that city, Anthony thought. I am glad I got *away* from there, away from those crazy people over there. I don't care if I never see that crazy place again!

But even as he thought it, Anthony felt the old sick fear begin to ooze around in his belly. It was the same fear that had driven him to go back across the bay the night that he saw Wally 4X at the mosque: the fear that some of the members might be looking for him. They *had* to be wondering where he went, Anthony thought. He had been gone more than two months and had not registered at any other mosque. They would have no choice but to consider him fallen away—and, he well knew, those who fell away were looked upon with great disfavor.

For a while now, ever since his clandestine visit to the mosque, Anthony had been considering getting in direct touch with Larry. He and Larry had been close almost since the day Anthony got out of San Quentin. There had been a couple of minor spats between them, some disagreement in Muslim philosophy and principle; but on the whole Anthony still considered Larry a friend, and felt—to some degree—that he could trust him.

This latest shooting, Anthony thought, could be just the excuse he needed to give Larry a call. He could say he saw it on the news and decided to get in touch to see just what was going on. He would not even tell Larry where he was; and if Larry asked, Anthony would make up some place and lie about it.

Glancing over at Debbie, Anthony saw that she was breathing the even, measured breath of someone sleeping peacefully. He eased himself off the couch and stood over her for a moment. She did not stir or open her eyes. Leaving the television on, he went quietly into the bedroom and got his coat. While he was in there, he checked on Anthony, Jr. The baby was sleeping as peacefully as its mother. Anthony put on his coat and quietly let himself out of the apartment.

Two blocks away, at a Chevron station, was an enclosed telephone booth. Anthony got a dollar's worth of change from the attendant. He still had Larry's number written on a Black Self Help business card Larry had given him at the Halfway House. He put in enough money for a trans-bay call and dialed. Larry answered on the first ring. Anthony tried to keep his voice steady.

"Say, brother, this is Anthony. What's going on?"

"Anthony? Anthony? Where the hell you been, man?" Larry's voice was nervous, hyper. "Where you calling from?"

"Texas," Anthony said. "I'm down here in Texas. What's happening up there, brother? I seen some bad stuff on the TV a little while ago."

"Hey, man, J.C. and Manuel been looking for you."

296

"Oh, yeah? What for?"

"They think you done wrong leaving like you did, man. They think you ran out on everybody."

"I didn't run out on nobody," Anthony said with a trace of irritation. "It's a free country, man. I don't have to ax nobody can I go here or can I go there—"

"Let me tell you something, Anthony," the younger man said self-righteously, "when you a Muslim, you either *with* your brothers or you *against* them! You understand me?"

"Sure, I understand. Hey, I'm always with my brothers, you know that—"

"Well, it don't look like it, man. Running off like that looked *bad*. It looked like maybe you was an *informant*."

"Who said that?" Anthony demanded.

"Couple of people," Larry replied evasively.

"Yeah, well those couple of people is *wrong!*" Anthony snapped. "I ain't been no informant on nobody!"

"I didn't say it, man," Larry protested. His voice rose to a nervous pitch, a shriek, like an addict begging for drugs. "I ain't never said nothing about no brother! I don't say nothing I be ashamed for Allah to hear. Did you ever hear me say anything about anybody? Say?"

"No, brother, I never did," Anthony said in a placating tone. "Calm down and stop yelling, man." In the booth, Anthony wiped sweat from his upper lip. Larry sounded like he was high on something. Anthony had seen him psyched up on more than one occasion, but had never heard his voice sound quite so shrill and— crazy. "Listen, man, will you do me a favor?" Anthony asked.

"What?"

"Just tell J.C. and the Man and anybody else who wants to know that you done heard from me and that I be in Texas, and that I ain't been no informant on nobody. Will you do that?"

"Yeah, I'll do that," Larry said, his voice still up. "I always be ready to help a brother, always. Allah knows I help my brothers."

"Yeah, right. Listen, maybe I'll be coming back in a few weeks, and when I do I'll call you up, hear?"

"Okay, man, okay."

They said good-bye and hung up. Anthony stepped out of the

297

booth. When the cool night air hit him, he discovered that he was drenched with sweat. He wiped his face with his palms.

Larry was as crazy as the others now, he thought. He shivered once, involuntarily. No way was he ever going back across the bay, he told himself again.

Hunching his shoulders to hide himself from the night, he hurried back to the apartment, to the baby, to Debbie.

In his cubicle in the Crime Lab, Mitch Luksich had gone to work immediately making a microscopic examination of the seven new pieces of evidence he had: four expended cartridge cases and three expended bullets. He got out a slug and casing from the gun used in the earlier shootings, in 1973, and a slug and casing from the gun used in the five shootings on the terrible night back in January. The new evidence, he was certain, would match one set or the other.

As he readied his microscope, he instinctively put the more recent casing-and-cartridge set nearest it to compare first. In the back of his scientist's mind, something told him that he would not be seeing any more evidence that matched the slugs from the earlier shootings. Luksich knew guns as few people did, but more importantly he knew the types of *people* who used guns: the collectors, cops, marksmen, designers, dealers—and amateurs. The men who were doing the Zebra killings were, Luksich was convinced, amateurs.

He had reached that conclusion early on in the case. Only gross amateurs would be running around trying to kill people with that kind of weapon and that kind of ammunition. A *real* killer, someone who knew the *tools* of killing, would not be firing standard ammo out of a small-bore weapon like the .32 that was being used. A pro would be shooting soft-nose slugs out of a .357 Magnum or a .38 Special with a five-inch barrel. *That* was the way to kill. With those types of weapons and that kind of ammunition, there would not have been people like Art Agnos, who did not even fall down for five minutes after he was shot; or Angela Roselli, who was already recuperated enough to resume walking; or Roxanne McMillian or Linda Story, both smallish females who had been hit at close range, yet survived.

They would all be dead now—if the Zebra killers were not amateurs.

When everything was ready, Luksich patiently and expertly examined first the four expended cartridge cases, then the two bullets taken from the body of Thomas Rainwater, then the single slug retrieved from Linda Story by the hospital. He compared them all with the sample set. They matched perfectly.

Luksich switched on his Dictaphone and got the facts down on record. "Lab number 74—2316," he said. "Thomas Rainwater and Linda Story. Description of Evidence: Four thirty-two APC expended cartridge cases. Two expended bullets from Thomas Rainwater. One expended bullet from Linda Story. Report Results: The four cartridge cases and three bullets from this homicide shooting were microscopically compared with those from 74-788, 74-789, 74-790, 74-791, and 74-792.

"Paragraph. The microscopic examination revealed that the cartridge cases and bullets from this case and those of 74-788 through 74-792 were fired from the same thirty-two-caliber automatic pistol."

Switching off the dictating machine, Luksich pulled the telephone over and dialed Homicide.

Linda Story's divorced mother, Jossie, had been watching television in the family home in Hayward, across the bay, the night her daughter was shot. Five minutes before she would have seen the news bulletin on her screen, the mother of another Salvation Army cadet telephoned her to ask if she had heard about the shooting. Mrs. Story was stunned.

A Salvation Army major, George Baker, came to the house and drove Jossie to San Francisco to the hospital. It was not until midnight, some three hours after the shooting, that Linda came out of surgery, comatose. Jossie Story cried at her bedside in the intensive care unit.

"I can't believe this happened," she said over and over again through her tears. "She's just an ordinary girl, just like any other girl. I just can't believe this happened."

Other officers from the Salvation Army Training School arrived and consoled Mrs. Story while they waited for Linda to wake up. By three o'clock in the morning, when Linda was still asleep, doctors decided to seclude her for the rest of the night. Major Baker took Jossie Story back home.

Linda woke up briefly just before noon the next day. By that time, her mother and the major were back at her bedside.

"Linda, honey, how do you feel?" her mother asked.

Linda, who remembered exactly what had happened, spoke through pale, dry lips. "I—feel—grateful," she whispered, "to—be—alive—"

The man who had shot Linda Story was not grateful that she was alive.

Yellow, standing on a street corner, read the morning paper with a tightly clenched jaw. Allah damn that white bitch devil! he thought. How could she have *lived?* The white bastard devil died; I stood and watched him die—

Yes, he told himself, you surely did stand and watch, didn't you? When instead you should have been seeing to it that the bitch devil died. You heard her screaming, you knew she was still alive, you should have done something about her.

I did, I did, he argued with himself. I fired another shot at her. But I must have missed.

You were close enough to make sure that you did *not* miss, his conscience chastised him. You were close enough to put the gun against her *head* and fire directly into her devil brain. But you did not. You kept watching the male devil, watching him walk, stagger, stumble away. You could not keep your eyes off the male devil. Why?

I don't know, Yellow silently answered himself. I don't know. Thoughts of the white homosexual flashed in his mind. Oh, no! No, it was not anything like *that*.

Why, then? Why, why, why? Was it because he was *all* white and you are only *part* white? Because he was pure and you are tainted? Because he was smiling, confident, and self-assured, and you are sneaky, weak, and inferior? Because he belonged to a smart, sharp, well-organized group, and you are only a member of a vile, disjointed, insane gang? Because he was entitled to wear a nice, bright, well-tailored *uniform*—and you were in sneakers and a ratty raincoat? Is that why you had to watch *him* die, instead of making sure she did? Because you were jealous of him, and she meant nothing to you? Was that it?

Yellow dropped the paper into the gutter. He walked away from the corner, terribly disturbed. For the first time in his life, he was consciously aware that something was driving him to kill. Some dark, terrible thing deep within him. Some awful thing that seized his mind and took over his body.

He did not know what it was, only that it had to do with white men and the color of his own very light skin.

And that he could not control it.

In the basement parking lot of the Hall of Justice, Inspectors Walt Ihle and Ken Moses of the Crime Lab set up a folding table next to a white 1970 Plymouth bearing license number DAD 368. It was the car that witness Frank Richardson had seen Yellow stumble against and touch when the young killer was fleeing from the scene of the Rainwater murder.

"The witness said the guy put his hand on the trunk," said Moses.

"Yeah," said Ihle, "but we don't know which side. You take the right, I'll take the left."

The two police technicians went to work. Using a dark gray powder made of mercury and black chalk, they carefully brushed the entire trunk lid with soft-bristle brushes. As they worked, they looked for latent, or hidden, prints: impressions made in perspiration or oil by the fingers or palms. They went over the shiny surface of the trunk square inch by square inch.

Whenever one of the men began to find a fragmentary impression of any kind, a surge of excitement went through him. Fourteen people dead, six others seriously hurt—and the answer to who was doing it might be right there in front of them: an invisible but undeniable link to a mad killer. Each time a fragment of a print appeared, Ihle and Moses worked more slowly, more carefully, more hopefully. And each time, when it turned out to be just another smudge or streak or tiny scratch, they forced themselves to take it in stride and continue their slow, methodical work.

Finally the trunk lid was finished. There were no usable prints of any kind.

Ihle and Moses looked at each other, mutual disappointment clouding their faces.

"The witness said it was the trunk that was touched," Ihle offered, "but the car might have been parked backward."

"You mean he might have touched the hood," said Moses. Some of his eagerness instantly returned.

"Sure, why not? It was nighttime. That lot wasn't all that well lighted. If the car had been parked backward, the witness might have *assumed* that it was the trunk that was touched."

"Let's dust the hood," said Moses.

"Let's," said Ihle.

They moved their table and equipment to the front of the car, each took one side again, and began a new round of slow, tedious work, made easier by a surge of fresh hope. But in the end it was all for nothing. There was not one usable print anywhere on the outside of the car that did not belong to the vehicle's owner. Either Yellow had been wearing gloves when he touched the car, or his hand had not stopped moving when he made contact, leaving not a latent impression but only a smudge.

Once again, the incredible luck of the Zebra killers had held.

While Linda Story remained highly sedated in the intensive care unit, and the remains of Thomas Rainwater were being released to the Nicholas P. Daphne Funeral Home, which was providing the funeral without charge, the remaining sixty-four cadets at the Salvation Army Officer Training School attended a special prayer service. The meeting was held to pray for three people: Rainwater, Linda Story, and the person who had shot them.

"Our feeling at this time is one of hurt, sorrow, and shock," said Captain Alfred Van Cleef. "But there is no hatred in us, no bitterness for the man who committed this tragic act. We know that Tom was ready for this spiritually. It is the rest of us who were not. His passing will leave a vacant space in all our lives. He was a popular young man—perhaps the most popular of all the cadets, as evinced by his election last month as student body president."

After the prayer service, reporters asked Captain Van Cleef if the school was making arrangements for any special security for its students.

"No, we have no such plans," the officer said. "We have asked the cadet body to use discretion when they go out, but we don't intend to put a shield around our lives."

"Has there been any indication of outrage or indignation among the other cadets?" he was asked.

"None at all. The feeling is a general sense of solemnity and introspection. We all know that we have lost a fine young missionary. Tom Rainwater had but one goal in life: to devote himself wholly to God and to orphan children. It is a terrible feeling to know that all his devotion and potential service, the work he would have done, the kids he might have helped, is all lost now. But we are not outraged or indignant about it. Because of it, I think each of us will work a little harder to help take his place."

The reporters, unaccustomed to such calm reasoning, left Captain Van Cleef feeling that they had been in the presence of an extraordinary man.

Vandyke was back in San Francisco again, and he was worried. In the back seat of the big Continental, riding across the bridge from Oakland to preside over a loft meeting, he found himself fidgeting with one fingernail after another. These so-called Zebra killings had got completely out of hand, he thought. Never in his wildest imagination did he think that an entire city—particularly one as urbane and sophisticated as San Francisco—would put forth such a massive effort to stop the killings of—of—*nobodies.* But, then, he never expected that some of the Death Angel candidates would be so stupid as to use the same weapon or weapons on all their victims, and that the collective killings would subsequently be connected so quickly. He had expected the men to use discretion and cunning; if not that, at least common sense. But some of them had bungled things from the very beginning.

He should have seen it coming, Vandyke chastised himself. As far back as the Hague thing, he should have seen it coming. When a grown man with a nineteen-inch machete cannot hack to death a helpless, bound, unconscious captive, something was vitally wrong. And those people who were shot at close range and did not die: that fellow Agnos, and more particularly the women involved—the Roselli and McMillian women, and now this Story girl—the whole thing had become ludicrous. In the name of Allah, why didn't those fools have the intelligence to shoot the people in the *heads?*

When the big car had parked behind the loft building and the door was opened for him, Vandyke, followed by his two aides, went inside and climbed the steep flight of stairs to the meeting. The men were all waiting for him, their black, brown, tan, and yellow faces shadowed in the poor lighting of the loft. In a few of those faces, eyes bulged out like great white oysters, reminding Vandyke of some old jungle movies he had seen as a child in Chicago. It looked like the natives were getting ready to make juju. Which, Vandyke reflected, was not too far from what they were doing.

"Good evening, my brothers," he greeted the group. "Tonight I want to do two things. The first is to congratulate you all on your recent destruction of numerous white devils. The black man's earth is much better off with that many fewer grafted snakes crawling about. You have all done splendid work for Allah during the past months. Now, however, I think it is time to move on to other work—and that is the second thing I want to talk about."

He clasped his hands behind his back and began to pace. The men's eyes followed him intently. I've got to make this good now, he thought. Must get them to stop the killings before they all go down—and take me down with them.

"It is time, I think, to put aside the destruction of the grafted white snakes—temporarily, at least—and move on to work of a more personal nature."

Skullcap and Rims exchanged surprised looks. Put it aside? The campaign had only just resumed.

"It has come to my attention," Vandyke continued, "that the local members of the Nation of Islam appear to be losing touch with our own people. I speak now of those who continue to worship at the churches of the heathen Christ, those who have not yet been guided to embrace Islam. We of the Nation seem to hold ourselves aloof from those unfortunate brothers and sisters who have not yet come to us. And this is not right, it is not proper. They need our help; we must step down to them and offer our hands."

Vandyke stopped and faced them. He held out his hand to them.

"I am therefore asking that the exalted Death Angels go out among our people and begin a new campaign to cleanse our people of the evils that plague them. Go out, my brothers, and help clean up the ghettos. Go out and help get rid of black pimps and their prostitutes—black and white. Help get rid of the black drug peddlers—those evil monsters who have paralyzed so much of the black race. Go out and find little black children who are not receiving any guidance in their lives and direct them to our temple so that they may be schooled in the way of righteous thinking."

Skullcap was frowning. The way of righteous thinking was the killing of grafted snakes. This very man had taught them that. And now he was telling them to stop? Before they were finished?

"My brothers," said Vandyke, "there are many things that need to be done in our black neighborhoods, much that we can accomplish. If you who are Death Angels go forth in the black community ready to do battle with the pimps, prostitutes, and pushers, then by the service you do your brothers and sisters, you will exalt the Death Angels to an even higher plateau than they have already achieved—"

"What about the ones who don't *be* Death Angels yet?" Skullcap said, rising to his feet in the middle of the group.

Vandyke's mouth remained open, with no words coming forth. He was surprised; it was the first time he had ever been interrupted at such a meeting. At each side of the room, his aides started toward Skullcap. Unafraid, Skullcap braced himself to meet them. Rims rose and stood beside him to show the aides that his friend was not alone.

"One moment!" Vandyke said sharply to his aides. This was no time, he quickly decided, for a show of authority. "As you were," he ordered his aides. He turned benevolently to Skullcap. "I beg your pardon, brother. What was your question?"

"I said, what about the ones who don't *be* Death Angels yet? The ones who don't got their wings yet? What do they do?"

"Why, exactly what the Death Angels do," Vandyke said with a smile.

"That not fair," said Skullcap. "Not fair to the ones who had to earn their wings. And not fair to us who has to *stop* earning ours."

Watch it, Vandyke cautioned himself. This can be touchy. People who are not very bright often have very fixed ideas about what is or is not fair.

"Your brother Death Angels are not selfish men," he told Skullcap. "They will not object to your working alongside them in such a laudable endeavor."

"But *I* might object to working alongside *them*," Skullcap argued. "Because I would feel less of a man if I had not earned the *right* to work alongside them."

"In the eyes of Allah," Vandyke told him, "we are all equal as brothers. Allah does not recognize or reward for individual acts, only for the spirit and intent which are in the heart."

Bullshit, Skullcap thought. Then a cunning idea materialized in his mind. Two can play at that game, sucker.

"Suppose," Skullcap said, "that Allah *moves* a man to keep destroying the grafted snake? Like this brother here." He put a hand on the shoulder of Yellow, who was sitting on the other side of him. "This brother was moved by Allah to destroy a white devil of the heathen Salvation Army. If a brother is moved like that, he be have to do what Allah commands. Am I right?"

Vandyke felt his spine stiffen. He had trapped himself. He should have known better than to bring Allah into it. It was too easy to justify something in the name of one's god. Human beings had been committing atrocities in the name of sacred goodness almost since time began. Even the Death Angels themselves were no exception. Even he *himself* would have been no exception had it not been for the fact that with him the religious part of it was simply a means to accomplish an end. The real motive was to drive whites out of San Francisco so that blacks could establish a Muslim city in America.

But sometimes one got carried away with using Allah's name. Sometimes it seemed that the simplest way to justify something was in the name of Allah. And sometimes doing it backfired. Like just now when this intense young man—what was his name? He was the young fool who had come to Chicago seeking a promotion. Well, no matter—this intense young man not only had interrupted him but had now virtually taken control of the conversation.

"Am I right?" Skullcap asked again.

Vandyke had no choice but to answer. "Yes, brother, you are right. "But I must caution you to be certain that you are indeed moved by Allah and not by false pride or vanity."

"I don't have no *false* pride," Skullcap said. "And I am never mistaken in what Allah moves me to do."

"I'm sure you're not, brother," said Vandyke.

For just an instant, Vandyke had a flash of realization that he had created a monster.

* * *

On the afternoon of the third day after he was murdered, funeral services were held for Thomas Rainwater at the Salvation Army Citadel. His parents, Mr. and Mrs. Arthur Rainwater, and fourteen-year-old sister, Joyce, of Ojai, traveled to San Francisco for the funeral.

During the services, the dead youth was eulogized by the highest and lowest ranks of his Salvation Army comrades: Salvation Army Commissioner Paul S. Kaiser, and Cadet David Chamberlain, who like Rainwater was a first-year student at the officers' training school.

Said Commissioner Kaiser, "Tom Rainwater was a good soldier of Jesus Christ. The person who killed him is obviously a very sick, mentally twisted individual. We all pray that he will swiftly be brought to a place where he can no longer be a threat to lives."

Cadet Chamberlain, in his eulogy, said, "Death cannot deprive him of being with us. Out of his loss will come a more determined congregation."

The services were strained and tearful, perhaps more so than at the usual funeral, for the pews at this funeral were filled with row upon row of clear-eyed young people whose faces were filled with bewilderment and hurt. Why Thomas Rainwater? their expressions seemed to ask. Why a young man who sought to do only good, to give only a helping hand, to speak softly in a world of shouters? Why did such things happen?

But there was no answer that day at the Citadel; there was only the question and the loss and the grief. And even had all the facts been known that day, they would have answered nothing. What rational person could have understood the insanity of one religion which could turn a young man into a killer who would prey on the life of a similar young man from another religion?

Monsters were not easily explained, even in eulogies.

It was Easter Sunday, thirteen days after Thomas Rainwater's murder.

It was a bright, sunny day, and in San Francisco's Golden Gate Park an unusually large number of families and couples took advantage of the pleasant weather to enjoy an Easter picnic. Among those doing so was Bernice White and her five children, two of those teenage boys: Terry, fifteen, and Timothy, fourteen. For several hours that afternoon, Mrs. White and her children ate and played games and enjoyed their family outing.

In another part of the city, a young merchant seaman named Ward Anderson boarded a city bus and rode across town to the marina area near Fisherman's Wharf to visit a friend for a few hours. Anderson was a tall, slim young man who was dressed in the functional clothing of a sailor: jeans, wool shirt, waterproof jacket. At the time, he was signed on board a geological survey vessel, but he had the whole day off.

While the White family had its picnic and Ward Anderson visited his friend, the two Black Muslims known as Skullcap and Rims had a philosophical discussion on the subject of murder.

"I say it be all right to keep on destroying the blue-eyed devils," Skullcap said. "And the man from New Mecca, he say so too. You heard him."

Rims grunted and nodded vigorously. They were sitting at the table in Skullcap's apartment, drinking herb tea. "That man from New Mecca, he didn't be *want* to say it be okay," Rims said with a grin. He pointed a finger at Skullcap. "But you be *make* him say it. You pretty smart."

Skullcap shrugged off the compliment with what little modesty he could muster. "What I did was for the good of all the brothers," he said, trying to emulate the calm but authoritative expression of Vandyke. *That son of a bitch,* he thought. *I got back at him good for the way he treated me in New Mecca: taking away all the Death Angel pictures, not promoting me to lieutenant, sending me back empty-handed. Well, I fixed his black ass good. I made him look* dumb *in front of everybody. They all know who be the smartest now. I be the leader of this bunch yet.*

"When you think somebody gonna kill white devils again?" Rims asked, squinting at Skullcap from behind his thick glasses.

"Only Allah knows that," his friend replied solemnly. "Allah will move someone to act when it is time." He paused a beat, then added, "But it wouldn't surprise me none if it happened today. This is the heathen holiday they call Easter, when the Jew named Jesus is supposed to have risen from the dead. That be zombie stuff, man, but the Caucasian intellect believes it. Maybe Allah will move somebody today to show the devils how wrong they be."

With that thought firmly implanted in Rims's head, Skullcap left him alone, saying that he was going to visit a new sister he had met at temple. If Rims did what Skullcap expected him to, then there could be no criticism leveled in *his* direction because of the resumption of the shootings. It would not have been *him* who had started it after the representative from New Mecca had suggested they stop. Even though he had confronted the man at the meeting, it would be another who would kill again first. Rims, not himself.

But he would certainly feel free to kill *after* that.

So he left the apartment. And Rims remained behind alone, mulling over what his good friend had told him.

At about five o'clock in the afternoon, at the Golden Gate Park picnic of the White family, the two teenage boys, Terry and Timothy, got ready to leave the park. They had been invited to eat supper at the home of a friend in the old neighborhood where they used to live.

"Don't you two be out late," Bernice White cautioned.

"We won't," the boys promised.

They left the park and rode a bus to their old neighborhood.

Ward Anderson, the young merchant seaman, spent the evening with his friend in the marina district. During the course of his visit, he smoked most of a pack of cigarettes he had brought with him. He made a mental note to stop and buy some more on his way back across town.

After Skullcap left him alone in the apartment, Rims took the .32 automatic from under the mattress where Skullcap kept it. He placed it on the table where he could look at it. Pouring himself another cup of herb tea, he sat back down and, as he sipped the tea, stared at the gun, waiting for Allah to move him.

At the home of their friend, the White brothers had supper and stayed for an impromptu Easter party that went on past early evening. At eight thirty, Terry told his brother that he was leaving. Timothy decided to stay a while longer.

"Tell Mom I'll be along later," he said.

Terry said he would and left. He walked over to Fillmore Street and got on a northbound bus to ride to Hayes Street, where he had to transfer.

At the other end of the same bus line, Ward Anderson, who had left his friend's house, boarded a southbound bus, also heading for

Hayes Street where he too would have to transfer. As he rode, he had an urge for a cigarette. Smoking was not permitted on the bus, but he would probably have time for one when he changed lines at Hayes Street.

In the apartment, Rims stared at the gun long enough to psych himself into picking it up and putting it into his belt. He put on his coat and left the apartment. Starting to walk aimlessly around, he waited for Allah to show him whom to kill.

Ward Anderson was the first to arrive at the Hayes Street intersection. He got off the bus, simultaneously reaching for the cigarette pack in his shirt pocket. Twisting a finger down into the pack, he found that it was empty. Damn! he thought, crumbling the pack into a ball and tossing it into the gutter. He looked around for someplace to buy a fresh pack. There was nothing open: it was Easter Sunday night.

As Anderson stood there coping with his nicotine fit, a bus arrived from the other direction and a husky teenage boy got off. Apparently also transferring, he crossed over to the bus stop where Anderson stood. Anderson bobbed his chin at him. "Say, you got a smoke on you by any chance?" he asked.

The teenager, Terry White, shook his head. "I don't smoke," he said.

Anderson walked over to the open entrance of an apartment building and sat on the outside steps. Several minutes later, two black women walked up to the bus stop to wait also. Anderson briefly considered asking them for a cigarette, but decided against it. They might get the wrong idea.

Hayes Street at this point runs uphill from Fillmore to Steiner, downhill from Fillmore to Webster. The bus the four people were waiting for would be coming uphill from Webster Street to Fillmore, so most of their attention was directed downhill from where they stood. None of them noticed the black man, his head lowered and hands shoved in his pockets, who was walking downhill toward them from Steiner Street.

Rims walked with his shoulders hunched, chin against his chest. Walking downhill, he did not need to raise his eyes to see where he was going. Down at the next corner, under the hazy glow of a streetlight, he could see several people waiting at the bus stop. He could not tell whether they were black or white. In one pocket, the cold handle of Skullcap's pistol had turned warm in his palm. Allah, give me a sign, he silently prayed.

Ward Anderson was the first to see Rims coming. He had stepped to the edge of the curb and looked down to see if a bus was coming yet. There was none, but several cars moved past him on the street. On the off chance that he could get a ride, he stuck his thumb up hitchhiker-fashion, but no one stopped for him. It was as he turned back to the steps where he had been sitting, the steps where the two black women now waited, that he glanced up the sidewalk and saw Rims approaching.

As Anderson stood there, with Rims still half a block away, an undercover Zebra unit drove by on Fillmore, heading south. The plainclothes officer in the passenger seat glanced out at the people at the bus stop. He saw nothing unusual. There was no reason to stop.

The Zebra unit continued on its way.

Anderson continued to stand there.

Rims continued to walk toward him.

Allah, give me a sign.

When Rims was close enough to him, Anderson said, "Say, man, you wouldn't happen to have an extra smoke, would you?"

Rims walked on past him, making a low, guttural grunt as he did. *His sign! That was his sign!* The white devil had spoken to him. He grunted again.

Anderson stared at him for a moment. Terry White, standing nearby, glanced over, then away. Rims stepped into the street and looked up and down, both ways. Anderson turned and took a step back toward the building. Behind him, Rims, eyes wide and fixed, drew the gun from his pocket and shot Anderson twice in the lower back.

The bullets ripped into Ward Anderson's body, tearing through his kidney and liver. He felt pain lace his right leg, felt it give away, and knew he was falling. "Son of a bitch," he said, and pitched facedown on the sidewalk. As soon as he hit, he braced his hands on the cement and raised himself enough to look up. He saw Rims running across the sidewalk toward the husky white teenager.

Terry White had just glanced at Anderson and Rims, then looked

311

away, when the shots sounded. He jerked his head back around and froze. By the time he realized what was happening, Anderson was on the sidewalk and Rims was running directly toward him. Terry did not even have time to think, much less react. Rims, the gun already leveled, fired twice more. The first bullet bore into Terry's right side just under the rib cage. It split his liver in half and coursed up to collapse his lungs. The second bullet, as he was twisting and falling, entered his left arm. Terry hit the sidewalk scant seconds after Anderson had fallen.

Rims, not even breaking stride, ran around the corner into Fillmore Street and ran north toward Grove.

Three blocks down Fillmore was the undercover Zebra unit that had passed the bus stop less than a minute earlier. It was just far enough away for the shots to be inaudible.

Within a square mile of the intersection of Hayes and Fillmore, where the shootings took place, there were nine other Zebra units cruising in various locations: a total of ten Zebra cars carrying twenty policemen.

Yet Rims got away.

He fled up Fillmore to Grove, ran around the corner on Grove—and disappeared. No one saw where he went—but he was observed fleeing around the corner. Yolande Williams, a seventeen-year-old black girl, had just driven her uncle and some friends back from Oakland. She parked the car on Grove Street and they all walked toward the uncle's house. Then, remembering that she had left the car unlocked, Yolande went back alone to lock it. When she did, she saw Rims run around the corner, shove the gun in his belt, and hurry down Grove Street. A moment later, the shadows engulfed him.

Within ninety seconds, patrol units had blocked the intersections of Hayes and Steiner, Fell and Steiner, Fell and Fillmore, Fell and Webster, Webster and Hayes, Webster and Ivy, Webster and Grove, and Grove and Fillmore. The latter—although the responding unit did not know it at the time—was the key intersection around the corner of which Rims had fled and disappeared. Police cars began to arrive on the scene in seconds. Scores of officers began to disperse into buildings, yards, alleys, within minutes. The area was completely sealed off as quickly as humanly possible.

But not quickly enough.

Rims escaped.

At the end of Day One Hundred Seventy-seven, there were twenty-two victims.

Quita Hague, hacked to death.

Richard Hague, his face butchered.

Ellen Linder, raped, ravaged, threatened with death.

Frances Rose, her face blown apart by close-range gunshots.

Saleem Erakat, tied up and executed.

Paul Dancik, shot down at a public telephone.

Arthur Agnos, surviving after his insides were ripped up by bullets.

Marietta DiGirolamo, thrown into a doorway and shot to death.

Ilario Bertuccio, killed while walking home from work.

Angela Roselli, surviving with nerve damage in her back.

Neal Moynihan, shot down taking a Teddy bear to his little sister.

Mildred Hosler, shot down as she walked toward her bus stop.

John Doe No. 169, kidnapped, tortured, butchered, decapitated.

Tana Smith, murdered on her way to buy blouse material.

Vincent Wollin, murdered on his sixty-ninth birthday.

John Bambic, murdered while rummaging in a trash bin.

Jane Holly, murdered in a public Laundromat.

Roxanne McMillian, surviving but paralyzed from the waist down.

Thomas Rainwater, shot down on the street as he walked to a market.

Linda Story, surviving with nerve damage after being shot down on the street.

Ward Anderson and Terry White, strangers, both shot down as they waited at the same bus stop.

Day 179

At the Hall of Justice the next morning, nearly fifty reporters, photographers, and television newsmen crowded into the conference room to question Chief of Inspectors Charles Barca about the most recent shootings. Barca, when he entered the noisy, smoky room, had in his hand the latest laboratory report from Mitch Luksich. It was brief and to the point:

Four expended .32 ACP cartridge cases. One expended bullet from Ward Anderson.

The four expended cartridge cases and one expended bullet from this shooting were compared to those from Lab. No. 74-788 through 74-792 and 74-2316.

Microscopic comparison revealed that all of the cartridge cases and bullets from all of the above cases were fired from the same .32-caliber automatic pistol.

As soon as Barca reached the podium, the rapid-fire questions began.

"Chief, were the two shootings last night Zebra shootings?"

"They were," said Barca. "I've just received a copy of the ballistics report. It was the same thirty-two-caliber automatic pistol."

"How many shootings is it linked with now, Chief?"

"This particular weapon has been positively connected with nine shootings: five murders and four attempted murders. But the department is convinced that these same killers are now responsible for a total of seventeen shootings involving eleven fatalities and six survivors." Barca was going all the way back to Saleem Erakat. The four prior victims—Quita and Richard Hague, Ellen Linder, and Frances Rose—had not definitely been connected to the Zebra killings as yet. The Hague case was a kidnap-hacking. Linder was a kidnap-sex assault. Frances Rose was similar to the street shootings, but it was not an open case: Jesse Lee Cooks had pled guilty to it and been sent to prison.

"Chief, are last night's two victims still alive?"

"Yes. Both Ward Anderson and Terry White were reported by the hospital this morning as being in stable condition. Each underwent surgery last night for his respective wounds."

"Chief, the last two shootings have involved two victims together. Does this indicate to you that the killers are doubling up? Trying to kill twice as many as before?"

"I don't know what it indicates," Barca replied patiently. "It may simply be coincidence, or it may be calculated. These gunmen are obviously sick people. They are mentally disturbed. It is very difficult to second-guess a maniac, a madman, a—" Barca's voice trailed off in frustration.

"Chief, do you feel that you—the department—is more or less helpless in this case?"

"Yes, I do," the veteran policeman admitted. "Helpless in the sense that I'm surprised how someone could be so lucky at not having been captured by now."

"Are you going to add more men to the manhunt?" a newspaper woman asked.

'We have the entire force mobilized now," Barca said. "It's impossible, of course, to cover everything, every square block in the city. But we are going to refine some aspects of the massive Zebra patrol operation. Just how, I'm not quite sure yet. I'm hoping, of course, that we can catch these killers right in the act."

"Sir, is the department still taking no official position on whether the killings are being committed as part of a black initiation rite of some kind?"

"I can only repeat what I have said in the past," Barca replied. "The department has no reliable evidence to support such a theory. There are, of course, as many rumors around as there are people in this room, and I'm sure individual police officers have their own private theories; but as far as the department is concerned, we are looking for two or more psychopathic killers. Two or more madmen. It's that simple."

One of the madmen was sitting in front of the television set, weeping. Rims was overwrought because both victims were still alive and he was not going to get credit for stinging either of them.

"They didn't die, man," he kept saying as a special news report on the collective shootings was being broadcast. "Them bastard devils didn't die!"

"Hey, brother, I know what you mean," said Skullcap. "I been there, remember?" He pretended to console Rims, but secretly he was glad that the big man had failed. If he himself started moving again now, he might well catch up with—even go ahead of—everybody else. He might still be the next one to win his Death Angel wings.

"I be right up close to them devils," Rims moaned. "I be right *next* to them! They both fall down. I don't see how they be still alive." He turned a pouting face to Skullcap. "You think maybe the TV be lying?"

Skullcap shook his head solemnly. "TV don't never lie, man."

Rims took off his glasses and dried his eyes on his shirt-sleeves. "Then it all be a mistake," he said.

"The TV?"

"No, man," he said irritably, "the stings. The stings be a mistake. Allah didn't move me none. If Allah be really move me, then the devils they be die. But they *don't* be die. So it all be a mistake. I just be a fool."

"Man, you not a fool—"

"Yeah, yeah, I be a fool. All my life. Dumb. Stupid. Idiot. Can't

316

learn nothing. Don't know nothing. Always be do things wrong. Always be get in trouble. Sometimes I think I be better off dead.''

Tears started to come to Rims's eyes again and Skullcap began to feel genuinely sorry for him. All the more so since with that pity came a pang of conscience brought on by the knowledge that it was *his* fault that Rims had gone out to sting in the first place. Skullcap had put the idea in his friend's head; he had suckered Rims into starting the killing again. Now, seeing the personal ordeal Rims was going through, Skullcap felt very badly about it.

"Hey, brother, come on, don't be so down about it,'' Skullcap said, draping an arm around his friend's big shoulders. "It don't be the end of the world. Those devils could still die. Maybe Allah just making them suffer.''

Rims shook his head. "No, they don't be die. Every devil that died since we started stinging, died the same night. The devils that lived until the morning, they didn't die at all. That be Allah's way of telling when a sting be failed.''

"Well, even if that be so,'' Skullcap reasoned, "it don't mean nothing bad 'bout *you*. It just mean Allah not ready for those particular devils to be destroyed yet. Man, look at all the stings that be gone bad for *me*. For a while there, it look like I never going to get *close* to no Death Angel wings. But then I start to catch up, and now everything looking good again. You just can't let yourself be so down, brother. Allah sometime put stumbling blocks in front of us. They be to let us know that what we have to do for Allah not always be easy. They be like a test.''

Rims sniffed. "You think Allah be testing me? That be why the devils lived?''

"No doubt about it,'' Skullcap said confidently. "You be tested just like I be tested before.''

"What I gots to do now?'' Rims wanted to know. He asked the question almost fearfully.

"Just be strong,'' Skullcap told him. "Be strong and dedicated. The next time Allah move you to do a sting, it turn out all right. You wait and see.''

Rims thought about it for a moment, his big head hanging like a chastised child. So much had turned out wrong for him in his lifetime, so many things had gone sour, misfired, fallen apart. The Muslims were the first things he had ever embraced that had embraced him back. More than anything he had ever wanted in the world, he wanted to be a good Muslim, to be accepted as a brother by his friends, to be a *permanent part of something permanent.*

Rims finally sighed a deep, wistful sigh that heaved his big chest and shoulders up. Then he looked at Skullcap and forced a half-smile.

"You good to me, brother," he said sincerely. "You the bestest friend I ever had."

"Hey, come on," Skullcap said, almost in embarrassment.

But deep inside himself, Skullcap was extremely pleased. Because *he* wanted acceptance too.

Coreris got in to see Terry White the moment the doctors at San Francisco General said it was all right. The husky teenager was awake but feeling miserable. Almost as white as the bandages on his body, he lay flat on his back, twenty-three stitches in his stomach, in constant pain because the drug they could only give him every four hours barely lasted half that long. Tense and uncomfortable, he was afraid to move because he had visions of tearing his stomach open and dying before a doctor could get in there and sew him back up.

Coreris sat next to the boy's bed and leaned forward. "How are you doing, son?" he asked.

"Awful," said Terry. "Terrible. I hurt all the time."

"Yeah," said Coreris. There was not much to say to that. "Do you know who I am?" he asked.

"Cop," said Terry.

"Right. Inspector Coreris. You just call me Gus, okay?"

"Sure." Terry licked his dry lips. "Look, I don't feel much like talking right now. I hurt bad."

"Just for a minute, Terry," said Coreris. "It's important. We want to get these killers before they hurt anybody else if we can. I want you to tell me what you remember about the man."

"I remember he shot me, man."

"I mean what he looked like, Terry. How tall was he?"

318

"I don't know. Taller than me."

"How much taller?"

"Five ten, maybe six feet. I don't know."

"How about his build? Was he skinny, stocky, what?"

"Kind of stocky, I guess. I don't want to talk anymore. I can't think straight when I'm hurting like this."

"You want to help us catch these guys, don't you, Terry?"

"Right now I don't care if you catch them or not."

"Just give me another minute," Coreris said. "What kind of hair did the man have?"

Terry sighed. "Short Afro."

"And what kind of complexion? Light, dark, what?"

"Man, it was night. The guy was black, that's all I know. Now leave me alone, please. I hurt bad."

Coreris went out to the hall where Fotinos waited. "Any luck?" his partner asked.

"Not much."

"Enough for a composite sketch?"

Coreris shook his head. "I doubt it."

Fotinos sighed in momentary disappointment. "Well, maybe we'll do better with Ward Anderson, the other victim."

"Yeah, maybe."

As they walked toward Ward Anderson's room, Coreris was deep in thought. His expression was fixed, reflecting intense concentration on the seed of an idea that had just sprung to life in his mind. It was true, Terry White had *not* given them enough of a description to warrant having a police department artist talk to him and try to work up a composite sketch.

But, Coreris thought, nobody knew that except Fotinos and himself.

Anthony Harris woke up in Oakland that morning after having a grueling nightmare. He came awake trembling, cold but slick all over with sweat, his hands shaking like a spastic.

Debbie did not wake up. Anthony eased out of bed and went into the bathroom. The linoleum floor was cold to his bare feet, but it did not bother him; he was too chilled all over to pay attention to

319

any isolated discomfort. At the sink he ran water until it was hot, then he splashed it liberally on his face and upper torso. It warmed him up just long enough for him to dry and hurry back to bed.

His side of the bed was slightly damp, so Anthony slid over close to Debbie. She purred in her sleep; she liked to cuddle with Anthony. Burying his face in her hair, he lay very still while her body warmed him.

Anthony had been having nightmares for several weeks—almost since his insomnia stopped. At first it had been blessed relief to be able to sleep again. The insomnia had been nerve-wracking, exhausting. The first night he had not suffered from it, he slept like a dead man. The next several nights were the same. He began to feel human again.

Then the nightmares started.

The first one was of Jesse Lee Cooks walking naked down a lane lined with elderly white people. They stood pathetically on each side of the lane, old and wrinkled and stooped. Jesse walked along with his powerful black body upright and strong, a long-bladed machete in each hand. As he came to one of the white figures, he would swing out and hack its head off. Left and right, right and left, both machetes swung like pendulums, lopping off heads, splashing the lane with blood.

Anthony had awakened the next morning shaken and tired, glad to see a new day. What a miserable fucking night, he had thought. Scary. Awful. He was greatly relieved that it was over.

Then it happened again. The very next night.

The second nightmare was about J.C. The two of them had come to blows at last. They were fighting out behind Black Self Help. All the others were standing around watching. Most of them were *for* Anthony, against J.C. Anthony was feeling good; he was winning. Then suddenly he turned white. Actually lost all the color in his face and body. After that, J.C. began to win. The others crowding around began to cheer unanimously for J.C. Anthony was completely outclassed; J.C. fought like Muhammad Ali: floating like a butterfly, stinging like a bee. *Stinging, stinging, stinging—*

Finally, when Anthony was completely beaten and about to drop, J.C. and all the others drew pistols and fired at him at once.

Bullets entered his white body from every direction and he fell dead.

When Anthony awoke the next morning, he knew instinctively that the two nightmares were not merely isolated bad dreams. He felt deep in his guts that they were the beginning of something terrible.

Each night they came. Each night a different one. Sometimes they were about Jesse Lee or J.C., sometimes about Larry or Manuel, sometimes even about the others at Black Self Help whom he knew only casually. Sometimes he himself was in them, sometimes not. But always the nightmares had one thing in common: they were invariably laced with blood. It flowed from deep hacks cut by a machete, or from ugly holes made by bullets, or from broken noses, eardrums, larynxes slashed by karate chops, or sliced throats opened by a garrote. They were horrible in scope and scene, sickening to his senses; at times Anthony was certain when he woke up that he could actually *smell* the blood from his dream.

As usual, he told Debbie nothing—and not telling her tormented him even more. He cared so deeply for her and she was so good to him, so trusting and loving, that it filled him with shame to deceive her so. But he did not know what else to do. There was so much he had kept from her, so much he was afraid of telling her, so much he had blocked out of his own mind and refused to admit anymore even to himself. He felt like a man torn apart inside, like two devils—no, not *that* word—two *spirits* were struggling to take him over. He had run away from San Francisco because he was afraid of the things that were happening there, he was afraid of the men he had fallen in with at Black Self Help, afraid of the stringent Muslim doctrines and restrictions, afraid of violating parole and being sent back to prison, afraid of losing Debbie, afraid of not ever being anything in life but a poor, pitiful nigger, afraid of—

Afraid of everything.

Admit it, Anthony, he thought, as he lay with his face pressed to the back of Debbie's head. Admit it, man. You are afraid of every fucking thing. You are the world's weakest man and biggest coward. If you weren't, you would have done something about the insomnia, and you'd do something now about the nightmares. You'd

321

stop running and stand and face things. You'd try once and for all to square yourself with the world. You would for once in your life face the truth.

The truth, he thought.

It had been so long since he had associated himself with the truth, that he was not sure he even knew how anymore. Maybe he could do it, and maybe he could not.

One thing he knew for certain. He had to do something.

Skullcap was ready to move again.

It was the second day following the Anderson-White shootings. Skullcap was *up*, way up. He felt good. Everything was falling into place his way—the way it should be.

It was Tuesday. The previous evening, at the regular loft meeting, there had been considerable discussion about the two shootings on Sunday night. Rims had come under fire from several Death Angels who already had their wings. Their criticism had been two-pronged: first, the representative from New Mecca had suggested in the strongest terms possible that the killing of the white devils cease for the time being—a suggestion that Rims had seen fit to disregard; and second, if he *had* to make a sting, he should have done it right and not let the devils live.

Rims, already emotionally upset over his failure, tried to defend himself to his peers, but as usual he became severely agitated and ended up babbling like an idiot. It had been left to Skullcap to come to his rescue.

"This brother say Allah moved him to sting the two white devils," Skullcap advocated. "What would you have him do? Is he be supposed to say, 'No, Allah, I can't do it right now because the man from New Mecca say no?' I mean, who he supposed to listen to—some mortal man or the spirit of almighty Allah?"

"If Allah had really moved him," said the Death Angel with the droopy eyes, "then the devils would have died."

"Not so," Skullcap argued. "Not so at all. I myself have had three misses, and I'll call any brother a liar who say *I* was not moved by Allah to make the stings. And as I look around this room, I see several others who also have had misses. You, brother," he pointed to Yellow, "had a miss just two weeks ago when that bitch devil from the heathen Salvation Army failed to die—and I *know* you were moved by Allah that night because I saw you and you told me so when you came to borrow my gun.'' He swept the room with his arm. "No one in here who has had a miss will get up and say that he was not moved by Allah to try the sting. I challenge anyone to do it!''

No one in the loft moved. Skullcap held their attention as rigidly as he had the night he debated with Vandyke. It seemed at last he was taking on the attitude and demeanor of a leader, and the other men apparently recognized it. When he spoke now, he was listened to with attention and respect. A few men in the group still shrugged derisively or otherwise showed disrespect, but they would come around in time, Skullcap was sure of it. His day as a leader of men was coming: he could feel it.

The loft meeting had concluded without Rims being reprimanded for what most of the men considered a sloppy, impulsive sting; and he had been let off only because of Skullcap's determined defense of him. After the meeting, several Death Angels had spoken to Skullcap to congratulate him on the spirit he had shown in helping a brother. And still later, Rims himself had thanked him profusely and pledged perpetual friendship and support. All in all, it had been a good night for Skullcap.

Now it was one night later, the Tuesday after Easter, and Skullcap was all dressed up in sport jeans, a waist-length blue jacket, shined shoes, and a supercool knit cap. He was on his way to see a new sister he had met at temple. They were going to spend a pleasant—although chaperoned—evening in her apartment. Afterward, because the night would still be young when he left his hostess at the respectable 9:00 P.M. time set down by Muslim dictates, he would go out alone and begin a series of stings that would put Death Angel wings on his photo the very next day.

He was *right*, he was *ready*, he was going to *move*. Without Rims, without Yellow, without even a car, he was going to make the night of the five shootings look like just a rehearsal.

Standing in front of the mirror, Skullcap adjusted the knit cap just so on his head, pulling it down on one side so that it covered his unusual hairline entirely. He looked good without fancy sideburns, he thought; he would never wear them again.

323

The last thing before leaving, Skullcap put the .32 automatic in his belt under his jacket, and slipped an extra magazine of bullets into his inside coat pocket.

Coreris had made up his mind to take an outside chance. A *far* outside chance. One that not even the chief, not even the mayor, would know about.

After leaving the hospital, he returned to the Hall of Justice and went directly to the office of Hobart Nelson, a police artist. "Hobie," he said, "I need a couple of sketches."

Nelson's eyebrows raised. Like everyone else at the Hall, he knew what Coreris's assignment was. "On Zebra?" he asked eagerly.

"On Zebra," Coreris confirmed.

Nelson picked up a pencil. "Who's the witness?"

"I am," Coreris said flatly.

"You?"

"Me."

Now Nelson looked at him with a frown. "You could be asking for a lot of trouble, Gus."

"Yeah, and I could be catching a gang of mad dogs too. I want the sketches, Hobie."

Nelson pulled a large drawing pad in front of him. "Okay, witness. Shoot."

Coreris sat down and leaned forward on his knees. "Start with the hair. Black, kinky, but very neatly trimmed. Medium hairline, with just a hint of a widow's peak."

Nelson's talented hand began to work. He concentrated intently, listening to Coreris but never looking up at him.

"A smooth, clean forehead, maybe just a couple of slight wrinkles. Ears close to the head, not protruding—"

Nelson shaded in the black hair and quickly drew the ears.

"Medium eyebrows. Medium eyes—make them just a shade close together. Nose narrow at the top, wide at the tip. I don't want a flat nose with big nostrils; I want *less* of a Negroid nose, but still more than a white man's nose. Does that make sense?"

"Sure," said Nelson. "Something like this—" Quickly he lined in a nose, shadowed the nostrils, and showed it to Coreris. "How's that?"

"Good," said Coreris. "Very good. You're a genius, Hobie. Now let's make the jawline slope in a little so the face won't be square. I want the chin flat on the bottom, but I don't want the face square. Know what I mean?"

"I think so." Nelson kept sketching, his hand moving with uncanny speed and skill. Literally in seconds he had made a nearly whole face appear on the page. "What kind of lips?" he asked. "Full Negroid?"

Coreris thought for a moment, then shook his head. "No. Thinner than most black lips. A well-defined upper lip, slightly thicker lower lip. And nice-looking, almost handsome."

"You got it." Nelson rapidly worked in a pair of lips that fit perfectly the rest of the face's features. Then he began to shade: a bit of shadow under the bottom lip, a little more to accentuate the cheekbones slightly, a touch at the inner corner of each eye. Nelson's hand moved here, there, everywhere—shading, erasing, wiping, intentionally smudging, adding a line, thickening a line, connecting a line—until the sketch was complete. He turned it around for Coreris to see. The detective stared at it for a long moment, then nodded.

"Perfect, Hobie. Excellent. Looks just like the son of a bitch. Now let's do suspect number two—"

Judo telephoned Yellow the night after the Anderson-White shootings, before Yellow left for the loft meeting. Yellow sounded unusually calm and collected, so Judo assumed at once that it had not been his sting. When Yellow made a sting, he stayed high on the experience for a week.

"What's shaking there, little brother?" Judo asked, trying to sound as casual as if he talked to Yellow every day.

"Where you at?" Yellow asked at once.

"What you want to know for? I ain't there, that's for sure."

"You hear the latest?" Yellow asked. "On the news? A friend of ours made another sting."

"I heard."

"You know, you not too popular with people around here right now."

"I don't think I ever was," said Judo. "Not really."

"You was with me, man," Yellow told him. "You and me, we

325

was *close* for a while. Then, I don't know, you changed, man.''

"I got tired of a lot of the shit that was going on," Judo said candidly.

"How come you run off like you did?" Yellow asked in a piqued voice. "Without telling nobody?"

"I just wanted to get out of it, man." Judo said. "It look to me like you and the others was going crazy. All you ever say was kill this, kill that, kill, kill, kill. That ain't no way to live, little brother. Can't no good come from shit like that."

"It is Allah's wish," Yellow said devoutly. "We not be supposed to question Allah's wish."

"Yeah, but *is* it Allah's wish, or is it the wish of that crazy sucker that always be visiting our meetings?"

"You speak like a nonbeliever," Yellow accused. "Like a heathen, an infidel."

"No, I just speak like I got a little sense of my own, is all. I ain't no robot and I ain't no zombie. I won't become like you and the others. I won't be no crazy man."

"If you not with us, man, then you *against* us," Yellow said coldly.

"Shit, man, I'm not *against* nobody. That's what I'm trying to tell you."

"You know we can find you if we want to. You don't be found yet 'cause we ain't looked. But alls we gots to do is put out the word. We can have every brother we know looking for you." Yellow paused a beat. "And not just you, either."

In the phone booth from which he was calling, Judo tensed. "What you mean, 'not just' me?"

Yellow did not answer.

"Hey, man, I say what you mean by that?"

"You figure it out," Yellow said. "It be your problem."

Judo heard Yellow hang up. He took the receiver from his ear and stared at it. His expression hardened, eyes narrowed to slits. Yellow's words reverberated in his head.

And not just you, either.

The two young white men in the Vega station wagon were tired and exhilarated at the same time. Dressed in shorts, sweat shirts, and tennis shoes, their hair matted with dried perspiration, they had just finished participating in a grueling game of lacrosse with the Golden Gate Lacrosse Club at Funston Park. In the back of the station wagon were their netted crosse sticks, the sponge rubber ball, their pads and helmets, and the thick Rosin gloves which were manufactured in Canada primarily for hockey players, but which so many lacrosse players had adopted.

"That was some rough game," said Jonathan May. He was a twenty-three-year-old cancer researcher at the University of California Medical Center.

"I like them that way," replied Nelson Shields IV. Also twenty-three, usually called "Nick," he was a handsome young man with delicate features and a quick, happy smile. "The rougher the game, the better the workout," he added.

May glanced at him with a grin. To look at Nick Shields, one would not have imagined him to be as tough as he was. But beneath the delicate features and slim, unmuscled body was a sinewy, wiry, hard-as-nails competitor, an avid outdoor sportsman who would—and could—play any game.

"You sure you don't mind taking the time to make this stop?" May asked.

"Not a bit," Nick replied. They were on their way to the home of Carl Connors, May's onetime employer, who owned the Pacific Rug Company. May was buying a small roll of carpet from Connors and had agreed to pick it up at the latter's home that evening.

"As long as we've got the station wagon," May said. "It'll save me a trip later."

"No sweat," said Shields.

Nick Shields was, if anything, a very agreeable young man. The son of a Du Pont executive, he was a native of Greenville, Delaware, and a former student at Hobart College in New York. He had spent the previous winter working as a fry cook in Aspen, Colorado, so that he could ski every day. Two weeks earlier, he had arrived in the Bay Area and temporarily moved in with friends, Virginia and Sheldon Crosby, who lived on a houseboat docked at Sausalito. With him from Aspen he had brought a black, mixed-breed little dog named Lady. While in a coffee shop there, he had seen the homeless dog picked up on the street by an animal control

327

truck. He had asked the waitress what would happen to the dog, and she had said, "I guess after a couple of days they'll put it to sleep." An hour later, Nick was at the pound, claiming the dog, paying a fine, buying a license. He had named her "Lady" and she had been with him ever since. The mutt literally worshiped Shields, almost as if she knew he had saved her life.

When May and Shields neared the Connors residence, at 231 Vernon Street, they passed the cross street of Shields, half a block away.

"Nice of them to name a street after me," Nick Shields said.

"You deserved it," May replied.

They parked in front of the Connors home and got out. "Why don't you go in for your carpet while I straighten out the back of the wagon so there'll be room for it?"

"Good deal," said May. He headed for the Connors front door.

Shields opened the hatchback of the Vega and began shifting their equipment around. Some of it was in a large canvas mailbag faintly stenciled Domestic on one side and U.S. Mail on the other. Shields had to remove the bag, along with one of the crosse sticks and several folded pads, in order even to begin his straightening job.

"This station wagon should be condemned by the board of health," Nick said to himself. He smiled briefly at his own joke and began whistling softly as he worked.

As Nick Shields was leaning into the cargo deck of the Vega, Skullcap came strutting around the corner half a block away. He felt good. His visit with the new sister had gone very well. She was tall and slim and very foxy-looking in her Muslim robes. She seemed to like him too—and that was important. If he was to become a respected leader in the mosque, he had to cultivate not only the men but the women as well. In theory, Muslim women had no status; their purpose in life was to give comfort and support to their men, and to bear children. That was in theory. In fact, there were some very influential women in the mosque, women whose opinions—when translated through their men—often had a direct bearing on mosque policy. So it was important to get to know, and be known *by*, some of the sisters. Skullcap, after an evening at his charming best, making good impressions on the sister *and* her chaperone, felt he had taken the first important step in that direction.

As he moved down the street, his lean, trim body picking up its natural swagger, he noticed a white man up ahead doing something at the back of an open station wagon. As he got closer, his eyes narrowed and flicked up and down the young man's body. Big jock, he thought derisively. Shorts, sweat shirt, tennis shoes, and what looked like a cargo deck full of athletic equipment. Skullcap grunted scornfully. A *white* jock—that was just plain pitiful. As far as sports were concerned, it was strictly a black man's world; whites just could not compete. They were too puny. This one that he was approaching, for instance: too skinny, obviously weak, pale—shit. Nothing. Probably dressed like that to try to impress someone. Stupid white asshole.

Skullcap glanced up and down the street; it looked deserted. Might as well get started, he thought. Got a long night ahead of me—

Skullcap drew the pistol from his belt. He walked to within four feet of Nick Shields and shot him three times.

The three bullets went all the way through Nick and exited the front of his body. The impact threw him forward; he hit the side of the hatchback opening and rebounded. In a split instant, he was sprawled on the pavement behind the car, arms and legs flung out wide, the mailbag of equipment lying across one knee, his glasses down below his chin. He died instantly.

Jonathan May was in the foyer, talking to his former employer's wife, Betty Connors. When the shots sounded, May pushed Mrs. Connors back into the house. Running to the front door, he looked out and saw Nick lying behind the station wagon. There was no one else to be seen. May hurried back inside and telephoned the police. Several minutes later, he and Mrs. Connors cautiously went outside where Nick lay. They were reasonably certain that he was dead, but they decided to stay with him until help came anyway.

May's call had been received at SFPD Communications at 9:27 P.M. The radio dispatch went out seconds later. It was picked up by Unit 3H-2, which was half a mile away at Orizaba Avenue and Lo-

bos Street. Unit 3H-2, was being manned by Officers Joseph De-
Renzi and Manuel "Mike" Coreris. The latter was the nephew of
Gus Coreris, who like Gus's son was also a San Francisco policeman. The unit rolled on the call and arrived at the shooting scene at
9:30. As soon as the patrolmen had determined that it was a homicide and a probable Zebra killing, they secured the area and began
the lengthy process of notifying the appropriate officers and
squads.

Skullcap had begun running the instant he fired the third shot.
But instead of running south on Vernon, which was the direction
he had been walking, he unaccountably turned around and ran
back in the direction from which he had just come. There was no
good reason for him to have done so; it was an instantaneous decision, made almost without thinking. Perhaps he did not want to run
past the man he had just shot down; perhaps he was subconsciously drawn back toward the only place in the neighborhood with
which he was familiar—the apartment he had just left; or perhaps
there was no reason at all: it might simply have been blind action.
But for whatever reason, he did run back the way he had just
come.

And almost got caught.

As he neared the corner that he had walked around several minutes earlier, he heard a door slam across the street. Stopping, he
froze in the shadows up close to a wooden fence. He saw a man
come out of a house across the street and look off in the direction
from which the sound of shots had come. He was in his undershirt,
smoking a cigar, and he had a pistol in his hand. He walked out and
stood next to the curb, staring. As he was standing there, the sound
of a faraway siren began.

Skullcap knew he had to move, had to get out of there. But he
did not dare step away from the shadowy cover of the fence: the
man in the undershirt with the pistol would see him for certain. As
an alternative, he quietly and slowly pulled himself over the top of
the fence and slipped down into the backyard of a house that faced
on the nearby cross street. He made his way across the dark, still
yard until he came to the next fence, bordering the adjacent yard.
Climbing it, he came down in a yard that was cemented. Walking
softly, he crossed it to another fence and a third yard.

The siren was getting louder now and Skullcap knew the police car would soon be there. And it would be only the first one; in mere minutes the entire neighborhood would be crawling with police.

He climbed another fence into a fourth yard. His face and body were beginning to sweat. How many yards were there to the next street? he wondered. And how long could he keep going before he encountered someone *in* one of those yards. He was a stranger in a strange neighborhood; anyone who caught sight of him was going to be curious about him, perhaps even point him out—

I've got to do something with this gun, he told himself. Got to get rid of it, hide it somewhere. Unless they catch me with the gun, can't nobody prove nothing.

He crept along one of the side fences to the back fence. The yards from the side-street houses backed up to the yards from the street he had run down. Peering into the one immediately behind the fence, he saw in the moonlight that it was a small, neat yard with a single palm tree growing in it. Directly next to it was a slightly larger yard with two tall elm and two tall pine trees. Thick, uncultivated grass and fallen pine needles covered the ground at the trunks of the trees; it looked like a part of the yard that was rarely used.

Skullcap hopped the fence, which was only chest-high, crossed the yard with the single palm, and peered into the overgrown area around the four trees. He was sweating heavily now and his eyes darted from place to place almost frantically. The siren had become very loud, screechingly loud; then suddenly it stopped. It had arrived at the scene, less than a block away. In the distance could be heard another, fainter siren. And another.

Got to *do* something! Skullcap thought. His teeth began to chatter, both from the fear inside him and the cool night air on his perspiring body. Come on, man! his mind screamed at him. Come *on!*

He snatched the gun from his waistband and held it next to his chest as he cringed up against the fence. His eyes were wide and unblinking, his whole body shivering, and from inside him came an occasional low, desperate whimper. He was like a ferret caught in a trap.

He knew he had to move. Forcing himself to act, he leaned over the low fence and tossed the gun into the wild grass and pine needles. Then he started hopping fences again, in a direction away from where he had heard the siren stop.

The second siren was the Code Three ambulance Patrolman Coreris had requested. It arrived nine minutes after Nick Shields had been shot. Steward Butler, after two minutes at the scene, pronounced the victim dead.

Patrolman DeRenzi had notified their company officers, Sergeant Cuneo and Lieutenant Abata, who rushed to the scene. Homicide, Crime Lab, Photo Lab, and the coroner were on their way. DeRenzi and Coreris began to search the immediate area for spent shell casings. They were still looking, unsuccessfully, when the elder Coreris, along with John Fotinos, reached the scene. Within minutes, Chief of Inspectors Barca was also there, along with Captain Taylor, Captain Schules, Lieutenant Ellis, and a dozen policemen from the surrounding area. Moses and Ihle of the Crime Lab arrived and joined the search for the shell casings.

Gus Coreris pulled his nephew Mike away from the area of the station wagon and directed him toward the opposite side of the street. "Those casings could have hit the vehicle and ricocheted," he said. "Check over in that area."

"Right, Unk. I mean, Inspector."

The elder Coreris's theory had been right: Mike found a casing twenty-five feet away. The Crime Lab men found the other two: Ihle located one inside the station wagon, buried in the athletic equipment; Moses found the third near a garage door where he had also located one of the slugs. The other two slugs that had passed through Shields's body were located under the Vega wagon.

"Did we get the surrounding area blocked off?" Coreris asked Fotinos after they had been there several minutes.

"Yeah, but not too quick," Fotinos said. "There weren't any units nearby. It took a few minutes to get them pulled out of the main area."

Coreris had been afraid of that. The main Zebra patrol zone was a six-square-mile area which included downtown, Alamo Square, South of Market, Japan Center, Jefferson Square, and the Panhandle. Thirteen of the nineteen incidents had taken place in that area. The secondary zone of patrol was a three-square-mile section from

Balboa Park to the South Basin, and Sutter Playground to Tompkins Street. Four other incidents had occurred within those boundaries. The two remaining incidents had been isolated. As was this new one, Coreris thought. He estimated that the Shields shooting was five miles outside the primary patrol zone, and three miles outside the secondary patrol zone. It would have taken the dragnet units several minutes to seal off the area. They might snag somebody in the net—but it was doubtful.

"Well," Coreris sighed, "we can't cover every block in the whole goddamned city. I wish we could."

"I'll check with patrol," Fotinos said. "Maybe we got lucky."

They did not get lucky. Skullcap did.

He finally came out of the maze of backyards onto Ralston Street, one street over and one street down from the scene of the shooting. From there he walked two blocks to Beverly and one block up to Garfield. Then he cut over one block to Junipero Serra Boulevard. There he composed himself as best he could and calmly—at least outwardly calmly—boarded a city bus. He had no idea that in making his escape from the scene of this, his last shooting, he had walked past the home of the survivors of his first victim. For at 230 Beverly was the family home of Saleem Erakat.

Skullcap's spectacular night of death had proved to be short-lived, but at the moment he did not care. He had acted like a fool by trying to start the evening with such an impulsive sting, but he was not chastising himself for it. He had almost been trapped at the scene, but he was not mentally berating himself. He had been forced—at least temporarily—to dispose of his gun, but that was all right too. *Everything* was all right—so long as he got away. He was almost physically ill with fear, but he still had enough composure to realize that the only thing that mattered was that he had *escaped*.

Allah is with me, he thought.

It was the first completely sincere Muslim thought he had ever had.

At the end of Day One Hundred Seventy-nine, there were twenty-three victims.

Quita Hague, hacked to death.

Richard Hague, his face butchered.

Ellen Linder, raped, ravaged, threatened with death.

Frances Rose, her face blown apart by close-range gunshots.

Saleem Erakat, tied up and executed.

Paul Dancik, shot down at a public telephone.

Arthur Agnos, surviving after his insides were ripped up by bullets.

Marietta DiGirolamo, thrown into a doorway and shot to death.

Ilario Bertuccio, killed while walking home from work.

Angela Roselli, surviving with nerve damage in her back.

Neal Moynihan, shot down while taking a Teddy bear to his little sister.

Mildred Hosler, shot down while walking toward her bus stop.

John Doe No. 169, kidnapped, tortured, butchered, decapitated.

Tana Smith, murdered on her way to buy blouse material.

Vincent Wollin, murdered on his sixty-ninth birthday.

John Bambic, murdered while rummaging in a trash bin.

Jane Holly, murdered in a public Laundromat.

Roxanne McMillian, surviving but paralyzed from the waist down.

Thomas Rainwater, shot down on the street as he walked to a market.

Linda Story, surviving with nerve damage in her back.

Ward Anderson, surviving but in serious condition after being shot down at a city bus stop.

Terry White, also surviving, also in serious condition, after being shot down at the same city bus stop.

And Nelson Shields IV, shot three times in the back as he was straightening out the cargo deck of his station wagon.

The one hundred seventy-nine days of terror had ended. The Zebra killers had assaulted twenty-three persons on the streets of San Francisco.

Only eight had survived.

Fifteen had been killed.

PART TWO
Aftermath to Terror

The Confession

When Anthony Harris picked up the newspaper and saw the two sketches Hobart Nelson had drawn for Gus Coreris, his entire body turned ice-cold.

Jesus Christ, he thought, *that's me!*

Not: Great Allah, that's me. *Jesus Christ,* that's me.

He stared at the reward poster reproduced on the front page. In letters two inches high across the top of the poster, it said:

REWARD
$30,000

Immediately beneath that, side by side, were two lifelike sketches of black faces: the original one that Coreris had described for Hobart Nelson, and a second one, very similar except that the face was slimmer, had a narrower, rounder chin, higher cheekbones, a little more hair, and was wearing a knit cap.

Below the pictures was printed:

THIS DEPARTMENT HAS BEEN AUTHORIZED TO STATE THAT THERE IS A REWARD POSTED IN THE AMOUNT OF 30,000 DOLLARS FOR INFOR-

MATION LEADING TO THE ARREST AND CONVICTION OF THE SUSPECT
OR SUSPECTS RESPONSIBLE FOR A SERIES OF MURDERS AND ATTEMPT-
ED MURDERS SINCE NOVEMBER 25, 1973, WHEREIN A .32-CALIBER
AUTOMATIC HAS BEEN USED TO DATE THERE HAVE BEEN 18 VICTIMS,
12 DECEASED AND 6 WOUNDED.

ANY INFORMATION
SAN FRANCISCO POLICE DEPARTMENT
HOMICIDE DETAIL—553-1145   DONALD M. SCOTT
INSPECTORS CORERIS/FOTINOS   CHIEF OF POLICE

The same edition of the paper ran a small item explaining the increase in the amount of the reward. The Arab community had posted the original reward of ten thousand dollars following the death
of Saleem Erakat. Later, the *Examiner* added five thousand, and
an anonymous San Francisco corporation put up an additional five
thousand. Now an anonymous "civic-minded citizen" contributed
five thousand more, and Mayor Alioto released the news that still
another five thousand had been authorized from city funds. The total came to thirty thousand dollars.

As he stared at the two sketches, Anthony was convinced that
the one without the cap was himself. And the one with the cap was
Larry Green.

Standing at the newspaper vending rack, he suddenly had the
strange feeling that he was being watched. Quickly folding the paper to conceal the sketches, he glanced around to see who might be
looking at him. There were several people nearby, some of them
looking at papers of their own as they waited at a bus stop. None of
them seemed to be paying any attention to him, Anthony thought.

Then he saw the little black kid.

The boy was nine or ten. He had wandered away from the bus
stop where his mother stood, and was looking at the next paper in
the vending rack. He stared at the sketches, then looked up at Anthony, seeming to study him. Anthony watched him for a moment,
watched the way his eyes went from the paper up to Anthony's
face and back again. Sweat popped out on Anthony's brow and upper lip.

That little kid knows, he thought frantically. His mixed-up mind
did not define for him exactly what it was that he thought the boy

knew; he simply panicked at the thought that someone might be thinking the same thing that he was thinking: that the face in the sketch was him.

Lowering his head, Anthony walked quickly away from the newspaper rack and the little boy. He hurried down the block and around the corner. Almost without thinking about it, he returned to the apartment. Debbie looked up in surprise when he let himself in.

"Anthony, what's the matter?" she asked in concern. "I thought you'd be to work by now."

"I ain't going to work today," he said despondently. "I'm sick."

He laid the newspaper on the arm of the couch and went into the bedroom. Debbie stared after him curiously. Then she looked down at the paper and saw the sketches. The breath caught in her chest.

"Oh, my God—"

The *San Francisco Chronicle*'s headline the day after the Nelson Shields killing aptly described what the authorities had decided to do. It read:

EXTREME MEASURE IN ZEBRA HUNT—
POLICE TO STOP 'A LOT OF PEOPLE'

The *Examiner* echoed the determination:

ALL-OUT HUNT FOR
RANDOM SLAYERS

Mayor Joseph Alioto, along with Police Chief Donald Scott, had already announced to the city what was going to happen. Said Alioto: "Police will begin stopping large numbers of black citizens throughout the city for questioning in the search for a suspect in the wave of random street killings. Officers have been supplied with the first complete description and sketches of the killers. We are going to be stopping people who resemble these sketches and descriptions—which means we're going to be stopping a lot of people. This is an extraordinary situation and it calls for extreme measures. We ask the cooperation of citizens and want to assure them that we will be mindful of their constitutional rights."

Chief Scott, participating in the unprecedented announcement, added, "The police department has blanketed the city with both auto and foot patrols in order to carry out this operation. The only persons who will be stopped will be those who match the descriptions of the suspects in the police drawing. We are partitioning the city into a grid of six police patrol zones and sending in an additional one hundred fifty specially picked officers—most of them detectives from elite bureaus such as Homicide and Crime Prevention, as well as veteran policemen from the district stations. The peak concentration of our surveillance will be between dusk and midnight. These men will carry out street searches of any blacks on the streets who resemble the sketches. This 'stop-and-search' tactic will also apply to motorists. We realize that some people are going to resent this effort. We are sorry for that. But extraordinary measures are called for in this case."

Dr. Washington Garner, black member of the three-man police commission, later added his own comments for the black community: "I know that many of you who are stopped are going to be angered," he said. "Especially those of you whom the police officers decide to search. But I would like to appeal to all of you not to resent it. I ask you all to remember that when the Nob Hill Rapist was at large, literally hundreds of white citizens were subjected to exactly the same tactic. Try to understand that this is not a racial issue."

There were some, however, who could not—or would not—understand.

Congressman Jerome R. Waldie, a Democrat from Antioch, California, immediately criticized Mayor Alioto. "Though I fully share the concern of the mayor and all people that the Zebra killers be quickly apprehended," he said, "we cannot justify the suspension of the civil liberties and constitutional guarantees of any class of Americans. Even in this worthwhile effort, the suspension of constitutional protection for young black males as a group is unwarranted and must be resisted. A philosophy such as the mayor and Chief Scott are following is exactly what led the Nixon Administration to condone wiretapping, burglary, and enemies lists. The police should be given every legitimate resource and cooperation they need to apprehend these vicious and insane killers, but they do not require and should not be given the right to suspend the Constitution as it applies to young black males.''

Paul Halvonic, general counsel for the American Civil Liberties Union, was more specific. "This is a racist outrage and a violation of the rights of every black man in the city. Our organization intends to pursue all appropriate legal action to halt these stop-and-search tactics as soon as possible.''

Benjamin James, an attorney for the National Association for the Advancement of Colored People, said his group was also looking into the possibility of some kind of injunctive relief. "The police are going a bit far,'' he said. "The descriptions they're talking about fit sixty percent of the young blacks on the streets.''

Black Panther leader Bobby Seale said the mass questionings placed "every black man in the Bay Area in jeopardy of losing his life. It is a vicious and racist action.''

While the political battle raged, Chief Scott's men quietly went into the streets and began the stop-and-search routine. They stopped more than a hundred black men the first night. The following day, there were more outraged protests.

The Reverend Cecil Williams, of a local black church, declared that the entire black community was under "a police state that could erupt into a racial war.''

Bobby Seale spoke out again. "If they are going to try to arrest every black man who may resemble the so-called Zebra killer, then why not arrest every white girl who may resemble Patricia Hearst?''

A group from the Progressive Labor party, about seventy-five strong, conducted a demonstration outside Mayor Alioto's home, chanting, "Alioto is a Nazi! Alioto is a Nazi!''

Stop-and-search continued. By the end of the second night, more than two hundred young blacks had been stopped. By the end of the third, three hundred. The police began issuing specially printed "Zebra Check" cards: identification cards about the size of a driver's license, containing space for an individual's name, address, driver's license number, Social Security number, and the date, time, and location where he was stopped. The officer making the stop had to sign the card and note his badge number. If the person was then stopped again, all he had to do was show the card along with his identification, and he was allowed to proceed without further delay.

The black organizations were not satisfied. They were determined to interfere with the police effort in any way they could. The threatened legal action began. A group of black residents, sponsored by the NAACP, filed suit in U.S. District Court to stop the police tactic, claiming it exceeded constitutional guarantees of personal freedom. The ACLU began preparing a similar case for filing.

Finally the two newspapers took editorial stands. The *Examiner* trod softly. "The only lead police possess is a composite sketch based on descriptions supplied by surviving victims. This description provides the basis upon which police are stopping all young black men who fit the general description. The process may prove ineffective. But it, plus saturation patrolling, is the only course open to the police."

The *Chronicle* was more precise. "The Zebra murders have brought out the police on highly visible, and reassuring, patrols of the streets. The patrols are called 'extreme measures' by Mayor Alioto, who invoked them, and since their purpose is to involve police in stopping and questioning black men who may resemble a Zebra suspect, the procedure has created a certain amount of restiveness and complaint from black citizens and organizations. It is, however, hard to accept such complaints as justifiable. If the killers are black, there would be no point in stopping white men for questioning. The discovery and taking into custody of the madmen is necessary for the peace of mind and the banishment of fear in the whole community. The police deserve every citizen's cooperation."

The city was paralyzed with fear, bewilderment, confusion. And again, the city's headlines were less than reassuring:

SHAKEDOWN SHAKES THE CITY

MOVE TO EXPAND KILLER HUNT

NET COMES DOWN BUT THERE'S
STILL A KILLER LOOSE

Anthony did not talk to Debbie for two days and two nights. He did not speak a word about anything, did not even talk to the baby as he usually did. For the most part he spent his time lying on the bed, staring up at the ceiling. When a meal was ready, Debbie would tell him so and he would get up and eat. But even at the table, he did not speak; he merely stared down at his food as if in a trance.

Debbie tried a dozen times to talk to him, to get him to respond to something she would say. She tried talking to him at the table, lying next to him on the bed, calling to him from the next room, even tried talking to him through Anthony, Jr., by holding the baby next to him and pretending it was the baby who was talking. But nothing worked. Anthony did not even look at her. He continued to stare at nothing, his mouth hanging open an inch, jaw slack, shoulders slumped. He was so peculiar-looking that Debbie had a brief, awful thought that maybe his mind had snapped. But she refused to let herself believe it.

In the evening, Debbie would bring the television into the bedroom and turn it on so that Anthony could see it. She lay beside him and watched it with him, making whatever comments she wanted to, whether he responded or not. He stared at the TV the same way he stared at her and the baby: with no recognition, no emotion, as if looking *through* it instead of at it.

When the news came on, invariably with an update on the massive Zebra manhunt being conducted across the bay, Debbie half expected to see some response from Anthony, a reaction of some kind. She knew that it had been the sketches in the newspapers that had plunged him into the morose condition he was in: that had been very obvious to her when he came back home without going to work, and dropped the paper on the couch. There was no question about the one sketch: it was Anthony. Not a perfect Anthony, by any means; but a *close* Anthony—enough to make it recognizable at least to himself and to her.

Of course, it was some kind of mistake; it had to be. Anthony had been there in Oakland with her on the nights when those people were shot in San Francisco. So he could not have had anything to do with it. Not the ones that happened recently anyway. The ones that happened earlier, back before they left, well—

Debbie *had* heard rumors now and again at the mosque: rumors about J. C. Simon and Larry Green and Manuel Moore and—yes, she had to admit it—even about Anthony. But they were not *specific* rumors; they were not rumors that actually said that someone did this or someone did that; they were vague rumors of who *might* have done something, who was *capable* of doing something, who somebody wouldn't *doubt* was involved in something. Nothing definite, nothing certain, just speculation. Of course, Debbie halfway believed the rumors insofar as they involved J.C. and the others, because she did not like them. She had started out liking them, especially Manuel, but eventually she came to dislike all of them, every man who worked for Black Self Help. They were, to her straight mind, troublemakers, every one of them. She called the place where they worked Black Self *Hurt,* and she disliked Anthony being associated with it or them. That was why she had not hesitated to give up her job at the bank and make the unannounced move to Oakland as soon as Anthony suggested it. To get him away from what she considered a bad influence. And because she was pregnant too, of course, and did not particularly like remaining in the same area with the baby's real father.

Secretly she had always dreaded the possibility that Anthony might have been in some trouble with J.C. and the others, and that he had been in such a hurry to leave San Francisco for that reason. She had never given much thought to what *kind* of trouble it was, and had never allowed herself to consider that it might be very *bad* trouble. But now, with Anthony acting the way he was, with the sketches in the paper that, to her, resembled both Anthony and Larry Green—again, not perfectly, but certainly closely enough—she was forced to consider the possibility that whatever it was that she did not know, it was worse—perhaps far worse—than she had imagined.

On the morning of the third day that Anthony had not gone to work, Debbie was sitting alone on the couch, again looking at the reproduced sketches and the reward notice in the three-day-old paper. As she was sitting there, Anthony came out of the bedroom and sat beside her. She noticed at once that his expression was different; he did not have the stupor look that had been on his face, in his eyes, for the past two days. He looked like the old Anthony now, *her* Anthony. She smiled her pleasure at seeing him, and he reached out and patted her hand. Then he bobbed his chin at the paper she held.

"Thirty thousand dollars a lot of money," he said.

Debbie nodded but did not trust herself to speak.

"How long you figure you and Anthony, Jr., could live on thirty thousand dollars?" he asked.

And with those words, she knew.

By the weekend, more than five hundred young black men had been stopped and searched by the Zebra units partolling the streets of San Francisco at night. The operation had turned up no leads to the Zebra killers—but it had reduced major crimes in the city by nearly a third. Major crimes—homicide, rape, robbery, aggravated assault, burglary, larceny over fifty dollars, and auto theft—had been cut back 30.7 percent. Because of saturation by police officers in the large areas considered primary Zebra operation sectors, which comprised some five hundred city blocks, many crimes which might have been committed, were not.

Despite the drop in the general crime index, however, the stop-and-search operation was continuing to generate criticism and protests throughout the city. The NAACP suit filed in federal court was calendared to the courtroom of U.S. District Judge Alfonso J. Zirpoli and set for Tuesday following the weekend. In other quarters, Dr. Carlton Goodlett, publisher of the small *Sun Reporter* newspaper, said that Mayor Alioto had begun a "drive against the black people of the community." The San Francisco Young Democrats called the police actions a "deliberate and desperate attempt by Alioto and Chief Scott to toy with public fear." Jesse Byrd, a black police officer who was also president of the predominantly black, eighty-member Officers for Justice organization, said that his group did not "approve of the gestapo-like tactics being used. We can only view this as another type of harassment." And Donald DeFreeze, the escaped convict who called himself Field Marshal Cinque of the underground Symbionese Liberation Army, sent a taped message to the news media in which he said that Operation Zebra was the white man's "means to remove as many black males from the community as possible." He predicted "block by block and house by house searches" that would result in the confiscation of all personal weapons.

Mayor Alioto himself was involved in one protest when a group calling itself the Coalition to Stop Operation Zebra held a demonstration in front of city hall. The group, estimated at one thousand persons, gathered shortly after 5:00 P.M. carrying picket signs which read, "Stop Alioto Storm Troopers" and "Smash Racism— The Rich Man's Tool, To Divide and Rule." As the crowd marched, it chanted, "The people say! This ain't the way!"

About thirty minutes after the demonstration started, Alioto and two of his aides emerged from the building and came down the steps, on their way to the mayor's limousine parked at the curb. The three men began easing their way through the crowd. One picket blocked the mayor's way and thrust a leaflet at him. Alioto accepted it with a smile. Then, as he continued toward his car, other pickets began spitting on him. One began hitting him over the head with a picket sign. His aides pushed the people aside and got Alioto into the car. Before the chauffeur could drive it away, the car was pounded on all sides and rocked back and forth on its shocks.

After Alioto successfully escaped, the demonstrators took over the steps of city hall and for the next hour heard speeches from young black men who told how they had been stopped and searched during Operation Zebra. A black nurse, Monique Von Clutz, then made a speech comparing the Zebra Check Cards being issued by police to similar black identification cards used in what she called "the racist Union of South Africa." Ms. Von Clutz said that she had a brother who was killed in Vietnam and another who was paralyzed. "They fought for this country," she said, "and now the police are going around harassing black men and giving out cards." A spokesman for a group called the Revolutionary Union then exhorted the crowd to help "build a mass movement to give the country back to the working classes."

Elsewhere there was support for Operation Zebra. California attorney general, Evelle J. Younger, said that, in his opinion, San Francisco police had "all the authority they need to stop a suspect who looks like the subject in the sketches." Younger, who was the man for whom Dick Walley of CII worked in Sacramento, was well aware of the statewide wave of black/white killings over the past several years. He agreed with Alioto that extraordinary crime called for extraordinary police action.

Instead of the demonstrations and protests influencing San Francisco officials in any way, they kept their minds directly attuned to their immediate goal: stop the killings. Far from considering any halt to Operation Zebra, they were already in the planning stages of expanding it. Chief of Inspectors Barca had drawn up a proposal to begin using reserve police officers to increase the strength and patrol capability of the regular force. The reserves, comprised of 150 backup officers, were normally used for crowd control at sporting events, parades, political rallies, motorcades, and the like, but Barca saw no reason why they could not also serve as "extra eyes" in Operation Zebra. The plan was sent to Mayor Alioto's office for immediate perusal.

In the meantime, the city had become a cripple. North Beach, the city's traditional nightlife district, was experiencing terrible business. Even though its main thoroughfare, Broadway, was one of the best patrolled areas in the city, "people," to quote one businessman, "were staying away in droves." Had it not been for Japanese tourists, who either did not know about the killings or felt safe anyway because they were Oriental, many North Beach clubs would have closed their doors entirely. The Condor, a club made famous by Carol Doda and her fantastic silicone-injected breasts, had once counted on their eleven o'clock and midnight shows as the heaviest of the evening. Now their early shows were packed, and after nine or ten o'clock the club was all but deserted. One club, trying to hype business, hired an eighteen-piece band and advertised an evening of ballroom dancing. Exactly ten customers showed up. Only a few of the clubs and better restaurants— primarily those with valet parking—did any kind of business at all.

San Francisco theater business was also off, its attendance down drastically. Even New York shows that had received rave reviews were playing to sparse audiences. One theater that frequently did a large business with out-of-town student groups reported that large blocks of such seats were being canceled because parents refused to have their children in San Francisco after dark.

Inexplicably, daytime business had also fallen off. Small neighborhood shopping centers in the middle- and lower-middle-class districts suffered a definite drop in customer flow. Even in the affluent sections of the city—those removed from any Zebra activity— shopping-area parking lots were less than half-filled. Supermarkets even reported a drop in business as customers just shopped quickly for essentials and hurried home. It was as if San Franciscans were so sick of it all that they wanted only to stay indoors in the safety of their homes until the madness ended. They fervently hoped that Operation Zebra would soon put an end to it all.

Then the unexpected happened.

U.S. District Court Judge Alfonso J. Zirpoli, acting on the suit filed by the NAACP-sponsored plaintiffs, ruled that the actions of the San Francisco Police Department in its stop-and-search operation were unconstitutional, and formally ordered a halt to the operation. The order handed down by the court expressly forbade the police from stopping and searching young black males simply because they resembled the sketches purported to be likenesses of the killers. In the future, the court said, officers would have to have independent information creating a reasonable suspicion that whoever they stopped had committed a crime or was in the process of committing one.

Just days after the shooting of Ward Anderson and Terry White, and the murder of Nick Shields, Operation Zebra was suspended.

Coreris sat glumly at his desk in the corner of Homicide and lighted a cigarette. He tossed the match at his ashtray. It missed and hit the desk. Coreris did not even bother to pick it up.

At the desk facing his, Fotinos first glanced around to be sure no one could overhear them, then lowered his voice to a confidential tone. "Cheer up, for Christ's sake, will you? It was a damn good idea, whether it worked or not."

Coreris shook his head. "All it did was make a lot of good cops work their asses off for a week. It got us nothing."

"Bullshit. It got the major crime rate down thirty percent all week. That in itself was worth it. Besides, who knows what might yet come of it?"

"Sure, sure," Coreris said. His expression of disenchantment remained fixed.

At another desk, the phone rang. Jeff Brosch, one of the young Robbery officers that Coreris and Fotinos had picked for the Zebra squad, answered it. He listened and conversed for a minute, then looked around at Coreris. "Hey, Gus, there's a guy on the phone says he's got some information on the Zebra killers. Wants somebody to come over to Oakland to talk to him."

Coreris grunted softly. Give me a quarter for every phony tip we've had on this goddamned case and I could retire early, he thought.

"Let's you and I handle it," Fotinos said. "A drive across the bridge might do you good."

Coreris shook his head. "No, I don't feel like it." He bobbed his chin at Brosch. "You and Carl take it."

Brosch nodded and resumed talking.

At five thirty that afternoon, Brosch and Klotz arrived at a predesignated meeting place to interview the man who had called. The meeting place was at a bank parking lot in Oakland. The man, wearing wraparound sunglasses despite the fact that it was getting dark, was Anthony Harris. He was leaning against the side of the building waiting for them.

Brosch and Klotz were cautious. They did not know who they were dealing with, and both realized that the meeting place was an excellent location for an ambush. Separating, their coats unbuttoned for quick access to their guns, they approached Harris.

"You the gentleman who called?" asked Klotz.

"Yeah, that's me," Anthony said.

The officers looked around apprehensively. "You mind if we pat you down?" Brosch asked. "Just so we know we can trust you."

"Whatever," said Anthony.

Brosch gave him a quick pat search and found no weapon.

"Want to take a ride?" Klotz asked him. "Beats standing out here where everybody can see us."

"Yeah, okay."

They got into the unmarked car and drove to a nearby supermarket parking lot. "Okay, Mr. Harris," Brosch said when they had parked. "What do you want to tell us?"

"First off, I got to be promised that my name won't be give to the papers or nothing like that," Anthony said. "And second, I want the reward for my old lady and kid."

"Sounds reasonable to us, Mr. Harris," said Klotz. "Providing you have good information for us."

"It's good information, all right," said Anthony. "I know all about the killings from the very beginning. In fact, they tried to make me a part of them."

"Who's 'they'?" Brosch asked.

"The Death Angels," said Anthony. "They be the ones who did all the killings. They killed them all, even chopped up that woman by the railroad tracks, everybody. They say all whites is blue-eyed devils. They wanted me to be part of it, but I skipped out on them. I don't go for killing women and kids and stuff like that."

Klotz and Brosch exchanged quick glances. "What kids are you talking about?" Flotz asked as calmly as possible.

"Three kids they tried to grab the night they hacked the woman," Anthony said.

Jackpot! thought Carl Klotz. He looked at Brosch and saw that his partner was thinking the same thing. This was *it*, this was *real*. The instant Anthony mentioned the three kids, they both realized it.

Because only the police knew about those three kids.

Only the police knew about the attempted abduction of Michele Carrasco and Frank and Marie Stewart two hours before Quita Hague was hacked to death. Only the police knew that a connection had already been made between the three men and the van described by the youngsters, and the man and van described by Richard Hague. Only the police.

And someone who had been there.

Anthony Harris agreed to accompany Brosch and Klotz back over to San Francisco. Within the hour Anthony was sitting in an interrogation room, facing Coreris and Fotinos. Klotz and Brosch were standing in the background. Coreris led the questioning, starting off slowly, easily. A tape recorder was turned on.

"Mr. Harris, it is my understanding that you have information relative to the particular crimes that have been occurring in San Francisco and are known as the Zebra slayings. Is that correct?"

"Right," said Anthony.

"And your main interest in giving us that information is the large reward that has been offered. Is that correct?"

"Yes. Exactly. And to stop the killing too."

350

"Yes. And I'm told you want protection for your wife and baby also."

"Right."

"All right, I think I can safely say that if you have information which results in putting a stop to these killings, that the reward will be yours. And I can guarantee the safety of your wife and baby. Now then, do you have information relative to the series of Zebra slayings?"

"Yes, I have."

"This information is based on personal knowledge?"

"Yes."

"All right then, why don't you just relate it to us in your own words?"

"Okay," said Anthony. "But first of all, I don't want my name mentioned at all. To the newspapers or anything."

"At this point, we guarantee you complete anonymity," Coreris said. He would have promised him the chief of police's job in order to start him talking. "Now what basics do you know of the Zebra killings?"

"Well, number one, I know the people who are involved in it. The main one is J.C."

"J.C. who?"

"J. C. Simon. He call hisself J.C.X. Simon."

Coreris glanced over at Fotinos. "Run a check on that name," he said in Greek.

"Right away," Fotinos replied, also in Greek. He rose and left the room.

"What's that you talking?" Anthony asked. "Chinese?"

"Yeah, Chinese," Coreris replied. "When did you first have contact with Mr. J. C. Simon?"

"I'd say about seven or eight months ago."

"How did you meet him?"

"At Black Self Help."

"By Black Self Help, you mean the movers on Market Street?"

"Right."

"Was he employed there?"

"Yes. Assistant manager."

"And he is directly involved in the Zebra killings?"

351

"Right. He be drive around sometimes and make a list of the places he want to do. To sting. To hit, you know. He drove me around one time and pointed out a market downtown. He say it be number one on his list."

Tiny fingers seemed to tickle the back of Coreris's neck. A downtown market, he thought. Saleem Erakat. "Do you remember the name of the premises?"

"No. It was a real small building. I didn't pay too much attention to it. I didn't know what he was talking about. Then he went back another time and he made a sting."

"He made a sting there?"

"Right."

"J. C. Simon?"

"Right."

"What type of vehicle was he driving on that particular day, Anthony?"

"A van."

The tiny fingers worked on Coreris's neck again. A van. The three kids. The Hagues. "Do you know what type of van?"

"It was a light, cream-colored van, more or less."

Fotinos came back in. "No criminal record," he said in Greek. "But I got a photocopy of his driver's license."

Coreris took the photocopy and held it up for Anthony to see. "I show you a California driver's license, number N-for-Nora, 402—464. It's issued to J. C. Simon, date of birth 5-8-46. Is this the J. C. Simon you are talking about?"

"Right," said Anthony, "that's him."

Coreris took back the photocopy. "All right, who else was involved that you personally know of?"

"Larry," said Anthony. "Larry Craig Green."

Without a word, Fotinos again left the room. Coreris asked Anthony a few more questions about the van while he waited for his partner to run the second name through the computer. After several minutes, Fotinos returned with another driver's license photocopy.

"Same deal," Fotinos said, still speaking Greek. "No rap sheet at all."

Coreris showed Anthony the second photocopy. "This is a copy of California driver's license number A-for-Adam, 15037, issued to Larry Craig Green, date of birth 2-12-52. Is this the Larry Green you are talking about?"

"Yes, this is him. That picture is Larry to a T."

"Are Larry Green and J. C. Simon affiliated in any way?"

Anthony was not sure what "affiliated" meant, but he understood the question enough to answer it. "Ah, they both live in the same apartment house and work at the same place."

"What are Mr. Green's duties at Black Self Help?"

"He's a mover."

"Do you know what type of auto he owns?"

"I believe a Dodge Dart, I think it was."

"What color is it?"

"White."

"Okay. Now tell me, what incidents do you personally know of that Larry Green was involved in?"

"Larry, he the one that chopped that woman by the tracks."

"By tracks, you mean railroad tracks?"

"Right."

Coreris turned to Carl Klotz. "Get me the photograph file."

Klotz left the interrogation room and returned a moment later with a large manila file folder. Coreris fingered through a number of glossy photographs while Klotz held the file. Finally he pulled one out. It was an eight-by-ten of Quita Hague as she had been found on the night of her murder. Coreris showed it to Anthony.

Anthony's eyes got very wide. "Oh, my God! This the girl here?"

"That's the girl, that's the woman," said Klotz. His expression was dark. He snatched another photo from the file and held it close to Anthony's face. "Here's when she was cleaned up and she was put in the morgue."

Anthony swallowed dryly. He stared fearfully at Klotz.

"This is what they were gonna do to those kids," Klotz said. "Three helpless little kids, this is what they were gonna do. And when that thing fell apart, an hour later this happened."

Coreris leaned forward on the table and cut back in before Anthony became too frightened. "Anthony, tell us who else you personally know to be involved."

Anthony tore his eyes away from big, angry Klotz. He wet his lips. "Let's see, there's Larry, and J.C., and—what's his name?—oh, yeah, Manuel. Manuel Moore." He pronounced Manuel's last name as "Moe." "He done time with me in San Quentin," he added.

Moore's name was run through the computer. His long and varied criminal record printed out on the Homicide terminal. Coreris showed it to Anthony.

"This is a criminal record of Manuel Leonard Moore," he said for benefit of the tape recorder. "California State Prison number B-for-Boy, 21009, date of birth 9-2-44. Can you identify him as the man you're talking about?"

"Yeah, that's Manuel."

"Based on your own personal knowledge, what Zebra crimes do you know of that Manuel Moore has been involved in?"

"Manuel, he done that woman in the laundry place."

Jane Holly, Coreris thought. In the Laundromat. He sighed quietly. The Hagues, Erakat, Holly. Four down, nineteen to go. He loosened his tie. It was going to be a long night.

For the rest of the night, Anthony Harris named names, made identifications, described killings. In addition to J. C. Simon, Larry Green, and Manuel Moore, he implicated in the Zebra killings and as being members of the Death Angels, Jesse Lee Cooks and four other men with whom he claimed to have attended loft meetings, and who were allegedly present on the night he was required to dispose of John Doe No. 169.

After identifying by name the men whom he knew in the loft that night, Anthony told of taking the body away. Carl Klotz questioned him on that.

"Whereabouts at the beach did you dump it?"

"I don't know," Anthony said. "I don't know much about the beach, you know. I think it was alongside the road there, more or less."

"Is that where you threw it?"

"I pushed it off. Pushed if off there."

"As you were driving, or did you stop and carry it?"

"No, carried it. Carried it, right."

"How far did you carry it from the truck?"

"About thirty or forty feet at the most."

"Can you show us where you dumped it?"

"I guess. It was nighttime. I never been on that beach down there."

"Who did the butchering?"

"I don't know. I don't know if Larry did the butchering or not in there. There was blood dripping out of it, you know?"

"You saw this?" Klotz asked.

"Right. I saw the blood, right. I picked it up and set it up there in the van and it got on my hands."

"When you dumped that package, did it smell bad?"

Anthony nodded. "Bad, ah—bad smell."

For a while the four police officers let Anthony talk extemporaneously about anything he wanted to, while they made mental notes of what he was saying. When he seemed to be winding down, one of them would toss a leading question at him and he would begin talking again. At various times he rambled on about the Muslims in general; the Fruit of Islam "military police"; the teaching of hatred for whites; the way the "officials" who conducted meetings would look for hostility in a person's face after preaching about how the whites cut open black mothers' stomachs; the pictures of men who had earned their Death Angel wings and had them drawn on each side of the neck in their photographs that were kept in the loft—

The loft, Harris said, was upstairs over the main floor of Black Self Help Moving and Storage. It was there—and in the apartment of J. C. Simon—that some of the stings had been planned. Fotinos questioned him about the loft.

"How many people can meet at the Black Self Help loft?"

"Twenty-five or thirty. If it was cleared out, it could hold more—about fifty."

"How often are these meetings held?"

"That's up to—nobody knows. You see, one day somebody will say there's a meeting there tonight at Black Self Help. Be there, you know. And they'll give you a small card—you know, number—to lick and press hard in your hand. Sometimes it stays in your hand for a while, but if you take soap and water, it comes right off."

"And you're admitted with this particular thing?"

"Right. It has to be identified with the number they have."

"When you go in, is everybody searched?"

"No. No one searches no one."

From time to time during the casual conversation part of the interrogation, one of the officers would drop in a quick question of some import, to which they would invariably receive a very valuable answer. Such as:

"Are you familiar with any weapons in the possession of Mr. Simon?"

"I remember seeing a thirty-two automatic."

Or: "To make the grade in the Death Angels, what does that consist of?"

"Well, you have to kill nine people—to take the heads of the enemy—nine heads."

"By taking the heads, does that mean decapitation?"

"Decapitation or just killing."

Or: "Do you know what other kind of transportation these men used, Anthony?"

"A black Cadillac."

"Who owns this black Cadillac?"

"The manager down at Black Self Help."

As the hours passed, Anthony began to get anxious about Debbie and the baby. He expressed his concern to Coreris. The detective nodded his understanding.

"We're concerned about them too, Anthony," he said. "We'd like to bring them over here and keep you all in protective custody for the time being. Is that agreeable with you?"

"Yeah, if that's what's best."

"Good. Now, I'm going to have the same two officers take you back across the bay to pick up Mrs. Harris and your baby, then they'll bring you back here and we'll have a place for you to stay."

"Not jail?"

"No, of course not. You're on our side now, Anthony."

Brosch and Klotz took Anthony and left. When they were gone, Coreris and Fotinos talked about the confession.

"Notice how everyone's a killer except him?" Fotinos said.

"Yeah."

"How much do you think he hasn't told us?"

Coreris grunted. "A hell of a lot. Some things he'll probably *never* tell us. But one thing's for certain: he'll tell us enough to put a stop to Zebra. And that's all I want right now."

"Amen," said Fotinos.

Anthony, Debbie, and Anthony, Jr., were lodged in a Holiday Inn near the Hall of Justice. Debbie was extremely nervous about the whole thing, but Anthony managed to keep her reasonably under control. She knew that what he was doing was for the best, but the presence of so many white policemen infused so suddenly into their lives was unnerving to her.

"You take the baby and go on into the other part of the room," Anthony told her the following morning when the interrogation was to resume. He was referring to a dressing and bath area that could be closed off from the main room. "That way you won't be hearing nothing that you don't need to know."

Debbie did as he asked. When she was gone, Coreris and Fotinos asked Anthony to tell them about Jesse Lee Cooks and the night of the Quita Hague killing, which by now had been connected with the Zebra attacks.

"I knew him in the prison house," Anthony said of Cooks. "How cold he was. He used to talk about killing all the time, you know. He was somebody who would go out and kill for the fun of it. Talk about going into an orphanage, you know what I mean? Going into a hospital, you know what I mean? This kind of off-the-wall stuff, demolishing everybody and this kind of stuff."

And later, when they were in the van with Larry Green, Jesse was "talking to Larry and telling him what it was like in San Quentin, and Jesse, he said something about he's glad he's out, you know, and he can pay his respects to, you know, his enemies."

Later still, when they were attempting to kidnap the three children off the street: "I know from looking at Jesse's eyes, you know, he had like, like *hurt* in his eyes, blood, murder, in his eyes, you know . . . and the way he was holding that girl's head, you know, around the mouth here, you know, holding it tight. . . ."

At first, Anthony referred to the killings and other incidents as being done by "them"—never with himself as a participant. It was always "they" did this, "they" did that. He claimed "personal knowledge'' of what had happened, but would not admit actually being present, except at the attempted kidnapping, where no killing had taken place. Coreris talked to him about it.

''Anthony, if you're involved in any way in these shootings, and you're afraid to talk, you're afraid you might be put up on charges for these crimes, I want you to know that you won't be. We'll offer you immunity so that you won't even be indicted or tried. But you have to understand that we need corroboration in this case. What I mean is, we have to back up what you're saying, we have to prove it. Otherwise, all this is just conversation.''

Anthony was still reluctant to admit more than just ''personal knowledge''—and he would not even explain what he meant by that. So Coreris decided to let him continue on that basis, for the time being anyway. At least, he thought, we'll be getting some facts—whether we can ever prove them or not.

Anthony talked about Quita Hague. ''They told her to get out, you know, and when she was getting out, they pushed her right on out. They had a real long skinny knife. They took the knife and walked over to the woman. Told her to shut up, you know, just put her head down there. And the woman screamed—''

Coreris and Fotinos exchanged glances. Only a person who had been there could tell the story that way—in spite of all the ''theys'' and ''thems.'' So the detectives let him keep talking. At one point he told them about a grisly find he made one day at Black Self Help. ''One day I forgot to clean the back up, and I smelled something that smelled a little strange, you know . . . the kind I smelled before in the penitentiary when a man got stabbed and it smelled like blood . . . blood . . . they told me to help get these packages on this truck . . . there were quite a few there . . . so I picked a package up, I set the package down in the truck, you know, and there was blood on my hand, and I asked what is this right here, and he said that's probably some old dog or cat cut up, you know, and don't worry about it. There were two or three different packages like that. . . .''

So John Doe No. 169 wasn't the only white devil butchered at Black Self Help, Coreris thought.

Anthony talked about J. C. Simon. ''. . . one time Larry told me, 'Don't bother him. He's very upset. He said something about, he just didn't have a high enough score, you know, to become a lieutenant . . . and he went to Chicago . . . said he had to kill a certain amount of people.' He had some pictures of him killing people . . . I seen some of them upstairs . . . and they showed me some pictures of a body hacked up . . . and told me I could lose all the fear in me because I could do the same to people.''

Little by little as Anthony talked, all of the attacks were tied in with one or another of the four men that he had been closest to: Cooks, Green, Simon, Moore. Their names and participation were linked with everyone on the long list of victims, and soon the pieces of Anthony's story fell so neatly into place that he could no longer reasonably deny his own implication. It was clear that he had been present at the Hague, Erakat, Dancik, Roselli, Smith, Wollin, Bambic, Holly, and McMillian incidents. Nine incidents involving ten of the Zebra victims—yet Anthony steadfastly claimed he himself had never killed.

Coreris and Fotinos talked about it out in the hall. "If we use him to get the others," Fotinos said, "we'll have to let him off the hook anyway. So in the long run it won't matter whether he killed anyone or not.''

"That's a hell of a way to have to look at it," Coreris said. "But we don't have much choice, do we?''

Fotinos shrugged. "Like you said before, the main thing is to stop the killings. Get the rest of those animals put away.''

"We're going to have to find a way to get him to admit being at the scenes first," Coreris said. "I think we'd better encourage him to get a lawyer. That way he'll know that he's got someone who can deal for him on the immunity thing.''

The detectives returned to the room and explained to Anthony the desirability of his having an attorney to protect his interests. Anthony did not know any attorneys, and Fotinos and Coreris were in no position to recommend one. It was finally decided to let Anthony select one at random. Fotinos opened the Yellow Pages to "Attorneys-at-Law" and Anthony reached down and put his finger on a name. The attorney was Laurence Kauffman. Anthony called him and the situation was explained to him. An appointment was made for Kauffman to come to Homicide the following morning, and from there Coreris and Fotinos would take him to meet his client.

* * *

At eleven o'clock the next morning, while Coreris and Fotinos were talking with Larry Kauffman, a Black Muslim named Jim 6X Peters* walked up to the desk at the Holiday Inn.

"Do you have Mr. Anthony Harris registered?" he inquired.

The clerk checked his guest list. "Yes, sir. Would you like to speak to him?"

"Just give me his room number; I'll go on up."

"I'm sorry, sir. We have to announce you. Hotel rules."

Peters smiled. "I see. In that case, ring him on the house phone for me. I'll announce myself."

Peters went to a house phone and the clerk rang Anthony's room. Anthony answered.

"Anthony Harris?" the caller said. "This is Jim 6X from the mosque. I have a message for you from the minister."

"What is it?" Anthony asked. It did not surprise him that the man was there.

"I'd rather not give it to you over the phone," Jim 6X said. "What's your room number? I'll come up."

"You can't come up," Anthony said. "My wife's still sleeping."

"Your wife? Oh, you mean Deborah. She can't be still sleeping; she just spoke to Sister Sarah on the phone a little while ago."

Anthony already knew that. He had caught Debbie on the phone when he came out of the shower. "You can't come up," he repeated.

"Why don't you come down to the lobby then?"

Anthony, his stomach quivering with fear, hung up.

Peters crossed to a pay phone and made a brief, urgent call. Just as he was hanging up, Coreris, Fotinos, and Larry Kauffman entered the lobby. Coreris had never seen Peters before, but was instantly suspicious of him. "I think we got some problems," he said to Fotinos. "Get upstairs and check on Anthony. Mr. Kauffman, you go with him, please."

After his partner and the attorney got on the elevator, Coreris walked up to Peters and showed his badge. "I'm Inspector Gus Coreris of the San Francisco Police Department. May I see some identification, please?"

---

*Since this person committed no actual crime, his name has been changed for the purpose of this narrative.

"Have I done anything, Inspector?" Peters asked with a smile.

"Not to my knowledge," said Coreris. "But the law states that all citizens must carry identification, and must show it when asked to do so by a police officer. May I see yours, please?"

Peters presented his driver's license. Coreris took out his notebook and copied down the information on it.

"May I ask what you're doing in this motel lobby, Mr. Peters?"

"Meeting friends," Peters answered. He took back the license Coreris handed him. "If you have no objection, Inspector, I'll wait for them out on the sidewalk."

Peters waited a moment, and when Coreris did not object, he walked out of the lobby. Coreris could see him standing at the curb, looking up the street. The detective picked up the house phone and called Anthony's room. Fotinos answered.

"Is Harris okay?" Coreris asked.

"Yeah, but I think our cover is blown," Fotinos said. "Debbie got nervous this morning and decided she needed to talk to a woman. While Anthony was in the shower, she called Sister Sarah, the wife of one of the Muslim ministers."

"Oh, Christ! Let me guess," said Coreris. "She told Sister Sarah where they were, right?"

"You got it," said Fotinos.

Coreris glanced out the lobby door again—just in time to see a black Cadillac pull up and four neatly dressed young black men get out and crowd around Jim 6X Peters.

"John, we got trouble down here," Coreris said. "Muslims coming out of the woodwork. I think you'd better get Anthony and his family out of here on the double. Get them over to the Hall. And don't come through the lobby. I'll do what I can down here."

Coreris hung up as the five Muslims entered the lobby. Three of them went directly to the elevator; Peters and the other one stood between it and Coreris.

"One moment, please, gentlemen," Coreris said, taking his badge out again. "I'm a police officer and I'd like to see some identification from each of you, please."

Peters shook his head. "Not just now, Inspector."

Coreris glanced up at the elevator indicator. The elevator was stopped on Anthony's floor. "Are you refusing to identify yourselves?" Coreris asked sternly.

"That is exactly what we are doing," Peters replied. He jerked his head at the three Muslims waiting for the elevator. "Take the stairs," he ordered.

Coreris saw the elevator indicator moving toward the upper-level parking area. He shrugged and smiled at Peters. "Well, if you don't want to identify yourselves, I guess you don't have to. Good day, gentlemen."

With a frowning, puzzled Peters following his every step, Coreris walked out of the lobby.

Outside, the detective hurried around the corner to the car in which he, Fotinos, and Larry Kauffman had driven over. Jumping behind the wheel, he lurched away from the curb and drove on screeching tires into the motel parking entrance.

The three Muslims who had hurried up the stairs were searching the hallways, one man to a floor. Their expressions were grim, fixed.

Coreris, on the spiral garage ramp, was careening around corners and pillars as he jammed the car upward to the top parking level.

When the Muslim on the second floor failed to find anything, he hurried up to the third floor. There he joined with the second man and they rushed up another floor.

Coreris skidded to a halt on the top level. Fotinos, gun drawn, guided the Harrises and Larry Kauffman from a fire stairwell and they all piled into the car. Coreris shot the car forward and began a speeding trip back down. Seconds after the car was out of sight, the three Muslims burst onto the upper parking level. They heard the screech of Coreris's tires and immediately began running down the spiraling ramp after the car.

But it was too late. Coreris reached the street far ahead of them. Putting the flasher on the dashboard, he sped toward the Hall of Justice.

Anthony, Debbie, and the baby were taken later that day to a room at the Stewart Hotel, near Union Square, where they had been preregistered under fictitious names. Three police details were assigned to guard them around the clock.

When Coreris found a moment later that day to sit down at his desk, he saw a phone message from a black police officer on the patrol detail. Coreris returned the call.

"I'd like to confer with you about something, Inspector," the black officer said.

"Go ahead," Coreris told him.

"Not over the phone. Are you going to be there for a while?"

"Sure."

"I'll come right over."

The officer arrived a few minutes later. Coreris took him into a private conference room. "What can I do for you?" he asked.

"I want to ask if you know of someone named Anthony that the department might be holding incognito."

Coreris's spine tightened. Watch this guy! his instincts warned. "Why do you want to know?" he asked the black officer.

"Some friends of mine asked me to find out."

"Are your friends Muslims?" Coreris asked bluntly.

The officer looked slightly surprised. "Yes, as a matter of fact. Can you tell me where this Anthony is?"

"I can," Coreris said, "but I won't. I will, however, tell you four other things. One: Anthony has an attorney representing him. Two: I have interrogated Anthony and in my opinion he has invaluable information which the department will protect at any risk. Three: I am going to formally report your inquiry to Chief Scott, Captain Barca, and the Intelligence Division. And four: If I were you, Officer, I wouldn't make any more inquiries about Anthony. You got all that?"

"I've got it," the black policeman replied tightly.

"Good. Anything else I can do for you?"

"I think not." The black officer strode to the door and stalked out.

The goddamned nerve! Coreris thought. He went back to his desk and told Fotinos about it. Fotinos shook his head. "What does he think we handle in this detail? Traffic warrants?"

"He must." Coreris pointed a finger at Fotinos. "You know, this thing is going to go sour on us if we're not careful. If those assholes are desperate enough to come out in the open with a *cop*, no telling what they'll do next."

"What worries me even more than that," Fotinos said, "is

363

whether J. C. Simon and those other animals might go underground on us. If their buddies decide to hide them, we'll be up the creek as far as making a bust.''

"You're right." Coreris drummed his fingers on the desk top. "I think I'll call Larry Kauffman and tell him we've got to get a formal statement from Anthony that will hold up in court. No more 'they did it' bullshit; we've got to have something solid. I just hope Anthony won't back out on us."

"He won't," Fotinos said confidently. "We're all he's got now. He can't go back out on the streets. Debbie burned all his bridges when she called Sister Sarah."

"That's right," Coreris said, immediately brightening. Picking up his phone, he called the Stewart Hotel and asked for the fictitious name under which Anthony was registered. Larry Kauffman answered. Coreris told him about the inquiry from the black police officer. "They want him real bad, Counselor," he emphasized to the attorney. "We've got to get him stashed somewhere permanently safe as quickly as we can. But we can't do it until he's formally gone on the record with something we can take to a grand jury. Until he admits personal participation, everything he's given us is just hearsay."

"I've already talked to him about that," Kauffman said. "He wants to cooperate further, but he's scared. He's afraid that after he talks, he might still be charged with something. It's not that he doesn't trust you guys; he just feels that you might be overruled by higher-ups. You have to admit he has a point."

"So what does he want?" Coreris asked.

"He wants his promise of immunity to come straight from the horse's mouth. He wants to meet with Mayor Alioto. Can you set that up?"

"If that's what he wants, we'll have to," said Coreris. "Let me get back to you."

Coreris told Fotinos what they had to do. They both got on the phone to try to locate the mayor. Within minutes they learned that he was out of the city; he had flown to Los Angeles on business. The detectives then began trying to locate Inspector Edward Sarraille, a police officer who was attached to the mayor's staff. After an hour, they finally contacted Sarraille. Coreris explained the urgency of the situation to him. Sarraille said he would try to locate Alioto in Los Angeles.

It was then past ten o'clock at night. Coreris and Fotinos sat back to wait.

In the downtown area, a black Continental moved methodically from one motel to another. At each stop, the routine was the same. A pleasant, well-groomed black man would go up to the desk and say, "Excuse me, I'm sorry to trouble you, but I'm trying to locate a cousin of mine who's staying with his family in one of the downtown motels. I'm a little embarrassed because I can't remember his last name; he's a distant cousin. But I wondered if you had a black man about thirty registered, with his wife and one infant—"

While this man was making inquiry at the desk, three other blacks from the Continental were strolling about the outside of the premises, checking for signs of a police guard.

The quartet had been searching since nightfall. They had started with the motels closest to the Hall of Justice and worked outward from there. One by one, they checked off every motel within a reasonable distance. They did not find the "cousin."

"The hotels," one of them finally said. "He may be in a regular hotel instead of a motel."

Midway through the evening, they started checking the hotels.

At midnight, Coreris received a call from Mayor Alioto in Los Angeles.

"What does it look like, Inspector?" the mayor asked.

"It looks good, sir," Coreris replied. "There's no doubt that the man has solid information."

"And he definitely wants to talk to me? The district attorney won't do?"

"He specifically asked for you, sir. He's afraid a guarantee of immunity from anybody else might not stick."

"Of course, you know I can't guarantee him immunity. All I can do is promise that we'll go to bat for him if he'll help us."

"I know that, sir. I think that'll be enough for him. He's painted himself in a corner."

"All right. I'll have to see what I can do in the way of a flight back up there. Stay at your phone; I'll get back to you."

"Yessir."

Alioto called back ten minutes later.

"All right, Inspector, I got on a TWA flight that will get me back to the city at three A.M. Have my driver and a red-light escort meet the plane. Then have your witness in my office at three thirty."

"Yessir."

In his office, a weary but optimistic Joseph Alioto met with Anthony Harris and Debbie Turner. Alioto would have liked to promise Anthony the moon if he wanted it, but he was determined to be scrupulously fair with the witness.

"Mr. Harris," he began, "I think that I ought to say right now, so there will be no question about it, that this is a constitutional matter, that you do have to understand that whatever involvement you have had, and whatever information you give with respect to that involvement, could be used against you in court.

"On the other hand, Mr. Harris, we are interested in solving this thing, and I, as the mayor of this city, would go to a judge and give him every assurance that you have come into this thing voluntarily, and helped us to secure certain evidence, and that you have cooperated. Whatever the law permits to be done in such cases, I will urge be done all the way down the line for you. So this is what we're talking about. If you feel under those circumstances, and with my assurance as I've just given it to you here, that you could be helpful to us—under those circumstances, if you want to tell us what you know about these killings on the streets of San Francisco, I promise that we will fulfill what I've talked to you about, and I will see to it that your wife gets the reward.

"Now then, your lawyers are here"—Alioto looked over at Larry Kauffman, who now had with him an associate attorney, Irving Hurd—"very capable lawyers, and they have heard, both of them have heard, what I have said about this whole thing."

"I'd like to read Anthony the Miranda Warning," Coreris said, "just for the record. Anthony, you have the right to remain silent. Anything you say can and will be used against you in a court of law. You have the right to talk to a lawyer, and have him present with you while you are being questioned. If you cannot afford to hire a lawyer, one will be appointed to represent you before any questioning, if you wish one. Do you understand each of these rights I have explained to you, Anthony?"

"Yes, sir," Anthony said.

"Having these rights in mind, do you wish to talk to the mayor and us at this time?"

"That's for sure," said Anthony.

And with that statement, Anthony Cornelius Harris began his formal confession to the Zebra crimes.

The Arrests

The arrest posse assembled at four o'clock in the morning on Wednesday, May 1, 1974.

There were more than one hundred officers. They were assigned to apprehend seven men who had been named by Anthony Harris as members of the Death Angels and participants in the Zebra killings. Besides J. C. Simon, Manuel Moore, and Larry Green, Harris had named Jesse Lee Cooks and four others. Cooks was already in Folsom Prison. The four others, like Simon, Moore, and Green, were to be taken into custody.

Forty officers were assigned to an apartment building at 844 Grove Street, where both Simon and Green lived: Simon in apartment two, Green in apartment seven. Five men, plus Coreris, Fotinos, and other homicide inspectors, were to assault Simon's apartment; another five, plus Dick Walley of CII and several more homicide inspectors, were assigned to take Green's apartment. The building itself was surrounded by ten additional men. The 800 block of Grove was sealed off by another twenty men.

A twenty-man team was also surrounding the premises of Black Self Help Moving and Storage, where two of the other suspects were known to be; and a second five-man team, along with a parole officer, was set to apprehend Manuel Moore at an apartment he had recently rented at 339 Fillmore, about four blocks from the Grove Street operation. The remaining two suspects were also under surveillance by sizable assault teams.

Coreris, Fotinos, and Dick Walley were sipping coffee from Styrofoam cups, standing on a dark street corner at the assembly point for the Grove Street assault team.

"It's been a long chase," said Walley. "Think they'll resist us?"

Fotinos shook his head. "They won't have a chance. Anyway, they're cowards, the whole goddamned bunch of them. Cowards don't resist."

"John's got this doctor friend who's guaranteed us a peaceful surrender," Coreris said.

"I hope he's right," said Walley. "Not that I'd mind blowing away these scum bags, but I keep thinking we might get lucky and catch one who'll blow the whistle on the whole gang—statewide."

"You're dreaming, Dick," said Coreris. "I don't think any one guy would know all that. Not even the main guy. These pricks are just too dumb to have that kind of information. I think the only way these dogs are going to be stopped are a few at a time, just like we're doing here."

An unmarked car pulled up and a Crime Prevention officer, Lieutenant Walter Braunschweig, got out. He motioned to two flak-vested assault sergeants, Edward Epting and Ralph Schaumleffel, who would lead the teams that would storm the two apartments. "Get your men in place," he instructed. "We hit in exactly ten minutes."

Coreris, Fotinos, and Walley quickly finished their coffee and moved into their respective positions. The Crime Prevention lieutenant, who was staging the overall assault, reached into the police car and took the radio mike. "Zebra Two, Three, Four, Five, and Six, this is Zebra One. Come in, please." From five different locations, including a roving patrol around the overall area, the assault team leaders responded.

"We're at minus eight minutes," the lieutenant advised. "There will be no more radio contact prior to the operation. Begin your respective assaults at exactly five A.M. Acknowledge."

Each of the teams acknowledged. The lieutenant tossed the mike into the car and picked up a riot gun. "Let's move in," he said.

Everyone moved quickly and quietly into place in the predawn

369

light. When all were ready, and the lieutenant's watch read five o'clock straight up, he spoke to an officer next to him and the officer flashed a battle lantern as a signal. Other lanterns, and spotlights, went on all around the building—and the assault began.

An officer with a steel crowbar hooked its neck around the doorknob of apartment two and smartly snapped it off. Another officer stepped in front of the door and kicked it open with one powerful thrust. The door slammed back on its hinges. Shotguns held at the ready, the officers stormed into the apartment.

In seconds, apartment two was awash with light from half a dozen battle lanterns, and shotguns, aimed and ready, covered every closet, corner, and crevice on the premises. The occupant of the apartment, J. C. Simon, sat up in bed in his underwear, eyes wide and bulging, face frozen with fear.

"I give up! I give up! Don't shoot!" he pleaded.

Not: *"What's going on? What's happening? What's the meaning of this?"*

Just: *"I give up. Don't shoot."*

The apartment lights were switched on. Coreris and Fotinos, guns drawn and aimed, stared at the terrified man on the bed; after a moment, his eyes focused in the light and he stared back at them. At that suspended moment in time, Coreris thought of Roxie McMillian and the man who said "Hi" before crippling her for life; and Coreris thought about Tana Smith, who had coped with and finally solved so many of her life's personal problems—just in time to be murdered. Only J. C. Simon knows what *he* was thinking at that precise moment. But whatever it was—and he must have been sure by now that he was not going to be killed in his bed; the officers were too calm, too mechanical in their duty—there was still no outraged indignation, still no demand for an explanation, still no behavior of any kind to indicate that J.C. *did not know why they were there.*

"Put your hands behind your back," Fotinos said, pulling out his handcuffs.

"Say, don't I be allowed to get dressed?" J.C. asked.

"We'll give you some clothes after we search the place," Coreris told him. He showed J.C. a folded document. "This is a duly authorized search warrant. At this time I am arresting you on a charge of suspicion of conspiracy to commit murder."

"Hey, man, I didn't commit no murder!" J.C. snapped. "This is a frame-up!"

"I'm going to read you your rights," Coreris said, ignoring the protest.

While Coreris read Simon his rights, Fotinos and the other officers methodically searched the apartment.

When Coreris was finished, he left Simon in the custody of one of the assault officers and walked down to apartment seven. There, in the middle of the living room, wrists cuffed behind him, Larry Green stood in his shorts. Standing nearby were his wife Dinah and her baby, both crying. A homicide inspector had just finished reading Larry his rights, and the young prisoner was vehemently protesting his innocence.

"I tell you, you got the wrong person!" he stormed. "I didn't do no murder! Turn me out of these handcuffs, man! You hear me? I didn't do nothing to be arrested for!"

After both apartments were thoroughly searched for weapons or other evidence—and none found—the suspects were allowed to dress and were taken out to waiting police cars. The assault lieutenant checked with other Zebra teams, listened to them one by one, then went over to Coreris. "Everyone's in custody, Gus," he said. "Black Self Help is secure and the boys from the Crime Lab have moved in to check the place out."

"Any guns found anywhere?"

"Afraid not, Gus. Sorry."

Coreris and Fotinos exchanged disappointed looks. They badly needed a gun that could be directly connected to one of the suspects. Two guns had been used in the shootings. Both were .32-caliber automatics. The first had been used to shoot Erakat, Dancik, Agnos, DiGirolamo, Bertuccio, Roselli, Moynihan, and Hosler. Eight victims, six of them dead. The second gun had been used to shoot Smith, Wollin, Bambic, Holly, McMillian, Rainwater, Story, Anderson, White, and Shields. Ten victims, six dead. The gun used in the Rose killing and the Ellen Linder sex attack, found in the possession of Jesse Lee Cooks at the time of his arrest, had been in custody since before the long string of shootings began. And in the Hague and John Doe #169 cases, no weapon had been fired.

"If we can't tie in a gun," Fotinos said, "maybe there'll be some

371

knives or meat cleavers with traces of blood on them at Black Self Help.''

"Yeah, maybe," Coreris said. There was little optimism in his voice, and Fotinos knew why.

Without a weapon, or some physical evidence, it was going to be almost impossible to convict the men.

The Gun

The two young black boys were playing a modified game of baseball—modified because there was only two of them and they had
no baseball field, only the backyard of one of the boys in which to
play. The yard was behind the Shields Street home of eight-year-
old Cleon Jones, who had been named after the star outfielder of
the New York Mets. The boy he was playing with was Darrell Bot-
ney, age ten.

The game they played was simple. One of them pitched, the other batted. When the batter made three outs by hitting the ball in
such a fashion that it could be caught by the pitcher, then the two
changed positions and the pitcher took his turn at bat. The only
rule was that the ball had to stay inside the yard; over the fence
was an automatic out.

Darrell, who was considerably stronger and taller than Cleon,
had trouble keeping the ball inside the fence. Cleon knew that and
purposely pitched easy hits to him, knowing that when he connected, there was a good chance the ball would go over the fence for an
out.

That was just what happened. Cleon pitched a good one—and
Darrell popped it into the next yard.

"That's it!" Cleon yelled. "You out!"

Darrell threw the bat on the ground and the two boys headed for the fence.

"Gimme a boost over," said Cleon.

Darrell cupped his hands and Cleon put one foot in them and was boosted to the top of the fence. He hopped into the next yard and began looking for the ball. The grass in the yard was wild and thick, covered by a layer of fallen pine needles. As Cleon walked, the needles made crunching sounds under his feet. Suddenly his toe hit something solid. The ball, he thought. He reached into the grass and found that it was not the ball at all.

It was a gun.

Cleon's father, F. A. Jones, called the police and Officers David Roccaforte and Gary Elsenbroich in Unit 3H-7 answered the call.

"My boy found this," said Jones, producing the pistol. "In the rear yard that backs up to our rear yard." The Jones family home was at 621 Shields. The rear yard to which Jones was referring extended back from a house on the nearest perpendicular street, at 271 Vernon.

Roccaforte immediately removed the magazine and checked the breech to make certain the weapon was not loaded. Then the two officers examined the gun closely. The weapon was a Beretta model 70, 7.65-millimeter automatic pistol.

Elsenbroich looked at his partner. "Seven-point-sixty-five millimeter is the same as a thirty-two, isn't it?"

"I think so," Roccaforte replied.

Both officers knew they were less than a block from where the last Zebra killing had taken place.

"We'd better call the Crime Lab," Roccaforte said.

At the Crime Lab, the Beretta pistol was first carefully processed for fingerprints. No usable prints were found. Next, it was photographed, top and sides, for identification. Then it was test-fired into a barrel of water in the lab's basement gun room, and the test bullet was retrieved and compared with laboratory specimens number 74–2686, the bullets and casings in the homicide of Nelson Shields IV.

The bullets matched.

"We got us a gun!" Coreris said jubilantly after the Crime Lab called him. "The lab has got a Beretta that some kid found a block from the Shields killing, and it matches the slugs in every case since Tana Smith!"

Fotinos began to count them on his fingers from memory. "Smith, Wollin, Bambic, Holly, McMillian, the two Salvation Army kids, Anderson, Terry White, and Shields. Jesus, that's ten of them. Any prints?"

Coreris shook his head. "No prints. But if we can trace that gun to one of those dogs we've got locked up, we're in business."

Coreris dragged the phone over and called the San Francisco office of the U. S. Treasury Department's Bureau of Alcohol, Tobacco, and Firearms. "Special Agent Lyman Shaffer," he told the girl who answered. A moment later, Shaffer came on the line. "Gus Coreris here, Lyman, how are you?"

"Good, Gus, good. How's Zebra doing?"

"Glad you asked," said Coreris. "We've found one of the guns and need to get it traced. Can ATF do it for us?"

"You bet. San Francisco's our city too, Gus. Send me a request in writing and we'll get right on it."

"Beautiful," said Coreris.

Lyman Shaffer was twenty-nine years old. He had been a special agent for ATF for two years, having joined the Treasury Department after spending five years as a Berkeley police officer, ending up in Homicide. He had known Coreris and Fotinos, also Mitch Luksich, since his Berkeley PD days.

When the request for the gun trace came in, Shaffer immediately put its description into the ATF's main computers in Washington, D.C. For purposes of tracing, the gun became: Beretta, Model 70, 7.65-mm semiautomatic pistol, blue steel, 3" barrel, serial number A47469.

In Washington, ATF tracer personnel took Shaffer's information and went to work. Under the authority of the 1968 Gun Control Act, ATF can assist any state or municipal law enforcement agency in tracing any firearm connected with any crime, whether federal or not. With the information on the Zebra gun, an ATF tracer made contact by overseas telephone with the gun files of the Pietro Beretta Company in Gardone, Italy. Within minutes, ATF was told that Beretta number A47469 had been sold in April 1968 to J. L. Galef and Son, a firearms importer in New York City.

ATF's New York office checked with Galef and Son. That particular handgun had been wholesaled to the J. C. Penney warehouse in Statesville, North Carolina. The Penney warehouse had in turn consigned the weapon to a Penney retail outlet in Tacoma, Washington. There, on July 31, 1968, it was sold to Peter David Puppo, a United States Air Force medic stationed at McCord Air Force Base.

Shaffer ran a check on Puppo; he had no criminal record. Now discharged, he had long since left the Tacoma area. A check with the Air Force showed that his mother lived in Santa Barbara. Shaffer drove down there and interviewed her. She said her son was living in a religious commune in Albion, California, a tiny coastal hamlet a hundred miles north of San Francisco. The Beretta, Shaffer told himself, was getting closer to home. Closer to Zebra.

Driving up to Albion the next day, Shaffer located and interviewed Peter David Puppo.

"Yeah," Puppo said, "I used to own that gun. Until about a year ago. I gave it to my roommate. Brad Bishop."

Bradley Eugene Bishop *did* have a record. He had been convicted in Marin County, California, of the sale of dangerous drugs, and at that time was a wanted fugitive for the same crime. For a time, he and Puppo had shared an apartment at 3721 Twenty-fifth Street—in San Francisco.

Bull's-eye, Shaffer thought. But it was not to be.

From Bishop's criminal record, Shaffer learned that his mother lived in Novato, California, just across the Golden Gate Bridge. He drove up and interviewed her. Mrs. Nola Bishop had not seen her son for about eight weeks, since he left to drive down to Los Angeles to look for work. What was he driving? Shaffer inquired. "A sixty-two Chrysler station wagon," Mrs. Bishop said. Shaffer ran a DMV check on the car. It was registered to Bishop and carried license plate number BFU 443. Shaffer also learned one other thing from Bishop's mother: his *grand*mother lived in Los Angeles.

376

Three days later, Shaffer was in Los Angeles. He spoke with the grandmother, Mrs. E. M. Bishop. "Brad came to see me about six weeks ago," she told him. "He said he was living in Downey and working for a construction company."

Shaffer moved on to Downey, a Los Angeles suburb twenty miles south. He began his search there by checking with all the licensed contractors in the area, but Bishop was not on the payroll under either his own name or the alias of James Andrew Wilson that he was known to use in the drug business. Next, Shaffer interviewed all postal carriers in Downey. None of them was able to help him. On a hunch, Shaffer put out a tracer on the Chrysler station wagon. Santa Monica Police Department responded. The vehicle had been picked up by them after being abandoned with a broken drive shaft. Shaffer went to Santa Monica and searched the car. Nothing. He interviewed residents of the area where it had been abandoned. Nothing.

The trail of Brad Bishop in Southern California was cold, so Shaffer went back up north. Through criminal records and other files, San Francisco ATF compiled a list of two dozen names of people who knew or had known Brad Bishop in the Bay Area. Shaffer began a methodical interrogation operation, tracking down each person and interviewing them regarding Bishop's whereabouts. Several people "thought" they knew where Bishop "might" be—but no one was certain. Among Shaffer's informants was one woman who said she had recently heard that Bishop was in Hawaii.

Shaffer teletyped Bishop's photo and record to the Honolulu Police Department. Three weeks later, Honolulu PD cabled Shaffer that Bishop had been located. Shaffer obtained a federal warrant charging Bishop, a felon, with violation of federal gun laws. The ATF agent flew to Hawaii. By the time Shaffer got to Honolulu, Bishop had left the island of Oahu and gone to Maui. Shaffer followed him. On Maui, an all-points bulletin was put out for Bishop. Maui police located him in Lahaina and he was taken into custody.

Shaffer telephoned Gus Coreris on the mainland. He had kept Coreris informed every step of the way in the long search for Bishop; now he wanted him to know that it was over. "I've got our man locked up on Maui, Gus," he told the detective. "This guy puts the

Beretta in San Francisco in April 1973. That's just eight months before the Zebra killers started using it.''

"Beautiful," said Coreris. "Hang on to that joker. I'll be there on the next plane."

Coreris grabbed Jeff Brosch and flew to Hawaii. The next morning the three of them interrogated Brad Bishop.

"Mr. Bishop," said Coreris, "we're interested in a Beretta automatic pistol—"

"I don't own a gun," Bishop said defensively.

"I know you don't. But you used to. You got a Beretta automatic from Peter David Puppo in March of last year in San Francisco. What did you do with the gun?"

Bishop shrugged. "I don't remember."

Coreris sighed dramatically. "You're sure?"

"Positive. I don't remember."

"Okay," Coreris said resignedly. "Sorry to have bothered you." He nodded to Shaffer. "Book him for murder."

The color drained from Brad Bishop's face. "What? Murder? Hey, man, what the hell are you talking about?"

Coreris put his face very close to Bishop. "We're talking about murder, Bishop. Murder committed with that Beretta automatic. *Six* murders, to be exact. All in San Francisco. And since you were the last one to have the gun—also in San Francisco—it looks like you're as good a suspect as we're going to find." He nodded to Shaffer again. "Go ahead, book him for murder. Six counts."

"Hey, hold it! Hold it now!" Bishop pleaded. "I didn't have nothing to do with any murders, man!"

"Then you'd better tell us what you did with that gun," Coreris said evenly. "And you'd better tell us *quick*."

"Okay, okay." Bishop lowered his eyes. "I sold it. For twenty bucks."

"Who to?"

"A guy named Ed St. Andre. He lives on Seventeenth Street in San Francisco. But he don't have it anymore; some dude named Dick Arzave ripped it off from Ed's apartment."

"How do you know that?" Coreris asked.

" 'Cause I helped Ed find the guy," Bishop explained.

Slowly, the detectives pieced together the story. Bishop had sold the Beretta to Edmond St. Andre, who had a police record for robbery. A week later, the gun had been stolen from St. Andre's apartment at 3562 Seventeenth Street. Bishop and St. Andre had narrowed the suspected thieves down to one person: Richard Arzave, who also had a criminal record. The two men confronted Arzave; he admitted stealing the gun—and selling it. Bishop and St. Andre made Arzave pay them seventy-five dollars for the gun and to overlook the theft. That was the last Bishop had heard of the gun or Arzave.

Coreris let Shaffer keep Brad Bishop to answer the federal gun law violation, while he and Jeff Brosch flew back to San Francisco to continue the gun trace. When they got home, they located Edmund St. Andre, who told them the same story Bishop had told them. He also gave them Richard Arzave's address in San Bruno.

Doggedly, the officers ran down Arzave. He admitted his role in the theft of the Beretta, his subsequent purchase of the gun from St. Andre, and his own sale of the weapon to one David Bonnelli, the proprietor of Atchinson's Pharmacy at 1607 Twentieth Street in San Francisco.

"How did the sale come about?" Coreris asked him.

"I work with Bonnelli's brother at the Gallo Wine warehouse in South San Francisco," Arzave said. "I mentioned to him that I had a gun for sale and he said he had a brother who might be interested in buying it. So he sent me up to the drugstore to see him. And I sold him the gun."

Back to San Francisco. At Atchinson's Pharmacy, David Bonnelli was very evasive with Coreris; he was clearly fearful of being implicated in a crime. Coreris reassured him.

"Mr. Bonnelli, this matter that we're concerned with is a very serious homicide. Believe me, I'm not interested in any possible minor charges for the illegal sale of a firearm or anything like that. I just want to know what you did with the gun. That's all I care about. Understand?"

"You're sure?" said Bonnelli. "This isn't some kind of trick?"

"No trick," Coreris promised. "What did you do with it?"

"I sold it to a customer," Bonnelli finally admitted. "For eighty bucks."

"Who's the customer?"

"Moo Moo Tooa," said Bonnelli.

"Who?"

"Moo Moo Tooa. He's a Samoan. You know, from Samoa."

Bonnelli could not tell the detectives where Moo Moo lived, and he had not seen him in several weeks. The Zebra Squad began a relentless search for the Samoan. An oversized, tattooed, former longshoreman and stevedore, he was known on the streets by a number of people, but no one was able to tell the detectives exactly where he lived. Then Coreris and his men got one of their rare breaks: Moo Moo walked into Atchinson's Pharmacy and David Bonnelli telephoned them at once. The detectives arrived before he left the store.

Moo Moo Tooa would have trusted the devil himself before he trusted a police officer. He had been in trouble with the law nearly all of his life, beginning in his early youth when he refused to register for the draft, down through years of brawling in South Pacific bars and being charged with assault and battery because of it. When Coreris questioned him about the Beretta, he said he had thrown it away.

"At first I pawned it," he said. "At the San Francisco Loan Association over on Sixth Street. I got twenty-five dollars for it in hock. Left it in there for about three months, I guess. Then I got it out and threw it away."

Coreris eyed the big Samoan skeptically. "You took it out of hock just to throw it away? Is that what you're telling me?"

"That's it. See, I had to sign some forms at the pawnshop, man. I was scared of them forms, you know. Like they connected me with that gun, see. I didn't want to be connected with no gun."

"No? Why'd you buy it then?"

Moo Moo shrugged his big shoulders. "Just an impulse. A spur-of-the-moment thing. It was a mistake. I didn't need no gun for nothing."

Coreris tried to reassure Moo Moo as he had Bonnelli. "I need to know where the gun went, Moo Moo," he told him. "I promise there won't be any charges pressed against you, no matter who you passed the gun on to or how you did it. If you traded it for dope or whatever, sold it to an ex-con, I don't care, understand? No charges. Just tell me what you really did with the gun."

Moo Moo shrugged again. "I threw it away, man."

Moo Moo stuck tenaciously to his story. A check with the pawn-shop showed that it had been left as security for a $25 loan on May 5, 1973, and redeemed for that amount plus interest on August 30, 1973. Within the hour after redeeming the gun, according to Moo Moo, he had placed the gun, in a paper bag, in a trash can on the northwest corner of Sixth and Mission.

"That doesn't make sense," Coreris challenged. "If you were going to throw the thing away, why not just leave it in the pawn-shop and forget it?"

"I told you," Moo Moo said. "I wanted the forms I signed torn up. Only way to get that done was to get the gun back."

"I think you're lying, Moo Moo," Coreris told him bluntly.

Moo Moo was unmoved. "That's your privilege," he said without rancor. He refused to change his story.

On the off chance that Tooa *was* telling the truth, the Zebra team contacted the Department of Public Works. They determined that trash truck number 793 had been assigned to the Sixth and Mission area on the day Moo Moo claimed to have thrown away the gun. The men assigned to the truck that day were James Reed and Thurman Spriull. Both men denied finding the weapon, and stated that they had never found any gun during their careers with the department. Both volunteered to submit to lie detector examinations to substantiate their statements.

Coreris went back to Moo Moo. He begged, pleaded, threatened, cajoled, attempted to bribe, and used every other approach he could think of to make the Samoan tell the truth about what he did with the Beretta. But Moo Moo's instinctive distrust of the police prevailed. He was unmoved by anything Coreris said. He had thrown the gun away—and that was that.

Coreris did not give up. At regular intervals he had Fotinos, Brosch, and Klotz locate Moo Moo and talk to him again. Each man tried his own personal style of persuasion on the big Samoan—and each man failed. Moo Moo Tooa was unshakable. But the detectives kept trying; it was four to one, they figured; maybe they would eventually wear him down.

They were right. The constant pressure applied by the detectives finally got to Moo Moo. But he did not change his story; he simply dropped out of sight. The Zebra Squad combed the Tenderloin for Moo Moo: they checked the flophouses, the bars, the hangouts; questioned people who knew him; alerted David Bonnelli again; put his estranged wife, Fatu, under surveillance; requested an all-points bulletin from the patrol division; and in general put out a dragnet for the big Samoan. All to no avail. Moo Moo Tooa, ever clever, ever resourceful, completely evaded location.

For Coreris and his team, it looked like the end of the line.

Then the situation got worse.

On September 12, 1974, sixteen days after Moo Moo Tooa had gone underground, he was walking out of a movie theater where he had spent the afternoon, when suddenly he clutched at his left armpit and fell to his knees. Then he pitched forward, dead. An autopsy later revealed a massive heart attack.

Now, for Gus Coreris and his men, this *was* the end of the line. The Beretta's chain of ownership had been broken, unequivocally, by death. The State of California would have to proceed against the Zebra defendants without the physical evidence of a murder gun—because unless there was some way to connect the Beretta with one of the defendants, they might as well not have the gun at all.

The luck of the Zebra killers was holding.

The Indictment

Seven men had been arrested for the Zebra crimes. The eighth, Jesse Lee Cooks, was already in custody. After a careful analysis of the statement given by Anthony Harris, and after numerous witnesses from the various crimes had been located and brought to the Hall of Justice to view lineups and identify suspects, it was finally decided by the district attorney to release four of the men. What Anthony Harris said, coupled with what Zebra witnesses saw, provided enough evidence to indict only J. C. Simon, Manuel Moore, Larry Green, and Jesse Cooks.

On May 16, 1974, fifteen days after they were apprehended, the four remaining defendants, on the basis of testimony from thirty-one witnesses, were formally indicted by a grand jury on one count of conspiracy to commit murder, three counts of murder, two counts of kidnapping, two counts of robbery, and four counts of assault with a deadly weapon. Based on only those crimes, which the district attorney felt could be proved beyond a reasonable doubt, the indictment read as follows:

In the Superior Court of the State of California In and For the City and County of San Francisco.

383

Clark Howard

People of the State of California,   No. 88244
Plaintiff

vs.

Manuel Moore, J. C. Simon,
Larry Craig Green, and Jesse Cooks, Defendants.

Indictment for Felony, To Wit: Conspiracy to Violate Penal Code Section 187 (Murder); *Green & Cooks*: Murder (187 P.C.); 2 Cts. Kidnapping (207 P.C.); 2 Cts. Robbery (211 P.C.); Assault With A Deadly Weapon (245a P.C.) *Moore & Simon*: 2 Cts. Murder (187 P.C.); Assault With A Deadly Weapon (245a P.C.) *Moore*: Assault With A Deadly Weapon (245a P.C.)
Count 1:

Manuel Moore, J. C. Simon, Larry Craig Green, and Jesse Cooks, defendants, are accused by the Grand Jury of the City and County of San Francisco, State of California, by this indictment, of the crime of felony, to wit: Violation of Section 182 Penal Code of California (Conspiracy), committed as follows: The said defendants, during the period of time between October 20, 1973, and April 30, 1974, at the City and County of San Francisco, State of California, did conspire and agree with each other and with other persons to violate the provisions of Section 187 Penal Code (Murder).

Overt Act No. 1:

That on or about the month of October 1973, in the City and County of San Francisco, State of California, in pursuance of and to carry out the object of the said conspiracy, Larry Craig Green, Jesse Cooks, Manuel Moore, J. C. Simon and others met in an apartment located at 844 Grove Street.

Overt Act No. 2:

That on or about the 20th day of October, 1973, in the City and County of San Francisco, State of California, in pursuance of and to carry out the object of the said conspiracy, Larry Craig Green and Jesse Cooks rode in a white Dodge van to the area of Chestnut near Powell Street.

Overt Act No. 3:

That on or about the 11th day of December, 1973, in the City and

County of San Francisco, State of California, in pursuance of and to carry out the object of the conspiracy, J. C. Simon and Manuel Moore rode in a Cadillac automobile at approximately 9:30 p.m. to the area of Haight and Buchanan Streets, at which place both men got out of the automobile.

Overt Act No. 4:

That on or about the 14th day of April, 1974, at approximately 9:15 p.m., in the City and County of San Francisco, State of California, in pursuance of and to carry out the object of the said conspiracy, Manuel Moore walked to the area of Hayes and Fillmore Street where he talked to two persons on the sidewalk.

Count 2:

Allegations As To Larry Craig Green and Jesse Cooks:

Larry Craig Green and Jesse Cooks, defendants herein, are further accused by the Grand Jury of the City and County of San Francisco, State of California, by this indictment, of the crime of felony, to wit: Violation of Section 187 Penal Code of California (Murder), committed as follows: The said defendants, on or about the 20th day of October, 1973, at the City and County of San Francisco, State of California, did murder Quita Hague, a human being.

Count 3:

Larry Craig Green and Jesse Cooks, defendants herein, are further accused by the Grand Jury of the City and County of San Francisco, State of California, by this indictment, of the crime of felony, to wit: Violation of Section 207 Penal Code of California (Kidnapping), committed as follows: The said defendants, on or about the 20th day of October, 1973, at the City and County of San Francisco, State of California, did forcibly steal and take Quita Hague and carry her into another part of the City and County of San Francisco, State of California.

Count 4:

Larry Craig Green and Jesse Cooks, defendants herein, are further accused by the Grand Jury of the City and County of San Francisco, State of California, by this indictment, of the crime of felony, to wit:

Violation of Section 211 Penal Code of California (Robbery), committed as follows: The said defendants, on or about the 20th day of October, 1973, at the City and County of San Francisco, State of California, did rob Quita Hague of a white metal ring with an emerald stone.

Great Bodily Injury Allegation as to Larry Craig Green (Section 213 Penal Code):

That in the course of commission of said robbery, said defendant, Larry Craig Green, with intent to inflict such injury, did inflict great bodily injury on Quita Hague.

Count 5:

Larry Craig Green and Jesse Cooks, defendants herein, are further accused by the Grand Jury of the City and County of San Francisco, State of California, by this indictment, of the crime of felony to wit: Violation of Section 207 Penal Code of California (Kidnapping), committed as follows: The said defendants, on or about the 20th day of October, 1973, at the City and County of San Francisco, State of California, did forcibly steal and take Richard Hague and carry him to another part of the City and County of San Francisco, State of California.

Count 6:

Larry Craig Green and Jesse Cooks, defendants herein, are further accused by the Grand Jury of the City and County of San Francisco, State of California, by this indictment, of the crime of felony, to wit: Violation of Section 211 Penal Code of California (Robbery), committed as follows: The said defendants, on or about the 20th day of October, 1973, at the City and County of San Francisco, State of California, did rob Richard Hague of a wallet, driver's license, and personal papers.

Great Bodily Injury Allegation as to Jesse Cooks (Section 213 Penal Code):

That in the course of commission of said robbery, said defendant, Jesse Cooks, with intent to inflict such injury, did inflict great bodily injury on Richard Hague.

Count 7:

Larry Craig Green and Jesse Cooks, defendants herein, are further accused by the Grand Jury of the City and County of San Francisco, State of California, by this indictment, of the crime of felony, to wit: Violation of Section 245a Penal Code of California (assault With A Deadly Weapon), committed as follows: The said defendants, on or about the 20th day of October, 1973, at the City and County of San Francisco, State of California, did assault Richard Hague with a deadly weapon.

Firearm Use Allegation as to Jesse Cooks (Section 12022.5 Penal Code):

In the commission of each of the crimes alleged in Counts 2, 3, 4, 5, 6 and 7, the defendant, Jesse Cooks, used a firearm, to wit: a pistol.

Count 8:

Allegations as to Manuel Moore and J. C. Simon:

Manuel Moore and J. C. Simon, defendants herein, are further accused by the Grand Jury of the City and County of San Francisco, State of California, by this indictment, of the crime of felony, to wit: Violation of Section 187 Penal Code of California (Murder), committed as follows: The said defendants, on or about the 28th day of January, 1974, at the City and County of San Francisco, State of California, did murder Tana Smith, a human being.

Firearm Use Allegation as to J. C. Simon (Section 12022.5 Penal Code):

In the commission of said offense, the defendant, J. C. Simon, used a firearm, to wit: a pistol.

Count 9:

Manuel Moore and J. C. Simon, defendants herein, are further accused by the Grand Jury of the City and County of San Francisco, State of California, by this indictment, of the crime of felony, to wit: Violation of Section 187 Penal Code of California (Murder), committed as follows: The said defendants, on or about the 28th day of January, 1974, at the City and County of San Francisco, State of California, did murder Jane Holly, a human being.

Firearm Use Allegation as to Manuel Moore (Section 12022.5 Penal Code):

In the commission of said offense, the defendant, Manuel Moore, used a firearm, to wit: a pistol.

Count 10:

Manuel Moore and J. C. Simon, defendants herein, are further accused by the Grand Jury of the City and County of San Francisco, State of California, by this indictment, of the crime of felony, to wit: Violation of Section 245a Penal Code of California (Assault With A Deadly Weapon), committed as follows: The said defendants, on or about the 28th day of January, 1974, at the City and County of San Francisco, State of California, did assault Roxanne McMillian with a deadly weapon.

Firearm Use Allegation as to J. C. Simon (Section 12022.5 Penal Code):

In the commission of said offense, the defendant, J. C. Simon, used a firearm, to wit: a pistol.

Count 11:

Allegation as to Manuel Moore:

Manuel Moore, a defendant herein, is further accused by the Grand Jury of the City and County of San Francisco, State of California, by this indictment, of the crime of felony, to wit: Violation of Section 245a Penal Code of California (Assault With A Deadly Weapon), committed as follows: The said defendant, on or about the 14th day of April, 1974, at the City and County of San Francisco, State of California, did assault Terry White with a deadly weapon.

Firearm Use Allegation (Section 12022.5 Penal Code):

In the commission of the said offense, the defendant, Manuel Moore, used a firearm, to wit: a pistol.

Count 12:

Manuel Moore, a defendant herein, is further accused by the Grand Jury of the City and County of San Francisco, State of California, by this indictment, of the crime of felony, to wit: Violation of Section 245a Penal Code of California (Assault With A Deadly Weapon), committed as follows: The said defendant, on or about the 14th day of April, 1974, at the City and County of San Francisco, State of California, did assault Ward Anderson with a deadly weapon.

Firearms Use Allegation (Section 12022.5 Penal Code):

In the commission of said offense, the defendant, Manuel Moore, used a firearm, to wit: a pistol.

Allegation As To Prior Convictions of Jesse Cooks:

Before the commission of the offenses herinbefore set forth in this indictment, said defendant, Jesse Cooks, was convicted of the following felonies:

(1) In the Superior Court of the State of California, in and for the County of Los Angeles, on or about December 10, 1965, the crime of Robbery, a violation of Section 211 Penal Code, and he served a term of imprisonment therefor.

(2) In the District Court of the United States for the Southern District of California, on or about January 24, 1966, the crime of Bank Robbery, a violation of 18 USC 2113(a) (d), and he served a term of imprisonment therefor.

Allegation As To Prior Conviction Of Manuel Moore:

Before the commission of the offenses hereinbefore set forth in this indictment, said defendant, Manuel Moore, was, in the Superior Court of the State of California, in and for the County of San Bernardino, on or about May 13, 1969, convicted of the felony of Burglary in violation of Section 459 Penal Code, and he served a term of imprisonment therefor.

A True Bill   John Jay Ferdon, District Attorney

(signed) *James T. Rodman*   By (signed) *Walter N. Guibbini*
Foreman of the   Assistant District
Grand Jury   Attorney

Names of Witnesses examined before the Grand Jury on finding the foregoing indictment: Louis Daugherty, M.D., Richard Hague, Inspector William Armstrong, Guy Bernardo. David Bienvineste, Chief Petty Officer L. C. Green, Yolande Williams, Mitchell Luksich, Inspector Gus Coreris, Anthony C. Harris, Jack Callas, Lynn Susoeff, Angela Roselli, Preston Demings, Jack Frost, Curtis L. Jones, Richard O. Williams, Denise R. Norman, Roxanne McMillian, Carol Matison, Linda Story, Terry White, Officer Bruce Marovich, Officer L. Manwiller, Officer James Ludlow, Officer Thomas Arnold, Officer Donal Merkley, Officer Stephen Gudelj, Officer Ricky Blim, Inspector Thomas Murphy, Shoji Horikoshi.

Order Assigning Cause And
Fixing Bail

It is hereby ordered that a bench warrant issue for the arrest of each of the within named defendants and that bail as to each defendant be fixed in the sum of $300,000 cash or surety bond.

It is further ordered that the within named indictment and cause be assigned to Department No. 23 for trial and determination.

Dated: 5/16/74

(Signed) *Clayton M. Arn*
Presiding Judge

(The foregoing Grand Jury Indictment has been reproduced verbatim except for the changing of one name.)

The Final Link

On January 5, 1975, just six weeks before the Zebra trial was to begin, Gus Coreris returned to his Homicide desk late in the afternoon and found a message from one of the lockup sergeants at the city prison. Coreris returned the call.

"Gus," the jailer said, "you ever hear of a guy named Arnold George Lucas?"

Coreris closed his eyes and plowed into his memory. "Lucas—Lucas—Arnold George Lucas. Yeah, I know him. Junkie. Small-time cat burglar and fence."

"We've got him over here in the cooler with a couple of burglary charges against him," the jailer said. "He asked me on the sly to get in touch with you. Says he's got something he wants to trade you."

"Did he say what it was?"

"No, just that it was something you'd be interested in."

Coreris thought about it for a moment. He had not had any contact with Lucas for several years, could not even think of any cases of his that Lucas would be connected with. Zebra did not even occur to him; Lucas, a freaky drug-addict type, was not even close to being Muslim material.

"All right, tell him I'll be over," the detective said finally.

Later that day he went over to the city prison. That was where, for the past nine and a half months, the four accused Zebra prisoners had been held awaiting trial. They were segregated from each other and from all other prisoners: J. C. Simon was in cell G-5, Larry Green in F-2, Manuel Moore in H-1, and Jesse Lee Cooks, who had been brought there from Folsom, in K-6. A special memo pertaining to the men had been issued by police captain J. William Conroy, who was in charge of the jail. It read:

> These prisoners are to be considered extremely dangerous. They shall be kept separated and no message of any kind, by any means, shall be transmitted from one to the other.
>
> Control of these prisoners is the task of City Prison personnel. Punishment is the task of the courts. Harassment of these prisoners, in any fashion, will not be tolerated. Custodial personnel are to be cautious, firm, but fair.
>
> Trusty bosses shall impress upon Trustys that they shall use the outside corridor exclusively when going to and coming from this area.
>
> The attorneys visiting room shall be inspected thoroughly following its use by any attorney visiting any prisoner.
>
> The medical staff shall be particularly attentive to feigned illness on the part of any of these prisoners, since escape from the City and County Hospital would be far easier than from this prison.
>
> Absolute tight security shall be instituted throughout the prison, effective immediately.

After they had been in custody sixteen days, a list of ten visitors, not including attorneys, was approved by the prison administration. Larry Green was allowed four visitors: Booker Green, his father; Cloteal Green, his mother; Dinah Green, his wife; and Dede Green, his sister. Manuel Moore was allowed three visitors: Gloria 2X Moore, who was listed as his wife; and Raymond Moore, his father, and Jean Moore, his sister, both of whom lived in Riverside County, 450 miles away. J. C. Simon was allowed one visitor: Greta X Burgess, who was listed as his wife. Greta Burgess lived in

San Francisco; in fact, lived down the street and around the corner from where the last Zebra victim, Nelson Shields IV had been killed. The backyard of her building almost touched the backyard where the Beretta pistol was found.

The other two approved visitors, who were allowed to visit all three prisoners, were John Muhammad, listed as their minister, and Joseph X Polite, his assistant minister.

Jesse Lee Cooks had no approved visitors. He had not requested any, and no one showed any interest in visiting him.

When Coreris arrived at City Prison, he had Arnold George Lucas brought to one of the attorney rooms so that they could confer in private. When Lucas was brought in, Coreris was surprised to see how healthy he appeared.

"You look like you're ready to start playing basketball again," he commented.

"I'm off the stuff," Lucas said.

"Sure," Coreris replied skeptically.

"No shit, Inspector," Lucas said. "I been off junk since last April, nearly nine months now. See for yourself," he said, rolling up his sleeves.

Coreris examined his arms. They looked clean, all right; all the tracks were old scars, from old needles.

"Well, good, Arnold, I'm glad to see it," said Coreris. "Now all you have to do is give up burglary."

Lucas grinned. "Come on, Inspector. A guy's got to live."

Coreris decided to get down to business. "What did you want to see me about, Arnold?"

"You're in charge of Zebra, right?"

"Right."

"Are you guys going to put Tom Manney on trial?" Manney was one of the eight men originally named by Anthony Harris, and one of the four whom the district attorney's office subsequently released after their arrests. He was the manager of Black Self Help Moving and Storage, and owned an older model black Cadillac.

"No, Manney wasn't indicted," Coreris said. "The D.A. didn't feel he had enough hard evidence to bring him to trial."

"That's too bad," Lucas said. "I was thinking I might be able to help you out if he went to trial. See, I sold Manney some guns now and then."

"Oh?" Coreris's interest came alive. "What kind of guns, Arnold?"

"I sold him a thirty-eight, a three-fifty-seven Magnum and two thirty-twos."

"What kind of thirty-twos were they?"

"Berettas."

Was it possible? Coreris asked himself. Could it possibly turn out like this? A million-to-one shot?

Wait a minute now, he cautioned. This is one smart kid you're talking to here. He reads the papers just like everybody else. Everyone in San Francisco must know by now that the Zebra gun is a .32 Beretta. And even if Manney *did* buy two Berettas from Lucas that still would not prove a connection. Unless—

A million-to-one shot, the detective thought. Like trying to pick a single star out of a summer night.

But stranger things had happened.

"Where did you get the Berettas, Arnold?" he asked the young burglar.

"One of them I got out of an apartment up on Nob Hill. The other I bought off a guy."

Coreris could feel himself getting closer to that star. "What guy?"

"A guy named Moo Moo. Big Samoan guy, used to hang out over on Turk Street."

That was it. Nobody but his own team and the district attorney knew about Moo Moo.

Coreris shook his head wryly. I'll be goddamned. The million-to-one shot had come through.

The final link—putting the murder gun into the hands of the men who worked at Black Self Help—had been forged.

The Trial

It was the longest criminal trial in California history. Beginning on March 3, 1975, it lasted until March 9, 1976—one year and six days.

One hundred eighty-one witnesses testified. Court stenographers reported three and a half *million* words of testimony. The transcript totaled nearly fourteen thousand pages, and was bound in 141 volumes.

There were four lawyers for the defense. Three of them—those defending J. C. Simon, Larry Green, and Manuel Moore—were retained by the Nation of Islam. The fourth was appointed by the court to defend Jesse Lee Cooks. As usual, Cooks was the loner. The Nation of Islam had disowned him when he pled guilty to the killing of Frances Rose.

The prosecution of the case was assigned to an assistant district attorney with ten years' trial experience: Robert Podesta. He was assisted by assistant district attorney Robert Dondero. Inspector Gus Coreris worked the trial with them, sitting at the counsel table throughout, making his own copious notes of the proceedings.

Anthony Harris, of course, was the superstar of the trial. He testified for twelve days—three on direct examination, nine under heavy cross-examination—freely admitting his participation in ten of the crimes, beginning with the Hagues and ending with the terrifying Night of the Five. He related how Larry Green had hacked Quita Hague to death, and how Jesse Cooks had tried to kill Richard Hague the same way. How he and J.C. and Manuel had gone out stinging after the Ali-Frazier fight, and how J.C. had shot and killed Tana Smith, and Manuel had shot and killed Jane Holly, and how J.C. had shot Roxanne McMillian in the back. But at no time in his testimony did he admit that he himself had ever personally assaulted or harmed anyone. He had been formally granted immunity by the court now, but he still maintained that there was no blood on his hands.

Arnold George Lucas was on the witness stand for several days, testifying to the vital link between the murder gun found in the yard near the Shields killing, and the same gun being put into the area of activity at Black Self Help by his sale of that gun to one Thomas Manney, the manager of the Muslim moving company.

Mitch Luksich testified for six and a half days to prove that the Beretta found in the yard, the Beretta purchased by Lucas from Moo Moo and sold to Manney, was indeed the same weapon that had killed Tana Smith, Vincent Wollin, John Bambic, Jane Holly, Thomas Rainwater, and Nick Shields, and had gravely wounded Roxanne McMillian, Linda Story, Ward Anderson, and Terry White.

Besides those three major witnesses, the state elicited testimony from 105 others whose stories helped fit together the jigsaw puzzle of death. Some of those witnesses:

Thirteen-year-old Michele Carrasco, who remembered the night she and her two friends were almost kidnapped by three black men. Michele identified Jesse Lee Cooks. She also remembered that one of the others was very light-skinned, but could not definitely say that it was Larry Green.

Richard Hague also identified Cooks, but failed to identify Green.

Police officer Bruce Marovich recalled seeing Cooks and Anthony Harris next to the van across the street from where Quita and Richard Hague were kidnapped.

David Paul Bienvineste, the young florist who ran to the nearby hospital to get help for Tana Smith—and was refused—testified that he was "ninety percent sure" that the gunman who killed Tana was J. C. Simon.

L. C. Green, the black Navy petty officer who had shared Jane Holly's newspaper in the Lightning Laundromat, positively identified Manuel Moore as her killer.

Ward Anderson and Terry White, shot down at the Hayes-Fillmore bus stop, both positively identified Moore as their assailant.

Yolande Williams, the young black woman who was returning to lock her uncle's car two blocks from the Anderson-White shootings, testified that it was Manuel Moore who had run into the 800 block of Grove Street, tucking a gun in his belt. It was in that same block, at 844 Grove, that Simon, with whom Moore frequently stayed, and Green, both had apartments.

Many others also testified. Carolyn Patton, to whom Anthony Harris had been briefly married, reluctantly testified that Quita Hague's ring, recovered from her by Inspector Gus Coreris, had been given to her by Anthony. The pawnshop owner testified that Anthony had pawned Saleem Erakat's wristwatch. It was thus proved beyond any doubt that Anthony was telling the truth—up to a point—about his own participation. All that remained was for the jury to believe that he was telling the truth about the participation of J.C., Manuel, Larry, and Jesse.

One person who did not testify at the trial was Eduardo Abdi, the little man who had been at the scene of the Paul Dancik murder, the one who had told the first officers on the scene that he and Dancik had been "working on a case together," and then had disappeared.

The prosecution did not know what possible link Abdi might have had with Dancik, but it was taking no chances that the defense might produce the man and sabotage their case. So it told Coreris to find him. Coreris assigned Jeff Brosch to the job. Brosch tracked Abdi to Albuquerque, New Mexico, and spent days trying to locate him. Finally, after riding in Albuquerque radio cars on patrol night after night, he found the little man.

It did not take long for Brosch to decide that the prosecution had nothing to worry about. Abdi was an itinerant preacher who followed the migrant crop workers and preached to them in the field.

397

He had an incredibly vivid imagination and often gave it full rein. That was why he had made the unusual statements to the officers at the Dancik scene that night. In actuality he had never known Dancik, and had not even got a good look at the man who shot him. He had just let his imagination take over.

Jeff Brosch, after a long, hard job of man-hunting, returned to San Francisco to tell the prosecution to forget Eduardo Abdi. He could not hurt their case.

For eighty-eight trial days, through one hundred eight prosecution witnesses who filled nearly eight thousand pages of transcript, the state painted a damning word picture of cold-blooded murder.

Then the defense began.

First it attacked Anthony Harris. He was pictured three ways:

One, he was crazy. This was supported by evidence that at the age of fourteen he had been placed in the Pacific State Hospital as a mental defective. He was subsequently transferred to the Patton State Hospital, another mental institution, from which he escaped at age fifteen. After his escape, he was arrested for several burglaries, and from then on was sent to ordinary penal institutions rather than mental health hospitals,

Two: Anthony was out for revenge. He believed that J. C. Simon had been involved in the death of his brother, Pinky Harris, who allegedly had been killed by the Muslims in Southern California. This allegation was never proved or disproved.

Three: Anthony himself was the Zebra killer, had committed most if not all of the crimes himself, and had even bragged about some of them to the defendants. As proof of this, they pointed to the fact that although Anthony claimed he remained outside as a lookout during the Erakat robbery-killing, his palm print had subsequently been found on the inside of the washroom door where the Arab grocer was murdered.

The defense also sought to cast doubt on the rest of the prosecution testimony. A former girlfriend of David Bienvineste testified that he had told her on numerous occasions that he was "not sure" whether J. C. Simon was the killer of Tana Smith. And a female acquaintance of CPO L.C. Green said he told her that he had dropped his glasses during the Jane Holly killing and saw only a blurred heavyset black man. Another witness in the Laundromat said that CPO Green was so dumb struck with fear that he could not have identified anyone.

Thomas Manney testified that Arnold Lucas was a liar and that he had never bought guns from Lucas. He denied that the Black Self Help loft had ever been used for meetings of any kind, saying that it had always been too filled with stored furniture for such use. His statement lost some of its credence when the prosecution, on cross-examination, introduced police photographs taken on the morning of the arrests, showing the loft set up for a meeting.

Finally the defendants themselves testified. Manuel Moore was first. Affable, easygoing Manuel made a good impression—but became confused under pressure, as was usual with him, and ended up telling conflicting stories about what he had done on the Night of the Five.

J. C. Simon's testimony was a disaster. Ever his own worst enemy, Simon spent his valuable time on the stand trying to make a fool out of the prosecutor. The result was that he himself looked like a fool. He even insulted the jury's intelligence by claiming to have had a visitation from Allah Himself, who left a set of Muslim laws for him to read.

Only Larry Green fared halfway decently. More poised and articulate than he had ever been in his life—evidence that the ten months in jail and year-long trial had matured him greatly—he made the most favorable impression of all on the jury. As his attorney pointed out, Larry had not been placed at any crime scene by anyone at the trial except Anthony Harris.

Jesse Cooks, disdainful of the entire trial, did not deign to testify.

Finally it was over.

Superior Court Judge Joseph Karesh, a paragon of patience during the long, tiring process, instructed the jury in seventy-four possible verdicts it had to select from in determining the murder, conspiracy, assault, kidnapping, robbery, and other charges brought against the defendants.

Then the jury retired to consider its verdict.

"Well, it's almost over," Fotinos said.

"Yeah," Coreris nodded. "I wish Dick could have been here for the verdict," he added sadly.

Coreris was talking about Dick Walley, the CII man who had been so helpful to them since the beginning. Several months earlier, when Coreris and Fotinos were concentrating on lining up witnesses and getting their statements for the impending trial, Dick Walley had invited Coreris out for a drink one night.

"Think you can carry the ball on Zebra without me, old buddy?" he asked.

"If I have to, I guess I can," Coreris said. "You leaving CII?"

"I'm leaving a lot more than that, Gus," the special agent said. "I'm dying. I've got terminal cancer."

Coreris felt sick inside. There was so much to say yet there was nothing to say. Here was a man who, next to Fotinos and the rest of the Zebra team, had worked as hard on the case as anyone—harder, perhaps, because he was working on other killings, other hackings, all over the state. And now, when they were about to see the fruits of their labor, when they were about to bring the dogs to trial and show them to the world for the mad animals they were, Dick Walley was to be denied that satisfaction by a creeping cancer that was eating away his life.

Coreris shrugged uncomfortably. "Jesus, Dick. I don't know what to say."

"There's nothing *to* say," Walley replied. "I'll handle it. I just want to be sure that Zebra will be finished up okay."

"It will," Coreris promised. "It will."

Because of the complexity of the evidence, along with the record-setting length of the trial—a year and three days—it was expected that reaching a verdict would be a long, quite involved process for the jury.

It was not.

The jury took just eighteen hours to reach a unanimous conclusion.

All four defendants were found guilty on all counts charged against them.

The jury had believed Anthony Harris.

400

Because of the surprising swiftness with which the verdict was reached, there were only a few people in the courtroom when the jury returned. Among those few were Coreris and Fotinos. They watched the four defendants as the many guilty verdicts were read and the jury polled.

J. C. Simon stared straight ahead, his jaw set, lips tight.

Jesse Cooks looked down at the floor, almost bored by it all. He moved his shoulders as if trying to work some stiffness out of them.

Manuel Moore and Larry Green looked at each other and smiled and winked. Larry kept glancing over his shoulder, wishing his family were there. Moore grinned idiotically at anyone who would look at him.

Then it was over and the prisoners were being taken out and the courtroom was clearing.

"Well, that's that," Fotinos said. "Chalk up another victory for the good guys."

"Yeah." Coreris thought briefly of Dick Walley. "All the good guys," he said.

The detectives walked down the wide corridor to the elevators.

"Those four touched a lot of lives," Fotinos reflected. The names streamed through his mind: Roxie McMillian, Tana Smith, Quita Hague, all the others. "A lot of lives," he repeated quietly, almost to himself. Then he looked at his partner. "No more death penalty, so they'll all get life sentences. Think they'll ever get out, Gus?"

Coreris grunted softly. "Don't they all?" he asked.

The elevator came and they stepped aboard side by side.

Afterword

This book is being published in October 1979, six years to the month after the death of Quita Hague, the first Zebra victim. Three days after her murder, Quita was cremated at Cypress Lawn Cemetery in Colma, California. Her ashes were scattered at sea.

Richard Hague, Quita's husband, was still living in San Francisco at the time *Zebra* was written. He was contacted twice through an intermediary but declined both times to be interviewed.

Ellen Linder also still resides in the Bay Area. She has fully recovered from her ordeal and, intelligent and self-assured woman that she is, has not let it affect her subsequent life.

Frances Rose's body was returned by her family for burial at Sunset Memorial Park in South Charleston, West Virginia.

Saleem Erakat was buried after a large funeral at Woodlawn Memorial Cemetery in San Francisco. He is still mourned today by his family, which has a large, framed picture of him displayed in the grocery store that they still operate.

Paul Dancik was cremated and interred at Cypress Lawn in Colma.

Arthur Agnos still resides in the Bay Area. After his recovery, he was a successful candidate for the San Francisco city assembly, where he serves today.

Marietta DiGirolamo is buried in Olivet Memorial Park in Colma.

Ilario Bertuccio is buried in the Italian Cemetery in San Francisco.

Angela Roselli still lives in the Bay Area. She is still pursuing her education. She still suffers pain from her wounds.

Neal Moynihan is buried in Holy Cross Cemetery in San Francisco.

Mildred Hosler is buried in Olivet Memorial Park in Colma.

John Doe #169 was held in the morgue by the San Francisco coroner's office for the statutory period required by law. He was never identified. After one year he was buried in the Potter's Field section of Woodlawn Cemetery.

Tana Smith was cremated and her ashes spread at sea near the coast of San Francisco, the city she loved so much.

Vincent Wollin was cremated and interred at Cypress Lawn in Colma.

John Bambic was buried in Holy Cross Cemetery in San Francisco.

Jane Holly was cremated and interred at Woodlawn Memorial Park in Colma.

Roxanne McMillian now lives some distance from San Francisco. She continues to suffer daily physical pain. Her husband has left her. Her income is extremely limited. Yet she maintains a positive, determined attitude. She has her own apartment and has learned to drive a specially equipped car. Her son, an infant when Roxanne was shot, has started his first year of school. He knows his mother was hurt by a "bad" man—but Roxanne has never pointed out to him that the man was black. And never will.

Thomas Rainwater is buried in Santa Barbara, California.

Linda Story is still a member of the Salvation Army. She works with young people in one of the Western states and, like Ellen Linder and Roxanne McMillian, is continuing her life in a positive, commendable manner. She too still suffers pain from her wounds.

The whereabouts of Ward Anderson, the seaman, could not be determined.

Terry White was still in San Francisco at the time the book was completed.

The last victim, Nelson Shields IV, was cremated and his ashes interred near the family home in Delaware. His father, Nelson Shields III, now heads the antigun lobby in Washington.

The men convicted of the Zebra crimes are, of course, still in prison after only six years.

J. C. Simon is in Folsom. He recently engineered a coup to take over leadership of the Muslim faction in that institution. His move may eventually prove successful—but at the time of this writing he has been relieved of his job in the prison laundry and confined in the SHU (Security Housing Unit) with limited privileges.

Jesse Lee Cooks is also in Folsom, and also in the SHU—not for any specific violations but generally because he is considered one of the more dangerous inmates in the institution.

Larry Green and Manuel Moore are both in San Quentin. Manuel, in his own affable way, made his usual effort to be agreeable and get along in prison. But Larry, with his blatant racist attitude, immediately incurred the enmity of the white population. On January 17, 1978, Larry was stabbed by a white inmate attempting to kill him. He recovered from his wound but, for his own safety, was confined in the AC (Adjustment Center), the prison's maximum security lockup. Because Manuel Moore was commonly known as one of Green's crime partners, he too was segregated from the main line. Both are still in the AC, where they will probably remain for several years.

Gus Coreris retired from the San Francisco Police Department and became an investigator for a large insurance company. He still resides in California, though no longer in San Francisco.

John Fotinos is still a homicide inspector for SFPD. By the time *Zebra* is published, he will have completed thirty years of police service and probably will have retired.

Jeff Brosch and Carl Klotz are still homicide detectives.

San Francisco, where it all happened, continues to be the West's jewel city by the bay, retaining all the charm and ambience that make such diverse people as Tana Smith and J. C. Simon fall in love with it. It is a delightful city, a fascinating city, a city of many hopes and dreams and much happiness—and sometimes terrible tragedy. It is to be hoped that it will never again be shrouded in the kind of terror created by the Zebra crimes.

I hope no place will.